D0231537

Supreme Gallantry

Other books by the same author

In Full Flight
Coastal Ace
Warburton's War
Faith, Hope and Malta G C
Clean Sweep
The Spooners of Middle England (genealogical)

Supreme Gallantry

Malta's Role in the Allied Victory
1939–1945

TONY SPOONER

DSO, DFC

JOHN MURRAY
Albemarle Street, London

A catalogue record for this book is available from the British Library

ISBN 0-7195-5706 2

Typeset in Great Britain by Servis Filmsetting Ltd., Manchester
Printed and bound in Great Britain by The University Press, Cambridge

To those who gave their all in and around Malta
during the Second World War

Contents

Illustrations

ACKNOWLEDGEMENTS

The author and publishers would like to thank the following for
permission to reproduce illustrations: Plates 2, 3, 10, 11 and 12,
Imperial War Museum; 4, F/Lt S.W. Lee; 5, 6, 7, 13, 20, 22, 23, 24, 25,
26, 27, 31, 32, 33 and 34, Royal Navy Submarine Museum, Gosport;
9, 14 and 18, *Aeroplane Monthly*; 17, J.R. Eric Cameron; 19, Arthur
Aldridge; 21, Patrick Gibbs; 28, Frederick Galea; 29, Dallas Schmidt;
and 30, Keith Durbidge.

Acknowledgements

THERE IS ALWAYS a risk, when giving thanks for help with a book which has taken a year and more to research and write, that the names of some valuable helpers might be omitted unintentionally. However, while hoping that not too many names have been forgotten, I would like to give my sincere thanks to the persons whose names follow. I also take this opportunity to apologize for having to omit much of the material sent to me. A book over twice this length could have been compiled.

In the list of names which follows ranks and decorations have been omitted as they are not known with accuracy in every case. It is difficult to determine exactly when an individual was promoted and when decorated. The ranks held during the war around Malta differ widely from those held subsequently.

With these limitations, my thanks go to:

Royal Navy (mostly submariners): Walter Alpino, Ken Aylwin, George Brough, David Brown (MOD, Naval Historical Branch), 'Tubby' Crawford, Jim Gilbert, George Hunt, Brian Hudson, Harry Jones, Christopher Lowe, Sir Ian McGeoch, Sir 'Rufus' Mackenzie, Lennox Napier, Sir John Roxburgh, Ray Steggles, Ian Stoop and Sir Tony Troup.

The enormous assistance of the RN Submarine Museum, Gosport, was invaluable. Special thanks therefore to: Jeff Tall, Director, Gus Britton and others. My further thanks to these two and Debbie Corner for assistance with many of the photographs which appear.

Fleet Air Arm: Ivor Cooksey, Pat Garthwaite, Anthony Gillingham, Katherine Hollins, Ivor Jeffries, Roger Kerrison, John Leech, Jeff Powell and Frank Walker.

RAF (RAAF, RCAF, SAAF): Arthur Aldridge, Jim Allen, 'Tony' Anthony, Artie Ashworth, David Beaty, Sir Ivor Broom, Eric Cameron, Gil Catton, John Clements, Philip Dawson, G. Day and Richard King (both of the MOD, Air Historical Branch), Cas de Bounevialle, Freddie Deeks, Keith Durbidge, Peter Eastcott, Hugh Fallis, Pat Foss, Patrick Gibbs, Robert Ginn, Eric Gittings, Al Glazer, Les Gully, David Gunby, Deirdre Hartman, Desmond Haynes, Jack Hoskins, Frank Laughlin, 'Laddie' Lucas, Bert Markland, Roy Nesbit, Fred Oldfield, Bryan Quinlan, Mickey Reid, Peter Rothwell, Dallas Schmidt, Frank Smith, Alex Stittle, Reg Thackeray and Lloyd Wiggins. My thanks also to Eric Cameron, Des Haynes, Bryan Quinlan and Dallas Schmidt for supplying illustrations.

If the names of those who supplied Allied Air Force material far exceed in numbers those of our Navies, it may be put down to the fact that, even in Malta, the war to many in Air Force blue still seemed at times to be 'a bit of a one-off adventure', albeit a dangerous and terrifying one. Very few were Regular Air Force men with career prospects. Most (including the author) had never before served in a Regular fighting Service. Consequently, their wartime antics became etched in their minds.

By contrast, the young Navy officers who commanded the submarines which inflicted most damage upon the enemy, were all pre-war Regular officers who, if they survived, were to continue in that fine Service post-war; several rose to admiral's rank. To them, this was the job they had chosen and the war was the fulfilment of what they had been trained to do; their wartime experiences constituted a step in a lifelong career. Moreover, they were part of a Service with long and cherished traditions, one of which was that the British Royal Navy was a silent, as well as a deadly efficient, Service. Unlike their RAF counterparts, they did not so readily respond to the opportunity to relate their wartime experiences. However, their contributions to this book have been invaluable.

I also wish to thank the ladies who kindly assisted with proofreading my typescript, namely Arlette Tedder and Queenie Barnes. My thanks also go to Charles Carnes (Ultra), Guildhall Library (D.T. Barriskill), Frank Rixon (Army details), Otto Kretschmer (U-boats), Paul Tenholt (U-boats), Eddie Leaf for help with charts and photographs (in particular, the chart which appears on page 330) and Mark Thackeray for excellent sketches.

Tullio Marcon, Italian historian, and Jürgen Rohwer, German historian, both helped me with information obtained from their research into the other side of Malta's peculiar and unique war.

The friendly assistance of Grant McIntyre, and that of other members of John Murray's staff, is much appreciated.

My special thanks go to Admiral of the Fleet Lord Lewin, who first conceived the idea of someone writing a book to show what Malta achieved in the Second World War and followed this up with appropriate introductions. My further thanks to him for the thoughtful Foreword.

Finally my very special thanks to my wife Anne who, by mastering a sophisticated word processor, has typed and retyped my voluminous papers with skill and devotion. Without her help, I doubt that this book could have been produced during the current millennium.

Tony Spooner

December 1995

Foreword

by Admiral of the Fleet Lord Lewin

Some modern military historians argue that sustaining Malta throughout the critical earlier years of the Second World War was not worth the immense cost in men and material. It is said that the contribution made by forces operating from this island base had little impact on the course of the war. This book proves them wrong. Malta was the thorn in the flesh of the Axis commanders in the Western Desert: the skill and determination of the sailors and airmen attacking the Axis supply lines, the resolution of those who kept Malta supplied and, above all, the courage and fortitude of the Maltese civilians ensured final victory in North Africa. Tony Spooner's wide research into German and Italian archives, recording the views of the commanders of the time, his assembly of logistical statistics, the recollections of many who played their part and his own personal involvement combine to make this a compelling and convincing account.

The crucial year was 1942. The progress of the war had been a succession of disasters: the Norwegian campaign, ending in defeat and evacuation; the fall of France and the evacuation from Dunkirk; the loss of the Channel Islands; and the transport of the army to Greece, its defeat and evacuation, first to Crete, then back to Egypt. Singapore had fallen. In North Africa Rommel's armies were poised to sweep through Egypt to the Suez Canal and beyond. Surrender of Malta and its people to the Fascist dictators and the imprisonment of some 30,000 servicemen – evacuation would have been impossible – would surely have resulted in the resignation of the Churchill Government and would have changed the course of the war. Malta had to be held at all costs.

In the early months of 1942 Malta was bombed until it appeared to the enemy that there was nothing left to destroy. Spitfires ferried in by aircraft-carriers enabled the Royal Air Force to win a victory that bears comparison with the Battle of Britain, but supply convoys failed to get through and by August Malta was on the brink of starvation. In the biggest single Royal Navy operation of the war five merchant ships of a convoy of fourteen were fought through, bringing urgently needed fuel, ammunition and food, just enough to maintain the fight and avoid surrender. In October came El Alamein. Strike-forces from Malta helped to keep Rommel short of supplies and he was forced back. In November the Allied landings in Algeria exposed the Axis to a second front. The interdiction of their sea lanes continued apace and, after the enemy's defeat in Tunisia, the forces based on Malta prevented the escape of some 400,000 men who played no further part in the war. In the following year Malta was the springboard for Operation Husky, the invasion of Sicily which marked the Allies' return to continental Europe.

Malta was the key. The naval and air strike-forces operating from this besieged island fortress made a contribution to the successful prosecution of the war far beyond all reasonable expectation.

Preface

WRITING ABOUT EVENTS which took place more than half a century ago, and a thousand miles away, has its problems. Much of this book is concerned with ships which were sunk in the Central Mediterranean during the Second World War; how they were sunk, and by whom. But in the course of research it soon became apparent that there were discrepancies between personal recollections and official records, as well as between the different official records.

This is not surprising. In some other theatres of war the official records are, no doubt, accurate and splendid – especially, it is suspected, when little of consequence was taking place. In Malta, however, under the unique circumstances in which the participants found themselves, almost the last thing anyone thought about – and the author was there at the time – was the keeping of correct and up-to-date day-to-day records. Recording for posterity, if it was considered at all, was a very low priority. Some units indeed kept no records at all – partly, given the threat of invasion, for security reasons, lest the records fall into enemy hands; and partly for want of personnel.

As the island, at the outset of its war, had no official RAF base other than a small flying-boat station at Kalafrana and no RAF airfield until Luqa was completed in about July 1940, there had been no need pre-war for the presence of RAF administrative personnel. Then, when aircraft such as the first handful of Hurricanes and the few Marylands of 431 Flight (predecessor of 69 Squadron) began to arrive, they had no room for 'pen-pushers', any more than had the detachments of Blenheims and Wellingtons that were to follow. If spare spaces in such aircraft could be found, they were given, not unnaturally, to desperately needed ground maintenance men – fitters, riggers, armourers and the like.

When the author himself flew out to Malta on 1 October 1941, alongside two other pilots and crews in three aircraft, the only non-operational personnel carried was one radar expert. The unit which he commanded for the best part of the next six months – the Special Duties Flight (SDF) – operated without any Flight Office or administrative personnel. No one in authority suggested that records should be kept; as a result, none were.

In those cases where squadron records are available at the Public Record Office for periods of service in Malta, even here the accounts may be suspect, since some are known to have been compiled weeks or months after the events recorded, often by persons who were never even there. As Reg Thackeray of 40 Squadron recalls:

> 40 Squadron's Operation Record Book for Malta is a shambles. An HQ echelon remained in Beurat [North Africa] continuously and all the daily and monthly sheets are signed by W/Cdr D.R. Bagnall who did not become CO until May/June 1943 by when 40 Squadron, having left Malta, may have been having a quiet time in Kairouan, Tunisia. There must then have been an opportunity to collect together all the notes made during the previous six months . . . there are many errors and omissions, inevitable in the circumstances.

In short, the daily record sheets were eventually made up six months after the event, during a lull in the action, and signed by an authorizing officer who may never have been in Malta. For these reasons the RAF records in the Public Record Office at Kew, insofar as they relate to Malta for the period 1940–1943, cannot be taken as a sole, or infallible, source.

For the Royal Navy, too, the situation was similar. At the outset of the war with Italy, the Navy had largely pulled out of Malta, owing to its proximity to Sicily, and the submarine base at Manoel Island was not officially created until January 1941. There, too, priority was given to bringing in operational personnel, rather than clerical staff. There may even have been a shortage of paper, judging by the habit of Captain G.W.G. Simpson, who first commanded the submarine base, of issuing instructions for week-long patrols on the backs of old railway or cloakroom tickets.

Unexpected difficulties arose when research disclosed that even official reports of enemy sinkings did not agree with one another. Contemporary reports frequently distorted information for the purposes of propaganda. The Italians issued one list, the German naval historian Jürgen Rohwer has prepared another. Both the Navy and Air Historical Branches of the Ministry of Defence, helpful as they were to the author, have compiled individual lists and Lloyd's of London compiled yet another. While all these have been of great use, they do not in every case agree.

One difficulty in compiling a list of ships sunk during a war is that ships do not always sink where they are hit. A submarine or air-craft – and about 95 per cent of the ships sunk in the area were sunk by one or the other – does not stay around in order to record the details. To give an example, it is known that the enemy ship *Amsterdam* was hit and 'sunk' by the submarine *Umbra* on 23 October 1942. It appears, however, that she was not actually sunk, and that not until 20 January 1943 were attempts to salvage the ship finally abandoned. Most attackers, immediately after an attack, are far more concerned with avoiding the counter-attacks and getting back to base, at times damaged, in one piece.

Even successful attacks carried out by surface ships do not always lead to certainty about what happened. In the first place, the major-ity of these attacks took place during night actions. A further diffi-culty is that in the Central Mediterranean the sea lanes used by both sides were liberally strewn with mines. These are known to have accounted for many enemy losses but exactly when and where can seldom be established: it is all too easy to attribute a successful air or sea strike to a loss caused by a mine or vice versa. For these and other reasons it is not possible to match every sinking with a claim by an attacker.

Another problem facing a historian attempting to discover who sank what, is that a number of ships were attacked and sunk by a variety of attackers during the same night. The period 1–3 December 1942 is a clear example. During that short period, a dozen or more enemy ships were hit, and for the most part sunk, in the same Tunisian waters during operations carried out, usually at night, by Royal Navy Force K, Royal Navy Force Q, Allied sub-marines, Fleet Air Arm (FAA) Albacores of 828 and/or 821 Squadrons, torpedo-carrying Wellingtons of the SDF and/or 221 or 69 Squadrons, as well as by Beauforts and Beaufighters. Most, if not all, were sunk by units operating from Malta or in waters over which either the Royal Navy or the RAF had operational control. On top of this, mines which had been laid by Allied submarines, by

Royal Navy surface ships and by RAF aircraft are thought to have accounted for at least two of the enemy sinkings. In these circumstances it is next to impossible to determine with certainty who or what was responsible for which sinking.

These matters are perhaps best left to the purists to resolve. The aim of this book is to describe operations in the area over and under which Malta exercised control, and where the enemy suffered heavy losses owing to Malta's firm presence as an Allied base for both warships and aircraft. Working closely together, the two Services combined to make life extremely difficult for the enemy armies in North Africa – a vast area which contained virtually none of the fuel (oil had not then been discovered in Algeria) nor other materials necessary to the Axis powers for fighting the war. Everything they needed, including food for their armies, had to be shipped from Europe and, whether the fighting was taking place in Libya, near Egypt or in Tunisia, Malta – positioned as it is at the crossroads of Central Mediterranean sea traffic – was instrumental in ensuring that the enemy's supply routes were constantly under attack.

Given that the official record is at its most fallible when the heat was on, where there is a possible conflict between official reports and personal recollections, this book tends to favour the accounts of the men at the sharp end of the action, particularly if these are supported by a pilot's Log Book entry or a submariner's Patrol Report compiled at the time. These were made up on a daily basis and had to be countersigned each month by the senior officer present. Moreover, for all that memory can play tricks, such personal recollections are often indelibly etched in the minds of those concerned, relating as they do to moments when life itself hung in the balance.

These records form an indispensable source for this book, and extracts from them are assembled in two chapters in particular, Chapters 8 and 10, which deal with the individual recollections of aircrew and submariners who served in Malta at this period. Another valuable source of information has been the *Times of Malta* – the daily English-language newspaper – which regularly reported events in the Allied campaign, if perhaps with a bias towards its successes.

Apologies are owed to many, especially to most of the successful submarine commanders, for the failure to mention their many gallantry awards. Almost every commander who survived Malta richly deserved the DSO and DSC (often with bars) which were awarded them. Many distinguished pilots and other crew members, in the Royal Navy, Fleet Air Arm and the RAF, were likewise decorated. Unfortunately, it is next to impossible to know exactly when these awards were made and, rather than get it wrong on occasions, these well-earned decorations have often been omitted. Wartime ranks may also, on occasions, be incorrect as, especially in the RAF, rapid promotions, at times 'to fill dead men's shoes', were frequent in Malta.

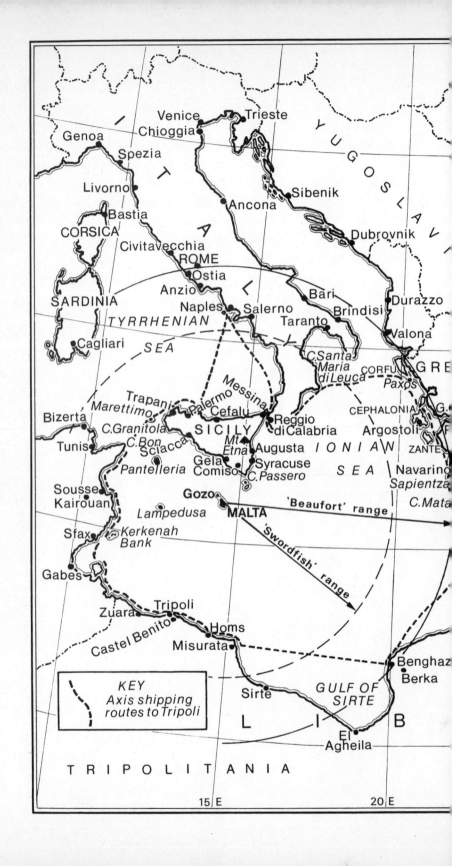

KEY
Axis shipping
routes to Tripoli

MALTA versus
TRIPOLI/BENGHAZI

45N

MILES
0   100   200   300
0   160   320   480
KMS

BULGARIA

40N

AEGEAN

T U R K E Y

Athens
Piraeus

Naxos

35N

C Y P R U S

Maleme
Suda Bay

CRETE

Beirut

*B
O
M
B
A
L
L
E
Y*

Haifa

el Hilal
Ras el Tin
Tobruk
   Bardia   Sidi
El   Barrani
Adem   Alexandria
     Sollum
       Mersa
A   Matruh   El Alamein
            Alam
          Halfa
    Qattara   Cairo
    Depression

30N

E G Y P T

25 E   30 E

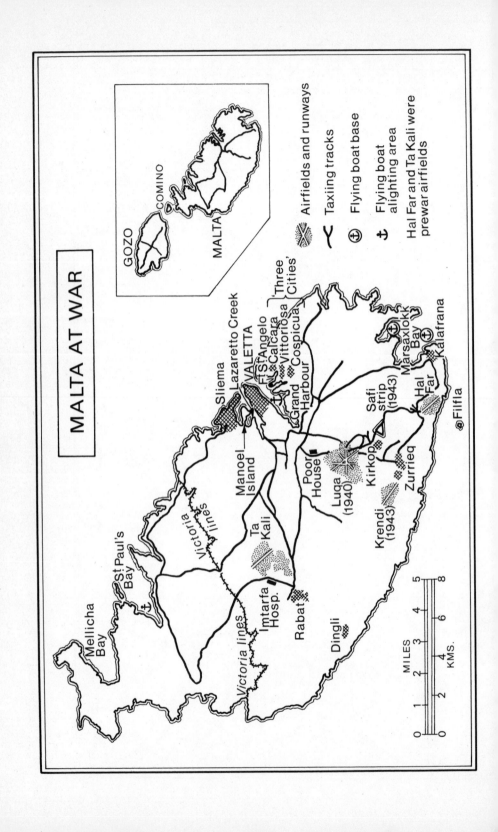

MALTA AT WAR

GOZO
COMINO
MALTA

Airfields and runways
Taxiing tracks
Flying boat base
Flying boat alighting area

Hal Far and Ta Kali were prewar airfields

Mellicha Bay
St Paul's Bay
Sliema
Lazaretto Creek
Manoel Island
VALETTA
Ft St Angelo
Ca Cara
Vittoriosa
Cospicua
Grand Harbour
'Three Cities'
Victoria lines
Victoria lines
Imtarfa Hosp.
Rabat
Dingli
Ta Kali
Poor House
Luqa (1940)
Kirkop
Krendi (1943)
Zurrieq
Safi strip (1943)
Marsaxlokk Bay
Hal Far
Kalafrana
Filfla

0   1   2   3   4   5
MILES
0   2   4   6   8
KMS.

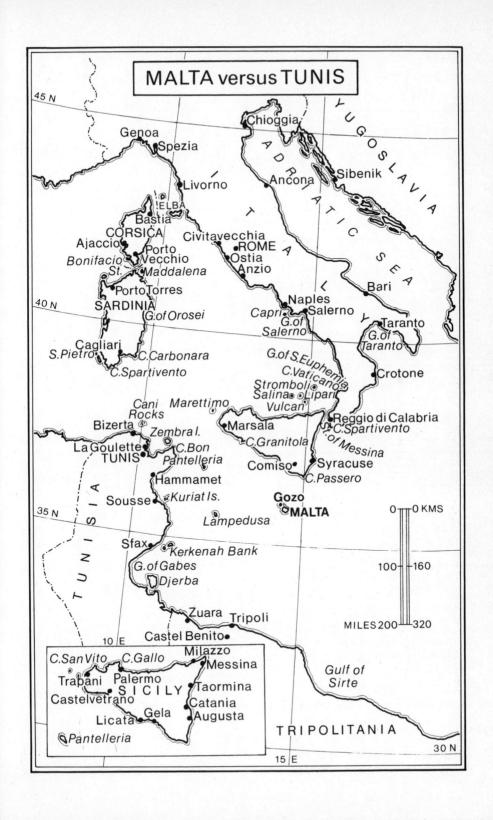

MALTA versus TUNIS

Abbreviations

AA	Anti-aircraft
AOC	Air Officer Commanding
ASDIC	Allied Submarine Detection Investigation Committee
ASV	Air-to-surface vessel
C-in-C	Commander-in-Chief
CO	Commanding Officer
Cr	Cruiser
Dr	Destroyer
E-boat	German motor torpedo-boat
FAA	Fleet Air Arm
GOC	General Officer Commanding
HAA	Heavy Anti-Aircraft
JG	*Jagdgeschwader* (Fighter Group)
KG	*Kampfgeschwader* (Bomber Group)
LAA	Light anti-aircraft
MTB	Motor torpedo-boat
MV	Merchant vessel
NJG	*Nachtjagdgeschwader* (Night Fighter Group)
OKW	*Oberkommando der Wehrmacht* (German Armed Forces General Staff)
PRU	Photographic Reconnaissance Unit
PV	Patrol vessel
RAAF	Royal Australian Air Force
RCAF	Royal Canadian Air Force
RDF	Radio direction-finding
RNZAF	Royal New Zealand Air Force
SAAF	South African Air Force
SDF	Special Duties Flight
Sqdn	Squadron
TB	Torpedo-boat
TLC	Tank (or Troop) landing-craft
U-boat	*Unterseeboot* (German submarine)
USAAF	United States Army Air Force
VAM	Vice-Admiral Malta
W/T	Wireless telegraphy

Prologue

WHICHEVER LOYAL BRITISH subjects made sure, round about the year 1800, that Britain took possession of the island of Malta – as the Maltese themselves requested – knew what they were doing. Few islands anywhere in the world are more favourably placed, for strategic purposes, for a leading maritime power with a Navy: which was Britain's status at that time.

One glance at a map of the Mediterranean shows that Malta lies a few miles south-east of the point where this great inland sea is reduced to its narrowest, with Cape Bon in Tunisia to the south and Sicily to the north. If this were not enough, it so happens that, in Malta, nature has created a magnificent natural harbour, protected on all sides and with water deep enough to take the largest warships, both then and now. At a time when, in the early part of the twentieth century, Britain could boast the largest Navy in the world, it was said that the entire British fleet could be accommodated in Malta's harbours, of which Grand Harbour stood out as the finest.

In the war between Britain and Italy, which began on 10 June 1940 when the Italian Fascist dictator Mussolini threw in his lot with the then victorious Hitler, Malta assumed an additional importance as a result of its proximity to Sicily.

Britons for generations, especially those with Naval connections, had long appreciated the supreme importance of the Maltese islands. Just as Gibraltar dominated the west end of the Mediterranean, and Alexandria the east terminus, Malta dominated the centre.

Let an American historian describe the importance of Malta during the Second World War. William Shirer in his *Rise and Fall of the Third Reich* wrote:

The key to that conquest [of Egypt] actually was the small island of Malta . . . It was from this British bastion that bombers, submarines and surface craft wrought havoc on German and Italian vessels carrying supplies and men to North Africa.

General Rommel in Egypt and his superior, Field Marshal Kesselring, C-in-C of the entire Mediterranean theatre of war, had no doubts about the importance of Malta, as these pages will reveal.

Today's popular tourist island was, fifty and more years ago, the rock which stood between the two Fascist dictators and their ambition to seize Egypt and thus open the way to the oil that lay beyond – a commodity which the Axis forces needed in abundance in order to have any chance of winning the Second World War.

1

The Cost

'They came from all Naval sources: Regular, Reserve
and Volunteer, and from all walks of life. They suffered
severe casualties and knew only too well the chill of
the vacant chair . . .'

Captain G. Phillips DSO, GM, RN, Foreword to
John Wingate, *The Fighting Tenth* (1981)

NO ONE SHOULD be in any doubt about what it cost Britain to defend and supply Malta during the Second World War. To try to minimize that cost would be to do an injustice to those who maintain that Malta was well worth its keep. No such attempt is made here. The cost in human lives, in ships, planes and other valuable cargoes of war was nothing short of stupendous. The question to be answered is 'Was it worth such a cost?'

To sustain and to launch attacks from this small island of only 91 square miles – a figure which makes it a mite smaller than the Isle of Wight – the Allied navies suffered the following casualties:

Aircraft-carriers: *Ark Royal, Eagle.*

Cruisers: *Cairo, Hermione, Manchester, Neptune, Southampton.*

Destroyers: *Airedale, Bedouin, Fearless, Foresight, Gallant, Gurkha, Hasty, Hyperion, Jersey, Kandahar, Kingston, Kujawiak* (Polish Navy), *Lance, Legion, Maori, Mohawk, Nestor* (Royal Australian Navy), *Pakenham, Southwold.*

Some of the Malta-based destroyers which were lost met their fate while at anchor or in dock in Malta. Much of the enemy bombing day and night was aimed at Malta's harbours. Some was very accurate.

One destroyer to meet this fate was *Maori* and one of its crew has

3

provided an excellent description of what it was like to have been on board, in the apparent safety of the Malta dockyard, during a night air raid. Tom Roxby was a radar (known then as Radio Direction Finding, RDF) specialist. He writes:

> On 12/13 February 1942, the *Maori* found herself in Malta anchored in Dockyard Creek. About 7 p.m. the ship's radio broadcast some popular songs including 'Now is the hour'. It would be fanciful to say a slight shiver of apprehension ran through me (hindsight premonition perhaps), for at a later hour a bomb was dropped amidships and exploded in the engine and gearing rooms. I was asleep in the Communications Mess. There was pandemonium and already the *Maori* was listing badly to port. The order was given 'Abandon ship'. Along with others I clambered down the side of the tilting fo'c'sle, hit the water, and managed to gain purchase on a nearby Carley float. It was evident the float could take no more men, so I struck out for a whaler from the destroyer *Havock*, and was pulled in. By that time blazing fuel oil was spreading on the water, the whaler had had its rudder damaged and we began to drift. By superhuman efforts the whaler crew, by alternate rowing, manoeuvred the boat away and eventually made *Havock*. The poor old *Maori* blew up and sank!

Maori, with her New Zealand associations, had adopted the then popular New Zealand folk-song 'Now is the hour' as the theme song of the ship's company. Over fifty years later, whenever Tom Roxby hears this haunting refrain, he lives again the memory of *Maori*'s last moments.

Another severe loss in Grand Harbour was the 40,000-ton floating dock, also sunk by German bombs. Tragically the Royal Navy also lost, steaming into Alexandria on 1 February 1943, the fast minelayer *Welshman* which had made several solo runs to Malta specifically to bring in each time 640 tons of urgently needed supplies. Another good friend of Malta's which was lost was the Royal Navy's 10,000-ton semi-tanker *Breconshire*, sunk in Marsaxlokk Bay on 27 March 1942. She too had repeatedly brought in urgently needed supplies, on more than one occasion braving 'Bomb Alley', the notorious passage between Crete and North Africa, alone and unescorted.

The Allied submarines which operated from Malta suffered the highest percentage of Allied naval casualties. Of the nearly 80 which were at one time or another based at Manoel Island near Sliema, or were visiting there, over 40 were lost. The smaller U-class submarines survived best but the losses of the ocean-going O, P, R and S-class submarines of the Royal Navy amounted to about 65 per cent.

The list of submarines lost is given below in alphabetical order. All were British except for the Free French submarine *Narwhal* and the Greek submarine *Glaukos*: *Cachalot, Glaukos, Grampus, Narwhal, Odin, Olympus, Orpheus, Oswald, P32, P33, P36, P38, P48, P222, P311, Pandora, Parthian, Perseus, Rainbow, Regent, Regulus, Saracen, Splendid, Talisman, Tempest, Tetrarch, Thunderbolt, Tigris, Traveller, Triad, Triton, Triumph, Trooper, Turbulent, Undaunted, Union, Upholder, Urge, Usk, Utmost.*

Originally the small U-class submarines were known not by names but by numbers, such as *P32, P33,* but at Winston Churchill's instigation they were later given names such as *Undaunted, Union,* etc. Several however were sunk before the naming of submarines commenced.

Submarines operating around Malta were especially vulnerable at those times when the seas were calm. They could then be seen through the pellucid waters of the Mediterranean and Adriatic even when submerged at up to a depth of 100 feet beneath the surface. The submarines were, at all times, vulnerable also to the thousands of mines which the enemy laid around the approaches of Maltese harbours. The submarine base on Manoel Island also suffered from bombing.

Losses were not restricted to the Allies. Scarcely a single one of the large numbers of German U-boats which were diverted from the Atlantic to the Mediterranean – and over 50 such vessels were so diverted – was ever to get back into the Atlantic. Virtually all were sunk. Italian submarines also suffered, the following alone being known to have been sunk by Allied submarines: *Acciaio, Capponi, Diemonte, Granito, Guglielmotti, Jantina, Malachite, Meduca, Micca, Millo, Porfido, Remo, Saint Bon, Salpa, Tricheco* and *Velella.* In all, about 74 Italian submarines were lost in the Mediterranean, most of them going down in the Eastern or Western Mediterranean, not around Malta.

In addition to ships lost while defending, supplying or operating offensively from Malta, many others were damaged, some so seriously that they were under repairs for up to a year, the aircraft-carrier *Illustrious* being one such casualty.

Among the major British vessels damaged were:

Battleship: *Nelson*.

Aircraft-carriers: *Furious, Illustrious, Indomitable*.

Monitor* (disguised as a battleship): *Centurion*.

Cruisers: *Arethusa* (twice), *Aurora, Birmingham, Cairo* (later sunk), *Cleopatra, Gloucester, Kenya, Liverpool, Manchester, Newcastle, Penelope*.

At least a score of destroyers were also damaged, whilst a number of Fleet Auxiliary vessels, corvettes, minesweepers, navy tugs, drifters and other vessels were either sunk or damaged. The total number of naval ships sunk or damaged as a result of the decision to keep Malta in business as a base from which to launch attacks must far exceed in numbers the total strength of the British Navy of the 1990s.

The cost in human lives is difficult to assess with accuracy but that, too, was appalling. The submarines alone lost about 1,700 men and the numbers killed when the cruiser *Neptune* was mined approached 1,000 as she was carrying an additional complement of about 160 Royal New Zealand Navy seamen prior to her being handed over to that service. Only one on board lived to tell the tale. Another 150 lives were lost when *Welshman* went down; a similar total was lost when *Illustrious* was hit and damaged: these included a number of Fleet Air Arm and RAF personnel on board. Losses aboard the damaged cruiser *Arethusa* totalled over 150 and when the aircraft-carrier *Eagle* was sunk, 230 men were lost. Even some submarines went down with more than 100 persons on board, since they would often be carrying many extra passengers crammed within. It has to be remembered that, after June 1940, no passenger ships were operating either into or out of Malta. Personnel travelling between Malta and either Gibraltar or Egypt – until May 1943, the nearest Allied territories firmly in Allied hands, though both more than 800 miles distant – often had to be transported in Navy ships or in RAF aircraft, many being carried within the limited confines of submarines or in the fuselage of bombers, often in appalling conditions. Returning merchant vessels were also used as makeshift passenger carriers.

---

* A relatively small and slow type of warship with massive guns (often 15-inch), intended to bombard enemy ports and coasts.

Merchant Navy losses were at times as crippling as any. Although at the start most convoys reached Malta safely from both ends of the Mediterranean, from early 1942 onwards the Merchant Navy incurred losses which were terrible to bear. The loss of their cargoes was also damaging for those in Malta. The March 1942 convoy from Alexandria was heavily attacked and although three of the four supply ships reached the island they were all sunk soon after arrival with only about 5,000 tons of their 30,000 tons of cargo unloaded.* The eleven ships of Operation Vigorous, which in June 1942 were to bring relief to much-bombed and half-starved Malta, never reached the island at all having come under heavy attack in 'Bomb Alley' to the south of Crete and been obliged to turn back.

Fortunately for those on the beleaguered island two of the six merchant ships which comprised Operation Harpoon, which was attempting to reach Malta from Gibraltar at the same time as Vigorous, managed to reach Grand Harbour, Valletta, where *Troilus* and *Orari* were successfully unloaded. The supplies they brought saved the island from surrender. Sadly, the other four merchant ships of that convoy were all sunk.

In all, twelve merchant ships were lost *en route* to Malta, or in Malta, between March and August 1942. The most tragic in terms of loss of life was that of the *Waimarama*, loaded with ammunition, which exploded with the loss of 93 lives. The numbers on board were high because she was transporting – as did many merchantmen – a number of Service personnel to Malta, in this case Royal Navy and Royal Artillery men.

The RAF, and those who fought alongside it in uniforms of the RAAF, RCAF, RNZAF and the South African Air Force, also paid for the decision to defend and supply Malta. Before the war moved into Italy in 1944 to distances beyond a useful range of Malta, the RAF are recorded as having lost 547 aircraft in the air and about another 160 on the ground. These are considerable losses when it is remembered that the original RAF defence consisted of a handful of

---

* One of the three which reached Malta was the *Breconshire*. She was hit by a bomb when only a few miles away, was towed (or staggered) into Malta where, in Marsaxlokk Bay, she was finished off in another air raid and rolled over on to one side. The other two were sunk by bombs in Grand Harbour. Their slow unloading probably cost Lieutenant General Dobbie, Governor of Malta, his job.

obsolescent Fleet Air Arm Gladiators. A memorial in Floriana near Valletta records the names of 2,301 airmen of the RAF and kindred Air Forces whose only graves are the waters, or adjacent lands, of the Mediterranean: this is in addition to those known casualties whose graves are on the island.

Maltese civilians and British Servicemen, both on and off duty, also suffered greatly from the bombing. Although enemy bombs were largely aimed at military targets, inevitably, especially when their bombers were being chased by Allied fighters or harassed by anti-aircraft fire, many fell elsewhere. With 3,340 air alerts over Malta, the miracle is that casualties were not higher; it is also difficult to comprehend how any work could have been accomplished.

When Italy entered the war in June 1940, there were no RAF operational airfields in Malta although one, at Luqa, was in course of construction and was nearing completion. All RAF aircraft therefore had to operate initially from the relatively small Fleet Air Arm airfield at Hal Far, which had served the RN Mediterranean Fleet pre-war, or from the even smaller civil airport at Ta Kali (or Ta Qali).

In the air the fighter Hurricanes and the various Bristol-built aircraft, Blenheims, Beaufighters and Beauforts, suffered most heavily. The Hurricanes – and many were early versions of this famous fighter aircraft – were not a match for the considerably faster latest Me 109s which, from mid-1941 onwards, had been brought to Sicily specifically to gain air superiority over Malta. The attacking Blenheims, Beaufighters and Beauforts suffered appalling casualties on their low-level strikes against enemy shipping, the loss ratio often being about one in three of the attackers.

On the ground the Wellington bombers, the largest type capable of being used from Malta airfields, with their conspicuous high tails, made easily identified targets and this type suffered many casualties, as also did every other type on the three Malta airfields during those periods when the Luftwaffe had gained air superiority over Malta. Losses would have been much higher on the ground but for the policy of wide dispersal of aircraft and the building of hundreds of anti-blast pens in which to house them. It should be noted that it was the German Luftwaffe operating from Sicilian airfields and not the Italian Regia Aeronautica which accounted for most of this destruction.

The cost to the Fleet Air Arm (FAA) was equally crippling both in the air and on the ground. Throughout its stay in Malta, commencing from June 1940 when Swordfish of 830 Squadron (FAA) first flew in to Malta, the squadrons of the FAA operated from Hal Far as land-based aircraft under the operational control of the RAF. The torpedo-carrying single-engined Swordfish biplanes – with their fixed undercarriages and open 3-men cockpits, looking as if they had strayed by some time-warp accident from the First World War – were especially effective. By 1941 their crews had developed a method of torpedoing the enemy's ships at night which was to prove most successful. Possibly as a result of this they were reinforced by the arrival of slightly more modern, but still single-engined biplane, Albacores of 828 Squadron FAA which at least had enclosed cockpits and more sophisticated instruments and propellers but which also operated with their wheels permanently down. A year or two later Albacores of 821 and 826 Squadrons were also based at Hal Far, as also were a few visiting Fulmar fighters from aircraft-carriers. The latter became 800 X Squadron while in Malta. By mid-1942 the losses of both 830 and 828 Squadrons, from a variety of causes, had been so great that the remnants of both units were amalgamated into a single unit which was known as the (Malta) Royal Navy Air Squadron.

Apart from the casualties brought about by the loss of aircraft in the air – and these were heavy enough in both the RAF and FAA – many ground crews at all three airfields, Hal Far, Luqa and Ta Kali, and the maintenance base at Kalafrana, were much in the firing line. With air raid alerts often in force for more than 12 hours at a time, day and night, it became necessary for men working on damaged machines to continue to work until the bombs were almost dropping. As a result many lost their lives, from inadequate cover or reaching shelter too late, as happened at Hal Far when an air raid shelter into which the men had just huddled was hit by a bomb which caused it to collapse, killing all 16 inside.*

The Army likewise suffered many casualties, principally among those manning anti-aircraft guns during the frequent raids. The enemy planes had good reason to make these gun positions among

---

* Malta was without all heavy lifting equipment and it was not until about two years later, in 1943, that the bodies of those inside could be removed.

their prime targets and dive-bombers were able, on occasion, to reap a revenge upon those who had brought down their comrades. Although 150 British Heavy and Light Anti-Aircraft personnel were killed, about twice that number lost their lives in the various infantry regiments, partly because they were so often at the airfields assisting to repair bomb damage or were around the harbour helping to unload and carry away supplies. Inter-service co-operation reached new heights.

The gallant Royal Malta Artillery also paid heavily as a result of the decision to hold Malta as an Allied base. Although at first both the AA defenders and fighting regiments in Malta were well below the required strength to defend the island from either air attack or a possible invasion from the sea, gradually the numbers of men and guns were increased as all vessels destined for Malta – whether loaded merchant vessels, larger Naval ones such as cruisers, or submarines on their 'Magic Carpet' service – brought in Army and RAF ground personnel to the island.

At all times, as befitted a key British overseas Naval base, Malta was defended by a sizeable British Army presence, along with a number of big coastal guns. Pre-war there were at least four infantry regiments in Malta and by the time Italy declared war on Britain, this number had risen to about twelve, along with eleven anti-aircraft regiments: six heavy and five light. Most had arrived during the period September 1939–April 1940, but the numbers were steadily increased until, by 1941/42, it is estimated that the number of British troops on the island had risen to about 30,000. Among these were several corps of Pioneers, two troops of tanks, coastal gunners, four sections of Signals, and the usual REME, RASC, RAMC and other auxiliaries. About one quarter in all were Maltese who had flocked to join up in Britain's cause.* In addition, large numbers of Maltese had hastened to enrol in the ranks of the Royal Malta Artillery. About one third of all Army personnel were Maltese.*

These Army personnel required guns, ammunition, fuel and transport – especially AA guns, including replacement barrels for

---

* Maltese also served at the airfields with distinction and the Royal Navy, even pre-war, had hundreds if not thousands, of Maltese on board ships and at shore establishments.

those rapidly worn out, and a constant flow of ammunition with which to counter the almost incessant air raids. As was the case with the Navy, Merchant Navy, Allied Air Forces and Fleet Air Arm, every gun, bomb, plane and round of ammunition transported to Malta for use by the Army and the other Services meant a corresponding number of men, bombs, ships, planes and armament denied to the Allies elsewhere in a war which, after December 1941, had expanded to global proportions. All in all, the cost of supplying and defending Malta was enormous.

The cost of the war to the civilian population is beyond measure. Over 1,300 civilians died as a direct result of bombs – ranging from Dolores Degabrielle, at five days old, to Carmela Borg, aged ninety-one; others died as a result of lack of food or heat, or as a result of the primitive living conditions which the war imposed.

The number of buildings destroyed tells its own tale. In this tiny but densely populated island 5,524 private dwellings were totally destroyed, 9,925 damaged but reparable, and 14,225 damaged by bomb blast. In addition, 111 churches, 50 hospitals, institutions or colleges, 36 theatres, clubs, government offices, banks, factories, flour mills and other commercial buildings suffered destruction or damage – a total of over 30,000 buildings in all. This number is probably larger than the total number of buildings standing in the Isle of Wight – an island of similar size – today.

Could this enormous cost be justified? Was this small infertile rocky outpost worth such an expenditure of effort in the midst of a modern global war? Was it just pride or obstinacy that made the British War Cabinet decide to hold Malta at almost any cost or did it make sound military sense to do so? The chapters which follow will present the evidence, leaving readers to make their own judgement as to whether the cost of keeping Malta in business between 1940 and 1944 was excessive or whether the island earned its keep.

2

Early Days

June 1940–January 1941

'Because it is there.'
George Leigh-Mallory, on being asked why he was
determined to climb Mount Everest: on which
he lost his life in June 1924

FROM THE FIRST moment of the war between Britain and Italy, which
had commenced at midnight on 10 June 1940, Malta, being firmly in
British hands, began to make its influence felt. The very presence of
this long-held British military base so near to Sicily dictated that
Italy was obliged to keep a major part of its large air force, the Regia
Aeronautica, at Sicilian airfields and to keep virtually the whole of
its large fleet in ports such as Taranto, in southern Italy.

If Malta had not been there and in British hands, what then? Italy
at that time had a colony in what is now Libya. The Italian Fascist
leader, Benito Mussolini, also had ambitions to extend his African
possessions as part of his burning desire to control the
Mediterranean. It was an open secret, too, that there was a faction
favourable to Italy in Egypt, whose King Farouk, very much under
Britain's thumb at the time, was rumoured to have an Italian mis-
tress who may even have been planted upon him by Mussolini. Had
the Italian Air Force, and virtually the entire Italian fleet, not been
detained as a check on Malta, the chances are that they would have
been used to support the large Italian Colonial Army in Libya in an
attempt to seize Egypt.

Before 10 June 1940, the Italian Navy had been conscious of the
opposing French Navy. The two powers, along with Britain, had

12

vied with one another for nominal domination of the important Mediterranean sea routes. The dramatic events of June 1940 had changed the picture completely, to the advantage of the Italians. With unexpected swiftness, France had been overrun by Germany and was, by 10 June 1940, in the process of suing for an ignominious peace. Her claim to sea dominance anywhere was no longer valid. Britain was also in difficulties. Her fleets were having to cover the Atlantic waters where the German U-boats threatened; added to which she had lost an alarming number of ships during her vain attempts to prevent the Germans seizing Norway. Britain also had commitments in the Far East, India and elsewhere in the world. The many other wartime demands made on the British fleets inevitably weakened her Naval forces in the Mediterranean.

The fact that Italy had to keep large numbers of ships and planes to guard against a potential threat from Malta weakened her position in Central Africa. There, Italy had a long-established colony in Italian Somaliland and had added to this by her unprovoked seizure of the independent kingdom of Abyssinia in 1936. Italy's weakness in Central Africa enabled Lieutenant General Alan Cunningham, with a hastily assembled force, to defeat the Italians in both countries and by May 1941 reinstate the Emperor Haile Selassie on the Abyssinian throne. If the Italians had not had Malta to worry about, there might have been a far more formidable Italian Air Force in that isolated Central African theatre of war – one that Britain was only too pleased to be able to eliminate at an early date.

Although by its mere presence Malta posed a threat to Italy, the threat was potential rather than real in those early months of the Mediterranean war. The British Navy, which by June 1940 was having to safeguard its ships as never before, decided, with good reason, that it was risking too much to keep major Naval forces in the magnificent Grand Harbour, Valletta. Although the harbour could take everything that the British Navy cared to base there, it was deemed to be too close to the enemy bombers which Italy was known to be keeping in Sicily. Likewise, no permanent well-protected submarine base had been established on now isolated Malta. A scheme to construct underground submarine shelters had been started but had been abandoned during the years when UK defence budgets had been slashed to the bone. A few abandoned excavations opposite Manoel Island stood as testimony to that once purposeful plan.

The British Navy did, however, possess excellent workshops, dockyard and harbour facilities elsewhere in Malta which, in the struggle to come, were to prove invaluable assets to the submarines. Although no submarine flotilla was based at Malta on that fateful 10 June 1940, two submarines happened to be in port there as the place was being used to refuel, rearm, restock or service visiting underwater craft.

The RAF on Malta was even less well prepared. It had neither operational pilots nor an airfield from which to operate. More importantly, it had no operational aircraft although enterprising engineers, notably Squadron Leader Louks, the senior RAF engineer officer on the island, had assembled four of the Sea Gladiators which were in crates and in store at the Fleet Air Arm depot at Kalafrana. These were reserve aircraft of the aircraft-carrier *Glorious* which had been sunk during the Norwegian campaign.

The Sea Gladiators – which were single-engined biplane fighters of far from modern design and performance and which carried only four light .303 machine-guns – were formed into what was originally known as the RAF Hal Far Fighter Flight. They were flown by a small handful of RAF Administrative and other Staff Officers who happened to be on the island at the time.* Three of the Gladiators became known as *Faith*, *Hope* and *Charity* and wrote their names into the history books of the RAF. They did enough to show that the much vaunted Italian Air Force was far from being the efficient and determined force of which Mussolini had boasted. As a result, a small number of Hurricanes were soon flown in and the RAF began to operate both from Luqa, as soon as it was completed – it became operational on 28 June – and from Ta Kali, the small grass airfield which, pre-war, had been Malta's civil airport for the few light planes which operated commercial services between the island and nearby Sicilian and Italian airports.

The only established RAF-cum-civil air base on the island was the flying-boat station at Kalafrana which was equipped to take the

---

* George Burges DFC, who became their distinguished leader, was a Flight Lieutenant flying-boat pilot who was serving a term as ADC to the Governor. None were fighter pilots.

largest flying-boats of the day. This contained a well-stocked main-tenance store, which, in the years to come, would prove to be an invaluable asset to the RAF. The fact that the RAF managed to put up a show of force on 11 June when, near dawn, the Italian bombers first came over Malta, was very much due to local enterprise and the initiative of the RAF men on the spot using FAA aircraft and doing what they could to defend the island, thereby making up for the years of neglect perpetrated by various British governments in their determination to reduce defence expenditure. Otherwise the 55 Italian bombers* escorted by over twenty Macchi fighters had no opposition in the air.

Needless to say, the island was woefully short of all the anti-air-craft guns which the Services had requested. It also lacked Fighter Control services.

More by chance than by design, on 19 June a dozen Swordfish aircraft flew into the small FAA airfield at Hal Far, which then, as befits an island which had always been essentially Navy-minded, was the only official military airfield in Malta. These Swordfish had been hastily evacuated from their training base in southern France when that country was on the verge of collapse. Their FAA crews had first flown themselves to an airfield in Tunisia, then a French colony. However, in French Tunisia their future was still insecure and, by then, they had nowhere else to go within their limited range other than Malta. Arriving unexpectedly during an air raid, they found not a soul around Hal Far and the landing area blocked off by old cars and other obstacles to make it unusable to the expected enemy. Somehow these difficulties were avoided. Upon arrival in Malta this team of Swordfish changed their status from 767 Training Squadron to become 830 Squadron FAA, providing Malta with its first official strike-planes – if by a stretch of the imagination this ancient biplane could be called a strike-aircraft.

Before June was out, these open cockpit aircraft had raided the Sicilian port of Augusta where they dive-bombed oil storage tanks. Although it is doubtful if they did very much damage, a sub-sequent raid by other Swordfish from an aircraft-carrier did sink a destroyer and damage a cruiser in that same naval base. This was

---

* All were fast three-engined Savoia Marchetti (SM 78) bombers.

enough for the Italians. They attributed both raids to the Malta-based aircraft and henceforth decided to abandon Augusta as a naval base except for submarines and light craft. The presence of Malta so close to Sicily had struck a vital blow: if cruisers had remained at Augusta, as was normal, it would have been all too easy for Malta to have been bombarded, in a series of swift night sorties, by their 8-inch guns. There was nothing on the island at that time to have prevented this.

Indeed, plans to take Malta by force had first come under consideration by the Italians as far back as 1935 at the time of Mussolini's seizure of Abyssinia.* To enforce the sanctions and oil embargo imposed on Italy by the League of Nations – forerunner of UNO – British warships thereafter had done their best to prevent supplies being delivered to that part of Italy's colonial empire which consisted of Italian Somaliland, Eritrea and the newly overrun Abyssinia. In retaliation, and in an attempt to blunt the power of the British Navy, a plan to invade Malta was drawn up, but nothing came of it.

In 1938, Italy again considered the seizure of Malta. Mussolini, still in the black books of the League of Nations and Britain, was contemplating transporting a military force into her Tripolitanian colony but realized that she could not get away with this attempt to expand her North African territory without first seizing Malta. Accordingly a secret plan, DG10/42, for invading the island was prepared. This again was shelved.

In the spring of 1940, at a time when Italy was still neutral in the war, a further and more detailed plan was drawn up. To overcome the estimated 15,000 troops in the British-held fortress, Italy proposed to invest 40,000 troops in the capture of Malta. She envisaged having to lose all the 80 sea-craft required. Landings would first be made in the north with an attack being made upon the Victoria Lines defences, which lay across the centre of the island and constituted the Army's principal defences. Secondary landings would be made on Gozo, an island adjacent to and north of Malta,† and

---

* These details are contained in Tullio Marcon, *La marcata occupazione italiana di Malta*.
† Malta comprises a small group of islands of which Malta itself is much the biggest. Gozo is also well inhabited. Comino had only one or two buildings.

the tiny island of Comino which lies between the two. Her entire navy would be involved as well as 500 aircraft, mainly bombers. The planners then came face to face with the fact that the country lacked the means to carry out the operation with any chance of success.

After entering the war on the side of Germany in June 1940, this plan was brought up to date. It visualized the use of only 20,000 men but incorporated tanks. Landings were also envisaged at St Paul's Bay and on the island's less protected, but more intractable, west coast. The operation would be launched from Augusta and Syracuse where the assault craft would be assembled.

Although technical reasons have since been put forward to explain why Italy did not invade Malta soon after entering the war – that the Italians had overestimated its defences; that they needed 100 more landing-craft, and that Malta was no longer being used as a British naval base for large warships – it is likely that the real reason was that, in June 1940, the seizure of Malta by force was thought to be unnecessary. Mussolini had only thrown in his lot with Germany in order to be able to claim a share of the spoils. With the collapse and surrender of France, it seemed almost inconceivable to Mussolini that Britain would fight on and even more inconceivable that she, and her Allies, would eventually regain Europe and defeat the all-conquering Wehrmacht. It was also believed by many in the Fascist countries of Germany and Italy that the Fascist regime in Spain would decide to join the war on their side and that, in this event, Gibraltar would be seized and entrance to the Mediterranean be barred to the British; Malta would then be rendered largely impotent.

This failure to enforce an advantage was to have its effect. It did not take the Royal Navy long to appreciate that Malta, positioned astride the sea routes which Italian ships would have to take when supplying their Libyan colony, was almost an ideal place in which to base submarines. Since long-range sorties would not be required, the Navy opted to deploy a flotilla of their smallest type there – the Royal Navy's Unity, or U-class vessels, of about 500 tons. They would be based at Manoel Island, Lazaretto Creek, to the north of Valletta and adjacent to Sliema, to which it was attached via a causeway.

It can scarcely be claimed that Malta was initially on the offensive.

Even when against expectations and all odds it seemed that the
RAF could hold off the challenges of the Regia Aeronautica, and of
equal or greater importance, it was shown that the Maltese population was made of stern stuff and, in the main, was staunchly pro-
British, the island in June 1940 was not geared for launching an
attack.

Britain kept a number of submarines in the Mediterranean both
at Gibraltar, where the Eighth Flotilla was based, and in Alexandria,
where the First Flotilla was based. Between them they operated
mainly with the P, R, S and T-class vessels, all relatively large types
designed to operate with the fleets. With Malta so strategically
placed, it is not surprising that many of the submarines from both
these bases were soon calling in at Malta or making patrols from
there, using such facilities as were available.

During the early months of the war against Italy, a number of successes were scored from Malta although the submarine base was
still being developed and the Tenth Flotilla was not yet officially
created. On 20 June, when the war with Italy was a mere ten days
old, one of our submarines, on passage through the Mediterranean,
came across an Italian submarine and Lieutenant Rimmington, in
Parthian, duly sent it to the bottom. Other successes followed.
Truant, under Lieutenant Commander Haggard, sank the Italian
merchant ship *Sebastiano Bianchi* (1,545 tons) on 13 December and,
four days later, sank the tanker *Bonzo* (9,175 tons) – a very important
success. Both attacks took place in the waters east of Calabria
(southern Italy).

Parthian struck again on 3 January 1941, sinking the supply ship
Carlo Martinolich (4,210 tons), whilst *Regent* (Lt/Cdr Brownes)
accounted for the *Citta di Messina* (2,475 tons) on the 15th of that
month.

Even after Commander G.W.G. Simpson had arrived in Malta in
January 1941 to set up and take charge of the Manoel Island base
and to commence operations with the U-class boats, which were to
constitute the backbone of his Tenth Flotilla, other larger submarines still continued to score successes from, or around Malta.
Rover (Lt/Cdr Marsham) sank the *Cesco* (6,160 tons) on 14 February
in the Ionian Sea and *Triumph* (Lt/Cdr Woods) scored two successes
on 5 March 1941 off Calabria, sinking the *Marzamemi* and *Colomba lo
Faro*, both supply vessels of just under 1,000 tons.

The RAF also showed an early interest in Italian submarines. On 28 and 29 June 1940 Sunderland four-engined flying-boats of 230 Squadron, a type which then frequently called in at Malta, sank the Italian submarines *Argonauta* and *Rubino*. By contrast with the FAA Swordfish, the Sunderland was a large up-to-date aircraft which operated throughout the war. It carried a crew of about ten and was armed with several machine-gun positions. These last successes had even preceded the Swordfish's first attacks in June; attacks which 830 Squadron followed up on 6 July 1940 when they aimed their Swordfish at the hangars at Catania, a major Sicilian airfield and flying-boat base.

However, these were isolated air attacks and, while Malta's defences strove to deal with the Italian Air Force as best they could with their inadequate equipment and while the defences were building up, little by way of retaliation could be offered by the slender Royal Navy and RAF forces available on the island. These isolated attacks were, however, proving costly and when 830 Squadron Swordfish again attacked Augusta on 13 August, three of the nine aircraft failed to return. Aircraft of 830 Squadron also bombed an Italian submarine on 19 July but, as was apt to be the case when aircraft attacked submarines, the results were inconclusive.

When a submarine crash-dives in a swirl of spray as a bomb or depth-charge dropped by an aircraft explodes nearby, and when it does not again resurface, what is the crew of the aircraft to deduce? The aircraft cannot hang around indefinitely to observe results and, if it had sunk the submarine, what results would the crew expect to observe? A flying-boat might be able to land and look for evidence but a Swordfish certainly could not.

However, during September 1940, while the Battle of Britain raged over south-east England, the whole character and importance of Malta as a war base was changed. During that month, the huge Italian Colonial Army, under General Graziani, began cautiously to advance over the Libyan frontier into Egypt. The see-saw battle for control of the 1,000-mile strip of desert which lay between Alexandria in Egypt and Tripoli in Libya had begun.

In that instant, Malta was indirectly pitchforked into the front line of the Desert War and was to remain there until the Allied seizure of North Africa in May 1943. If an enemy army in the Desert were to succeed, then Egypt, the Suez Canal and the oilfields beyond would all come within the reach of the German and Italian dictators.

But to succeed in that barren desert, the invading armies had to receive a steady flow of war supplies from the factories of Italy and Germany; and to a lesser extent, even rations for its men. Those supplies had to reach them by ship. It only takes a glance at a map of the Central Mediterranean to appreciate that Malta was well placed to interfere with the ships carrying those supplies. Its strategic position was one reason why Nelson and Britain had accepted, and the latter held firmly on to, control of the island fortress for well over a hundred years.

The question now was whether or not the island could, after all these years of British control and, despite the recent neglect of successive British governments, justify the reasons for that control; whether the local populace would stand firm with Britain, and whether or not the men who found themselves there in September 1940 onwards still had the 'Nelson touch', that ability to fight relentlessly towards victory with, at times, no more than scant regard for the accepted precepts of the day.

The RAF was soon to send modern attack forces to be based in Malta. By December 1940, 148 Squadron,* operating twin-engined Wellington bombers, flew into the newly constructed Luqa airfield: the only one on the island large enough to take this 15-ton twin-engined bomber-type aircraft. The Air Officer Commanding (AOC) Malta, Air Commodore F.H.M. Maynard,† had instructions to attack the ports of departure and arrival of ships carrying supplies to North Africa. By 2 December 1940, ten Wellingtons had launched a night raid upon the large enemy port of Naples from which supplies to General Graziani's army in North Africa departed. Other raids on other ports followed.

As in Europe, the large, relatively slow Wellington bombers of

---

* A normal RAF squadron establishment was sixteen aircraft, with four in reserve. However, these numbers were seldom, if ever, attained in Malta.

† Not until Hugh Pughe Lloyd arrived in January 1941 was an Air Vice Marshal's post established. Throughout the war, AOC Malta came under the command of AOC Middle East in Egypt, but when a dynamic personality controlled RAF (and FAA) operations from Malta, the RAF in Malta was very much fighting its own war.

RAF Bomber Command were deemed too vulnerable for daylight use. However, unlike the experience of those then operating over Germany at night, the Wellingtons from Malta were able to find and hit their targets with great accuracy. The bright moonlight of the Mediterranean was an undoubted help, but in addition their targets were generally ports which stood out clearly on most nights. The Italians moreover, unlike the Germans, had no strong searchlight bands or large numbers of radar-controlled AA guns. As a result Wellington losses, due to enemy action over their ports at night, were almost negligible. Although the aircraft had twin machine-gun turrets fore and aft its six-men crew seldom had to defend themselves.

Over Tripoli in Libya, a frequent target, the Italians had a considerable number of guns which fired a colourful amount of ammunition without apparent aim. The effect was spectacular rather than frightening, as the author can testify. These factors encouraged the attacking bomber crews to drop their loads from lower altitudes than was the custom over Germany: another factor making for greater bombing accuracy.

The Wellington could carry up to 4,000 pounds of bombs in either sixteen 250-pound form, eight 500-pounders or lesser loads supplemented by a large number of small incendiary bombs. When they were thus loaded, the longest runway at Luqa was barely of sufficient length and after two aircraft had crashed immediately after take-off, the bomb load had to be reduced until such time as the village church, immediately in line with the take-off runway, was demolished. This was done with remarkable speed – an early example of how Maltese citizens co-operated with the RAF. Steps were also put in hand to lengthen the longest runway, an undertaking which was to be required more than once.

Meanwhile, in the course of November/December 1940, the British Army in the Desert had routed the vastly superior numbers of the Italian forces, in a brilliant offensive action conducted on the ground by Major General R.N. O'Connor. One consequence of this was that nearly 1,200 Italian aircraft had been either destroyed in the air or, more often, captured or destroyed on the ground by the fast advancing British Eighth Army. It was a blow from which the Regia Aeronautica never fully recovered, and henceforth the RAF in Malta had, for the most part, only the German Luftwaffe to worry about: although in December 1940, this force had yet to appear in the arena. Nevertheless, in size the Italian Air Force in Sicily was still numerically greater than the RAF in Malta.

Wellingtons of 148 Squadron were able to assist the work of the Eighth Army and add to the Italian Air Force's confusion when, on the night of 7 December, they raided the principal airfield of Tripoli, Castel Benito, and destroyed or damaged 29 aircraft parked there in neat rows. On that occasion, throwing all caution to the wind, some of the attackers, realizing that the AA fire was ineffective, swept down to a low level and gave their gunners, who seemed to have no enemy night fighters to fire at, the opportunity of blazing away at hangars and aircraft with the twin guns in their fore and aft turrets.

Not to be outdone by the newly arrived RAF Wellingtons, the FAA Swordfish of 830 Squadron also attacked Tripoli and on 10 December claimed three hits on ships which had arrived there.

Although it was not in itself an attacking force, the RAF had also sent, in September 1940, three Glen Martin (US-built) Maryland fast twin-engined fighter-bombers to Malta to serve as a photo-reconnaissance unit. They carried a crew of three: pilot, navigator/observer and a wireless operator-cum-air gunner (WOP/AG) who could operate either of the aircraft's upper or lower twin machine-gun positions. In Malta this type was only seldom rigged to carry bombs but the latest RAF cameras were installed. Its armament included two fixed forward-firing machine-guns in its wings. The three planes were given the name of 431 Flight. As their successes mounted, they were increased in number and shortly became 69 Squadron. This was the one permanent resident squadron at Luqa which never left the place and which was, through the next two years and more, to play an increasingly important role in supporting attacks from Malta whether by sea or air. General Werner von Fritsch, a member of the German High Command (OKW), never spoke more truly than when he stated, in 1939: 'The military organization with the best aerial photo-reconnaissance will win the next war.'

By fate and good fortune 431 Flight (69 Squadron), on arrival in Malta, included among its aircrews a young disgraced pilot who had been designated a navigator after a series of failures as a pilot in the air and many irregular escapades on the ground. But for the state of the war in September 1940, there can be little doubt that this irresponsible young officer would have been ejected from the RAF, but by then everyone with any flying skills was desperately needed. This officer was the remarkable Adrian Warburton who was later to become the symbol of the island's resistance and its ability to hit back, often in a highly irregular manner. Before the month was out Warburton was back piloting Marylands of 431 Flight (solely because two other pilots had gone sick and there was no one else to do it) and, along with his energetic CO, an Australian Squadron Leader E.A. 'Tich' Whiteley, was preparing the way for the most successful torpedo attack of the war in the Mediterranean.

Although no aircraft from Malta took part in the now famous Taranto harbour attack in November 1940, when three Italian battleships were sent to the bottom by Swordfish aircraft flown from the aircraft-carrier *Illustrious*, the debt that was owed to the Malta-based reconnaissance aircraft of 431 Flight was recognized by Admiral Sir Andrew Cunningham, the C-in-C Mediterranean Fleet in Alexandria, who signalled to the AOC Malta his appreciation of the photography and visual reconnaissances which 431 Flight had carried out over Taranto immediately before the attack. When attacking with torpedoes at night, it is essential to know exactly where the prize targets are, as well as the booms, nets and other defences.

Of the several flights over Taranto which 431 Flight had made in the period prior to the famous Swordfish attack, Warburton had carried out the most important ones of 10 and 11 November. That carried out on the 11th, the day preceding the night attack, was completed in atrocious flying weather with clouds almost at sea level. As a result, photographs would have been meaningless. Instead Warburton directed his crew to plot on paper the positions of the ships as he flashed past them at low level. His gunner was even directed to try to read the names of each ship while his navigator did the plotting. Because of the bad weather, no balloon barrage was flying.

When they escaped, having achieved surprise and not been seriously shot at, the crew compared notes. They found a discrepancy about the number of battleships in the outer harbour; one man made it five and the other made it six. 'We will have to do it all again,' remarked the intrepid Warburton. So in they went again, but this time to a hot reception. Having determined that there were only

five battleships, Warburton calmly flew his Maryland AR 705 back
to Malta. The results were immediately passed to *Illustrious* at sea.

How low did Warburton go in his Maryland? His navigator,
Sergeant Spiers, in a newspaper article published after the war,
recalls seeing the ripples made on the surface of the water by the aircraft's wing-tip. Even more substantive evidence is the ship's aerial
which Warburton brought back caught up in his non-retractable tail
wheel.

The successful Taranto raid established two facts: most importantly, that it was the British Navy with their aircraft-carriers
(the Italians had none) which dominated the Mediterranean, and
that Malta possessed, in 431 Flight, a superb photo-reconnaissance
unit. It was also an early example of RN–RAF co-operation, which
had commenced even earlier when it had been decided that, while
in Malta, 830 Squadron FAA should operate under RAF control.

It was no surprise that 431 Flight was soon to be given additional
aircraft and upgraded to squadron status. By January 1941, 69
Squadron was born and firmly entrenched at Luqa where nothing
subsequently attempted by the enemy was ever to cause them to
cease operations.

It was equally no surprise that Warburton was soon awarded the
first of the six* gallantry awards which were to be given him before
he finally departed from Malta. The rejected pilot, who had been
sent to Malta as a navigator by a kindly CO in the UK who did not
want to see him court-martialled, was on his way to becoming a
living legend.

The Taranto attack, thanks in part to the daring photographic and
reconnaissance feats of Warburton and Whiteley, changed the
balance of sea power in the Mediterranean for many months to
come. The decision to hold on to Malta, to supply and defend it, was
proving to be a sound one, although few could then have imagined
the enormous cost in ships, aircraft and men's lives that would ultimately be expended in the process.

---

* Two DSOs and four DFCs – one an American one.

3

The Tenth Submarine Flotilla

September 1940–April 1941

'Now, as formerly, the most dangerous British weapon
in the Mediterranean is the submarine, especially those
operating from Malta.'

Report from German Naval Council in the
Mediterranean, 9 September 1941

ALTHOUGH MALTA WAS a long-established Royal Navy base and
the home of Britain's large Mediterranean Fleet, by June 1940 conditions had already greatly changed. With Sicily almost within sight,
it was considered dangerous to continue to expose warships in
Malta's massive Grand Harbour to the risk of bombing. The decision was therefore taken, even before Mussolini threw in his lot with
Hitler, to move the Mediterranean Fleet to Alexandria in Egypt.

As a result, when Italy declared war upon Britain, there were in
Malta only a handful of visiting submarines and a few motor
torpedo-boats (MTBs). However Malta still possessed, in and
around Grand Harbour, its well-equipped dockyard with repair
and servicing facilities capable of coping with the biggest vessels
afloat. It also retained W/T facilities, which included 'Y' Listening
Service personnel to intercept and make use of every W/T message.
Although the Fleet personnel had moved away, there were sufficient dockyard men, wireless operators, shore personnel, stores and
machinery to justify the presence of a Vice Admiral and Wilbraham
Ford was duly appointed Vice Admiral Malta (VAM).

Even when the Royal Navy in Malta had dominated the Central
Mediterranean, there had never been a separate submarine base as

such. The considerable number of RN fleet submarines operated from a floating base and a depot ship moored in Grand Harbour. In 1934 a start had been made to create bomb-proof submarine pens by tunnelling into the rock face to the north of Lazaretto Creek opposite the former leper hospital buildings on Manoel Island, a few miles north of Valletta. However this excellent plan was soon abandoned in a politically motivated cost-cutting exercise.

From June 1940, once Britain had decided to try to hold on to Malta, a few of the larger types of submarines commenced operations in the waters around Malta but, after suffering 50 per cent losses, it was decided that the smaller, relatively new U-class submarines would be better suited to the conditions. It was further decided to create, as hastily as possible, a submarine base away from Grand Harbour on Manoel Island where the strongly built stone buildings of the former leper hospital could be used as a shore establishment. This task was given to a former Navy Officer, R.G. 'Pop' Giddings, who had retired to Malta and who had become the representative of a well-known firm of wine merchants. The Manoel Island base, when fully functioning, went by the name of HMS *Talbot*.

Back in the UK, the decision was made to form a submarine Flotilla based in Malta to be named the Tenth Flotilla and Admiral Sir Max Horton, the Flag Officer Submarines (FOS), appointed Commander G.W.G. Simpson to command the new unit.

Pending the availability of the U-class submarines, in September 1940 Lieutenant Commander R.G. Mills was sent to Malta with four of the new larger T-class submarines, one of which he also commanded in person. Commander Simpson, commonly known by his nickname of 'Shrimp', was to follow in January 1941. There he would become Captain Simpson with the title 'Captain (S) 10'.

By 20 September 1940 several T-class boats were on patrol from Malta and, though operating with some success, also suffered heavy losses. They were found to be too large and unwieldy for the waters round Malta, and within weeks three Malta-based submarines had been lost, together with many pre-war trained officers and men.

Administratively, the Tenth Submarine Flotilla came initially under the command of the First Submarine Flotilla in Alexandria, which itself was part of the Mediterranean Fleet under Admiral

Sir Andrew Cunningham operating from its Alexandria base. However, in practice, the Tenth, once established and with Commander Simpson in charge, operated as an independent unit and was given a very free hand by Admiral Cunningham. For someone of 'Shrimp' Simpson's outstanding qualities and strong views, this suited him well. 'Shrimp' Simpson was an experienced submarine commander and one who, in pre-war days, had made quite a nuisance of himself in certain exalted quarters of the Admiralty by expressing doubts upon the efficiency of the Asdic underwater device, which the Admiralty was claiming at the time had virtually rendered the submarine useless as a weapon against ships equipped with this device.

In pre-war sea trials against naval vessels equipped with Asdic, a younger Simpson, in charge of a submarine, had managed to penetrate the destroyer screens and score theoretical hits against such famous battleships as *Nelson*. In Simpson's mind, it proved his point. However it did not result in any change of heart in the Admiralty.

Earlier in his career 'Shrimp' had obtained the details of the U-boats which, in defiance of the Versailles Treaty, Germany was building and designing for the Finnish Navy, to which Germany was also sending officers for training on these excellent boats. His detailed report describing this potential menace to Britain had been filed and largely ignored, although once hostilities began, some consideration was belatedly given to it.

Now Cunningham's instructions to the newly appointed flotilla commander were brief and to the point. Because of torpedo shortages, Commander Simpson was to sink only southbound shipping, except for tankers, large transports and warships which could also be attacked when heading back to Italy. His main job was to stop supplies reaching North Africa. 'If you don't get results, I will soon let you know. Until then, you have a free hand' were the words completing his briefing. This was music to his ears. He was always his own man, a person who welcomed responsibility and one who was never bereft of ideas. A humane leader also, he went out of his way to study the idiosyncrasies of each of his submarine commanders and, within limits, allowed them to do things in their own individual way, as he himself preferred to do. He was also, at times, prepared to break the established rules in order to get things done.

Such qualities, together with a tough and determined fair-minded-ness, soon endeared him to all who served under him. Nominally Commander Simpson was subordinate to Captain (S) 1, Captain Philip Ruck-Keene, the Officer Commanding the First Submarine Flotilla in Alexandria but, thanks to former friendship and mutual respect, this never imposed a barrier between himself and the hierarchy above.*

Although the Tenth Flotilla was composed of small 500-ton Unity-class submarines (including the Polish *Sokol* of the same design) Captain Simpson, to give him the rank which he was to hold for much of his time in Malta, also found himself responsible for many larger submarines which visited Malta for long periods, coming in either from Gibraltar or Alexandria. In effect, Captain Simpson had operational control over all Allied submarines in the Central Mediterranean, irrespective of where those submarines might be based.

P, R, S and T-class submarines all appeared from time to time to operate from Malta. *Rorqual*, a 1,500-ton minelayer submarine, for instance, was twice commissioned to operate from there, and prob-ably spent twice as much time in Malta as many U-class submarines of the Tenth Flotilla. The *Clyde*, a submarine specially converted to carry supplies, also frequently operated under the command of Captain (S) 10.

The mainstay of the Tenth Flotilla, however, as it built up a strength of about ten submarines, was the small Unity-class vessels. U-class submarines were never designed as operational vessels but were intended to serve the Navy as, to quote the words of John Wingate in his book *The Fighting Tenth*, 'clockwork mice' in the train-ing of surface warships in anti-submarine detection. However, with war clouds looming over the horizon, in the late 1930s they were put into production as operational vessels. The first ones were all built at the Vickers yards at Barrow-in-Furness and the first three to be launched in 1937 were *Undine*, *Unity* and *Ursula*.

---

* The Malta-based submarines remained officially part of the First Flotilla based in Alexandria until September 1941, when they were officially designated the Tenth Flotilla and Commander Simpson was promoted Captain. However, it is conve-nient to refer to the Tenth Flotilla and Captain Simpson throughout. In September 1941 their operations underwent no change, other than in name and status.

As fighting submarines, the U-class had many disadvantages. With a maximum of only 10 knots, they were woefully lacking in speed. This meant that their chances of being able to catch up, and overtake, even merchant ships were slight and the chance of their manoeuvring to head off an enemy warship was almost negligible. At only 500 tons, conditions on board were more cramped than was usual, even in a Service where living conditions were always both insanitary and overcrowded. A total crew of about thirty-two was required, including four officers.

As well as being too slow and small, the U-class boats initially suffered from having an almost totally useless 12-pounder gun; later a more effective 3-inch one replaced this ancient weapon. Their size limited them to ten torpedoes, four of which could be fired in quick succession.

On the asset side, they could dive with a rapidity that was unmatched. A good crew could get under the waves in about 16 seconds. They were also easy to build, relatively simple in design and, as such, made an almost ideal boat for a first command. Their crews also found several uses for the Asdic on board. However, they were always difficult boats to trim accurately and when supposed to be at negative buoyancy they were apt to bob up to the surface in bad weather and also whenever a succession of torpedoes was being fired.

The history of British submarine operations in the Mediterranean in the early part of the war did not make for confidence. By the time Commander Simpson had got himself to Cairo *en route* to Malta, nine British submarines had been lost although nine Italian merchant vessels, along with one Italian submarine and one of their torpedo-boats, had been sunk by Mediterranean-based Allied submarines, making in all a total destruction of 37,000 tons of enemy shipping. The loss of nine trained and experienced submarine commanders was particularly serious. These losses were mostly attributed, at the time, to enemy mining, as there seemed to be a reluctance to admit that the real causes of seven of the nine losses were Italian destroyers and torpedo-boats which were proving to be efficient submarine hunters. It was also significant that of the 37,000 tons sunk about half had been accomplished by just one submarine commander, Lieutenant Commander Hugh Haggard in *Truant*. Many of the submarine commanders had not scored at all.

The Tenth Flotilla can be said to have been truly born on 14 January 1941 when the first of the Unity-class submarines arrived in Malta. This was *Upholder*, commanded by Lieutenant David Wanklyn. This was a happy event as 'Wankers' had been Simpson's First Lieutenant before the war on board *Porpoise*, a minelayer similar to *Rorqual*, and the two had operated well together. This was the same Lieutenant Commander Wanklyn (as he became in February) who was to write his name in glorious letters in the months to come. Just as Warburton's name is inevitably associated with the RAF in Malta during the Second World War, so is Wanklyn's name associated with the successes of the Malta-based submarines of the Tenth Flotilla.

Captain Simpson also found himself in charge of a small bunch of extremely brave young Army personnel who were the forerunners of persons whom we now refer to as Commandos. Led initially by a Captain Taylor of the Liverpool Scottish Regiment, they were to carry out at least seventeen raids on enemy targets in the adjacent territories of Sicily, Italy, Greece and Tunisia. Transported by one of the submarines of the Tenth to a beach, the commandos would go ashore in their two-man folding canoes, known as folbots, armed to the teeth with guns and explosives with which to blow up trains, demolish tunnels, bridges and the like. Owing to the country's mountainous interior the Italian rail system in Calabria and Sicily often ran close to the shore. The line also had to cross rivers and dive through tunnels. These points all made attractive targets for the soldiers once they had paddled ashore in the folbots. Spies also were occasionally carried or picked up.

The folbots, being collapsible and portable (they were sold pre-war in Gamages for holiday-makers), could be manhandled fairly easily into and out of the submarines. Before departing, the raiders would arrange a time and place to rendezvous with the submarine which had brought them in. Sadly, many a pick-up was never accomplished as losses were heavy and conditions often militated against a safe rendezvous.

The arrival of *Upholder* was soon followed by that of *Usk* (Lt Collett) and *Upright* (Lt Norman) as gradually the Tenth Flotilla grew in size to about ten small U-class submarines.

Much of the success which was to follow was due to a splendid engineering officer, Lieutenant Commander (E) Sam McGregor, who was later to find his hands more than full when the bombing of Malta reached its peak and the flotilla's Lazaretto Creek/Manoel Island base was identified and specifically targeted by the Luftwaffe. In Malta itself, Captain Simpson came under the command of Vice Admiral Malta (VAM) Wilbraham Ford, another outstanding sea-dog, tough and outspoken, who, long familiar with the island, knew how to get the best out of local facilities. Although both Captain Simpson and VAM Ford (soon to become Sir Wilbraham), had minds of their own, the pair got along splendidly and Simpson was able to carry on just as Admiral Cunningham had briefed him to do, with a 'free hand to act as he thought best'.

An early innovation, which showed remarkable foresight and was to pay handsome dividends, was the decision to start a piggery at the Lazaretto base. £300 was expended upon setting this up and, with the pigs fed partially on mess left-overs, by the time the base had to be abandoned at the height of the 1942 blitz, there were no less than 120 pigs' carcasses hanging up in the Government's freezer storage. Another brilliant piece of foresight was to hire local masons and carpenters to excavate and build safe underground living and storage quarters.

Lieutenant Commander Hubert Marsham was appointed as Deputy Captain (S) 10 and with a Mr Warne, generally known as 'Sunny' Warne, as Torpedo Officer and the long-retired Lieutenant Commander 'Pop' Giddings brought back from Naval Reserve to look after the buildings, the Tenth Flotilla settled down to work with an efficient base team all solidly behind their energetic leader.

One of the Tenth's early tasks was to play a part in the first large commando-style raid of the war using parachutists. The plan was intended to test whether such raids were feasible.

The operation was given the code name Colossus. The target was an aqueduct in Calabria, southern Italy, which was known to supply water to a large, partly industrialized area as far south as Brindisi. Eight twin-engined Whitley bombers – an obsolescent type of night bomber – were flown to Malta with a rising star, Squadron Leader Willie Tait, in charge. Four were to drop the 40 parachutists while the other four were to carry out a diversionary raid upon an adjacent target. Photographs of the target were as ever essential and a splendid set of pictures were duly obtained by Warburton from heights down almost to grass level.

The parachutists were dropped more or less on target, although the fall was as usual somewhat scattered. However the amount of explosive used, although correctly placed and detonated, failed to cause the towering aqueduct to collapse. Possibly Roman, it was doubtless built to last. However, a nearby railway bridge, though not a primary target, was blown up, so the venture was not entirely without success. Then things started to go badly wrong.

The aim had been for the party to get themselves to the mouth of the River Tragino where, five days later, they were to be picked up offshore by the submarine *Triumph* (Lt Cayley). Two unexpected misfortunes befell the raiders. First, snow began to fall and this made it impossible for the raiders to conceal their tracks as they headed for the coast; in due course, all were captured before reaching the river mouth. Secondly, one of the bomb-dropping Whitleys experienced engine trouble, was unable to maintain height and eventually had to crash-land. Regrettably it chose to do so close to the mouth of the River Tragino. This raised the suspicion in the minds of Captain Simpson and others that the secret details of the rescue by *Triumph* might have been leaked to the Whitley crew who had therefore chosen that area in which to crash-land, in the hope also of being picked up by *Triumph*. With a crew of 44 on board his submarine, Captain Simpson decided that, since security might have been compromised, it made sense to recall the submarine even before it could reach the rendezvous area. It was a hard decision but a necessary one in wartime conditions.

In the event, the decision turned out to be 100 per cent correct. None of the parachutists succeeded in reaching the area; all the raiders were taken prisoner except for a brave Italian, Sergeant Pecchi – a former Savoy Hotel employee and an ardent pro-British anti-Mussolini Italian, who had volunteered his services because of his local knowledge of the area around the aqueduct. When apprehended he was summarily shot as a traitor. He died in a just cause.

Again it was Warburton who, after the attack, photographed the fractured rail bridge and brought back evidence of the still standing aqueduct. Although the raid itself must be deemed a failure, it served to establish the feasibility of such commando-style operations, and these have since become an intrinsic element in every major country's military forces.

Squadron Leader Tait who had successfully led the air side of the operation was awarded the first of the four DSOs which were to come his way. By the end of the war he had become widely known as 'Tirpitz' Tait, having led the formation of Lancaster bombers which, much later in the war, dropped the massive 12,000-pound 'earthquake' bombs which caused the enormous German battle-ship *Tirpitz* to roll over in Trondheim Fjord.

By February 1941, when Operation Colossus took place, the Desert War had undergone a traumatic change. After the crushing defeat of the Italians in Libya by General O'Connor, Hitler had little option, unless he was to abandon for ever his dream of reaching the oilfields of Arabia, but to send German troops to North Africa to bolster up the remnants of General Graziani's defeated army. This army, once formidable on paper, had by then lost some 20 generals, 130,000 men, 845 guns and nearly 400 tanks, mainly through encirclement and capture.*

Early in 1941, to prevent a total Italian collapse in that theatre of war, Hitler sent the famous Afrika Korps, led by the then largely unknown General Erwin Rommel, to North Africa. These were the first German troops to take part in the Desert War. As a measure of protection for these troops, Hitler also moved the X Fliegerkorps from northern Europe to the Middle East. Many of these Luftwaffe units were stationed in Sicily as the German High Command had already come to realize that their shipping routes to North Africa were vulnerable to naval and air forces based in Malta.

Meanwhile, the Wellingtons and Swordfish kept up their attacks on ports such as Naples, Catania, Palermo and Tripoli without, however, encountering too much enemy opposition; the port of Tripoli and Castel Benito, its adjacent airfield, being targets which were frequently hit and damaged. However, the best way to deny supplies to North Africa unquestionably was to sink the ships trans-porting them southwards, which was why the Tenth Flotilla had been established in Malta. Swordfish of 830 Squadron were also

---

* John Terraine, *The Right of the Line*, p. 317.

used to lay mines outside Tripoli but Admiral Cunningham objected. He likened this to playing Russian roulette and persuaded the Admiralty that these torpedo-bombers should be used for their proper purpose rather than as minelayers.

Although the Tenth had been officially established in Malta during January 1941, at least one U-class submarine *Upright*, first under Lieutenant Brooks and then under Lieutenant Norman, appears to have been operating out of Malta from December 1940 onwards. However its first two patrols produced no results.

It was much the same story with *Upholder* under Lieutenant Commander Wanklyn. Although on his first patrol in Malta, 24 January–1 February 1941, he claimed a hit upon the important German merchant ship *Duisberg* (7,889 tons) without sinking it, the reports of his next three patrols could only record a number of misses. As he had by then expended over a dozen torpedoes (several torpedoes were usually fired in succession during each attack) without sinking a ship, Captain Simpson was in two minds whether to replace his former good friend and efficient First Lieutenant and give the command of *Upholder* either to the spare CO, who was always at hand in case of sickness or absence among the others, or to a replacement called in from Alexandria or elsewhere. Fortunately for the Allies, he decided to give the newly promoted Lieutenant Commander another chance.

These misses were extremely costly as it was during this period, January–April 1941, that the Afrika Korps was being transported to Tripoli: one particular convoy was missed by three different U-class submarines on the same day, 9 February 1941.

For these early patrols, the area assigned to submarine commanders was essentially the same, since the enemy was relying solely on the direct route to North Africa. Their ships, whether departing from Naples or from Palermo, would round the western tip of Sicily near Marettimo Island and then head south towards Cape Bon which lay in neutral, Vichy French-controlled Tunisia.* From there

---

* After the French surrender in June 1940, Hitler allowed the southern half of France a measure of freedom under a Government based at Vichy. Tunisia, then a French colony, came under the jurisdiction of the Vichy Government. Vichy France was not occupied by the Germans until late 1942 and was, technically, neutral although much under German influence.

they continued down the Tunisian coast, until turning east for their final short run to Tripoli.

Tripoli was the Italians' principal town and port in Africa. Its docks could cope with up to six ships being unloaded at a time. These were by far the best port facilities between itself and Alexandria, 1,000 miles away to the east.

Midway down the coast of Tunisia lies the Kerkenah Bank and the Italian island of Lampedusa. It was in the vicinity of these that the Malta-based submarines often lay in wait, as the likely shipping routes past these 'obstructions' could be assessed with accuracy. Kerkenah Bank itself was a natural hazard with a wide area of shallow water to be avoided. Captain Simpson also sent his few submarines to lie in wait close to Tripoli itself, although this position carried the additional hazard of mines, both magnetic and of other kinds, laid by the Swordfish aircraft of 830 Squadron immediately outside the entrance to that enemy port.

Mines were to be the bane of the submarines of the Tenth Flotilla throughout the war. Both Italian and German, they were laid in their thousands during the next three years. By the war's end the Italians had laid approximately 54,000 of these insidious weapons. Many had already been laid by 1941 and the narrows between Sicily and Cape Bon would soon become a favourite mining area for the enemy in their attempts to prevent Malta receiving supplies from Gibraltar. Malta-based submarines always had to tread warily in that channel, especially when in waters less than 70 fathoms in depth.

Even before Italy entered the war she seems to have been obsessed by the thought that her major naval ports needed to be protected by minefields. By June 1940, Italy had laid large fields of an estimated 19,000 mines around Taranto; around an area just north of Messina; outside Civitavecchia – a port near Rome – and outside Livorno. Mines were also laid all around Malta and Gozo.

After joining the war on Hitler's side in June 1940, large minefields totalling some 3,000 mines in all were laid around the northeast corner of Tunisia – Bizerta and Cape Bon both being heavily protected.

During 1941 protective minefields were laid in the vicinity of Augusta, Sicily, and Naples. The waters off the west of Sicily, from Palermo stretching all the way round to Cape Granitola and almost as far as Sciacca, were further mined. From about Cape Granitola, a long chain of mines were laid towards Pantelleria and on from that Italian outpost almost the whole way to Cape Bon. This blocked off much of the Sicilian Channel through which ships heading for Malta from the west would have to pass.

Fear of attack upon their ports further north also induced Italy to lay mines in large numbers outside Livorno, Spezia and Genoa on the Ligurian coast and outside Venice, Trieste, Ancona, Bari and Brindisi on the Adriatic, although there was in fact little likelihood of attack in the northern Adriatic. Other minefields were laid around Sardinia – the Bonifacio Channel between Sardinia and Corsica being heavily mined.

In the relatively shallow waters of the long Mediterranean coast-lines, mine-laying by both sides became an effective war weapon. In particular, the heavy and persistent mining of the Sicilian Channel between Cape Granitola, Pantelleria and Cape Bon was a per-manent anxiety for Captain Simpson and the commanders of the submarines which operated under his control. It took courage, dis-cipline and skill to get past these deadly obstructions unscathed, even after a safe passageway had been reconnoitred, late in July 1941, by Lieutenant Commander Dick Cayley when on his first command in Malta in the submarine *Utmost*.

Despite these hazards and some early misses, successes were scored. *Truant* sank a ship estimated at 3,000 tons off Tripoli on 8 February 1941, *Utmost* damaged another on 12 February and *Unique* (Lt Cayley) damaged yet another, also unidentified, a week later. *Ursula* hit, but again failed to sink, a transport on 22 February and *Regent* sank a ship, name unknown, a day later outside Tripoli. Even so, these successes, and a few achieved by the Swordfish of 830 Squadron, did not prevent the enemy from receiving 49,084 tons of supplies in January, 79,173 tons in February and 92,753 tons in March; whilst during these same months the enemy landed a total of 51,955 of the 53,023 men who had set forth to reinforce the armies in Africa. These figures, which have been supplied to the author from official Italian data by the Italian historian Tullio Marcon, show that only 11,652 tons out of 232,662 tons of supplies destined for North Africa failed to reach their destination: almost 95 per cent of the supplies arrived safely in North Africa, as well as nearly 98 per cent of the personnel shipped. (See Appendix IV.)

*

It seems appropriate to pause here to consider the role and qualities required by submarine commanders. They were a special breed of men, especially the few who achieved outstanding successes. Throughout the history of modern warfare, submarine commanders have either possessed, or failed to possess, the indefinable knack of sinking enemy ships. In most cases this knack was only acquired through early experience or failure. A few caught it direct; more than a few never acquired it, although virtually all were efficient skippers of their crafts.

To hit and sink a ship in daylight the submarine in most cases, in order to avoid detection, needed to be under water, with only its periscopes visible. There its commander, who alone could see what was happening above the water via the raised periscope, had to make judgements about the enemy ship's course, speed and depth below the water-line. He also had to estimate the angle of attack which it presented. Sea conditions had to be taken into account and at least half an eye kept upon accompanying escort ships and marauding aircraft in the area.

In the small U-class submarines, the torpedoes all ran straight (or were *supposed* to run straight, though occasionally a commander had to dive his submarine hastily when a 'circler' ran wild, turned back and threatened his own vessel) and had to be fired from the bow tubes with the submarine heading in the desired direction of attack.

The enemy's course had to be estimated by eye but it helped greatly, as was often the case for Malta-based submarines, to know where the enemy vessel was heading. On the other hand, some ships deliberately adopted zigzag tactics which also had to be taken into account. The enemy's speed was estimated by known factors – many Mediterranean convoys went at 8–16 knots. Speed could also be assessed by experienced commanders from the bow wave patterns and/or by being advised by the acoustic operator in the submarine of the propeller revolutions of the enemy.

The angle of attack was always difficult to assess by eye but, if given the enemy's speed and course, a mechanical Director Angle machine – a massive forerunner of today's neat computers, which acquired the nickname of the 'fruit machine' – could calculate this angle accurately provided correct data was given to the operator. Range – perhaps the most important parameter of all to be assessed

– was estimated by the height of the enemy's mast (or funnel). All these parameters had to be estimated at lightning speed while manoeuvring between escorting destroyers or torpedo-boats, and hoping against hope that the submarine's periscopes had not been observed.

It is understandable that some submarine skippers should never have managed to acquire the knack. It has been estimated that about 80 per cent of our shipping losses from U-boats in the First World War were caused by less than 20 per cent of German U-boat commanders; the situation in the Second World War was similar.

While all these requirements called for a man with a lightning-quick arithmetical brain – a rare enough feature – the commander also had to be a man possessing monumental patience. It was not unknown to have to stalk a target unobtrusively for twelve or more hours in order to get the submarine into the right place at the right moment, away from the escort vessels and at the range and angle of attack most likely to produce a satisfactory result.

Qualities of patience do not often go hand in glove with a razor-sharp decisive mind. Yet both were required and the commander might have to switch from one mode to the other in a flash when, during a careful stalk, something unexpected occurred, such as the sighting of an enemy plane in an attacking dive, or the report of noises of another, probably hostile submarine detected in the vicinity by the submarine's sensitive listening equipment. It is no wonder that Winston Churchill said of them, 'Submarine COs are worth a million pounds each', and that Admiral Sir Andrew Cunningham wrote to the Admiralty in London in September 1941: 'Every submarine that can be spared is worth its weight in gold.' This is confirmed by Admiral Sir Max Horton's advice to Captain Simpson which was 'To treat your submarine commanders as Derby winners'.

Captain Simpson must, however, have had doubts about the value of his commanders during the first three or four months of his command of the Tenth Flotilla. The facts are (according to official Italian records) that in the period January–April 1941 the enemy sent 321,259 tons of supplies from Italy to Libya and that all but 18,777 tons – that is, 94 per cent – duly arrived there. In numbers of personnel transported to Libya the enemy did even better in the same period. Of the 73,991 sent by sea, 71,881 – 97 per cent – duly arrived (including Rommel who reached Africa on 14 February 1941). These landing successes by the Axis powers markedly changed the character of the Desert War as a large number of those who made the journey safely to Tripoli – virtually no other port was then being used in North Africa by the enemy – comprised Germans of the Afrika Korps. With Germans to face as well as Italians, the task of the British Army in the Desert was now much more difficult.

It is interesting to speculate what Hitler might have done if (say) 50 per cent of the Afrika Korps sent during the first four months of 1941 had been lost at sea. As it was, by April 1941 Rommel took full advantage of a decision by Britain which seriously weakened the land forces opposing him. General Wavell, GOC Cairo, on instructions from the UK, was obliged to send many of his best troops to Greece, which had just been invaded by Germany. As a result, Rommel was able to strike back, with surprising effect, soon after his arrival.

In no time, thanks also to errors which allowed him to capture British fuel, he had the Eighth Army on the run and was gaining ground by leaps and bounds. Soon, all the gains won against the Italians by General O'Connor had been lost except for the port of Tobruk where the Australian 9th Division, although surrounded and bypassed, was holding out magnificently.

By May 1941, by when the Swordfish of 830 Squadron had also begun to master the difficult art of torpedoing enemy ships at night, the submarines of the Tenth, especially one commanded by the tall bearded Lieutenant Commander Wanklyn, began to strike hard. Henceforth, for almost the entire next two years, General Rommel was never assured of receiving the steady flow of supplies which he needed if he wished to sustain his momentum and achieve his aim of driving the British Army, not just out of Libya, but out of Egypt as well.

This aim had never been part of his initial brief which was simply to hold his ground and ensure that the northern coastal province of Tripolitania, and the port of Tripoli in particular, remained firmly in Italian hands. His long victory march from Agheila to within sight of the Egyptian frontier – an advance of nearly 800 miles – was strictly against his specific instructions, but was condoned as a successful *fait accompli*. Although a few wise heads in Berlin realized that Rommel, by advancing so far, was setting himself an almost insuperable supply problem, Hitler and others were swept up in the euphoria of his swift advance, especially as it took place during the months when action on the huge Russian fronts was at a standstill; literally frozen.

It had not been all gloom for Captain Simpson and his Tenth Flotilla. *Unique* under the command of Lieutenant Commander Collett and *Truant* (Lt Haggard) – one of the four T-class submarines which had been sent to Malta ahead of the Tenth – had scored successes as early as February 1941. *Upright* (Lt Wraith) followed this up by sinking the 5,000-ton Italian cruiser, *Armando Diaz*, in a brilliant night attack. *Regent*, another larger submarine under Captain Simpson's orders, also sank or damaged a transport off Tripoli, where *Ursula* had also struck. However as the aforementioned figures show, most men and supplies were arriving safely in Tripoli's big harbour.

One reason for the initial lack of success of the Tenth Flotilla was that Captain Simpson had orders to send his 'million pounds' submarine commanders on a number of cloak-and-dagger raids, the value of which he personally doubted. (History proved him right.) It galled him particularly to know that his submarines were having to expose themselves close to enemy beaches at night, virtually stationary, while awaiting the return of the commandos in their flimsy canvas folbots. As an experienced ex-submariner, along with his experienced Staff Officer Operations (SOO), Lieutenant Commander Bob Turner, this seemed to Simpson an inappropriate use of such sophisticated specialist weapons. Sadly, many of the raids to pick up spies were compromised and this added to the risks being taken. Lieutenant Commander Cayley, in particular, seemed to be given these assignments more often than most although he was one commander who had rapidly acquired the all-important knack of torpedoing enemy ships.

On 9 March Lieutenant Commander Cayley struck again, hitting and sinking the *Cap Vita* (5,683 tons). Next day, Lieutenant Collett in charge of *Unique* sank the *Fenicia* (2,584 tons), but it was to be his sole success in six patrols, each of about twelve days, and he was soon to be replaced. Towards the end of the month Cayley had a further success when he sank the German troopship *Heraklea* (1,927 tons) off the Tunisian coast. As the escorts busied themselves picking up survivors from the water, the Lieutenant Commander allowed various members of his crew to observe what was taking place via the submarine's periscopes.

Although Captain Simpson held the view that military personnel plucked from the sea by a destroyer constituted a legitimate war target – and it would be hard to argue otherwise – most of his commanders allowed such humane rescue work to proceed un-molested. Captain Simpson left it entirely to the discretion of each submarine commander and there was at least one who shared Captain Simpson's views. On the whole, compassion ruled and sur-vivors were picked up; much as airmen on both sides regarded it as almost a crime to shoot at a man dangling at the end of a parachute, or to 'stream' the 'chute by flying close to and above it – an action which caused it to descend at speed.*

It could also be argued that the submarine skipper who did not attack the rescuing destroyers was being rational as well as humane. A destroyer thus engaged upon rescuing soldiers from the water was fully occupied, and was therefore in no position to search for and engage the submarine. Nor could depth-charges be dropped without the risk of injury to those in the water.

Meanwhile, in April, the 1,500-ton minelayer submarine *Rorqual* (Lt/Cdr Dewhurst) accounted for the tanker *Lauro Carban* (3,700 tons), which hit one of its mines. Earlier it had sunk with a torpedo an Italian submarine, the *Capponi*. But despite these successes, the bulk of the supplies and personnel heading for North Africa and intended to sustain the newly appointed Rommel continued to arrive.

However, a major set-back to the Afrika Korps, and an event which reduced the percentage of supplies which arrived safely in Africa in April 1941 to 91 per cent for that month, took place on the night of 15/16 April when the Royal Navy's 14th Destroyer Flotilla, based in Malta, composed of *Jervis, Janus, Mohawk* and *Nubian*, under the command of Captain Mack RN, attacked at night an escorted convoy of five, mainly German, cargo ships and sank the lot. *Sabaudia* (1,500 tons), *Aegina* (2,447 tons), *Adana* (4,205 tons),

---

* Wing Commander Bob Braham, a dedicated night-fighter 'killer ace', was once about to commit this 'crime' but was talked out of it by his (Jewish) radar operator. The Luftwaffe night-fighter Heinz Vinke thus lived to fly and fight again. Wiser by experience, he was to claim 54 kills of big four-engined bombers. Who was right?

Isetlhon (3,704 tons) and *Arta* were the victims, along with the Italian destroyers *Targo*, *Lampo* and *Balendir*. During the engagement the destroyer *Mohawk* was torpedoed and sunk by the Italian destroyer *Targo*, just before she also went under. This success showed that when it came to night fighting, probably aided by radar, the British Navy held the upper hand in the Mediterranean.

Upholder under Lieutenant Commander Wanklyn later made a contribution to this victory. A few days after the successful naval battle, when patrolling off the Kerkenah Bank, 'Wanks' came across the remains of the *Arta* and of a destroyer. Both had finished up, after their mauling by the 14th Flotilla, aground on the notorious sand-bar. The crew of *Upholder* boarded the supply ship and noted that it had clearly been used to transport soldiers. With demolition charges they blew up both the enemy ships and returned with German helmets and other war souvenirs. This action took place during this commander's fifth Malta patrol by which time, to Captain Simpson's personal delight, his former No. 1 had already proved that he had acquired the knack of sinking enemy ships. Then, on 25 April 1941 *Upholder* came across the *Antonietta Laura* (5,428 tons) and duly sank her with a well-aimed torpedo. Six days later he fired a salvo at a convoy of five supply ships accompanied by four destroyers. The weather was very rough, which made viewing through the periscopes, and his task, many times more difficult. In spite of these problems, three hits were scored and the German *Leverkusen* (7,386 tons) and the *Arcturus* (2,586 tons) were both sunk. 'Wanks' was deploying his knack with a vengeance.

One of the Tenth's bigger submarines, the *Truant* (Lt/Cdr Haggard), had played an unusual role on 21 April 1941, acting as a 'marker buoy' to guide a battle fleet from Alexandria to an exact position just outside Tripoli harbour. Once there, and equipped with photographs taken by Warburton the day before, a number of big naval ships, commanded by Admiral Cunningham in person, proceeded to plaster that busy port with their massive guns. For an hour from the break of dawn Tripoli was bombarded and many port facilities were set on fire before the fleet returned unscathed to its Egyptian port. *Truant* had earlier sunk a schooner, the *Vanna* which, though only 270 tons, was being used to transport petrol to Axis forces in North Africa. This was perhaps a forerunner of events to come: a sign that almost everything that could float was being used to supply Rommel and his troops with the life-supporting fuel that his vehicles, and Luftwaffe aircraft, had to have in constant supply in order to operate effectively.

Before April was out, *Tetrarch* under Commander Mills, the same senior submarine commander who had held the fort in Malta in late 1940 and early 1941, pending the arrival of Captain Simpson, may also have hit and sunk the tanker *Persiano*.

The Tenth was beginning to get its eye in, as May was about to demonstrate. By then, too, the RAF had introduced a new element into the struggle to sever Rommel's supply lines. Although throughout the earlier period the Wellington bombers had continued their nightly pounding of enemy ports, with the assistance at times of the Swordfish of 830 Squadron, it was difficult to assess positive results. Both types of aircraft had, for example, laid on a maximum effort over Tripoli during the night of 21 April 1941, immediately before the battle fleet from Alexandria had bombarded the port. This had the effect of fully occupying the defences while concealing the fact that naval shells, and not bombs, were later to fall.

This operation was a good example of air–sea co-operation and how the Services in Malta and Alexandria worked in harmony. The big ships had come from Alexandria. The submarine 'marker buoy' had sailed from Malta. The diversionary air attacks had been carried out by FAA Swordfish from Hal Far airfield and RAF Wellington bombers from Luqa. Yet it had all worked as planned and had been accomplished without loss. Co-operation between the two distant bases and the three Services was exemplary.

Rommel, by later April 1941, had advanced to the Egyptian border and had Tobruk surrounded and cut off. However, the signs were that although the Axis was victorious on land in the Desert, the disruption of his supply services from ships, submarines and aircraft based in Malta was beginning to be of concern to him.

It was a concern that was to grow.

4

Successes and a VC

April–October 1941

'As the Fuhrer knows, our North African supply
shipments have suffered additional heavy losses.'
Admiral Raeder, Summer 1941

MAY 1941 WAS, in several respects, a significant month of the war in
Africa and the Middle East. On the debit side, the British intervention in Greece, and then Crete, was a total disaster. It had weakened
the Eighth Army* to the point where a small force under Rommel
had driven it back about 800 miles with surprising ease. The
Greek/Crete withdrawals had also caused so many disastrous
casualties among Admiral Cunningham's Naval forces, which
had been given the unenviable task of trying to evacuate Allied
troops, that he was obliged to advise the Admiralty that he could
no longer risk his ships on this task. German dive-bombing, with
Ju 87s and 88s, had achieved what the large Italian Navy had failed
to do.

On the credit side, the small army under Lieutenant General Sir
Alan Cunningham had completed their victory over the Italians in
Eritrea and Abyssinia and – perhaps of greater significance –
another small force, supported by an air force composed largely of
hastily modified Oxford and other training planes, had put down a

---

* The British Army in the Desert was originally called the Army of the Nile or
'British Army in the Middle East' but soon became the Eighth Army. Many
Australian troops, as well as some New Zealand, Indian and South African units,
were included.

German-supported rebellion in Iraq where the RAF had for many years maintained a big base at Habbaniya. With Britain already controlling what is now Israel, and a Free French force, supported by Commonwealth troops, about to take control of Syria, these successes effectively put paid to Hitler's plans to reach the oilfields of Arabia via the Middle East/Levant back door.

May 1941 was also the month when the submarines based in Malta revealed all too clearly the vulnerability of the supply line between the Axis armies in the Desert and Italy, their only source of supply. During this month Hitler and his foreign secretary Ribbentrop held secret talks with Vichy France; on the agenda was a request that the French Admiral Darlan – the Governor of French-dominated Tunisia – should allow supplies to Tripoli to go in via his ports and through his territory. Darlan had little choice other than to agree in principle but, with characteristic French diplomatic procrastination, he managed during the months ahead to raise so many technical objections that, much to the Allies' relief, this route was never employed by the Axis powers.

There seems little doubt that what lay at the back of Admiral Darlan's mind was the genuine fear that if he sided so openly with Britain's enemy, then his cities, where a not unpleasant war was being enjoyed by large numbers of French administrators and citizens, would be bombed by Malta-based aircraft – yet another example of Malta's strategic value to the Allies. The Axis powers were thrown back on their regular supply lines.

In this month the Tenth Flotilla began to score with consistency. Lieutenant Commander Wanklyn's success in sinking the *Leverkusen* and *Arcturus* on 1 May was just the beginning. *Urge*, commanded by Lieutenant Tomkinson ('Tommo'), had two weeks earlier sunk the 10,535-ton *Franco Martelli* when on his way from the UK to Malta. 'Tommo' was an old friend of 'Wanks' and both were to become successful – almost rival – ship destroyers.

By this time many in Malta were speculating among themselves upon the source of the excellent intelligence which was being received as the basis for many sea and air operations. For aiding the battle in the Mediterranean, from early 1941 onwards, were 'Ultra' reports received from the UK. These emanated from Bletchley Park, Middlesex, where Britain's most senior Intelligence officers were intercepting and unscrambling the enemy's secret W/T messages. Coded by means of the 'Enigma' machine, which was capable of scrambling messages into trillions upon trillions of possible combinations, this system was considered impenetrable by the Germans. Only a person in possession of another Enigma machine and knowing the code being used could possibly interpret the messages.

However, pre-war, both the French and particularly the Polish Intelligence Services had got wind of the principle being used and when war was declared they shared their knowledge with British Intelligence. The Poles had even manufactured what they considered to be a reasonable facsimile of an Enigma machine. In an attempt to reduce the number of possible combinations to manageable proportions a brilliant young Cambridge University mathematician working for British Intelligence, Alan Turing, duly constructed what was called a 'bombe'. This was in effect a huge early form of computer containing about 1,500 radio valves. In size it occupied one side of a normal room. The bombe enabled the team of cipher experts assembled at Bletchley Park to sort the various combinations and work out the possible codes to apply to their version of the German Enigma machines.

As war progressed, examples of Enigma machines were captured: one from a stricken U-boat in the Atlantic and another during a raid upon the isolated Lofoten Islands, near the Arctic Circle off the coast of Norway.

The enemy changed their codes at about six-monthly intervals and each Service had its own codes broken down by region and function. For example, the German Navy used a different code for its U-boats and its surface ships and different codes for the Baltic, Atlantic and Mediterranean. Once the Italians had joined the war and begun to use a similar Swedish-made machine, known as the C38, there would be about fifty different codes in use simultaneously, some of which were relatively easy to decode, while others took months to solve.

It was fortunate for Malta that there were no underwater cables between Italy and the Italian North African colonies, as this meant that all urgent messages to Tripoli and Benghazi regarding sailings from Italy – including destination, route and escorts – could only be sent by W/T and could therefore be intercepted. On the other hand commercial cables* existed between Malta and both Alexandria and Gibraltar – and thence to the UK. These cables enabled Alexandria, Malta and the UK to exchange information, especially Ultra reports, without fear of it being known to the enemy.

In Malta, only Charles Carnes, a RN Reserve officer who had been called up and, after the Mediterranean Fleet had departed to Alexandria, been placed in charge of the Base Cipher Office in Fort St Angelo, was allowed to read Ultra messages. Consequently at all times he had to say where he could be found. He passed Ultra reports only to the VAM who probably shared the information with the AOC Malta.

It was not until twenty-five years after the war that Charles Carnes first heard about the Enigma machines, the existence of Bletchley Park, the bombe, or knew from what source Ultra reports were obtained. It is reasonable to suppose that the VAM, and most other recipients, were kept equally in the dark about Ultra. All that it was necessary for them to know was that the reports came from an unusually reliable source. Charles Carnes, for example, thought that they were from an exceedingly well placed agent in Naples. His views were shared by many of those in Malta who referred knowingly to 'the man on the end of the pier'.

Meanwhile the RAF was adding its weight to the supply struggle. According to Ultra intercepts, 'The RAF sank three ships on 4 May and one contained Luftwaffe petrol.' Although it is not clear which aircraft accounted for these losses, it would seem that they could either have been Wellington bombers on night raids of enemy ports or the Swordfish of the FAA using torpedoes or mine-laying. Alternatively, the damage might have been caused by Blenheims. These were smaller twin-engined daylight bombers, manned by a three-man crew and carrying four 250-pound bombs. They came from 2 Group in the UK, one squadron at a time, each relieving the other at about eight-week intervals, commencing in April 1941 when 21 Squadron led by Squadron Leader Pepper arrived. Their pilots reported that they had damaged two merchant ships during

---

* These Cable & Wireless cables were taken over, in part, by the military who exercised a priority.

one of their first attacks on 2 May. Blenheims were never in a good position to observe accurately the result of their attacks. They attacked in daylight from low level under almost suicide conditions and suffered losses of about one in three from the guns of the escort ships, or those now mounted on the supply ships themselves. Those who survived escaped as quickly as they could and never hung around to record results.

Upholder struck again on 6 May when she and her commander, Lieutenant Commander Wanklyn, sank the *Cagliari* (2,322 tons). This was confirmed via Ultra which offered the additional information that 'several units of the 15th Panzer Division *en route* to Egypt had been sunk': the 'several' implies that some might also have been on board the three ships earlier reported as sunk, as well as on the *Cagliari*.

Night bombers, according to Ultra, accounted for 'four ships sunk in Benghazi harbour' on the night of 8/9 May, but whether by Wellingtons from Malta or from the Middle East was not stated. It is also not known whether the four ships in Benghazi were sunk before or after they had discharged their cargoes. But even if unloaded, the loss of the ships would have been a telling blow. The Italians were beginning to realize that their shipping supply was dwindling and was not being replaced by new building, one reason being that shipyards were kept busy repairing the many ships which were damaged. When reporting the four ships sunk in Benghazi harbour, the Ultra intercept added: 'with serious consequences due to the petrol lost' – given a clear indication that one, at least, was a laden tanker and that petrol supplies were a worry to the enemy. A few days later Ultra reported 'more fuel lost in another raid on Benghazi'.

As early as 12 April 1941, a Swordfish pilot of 830 Squadron reported a possible hit on another merchant ship. It was even more difficult for these crews to report positive results. Owing to their lamentable lack of speed – they cruised at much the same speed as present-day traffic in the fast lane of a motorway – they had been compelled to operate their torpedo-carrying sorties only at night. To have done otherwise would have led to swift elimination of the squadron. To attack at night in their obsolete biplanes with their fixed undercarriages and unheated open cockpits, they flew in formation. Only the leader carried a fully qualified observer. He also carried flares and occasionally had on board the benefit of an early form of air-borne radar known as ASV (Air to Surface Vessel). Thus laden, the leader was unable also to carry a torpedo.

Assuming that the leader could find the enemy ships in the dark – no easy task over a featureless sea, even if aided by Ultra-obtained information – he would then act as a flare-dropper to illuminate the scene for those following him. The operation required much pre-planning and the development of an entirely new tactical plan whereby the leader broke away so as to get behind the ships and illuminate them at the precise moment when the others were running in to drop. It had taken months to perfect the manoeuvre and much was owed to their (Observer) CO Lieutenant Commander Howie, whose aircraft usually led the night formations.

Unbeaten (Lt Woodward) was the next submarine to strike. On 14 May 1941, he sank a large schooner of over 1,000 tons near Tripoli and went on to hit another ship with his gun in the Benghazi area. *Urge*, with Lieutenant Tomkinson very much in charge, sank the *Zeffero* (5,165 tons) on 20 May during a patrol down the Tunisian coast, and damaged the *Perseo* (4,800 tons) on the same date. The Blenheims had also hit and damaged this latter ship. Many enemy ships were finally disposed of after first being hit by a Malta-based aircraft, then sunk by a Malta-based submarine, or vice versa. The two Services worked closely together with RAF and RN Ops Rooms adjacent to one another at the Lascaris underground site.*

Upholder, now on her sixth patrol out of Malta, damaged the tanker *Capitaine Dizmiani* on 23 May and sank the big troop transport *Conte Rosso* a day later. This was a prize target of 17,879 tons and cost the lives of 1,568 troops. It was sunk south-east of Sicily, doubtless having been first reported via Ultra, and resulted in the award to Lieutenant Commander Wanklyn of the first Victoria Cross to be given any serviceman stationed in Malta.

The attack was a brilliant and daring night attack. The troop-ship was travelling at 21 knots – twice the maximum speed of *Upholder*

---

* In June 1940, it was decided to set up an RAF Control Room adjacent to the Navy Ops Room in an underground area (Malta has many such chambers going back to earlier sieges) underneath the St John's Cavalier Bastion in Valletta. It was entered via a sloping tunnel. This became the Lascaris Operational Control centre for the RN and RAF.

– and was being escorted by a number of destroyers. Normally, propeller noises made by destroyers could be picked up by the submarine's listening equipment, but this device was not functioning in *Upholder* at that time. As Wanklyn was about to fire his torpedoes, one of those escorts appeared out of the darkness and nearly rammed his submarine, forcing him to crash-dive. However the bearded Lieutenant Commander brought *Upholder* back rapidly to periscope depth and fired his torpedoes with a lightning-quick estimation of the correct amount of deflection angle to be used. After the attack he was, as usual, depth-charged by some of the enemy destroyers and his lack of listening devices made it extremely difficult for him to evade these. In all thirty-seven depth-charges were counted by the crew beneath the waves but, as his VC citation adds: 'with the greatest courage, coolness and skill he brought *Upholder* clear of the enemy and safe back to harbour'.

It is possible, even likely, that the sinking of this large troop-carrier may have been instrumental in dissuading the Italians from using their huge fast transatlantic liners as troop-ships. Italy possessed, in the *Rex* and *Conte di Savoia*, two 50,000-ton liners capable of 30 knots which could easily have carried up to (say) 10,000 troops each to North Africa in a swift night trip between Palermo and Tripoli: much as the British transatlantic liners *Queen Mary* and *Queen Elizabeth* were used to transport tens of thousands of US troops across the Atlantic to the UK, in rapid unescorted dashes which defied attack in those U-boat infested waters.

Regarding Italy's failure to deploy these splendid ships the eminent historian Tullio Marcon surmises:

> The use of the *Rex* and *Conte di Savoia* would have caused a strong enemy action against them [correct]. If sunk, the loss of men would have been higher than the ones with smaller ships, not to mention the inevitable shock on public opinion. Mines, and some difficulty in Tripoli to attend them, were, I presume, two other good reasons for not using them in the Second World War.

Even so, June 1941 proved to be the month when the enemy landed a then record tonnage of supplies in North Africa. Although more than another 8,000 tons were admittedly lost at sea, 125,076 tons were reported to have arrived. The figures for personnel were even more encouraging to the Axis powers. They show that every one of the 12,886 men transported across the Mediterranean in June 1941 arrived safely. This was a most satisfactory situation for Rommel and his armies, in a period when the opposing armies in the Desert were doing their utmost to build up supplies for a renewal of the battle which both sides knew had soon to occur.

The British, now under General Auchinleck, were being constantly urged by Churchill and the War Cabinet to counter-attack and to push Rommel back towards Tripoli. Rommel, having defied orders and advanced so far, was anxious as ever to press further forward into Egypt. He also had what amounted to an obsession with Tobruk. This Libyan port had so far eluded recapture. It was surrounded and lay a hundred or more miles behind where his front line had come to rest, at the Libyan-Egyptian border. It therefore constituted a threat to Rommel's rear and, thanks to strenuous efforts by the British Navy operating from Alexandria, was being supplied and maintained in such strength that he was unable to break down its considerable defences.

Rommel's obsession with Tobruk was more than a fear of having it at his rear. He also believed that its capture would solve his nagging supply problem. It is one thing to land 125,000 tons of supplies in North Africa, with a substantial percentage now being landed in Benghazi as well as Tripoli. It was quite another matter to get these supplies to the armies and airfields of a now distant front line. In fuel costs alone, about 10 per cent of the petrol was consumed in transporting the other 90 per cent to where it was most wanted. The long journey also used up personnel and wore out lorries at an alarming pace. All supplies had to be driven along a single coastal road, the Via Balbo. Built pre-war by Mussolini, this road was often the target for Allied aircraft, surface ships and even, occasionally, the submarine's one gun. These raids caused damage and constant delays, as well as physical loss of supplies. In his anxiety to gain supplies, without which he could not advance his exhausted troops, the port of Tobruk appeared to Rommel like a mirage in the desert. Expectation was overcoming reason. As he was later to find out, possession of the port of Tobruk, with its very limited facilities, its lack of storage tanks and its extremely vulnerable position, was not the answer to his besetting supply problems.

A few successes were claimed in June 1941 by the submarines and aircraft operating from Malta. In the first few days of the month, the Blenheims hit the *Beatrice C* (6,132 tons) and so damaged her that she later had to be sunk by one of her own escorts. They also sank the *Montello* (6,117 tons). In the same period, *Unique* (Lt Collett) sank the *Arsia* (735 tons) but missed hitting three cruisers. However, for the following two to three weeks, no positive successes could be claimed.

The Blenheims had also struck late in May. On the 26th a strike, led by their leader Wing Commander Pepper, hit a ship which was later seen to be abandoned. On the next day aircraft from 82 and 139 Squadrons – 139 was relieving 82 Squadron and operating with the remnants of that squadron during the changeover period – damaged the *Foscarini Marco* (6,342 tons). The Blenheims closed the score for that month by sinking, or damaging, the *Florida* (3,314 tons).

Upright also took part in a successful demolition job on a railway viaduct in east Calabria, carried out by the young soldiers in their folbots. This commando-type raid was led by the youthful Lieutenant Dudley Schofield. However, none of the submarine crews enjoyed these raids. They had to endure anxious periods waiting on the surface, with the dawn light breaking the sky, for the return of the furiously paddled canoes.

Although official Italian figures for losses in June 1941 claim that only 8,000 tons of supplies and no personnel were lost during this month (and if they were anything like as inaccurate as were the absurd broadcasts from Rome Radio at that time, they must be suspect), the number of ships hit and sunk would seem to indicate that considerably more might have been lost.* No country at war ever fails to minimize its own losses, whilst propaganda dictates that much has to be made of the opposing side's losses; and although post-war analysis, in a dispassionate era of peace, tends to be more accurate, with the best will in the world claims and losses still never match.

Despite these apparent successes, June was the month when, almost abruptly, the non-stop air raids on Malta by the efficient Luftwaffe from bases in Sicily practically ceased. Up to then, com-

* The official post-war list, as supplied by Tullio Marcon, appears as Appendix IV.

mencing early in January 1941, the island had been subjected to Luftwaffe raids several times each day – and also spasmodically at night. These had wrecked the 'Three Cities' – the area around Grand Harbour – caused much damage to the harbour facilities and had flattened practically every building in and around the three airfields of Hal Far (FAA biplanes), Luqa (twin-engined bomber and reconnaissance aircraft) and Ta Kali, the fighter airfield.

Thanks to information supplied by Richard King of the Air Historical Branch of the MOD, the numbers of German aircraft which were moved to Sicily specifically in order to attack Malta are now known. When it is considered that Malta, in 1941, could only field, at most, two or occasionally three squadrons of Hurricanes which were rapidly reduced to a mere handful of aircraft, the numbers of enemy aircraft which they were up against is truly formidable. These aircraft, moreover, were more modern than the outmoded Hurricane I fighters which at that time constituted Malta's sole defence.

As early as January 1941 the Luftwaffe had moved 11 Ju 88s and 28 Heinkel 111 bombers to Catania; 44 Ju 87 dive-bombing Stukas to Trapani; 25 Me 110 long-range fighters and another 5 Ju 87s to Palermo and a few more He 111s to both Comiso and Trapani. It was these aircraft, often accompanied by dozens of Italian fighters, which were responsible for the blitz which almost totally destroyed the 'Three Cities'.

By February 1941, the strength of Fliegerkorps X in Sicily had grown to 243 aircraft of which 92 were bombers, 73 dive-bombers and 54 Me 110 twin-engined fighters. Others were reconnaissance aircraft and 7 were night fighters. However, owing to Hurricane successes, Malta AA fire and the inevitable accidents plus wear-and-tear losses, the number of serviceable German aircraft was barely 150: but this was still many times the number of Hurricanes, assisted by a Fulmar or two, ranged against them.

The numbers steadily grew until, by 22 March 1941, the strength of the Luftwaffe had grown to 316 aircraft of which 169 were serviceable. By then, ominously, the efficient single-engined Me 109 fighter had begun to appear in the form of fifteen belonging to 7/JG 26. Of the enemy bombers, 87 were (coincidentally) the Ju 87 dive-bombers but the mauling which this type was receiving was to lead to their steady reduction in subsequent months. By April 1941, only one Ju 87 unit remained, with a nominal establishment of 39 aircraft.

Soon after April 1941, the Me 110s were being replaced by the more effective Me 109s, and the He 111 bombers by the very useful Ju 88s. This was a trend which was to persist. Only Germany's best aircraft were henceforth sent to Sicily.

During May 1941, the Italian Air Force fighting alongside the Luftwaffe in Sicily had a strength of 60 bombers, 112 fighters and 43 reconnaissance aircraft. This meant that Malta's few Hurricanes were up against a total of close to 400 enemy aircraft, with the Germans still largely relying upon Italian fighters to protect their bombers.

However, the virtual disappearance of the Luftwaffe from Sicily in June 1941 changed the situation. Towards the end of that month, it had become obvious that the air raids on Malta, now carried out by the Regia Aeronautica from Sicily, were far less fearsome than had been those of the Luftwaffe previously. On 22 June 1941 the reason for the absence of the Luftwaffe became apparent. At dawn on that fateful morning, Germany launched a vicious and unprovoked attack upon Stalin's Russia. In 1939, Hitler and Stalin had signed a non-aggression pact which had given Hitler the assurance that his back was protected. This assurance enabled him to attack Poland a few weeks later and so precipitate the Second World War. Now in June 1941 Hitler turned the full fury of his war machine – the Wehrmacht – against his alleged ally. The bombers and fighters which had given Malta such a hard time were now ranged against the USSR.

Although Ultra reports that 'a tanker blew up in Benghazi',[*] this action may have been due to a Wellington raid from the Middle East rather than to one from Malta. By and large Middle East Wellingtons raided Benghazi whereas those based in Malta, when heading for Africa, raided Tripoli. The intention was to give neither enemy port a respite, but unquestionably some raids upon Benghazi were also carried out from Malta especially during those periods when the enemy stood on, or had crossed, the Egyptian frontier. Benghazi was then closer to Malta than to any other airfield in Allied hands.

---

[*] See Ralph Bennett, *Ultra and Mediterranean Strategy* (1989).

Ever keen to take the fight to the enemy, AOC Malta Air Vice Marshal Hugh Pughe Lloyd, who was controlling all FAA aircraft, retained a few FAA Fairey Fulmar fighters which had flown in from the aircraft-carrier *Illustrious*. These were designated 800X Squadron and were used by him on night intruder raids on enemy airfields in Sicily. Never for one moment did this pugnacious RAF leader consider that bombed and beleaguered Malta was on the defensive even at the times when there was practically nothing within his command with which he could strike back.*

The next U-class submarine to strike was *Union* when on 22 June her commander, Lieutenant Galloway, sank the *Pietro Querini* (8,004 tons). Sadly, it was to be his only success: on his next patrol in July he failed to return, probably one of several victims of a torpedo-boat.

By July, *Undaunted, Usk, Regulus* and *Triton* had already been lost – the *U*'s to Captain Simpson in April and May 1941, the two others to his predecessor, Commander Mills, the previous December. More losses were to follow. Before long the *Cachalot*, a mine-laying submarine which had helped to supply Malta, was lost to the torpedo-boat *Papa*. As was normal with supply-carrying submarines, she was also transporting passengers as well as cargo. *Papa* gallantly assisted by saving all the 91 persons on board, to the great credit of her Italian commander.

Few attacks made by submarines ever escaped without a cascade of depth-charges being dropped around them. Damage on board was frequent. At times this was only slight, with just the lights going out, cork falling from above† and minor fittings failing, but even these occurrences must have been terrifying to the men on board. To be operating in darkness underwater is bad enough, and the chances of being able to escape, in the event of the submarine suffering fatal damage, were known to be negligible. As it was, several submarines of the Tenth Flotilla which had survived these

---

* The author clearly recalls overhearing a conversation in the Sliema Club when an RAF officer casually asked the AOC, 'How goes the defence of the Island, sir?' Like a shot, and with a withering look, the answer came straight back: 'Malta is on the *offensive* and don't you ever forget it.' Yet at that time, March 1942, there was scarcely a serviceable aircraft, bomber or fighter, on the three airfields.

† To counter dampness, the 'ceilings' of the submarines were lined with cork, which too easily came adrift.

depth-charge attacks, had dived, at times temporarily out of control, to depths way beyond the limit of 250 feet where even the reinforced hull, inside which the men worked, was liable to collapse under the enormous water pressures.* Some of the Malta-based U-class vessels had been forced down to about 350 feet where ominous noises, caused by the steel hull being distorted, had added greatly to the concern of all on board.

On 22 April 1941 *Wachtfels*, a German supply ship, was damaged by Blenheims of 82 Squadron, as also was the Vichy-French *Tembien* (5,584 tons) two months later. A number of ships with obvious French names were being used by the enemy, having been seized when the French surrendered or subsequently purloined. The Germans had also bought, or hired, lorries from Tunisia for use along the Via Balbo, to assist in getting supplies through to their far-distant front line.

Later in June 1941 a few more successes were scored. *Osiris* sank two caiques. *Esperia* (11,398 tons) was damaged by the remarkable Warburton of 69 Squadron who, on that occasion, had used his reconnaissance Maryland as a dive-bomber. *Enrica Costa* (4,080 tons) fell either to *Utmost* (Lt Cayley again) or to the Swordfish of 830 Squadron or to both. *Utmost* at the time was also on a train-wrecking patrol off the Gulf of Euphemia near Messina. As her log mentions the definite sinking of *Enrica Costa*, it is presumed that the Swordfish hit had been scored earlier.

Esperia, having survived with only damage from Warburton's Maryland attack, was again damaged, this time while in Tripoli harbour, by Blenheims of 82 Squadron, and on 29 June *Brarena* (6,996 tons), a Norwegian vessel seized by the enemy, was also damaged. However, after being repaired, she was to fall to the submarine *Urge* (Lt Tomkinson) on 2 July 1941, one of several victims whose numbers were beginning to mount in that month.

During the month of June, the enterprising Lieutenant Dudley Schofield, leading a commando force transported to the scene by *Upright*, blew up a train south of Naples, an event which must have brought the war closer to home for some of the Italians who, in the opinion of Marshal Kesselring and others, were not pursu-

---

* The stronger German Type VII U-boats could normally dive safely to about 800 feet and many had survived at depths of up to 300 metres (approx. 1,000 feet).

ing the war with the same deadly earnestness as were their German allies.

July began with a series of Blenheim successes when Wing Commander Atkinson led his formation into Palermo. The results claimed were one 10,000-tonner sunk, a 5,000-tonner also sunk and burnt out, another ship of 10,000 tons left with a broken back and three other vessels damaged. One of these was later observed on tow towards Naples. Blenheim losses for once were slight.

830 FAA Squadron with their ancient-looking Swordfish, generally dubbed 'Stringbags', were now getting into full stride. Aided by the Blenheims – the former attacking by night, the latter by day – they accounted for the *Sparta* (1,724 tons) and another ship. As well as the *Brarena*, finally sent to the bottom by *Urge* (Lt Tomkinson), a ship of 'about 8,000 tons' was claimed by the Wellingtons during one of their frequent night raids on Tripoli and the *Laura Consulich* (5,867 tons) was sunk by *Upholder*. 'Wanks' clearly intended to live up to the VC which had been awarded to him.*

Later in July the submarine *P33*, a submarine of the Tenth Flotilla which did not survive long enough to be given a name, sank near Tripoli the *Barbarigo*, another big 1,000-ton schooner. In the subsequent counter-attack, she was forced down to 350 feet and was fortunate to survive. Along with her sister U-class *P32*, she had only another month to live.

The tanker *Panuco* (6,212 tons) was hit and damaged by one of the gallant 'Stringbags' of 830 Squadron piloted by Lieutenant Osborn, one of their most experienced and successful pilots. *Panuco* had to return to Italy with her 6,000 tons of precious petrol; although she was to survive another fifteen months, in the end a torpedo dropped from the air, also at night but this time by a Wellington, was eventually to get her. A German ship – always a special prize – the *Preussen* fell to the Blenheims on the 22nd.

Seldom out of the picture, *Upholder* reported damaging a large unidentified supply ship late in July as well as damaging with a torpedo the 9,000-ton Italian cruiser *Garibaldi* on the 28th. On the same day *Utmost*, under Lieutenant Commander Cayley, who on

---

* The story is told that Warburton and Wanklyn were introduced to one another in a Malta club as: 'This is the famous Warburton and I want you to meet the famous Wanklyn VC. ' Both blushed red and, for a while, were too embarrassed to speak.

her way out to patrol around Sicily had blazed a safe trail through
the dense minefields to the west of that island, sank the *Federico*
(1,466 tons). Enemy mines laid in the Sicilian Channel between that
island and Cape Bon were a major problem to the Tenth Flotilla but,
thanks to Cayley's pioneering passage, a way past these huge minefields had been found. This was later much copied on orders from
Captain Simpson.

An unusual but extremely important success was achieved as the
month closed when *Upright* (Lt Wraith) attacked a huge floating-
dock on tow and scored two hits. The floating-dock was much
damaged. *Upright*, too, had to dive deep to escape the inevitable
counter-attack with depth-charges. A successful month closed with
Swordfish, led by a rare ASV-equipped version, damaging a 6,000-
ton ship.

During July 1941 one of the larger British submarines, *Talisman*,
arrived to replenish Malta with 5,500 gallons of 100-octane aviation
fuel. Submarines loaded with valuable supplies were, by then,
arriving in Malta about every twelve days. In the same month the
Royal Navy cruiser *Hermione* arrived in Grand Harbour for urgent
repairs to damage caused when ramming an Italian submarine.

The fact that only 62,276 tons of supplies were landed in North
Africa during July 1941 tells its own tale: this was less than half the
tonnage that had arrived in June.

August 1941 began with a Blenheim attack by 105 Squadron on
barracks at Misurata near Tripoli. This attack was successful in spite
of the loss of the CO, Wing Commander Scivier, who collided with
another Blenheim attacker while over the target. It was the first
operation from Malta of a young Sergeant Pilot, Ivor Broom,* who
was to become one of the most outstanding Blenheim pilots based
on the island. In this operation, he proved his worth by first leading
the surviving aircraft back to Malta after having seen his CO dive
down to certain death. Soon thereafter he returned to the target area
to guide back the seriously crippled Blenheim with which Wing
Commander Scivier had collided. It was not long before Sergeant
Broom's leadership qualities were noted by the AOC who commissioned him on the spot after all officer pilots of 105 Squadron had

---

* Later Air Marshal Sir Ivor Broom KCB, CBE, DSO, DFC and two bars, AFC.

been killed. Pilot Officer Broom then led many Blenheim raids. By the time he came to leave Malta, he had achieved a record, for Blenheims, of thirty-one operations from the island.

Swordfish were deployed to attack land targets when a formation dive-bombed, and set on fire, the naphtha storage tanks at Augusta, Sicily. Swordfish of 830 Squadron also hit a German ship of about 8,000 tons which was seen for the next two days to be beached and burning off the Italian island of Lampedusa. Blenheims then sank the *Nita* (6,813 tons). The *California* (13,060 tons) was likewise beached and burnt out but there is some doubt about whether or not she was a hospital ship and thus should, or should not, have been attacked. Another ship was hit inside the boom at Syracuse.

While all this was taking place, the war in the Desert continued to go badly for the British Eighth Army. Before he was relieved of his command, General Wavell, GOC-in-C Middle East, had twice tried to launch an attack in order to relieve Tobruk. He first launched 'Operation Brevity' on 15–17 May, following it with 'Operation Battleaxe' exactly one month later. Neither achieved any lasting success and only wasted precious fuel, men and tanks. These failures led to his replacement by General Auchinleck in August 1941. However, Tobruk still held firm, far behind Rommel's line, thanks to the Australian Division's determination and to the Royal Navy which kept it supplied from Alexandria.

Once in command General Auchinleck had to deal as best he could with Churchill's insistent demands that he go onto the offensive, that Rommel be driven back. After the German attack on Russia, and Britain's bold pledge to do whatever it could to aid this Communist dictatorship, it was anathema to Churchill to have British troops standing by, apparently idle, while tens of thousands of Russians were being chopped down daily. The 'Auk', however, was biding his time.

Although the British in Egypt were never as short of fuel as were their opponents, the closing of the Mediterranean by the German dive-bombers operating from airfields in Sardinia, Sicily and, by the summer of 1941, from Crete as well, meant that supplies from Britain to Egypt had to be transported the whole way around Africa in order to reach Port Said. U-boats were liable to intercept these convoys in both the North and South Atlantic and a few of their long-range Type IX boats were even lurking in the Indian Ocean, near to the Red Sea. Many supplies were thus lost *en route*.

Both land commanders were constantly demanding reinforcements. Rommel went to Berlin to request four Panzer Divisions from the Wehrmacht to enable him to take Tobruk; with that nagging thorn in his side removed, he hoped to be able to carry on and take Egypt. By coincidence, Auchinleck was in London at the same time informing Churchill that he needed to train up three fresh divisions before *he* could advance. Both Generals were also complaining that supplies destined for them were being lost *en route*.

Another important change of command was the replacement of Air Marshal Longmore AOC Middle East by Air Marshal Arthur Tedder, a university-educated airman with an acute tactical brain and one who understood the global aspects of the war better than perhaps any other airman of the war.* Tedder was also a strong advocate of the closest possible Army–Air co-operation.

The Germans in December 1941 also raised Marshal Kesselring to the position of C-in-C of Axis forces throughout the Mediterranean theatre of war, although his position was complicated by two factors. One was that Mussolini was nominally in charge of all Italian forces and, via his Supremo, Marshal Count Ugo Cavallero, retained a form of control over the Italian Army. If this was not complication enough, Hitler, while appointing Kesselring as the man in charge of all German forces in the Mediterranean, added the caveat that Rommel came under his (Hitler's) direct orders. In theory, Rommel also came under General Cavallero although, in practice, he more often than not chose to ignore him and even, since he distrusted Italians, to conceal his plans from him.

Ultra inadvertently added to the distrust of the Italians which so many Germans felt. When it became apparent to the Germans that advance notice of their shipping movements was somehow known to the Allies, instead of checking the security of their Enigma-transmitted messages, Kesselring became convinced that a highly placed Italian admiral was acting as a spy for the British. He also fell for the idea that the information came to the British from an agent in Naples. This idea had been set up as a smokescreen by the

---

* Tedder was to end up as Deputy Supreme Commander of all Allied land, sea and air forces in Europe.

British, who sent coded messages, which were expected to be intercepted and decoded, to a mythical agent in Naples, raising his pay and thanking him for his shipping messages. This ruse was intended to protect Ultra.

August 1941 saw other successful attacks from Malta. The Swordfish of 830 Squadron damaged, or sank, two Italian merchant ships and a cruiser on the 14th, and hit the *Maddalena Odero* (5,420 tons) two nights later; the latter ship was later finished off by Blenheims. Two tankers were hit off Beurat, a small port between Tripoli and Benghazi. Swordfish attacked Catania harbour, and Beaufighters – a tough, fast twin-engined fighter with a two-man crew and massive firepower,* now introduced to Malta which was enjoying a relatively quiet respite from bombing – attacked enemy airfields in Sicily. A schooner was also attacked towards the end of August when Blenheims claimed three hits on ships which were using the new Greek coast route to North Africa.

By then, given the success of Allied attacks on enemy ships on the direct route to Tripoli down the Tunisian coast, the supplies to Rommel, especially those to be unloaded at Benghazi, were often being sent through the Strait of Messina (or by rail to Taranto) and thence east, or even north-east, to the Greek coast before turning south to Benghazi. However, although this took the supply ships beyond the range of Malta-based Swordfish – and made attacks a lot more difficult for the Blenheims – it added considerably to the mileage and hence the time. To double the enemy's mileage was, at a stroke, to halve his shipping.

As Benghazi only had limited docking facilities, many ships taking this longer route finally had to complete the semicircle and sail another 200 miles eastwards across the Gulf of Sirte from Benghazi to Tripoli. Also, while discharging their cargo at Benghazi, they were liable to be damaged or sunk by bombs dropped almost nightly by Wellington aircraft from Malta or from Egypt on what became known as the Middle East 'Mail Run'. Even if no ship was damaged by the night raid, the attack itself would have caused all

---

* Designed as a long-range day or night fighter, the Beaufighter packed a punch of 4 × 20 mm cannons and six .303 machine-guns. It was later used as a bomber, PR aircraft and torpedo-bomber.

unloading to be suspended. The Malta-based Wellingtons likewise had the same effect of suspending operations from Tripoli during their frequent all-night nuisance raids.

The Wellingtons of 38 Squadron, for example, now able to operate more freely from Malta's relatively undisturbed airfields, dropped 22 tons of bombs and a ton of small incendiary bombs on Tripoli on the night of 22 August. Another raid on that port resulted in the *Riv* and three smaller ships being sunk, and the Swordfish on the 30th sank the *Egardi* (861 tons). These successes did not go unnoticed in London, and Sir Archibald Sinclair, the Minister for Air, sent the AOC Malta the following message:

> [We have noted] the audacious attacks by the Beaufighters on enemy air bases, the steady and deadly slogging of the Wellingtons at the enemy ports, the daring and dextrous reconnaissances of the Marylands, culminating in the tremendous onslaughts of the Blenheims and Fleet Air Arm Swordfish on Axis shipping in the Mediterranean. You are draining the enemy's strength in the Med.

To which Air Vice Marshal Hugh Pughe Lloyd replied: 'The hunting is certainly good and the hounds are in fine fettle.'

The Tenth Flotilla had also been active: *Upholder* sank the *Enotria*, a 852-ton trawler, in mid-August north of Sicily. This was followed by the sinking, at last, of the 11,398-ton *Esperia* by *Unique*, this time commanded by Lieutenant Hezlet (later Vice Admiral Sir Arthur Hezlet), who was Captain Simpson's spare, or reserve, submarine commander. *Unique* was operating off Tripoli in company with *Urge* and *Unbeaten*. They were hunting for four fairly large liners whose presence in the area had been disclosed by Ultra, and which were known to be carrying troops in response to Rommel's pleas.

Upholder (again) sank the German *Luissin* (3,998 tons) and *Triumph* damaged the big 8-inch gun cruiser *Bolzano*. *Urge*, with Tommo in command, when operating in the Marettimo Island area immediately west of Sicily, damaged both the *Aquitania*, a tanker of 4,871 tons, and the liner *Duilio* (23,600 tons).

September 1941 might, with justification, be called *Upholder's* month. Ultra again advised Middle East and Malta that four Italian liners crammed with troops would be attempting to reach Tripoli. However, with the loss of the *Esperia*, they were down to three, the *Oceania*, *Neptunia* and *Vulcania*. All were *en route* to North Africa to swell the numbers of the Afrika Korps. As was usual with fast ships, they were routed well to the west of Malta: first proceeding towards Cape Bon, then moving down the Tunisian coast towards Zuara, thence east along the African coast to Tripoli. It was only a few days after the German High Command had reported to Hitler: 'Enemy submarines definitely have the upper hand. German and Italian naval and air patrols . . . are inadequate both in numbers and equipment. There are constant shipping losses.'

Upholder, along with *Unbeaten*, *Upright* and *Ursula*, were all rushed to the area of probable interception, spread out across the anticipated track of the convoy. Some of these small submarines had only just returned to Malta where the crews were hoping for a well-earned rest. But the size of the prize on offer was too tempting for most commanders to miss, even though Tommo in *Urge* decided against sailing so soon. The prospect of a major kill drove others to shorten their rest periods.

Unbeaten (Lt Woodward) sighted the three liners and eventually got his report through to the others. He himself could not attack as he was behind the convoy and lacked the speed to catch it. Wanklyn in *Upholder* was doing his best to get into an attacking position before the big ships, with their half-dozen destroyer escorts, slipped by. Lieutenant M.L. 'Tubby' Crawford, his First Lieutenant,* gives an excellent account of the attack:

> By skilful manoeuvring Wanklyn was able to fire his torpedoes as two of the big ships overlapped making a large continuous target. The yawing of the submarine (there was quite a big sea running and the submarine's gyro-compass was out of action making it difficult to hold a steady course) caused him to vary the normal sequence of firing. The first torpedo was aimed at the bow of the leading ship but the second was fired at the stern of the rear ship. The third and fourth torpedoes (the Unity-class vessels could only fire four before having to reload – a laborious process) were spread across the centre of this large target as the submarine swung back. The range was about 5,000 yards. *Upholder* then dived and, after what seemed like hours,† at least two, and possibly three, torpedoes were heard to explode.

---

* Now Captain M.L. Crawford DSC (Rtd).
† At 40–45 knots the torpedoes with nearly three miles to run would not reach the target for about three and a half minutes.

According to Tubby Crawford no counter-attack was made, presumably because the destroyers were being fully utilized in picking up survivors from the *Oceania* and *Neptunia*, both of which had been hit. By the time Wanklyn ventured to surface, some forty-five minutes later, one liner had disappeared completely, presumably sunk, and the other was stopped with destroyers busying themselves alongside. The third big ship could be seen steaming rapidly away. Wanklyn then dived his submarine in order to complete the complicated reloading procedure and, as dawn was about to break, he rose to periscope depth and drew closer in order to sink the still stationary liner. Three destroyers were around the damaged ship and, before Wanklyn could fire again, he had to dive deep to avoid being caught. *Upholder*, reports Crawford, 'was now so close to the target that the only solution was to dive *under* the stricken liner and come up on the other side and fire his torpedoes that side. Two more hits were scored and these sent the liner to the bottom.'

Meanwhile Lieutenant Woodward in *Unbeaten*, having passed his sighting report, had been following in the wake of the convoy in the hope of coming upon a damaged straggler which he could then finish off. Having almost caught up with the stationary damaged liner, he was gleefully closing in from the other side when, to his amazement, the big ship, hit by *Upholder*'s second salvo, disappeared beneath the waves before he could deliver his *coup de grâce*.

If Lieutenant Commander Wanklyn had not already been awarded a VC, it seems likely that this brilliant performance might have merited this prestigious award. As before, when sinking the *Conte Rosso*, he achieved his success in spite of there being a major fault with his submarine. Moreover he had hit, initially, the two big liners *Oceania* and *Neptunia*, each of 19,500 tons, solely by eyesight* and a swift estimation of the large amount of deflection to be applied at the 5,000-yard range. For a 10-knot submarine to score one or more hits upon two 18-knot vessels at such a range with a single salvo of four torpedoes, was an astounding feat.

Ursula (Lt Hezlet) tried to sink the sole survivor, *Vulcania*, with a long-range torpedo shot but she escaped – owing, it is thought, to

---

* There was a Director Angle 'computer' on board, but this required time to be set up.

her ability to steam at 23 knots, which was faster than Hezlet had estimated. Previously, *Vulcania* may have been inhibited by the need to stay in convoy with the two slightly slower liners. Having seen the other two ships stopped and sunk, *Vulcania* then had every reason to go hell-for-leather for the relatively few miles which separated her from Tripoli.

Convoys had also been trying to reach Malta as well as Tripoli. The island fortress was as much in need of supplies as was Rommel. In July 65,000 tons had arrived from Gibraltar, via Operation Substance, when six merchant ships accompanied for most of the way by one aircraft-carrier, one battleship, four cruisers and seventeen destroyers had fought their way towards the island for the loss of the destroyer *Fearless*: the cruiser *Manchester*, the destroyer *Firedrake* and the MV *Sydney Star* also being damaged.

No supplies for Malta arrived in August 1941 but a mammoth 85,000 tons was duly delivered from Gibraltar in September, via Operation Halberd. This consisted of a convoy of nine supply ships escorted, until near the narrow channel between Cape Bon and Sicily, by an even bigger Navy force of one aircraft-carrier, three battleships, five cruisers and seventeen destroyers. One cargo ship, *Imperial Star*, was lost and the large battleship *Nelson* was torpedoed and damaged. These two successful convoys were to save Malta.

The similarity between the plight suffered by the two enemies is heightened by the fact that both sides had been compelled to use priceless submarines as somewhat inefficient supply carriers. Just as *Rorqual* and *Cachalot* were thus reduced to the relatively humble, but vital, status of small freighters, so it was reported by Ultra, aided by the Allies' Middle East 'Y' Listening Services which first picked up the Enigma/C38 messages, that between 6 and 20 August Italian submarines had brought to Bardia, a minor port some 100 miles east of Tobruk, 192 tons of ammunition, fuel, food and spare parts – almost exactly the same kind of load as Allied submarines were carrying. The spare parts were probably for lorries as well as for aircraft and tanks, as the arduous journeys carried out in the summer heat of the African Desert along that dust-laden coastal road was causing havoc with every form of transport. Damage caused by marauding low-flying aircraft was also adding to the Axis's transport and maintenance problems.

September 1941 was also an excellent month for 830 Squadron although Lieutenant Commander Francis D. 'Frankie' Howie, their dedicated leader, had departed from Malta with a well-deserved DSO. The tall bearded Lieutenant H.E.H. 'Pancho' Pain took command until a more senior officer from the UK was posted in. Meanwhile Pancho made an excellent job of it.

Lieutenant Charles Lamb, a senior and very able pilot who had been sent by Vice Admiral Dennis Boyd, Vice Admiral Aircraft Carriers Middle East, to Malta to strengthen 830 Squadron, torpedoed a destroyer outside Tripoli on an night early in September, when he also observed an ammunition ship blow up in that port with a flash seen sixty miles away. (Was it caused by a Wellington, sabotage or accident?) On the same night the Fulmars of 800X Squadron damaged a number of aircraft on Catania airfield, the enemy's principal airfield in Sicily. That night 38 Squadron carried out a big raid on Tripoli, in which thirteen Wellingtons took part: they could easily have been responsible for the huge explosion noted by Lamb.

Charles Lamb and others in 830 Squadron also sank or damaged the *Andrea Gritti* (6,338 tons) and the *Pietro Barbaro* (6,330 tons) during the first few days of September. For once, Ultra disclosed the cargo of a sunken ship, that of the *Pietro Barbaro*: this consisted of 3,500 tons of bombs, 4,000 tons of ammunition, 5,000 tons of food, one entire tank workshop, 25 engines for Me 109s and 25 cases of glycol coolant for the engines of these excellent single-engined Luftwaffe fighters.

One reason why cargo manifests were so seldom extracted from Ultra intercepts was that the German Army was far more security-minded about the use of their army codes, and not until quite late in the Desert War were the decrypters at Bletchley Park able to unscramble this particular code, known as 'Chaffinch'. By contrast, the Luftwaffe and German Navy codes – both were changed after about every six months – were usually unscrambled and read within days of being first used.

A paradoxical situation arose with regard to Italian Navy codes. When Italy entered the war, they were using a series of naval codes which were changed almost daily and which were not being unscrambled by our decoding experts. They were being sent by normal W/T means and were being intercepted by our 'Y' Listening

Service teams in Malta, Egypt and elsewhere. However, the Germans soon persuaded the Italians that machines such as their Enigma were far superior and absolutely foolproof. Accordingly, when the Italians bought the Swedish version known as C38, this was soon being read and unscrambled by the experts at Bletchley Park as easily as were the German signals sent by their Enigma machines.

It was the ability of Bletchley Park to intercept, unscramble and decode these German and Italian naval machine-made codes which enabled the Ultra team to obtain the essential shipping information in time for forces in Malta to take advantage of it. However, an aerial reconnaissance had first to be carried out in order to confirm the ship/convoy position and also to give the enemy a reason to deduce why their movements had become known; then an attack was made. Occasionally an attack would be made based solely on Ultra information. In the latter case, arrangements were then made to send the signals which they knew would be intercepted by the enemy and which purported to reward the mythical agent in Naples.

Until Chaffinch could be read by Bletchley, the vital additional information about what the ships *en route* to Africa were carrying was not normally available, although that information was regarded as almost essential if Allied generals in the field were to know what Rommel had in mind and what he needed most. Once given the cargo information, Rommel's intentions could be deduced. Later, however, the enemy sent routine returns of his tank strength, his desperate fuel situation and his chronic shortages of both ammunition and food. These were then picked up by the Ultra team and relayed to the Middle East. By the time Rommel was planning to advance from El Alamein, in late August 1942, his intentions were known to the GOC-in-C Cairo and to General Montgomery. Rommel's defeat at the Alam Halfa ridge followed.

From about September 1941 onwards Malta received relevant Ultra signals direct from London. Earlier they had been sent to only three persons in the Middle East and, after being digested there, were relayed to Malta by appropriate signals, probably using the one underwater cable link which the Italians had not cut. Later, in order to speed up delivery, Ultra signals were even sent direct from Hut 3 at Bletchley to the Middle East and Malta.

As well as the Swordfish of the FAA and the Wellingtons of the RAF, the Blenheims also struck hard during September 1941, although by then the enemy's murderous anti-aircraft fire was devastating these low-level attackers. Britain's lack of an effective dive-bomber was all too evident. The Blenheims, not being dive-bombers, came under fire when first sighted, usually still a mile or two away. At that range they had to contend with the big guns and shells fired by the destroyers: guns of up to about 4.5-inch calibre. These shells threw up alarming fountains of water among and around the attacking formations. Later, fire from the Bofors and pom-pom guns and a host of machine-guns would come pouring their way. The Blenheim casualties included aircraft which, in their determination to score a hit, crashed into the masts of the ships they were attacking. Other Blenheims were lost in mid-air collisions over the target as aircraft tried to turn and weave their way from the withering flak.

The *Caffaro* (6,476 tons) was damaged or sunk by a combination of Blenheims and Swordfish: Wellingtons may also have been involved. The *Alfredo Oriani* was hit and probably sunk by 105 Squadron Blenheims, and the *Nicolo Odero* (6,003 tons) fell either to Swordfish or Wellingtons. The latter aircraft, in a night attack, dropped 24,500 pounds of bombs on or around the ship. Blenheims again attacked at low level on 17 September, claiming damage to a liner and a merchant vessel. The *Monselet*, a French vessel of 3,372 tons, fell to 107 Squadron Blenheims which had come to Malta to relieve what little was left of 105 Squadron. On the 21st a hit was claimed on a 'large liner', almost sure to be the *Vulcania*, probably then on her return to Naples northwards. *Marigola* (5,996 tons) was first damaged by Swordfish on the 23rd before being sunk later by submarine gunfire, and finally *Upright* closed the score for the month when, still commanded by Lieutenant Wraith, she sank the *Albatros*, an Italian torpedo-boat, on 27 September.

One difficulty for the submarines of the Tenth Flotilla was that torpedoes were always in short supply. At times they were obliged to use obsolescent Mark IV models, some of which happened to be in store in Malta. These were inferior to the Mark VIII. For one thing, their depth setting could not be altered once positioned in the tubes. The use of the Mark IV led to several ships, with either too deep or shallow a draught, being allowed to pass within range unmolested. Mark IVs were also more liable to run wild and circle round to attack the submarines which had only just ejected them. Nor were the more deadly Duplex pistols readily available in Malta. These were designed to detonate the explosion heads of the torpedo by magnetic impulses when passing immediately under a ship's hull. In theory at least – and usually in practice too – this was sure to break the back of the vessel. The submarine commander only knew that he had scored a hit when the ship's funnel gave off a peculiar puff of smoke just as her back was broken. With that, the ship could be declared a certain total loss.

The Tenth Flotilla had also been active during September 1941 when engaged on its other task: that of taking part in cloak-and-dagger raids, though the success rate of these was not improving, often to the cost of brave young men.

One unusual operation into enemy-held territory was carried out with courage and resourcefulness, not by the folbots, but by a Swordfish piloted by Charles Lamb. His task was to carry out a night rescue of an agent in Tunisia. The agent, who had been rumbled, was somehow briefed to jump from a train near Sousse and Lamb had to pick him up in the dark from a field (which he had never before seen) and fly him back to Malta. To make the impossible task even more impossible the Swordfish, with engine ticking over, would have to be refuelled in the field while awaiting the agent's arrival. Refuelling could only be accomplished by carrying the fuel in tins which were stowed alongside the observer in the open rear cockpit of the Swordfish.

Miraculously Charles Lamb found the right field, landed safely, taxied back to be in a position for a rapid departure and, with the engine still noisily ticking over, he and his observer, Sub Lieutenant J.M. Robertson, then faced the dangerous task of refuelling. As the fuel tank was only just behind the whirling propeller, this in itself was no easy task. Even lifting up the 40-pound tins was arduous enough. Not until near dawn, after an hour or more of anxious waiting behind enemy lines, did the agent appear, and this highly improbable rescue mission was safely accomplished.

Sadly, this remarkable pilot, who well earned his DSO, was later captured on a similar operation, and spent the rest of the war in a POW camp in the Sahara where British prisoners were brutally treated by sadistic French guards. On the occasion of his capture, Lamb was landing an agent, again in Tunisia, on a supposedly dried-up lake. The lake, however, was boggy and the Swordfish tipped over on to its nose, smashing the propeller. 830 Squadron had lost an outstanding leader and pilot.

Lieutenant Tomkinson in *Urge*, after further hitting the *Marigola*, opened the score for October 1941 by sinking the *Maria Pompei* (1,407 tons). But on the whole this was a quiet month for the Tenth Flotilla with only *Ursula* damaging the *Beppe* (4,859 tons) and the Polish submarine *Sokol*, also a Unity-class boat of the Tenth, sinking the *Citta di Palermo* (5,413 tons). *Sokol*, under the dynamic Commander Boris Karnicki and his Polish-speaking crew, also sank another ship by gunfire after his torpedoes had caused her crew to abandon it. However, this stationary target did not sink until many rounds from the inefficient 12-pounder gun had been fired at her. *Sokol* operated with an English liaison officer, Godfrey Place, on board but otherwise was treated just the same as the other submarines of the Tenth. On his return to Malta flying the Jolly Roger, which depicted his sinkings, Boris was delighted to find the Polish leader General Sikorski on the island. The General decorated him with a high Polish honour, the Virtuti Militari, unpinning his own medal and affixing it to Karnicki's chest.

Admiral Sir Max Horton, Flag Officer Submarines, also honoured Captain Simpson with a visit at the same time. Sir Max talked with all commanders not on patrol, encouraged them to relate their grievances, and went back to the UK suitably impressed, intent on seeing what could be done to improve the serviceability of their submarines and to ameliorate the working conditions of their crews.

October 1941 was, however, an active month for both the FAA and RAF. The four Fulmars, often led by a pilot, Petty Officer Sabey, continued with their intruder raids on Sicilian airfields such as Comiso, Gerbini, Catania, Trapani and Marsala, and the Swordfish went from strength to strength. Both Edgar Bibby and Myles Osborn led successful night torpedo attacks, with pilots Taylor, Cotton, Downes, Coxon, Stew Campbell, Nottingham and others scoring successes which resulted in the sinking of the *Rialto*, a tanker of 6,089 tons, the *Paola Podesta* (863 tons), the *Zena* (5,219 tons), the *Casa Regis* (6,485 tons), the *Bainsizza* (7,933 tons) and the *Caterina*.*

The Blenheims, often led by the recently commissioned Pilot Officer Ivor Broom, also scored many daylight successes. Some of their sorties now took them towards the islands off the Greek coast, as the successes of Allied submarines, Swordfish and the Blenheims themselves in the Central Mediterranean forced the enemy to resort more and more to the easterly approach to North Africa. The Blenheims also struck at ships at Zuara outside Tripoli, sinking among those they attacked the *Achille* (2,415 tons); they also sank an unknown vessel on 7 October and struck a ship outside Tripoli on the previous day.

During September 1941, a new type of Wellington equipped with ASV had arrived in Malta. A significant innovation, they carried out reconnaissance duties at night[†] to supplement the 69 Squadron Marylands which were performing so well shadowing enemy ships by day. Under the author, then a junior officer whom the AOC had promoted to command this new unit which went by the name of the Special Duties Flight (SDF), a number of novel operations were subsequently developed in co-operation with both the FAA Swordfish at Hal Far and a Royal Navy strike-force, Force K, which arrived on 21 October, to be based in Grand Harbour. These Wellingtons, with their rows of additional ASV aerials on top, along each side, and under the wings were quickly dubbed 'Sticklebacks' for obvious reasons and also 'Goofingtons' for no particular reason. They owed much to a brilliant Canadian ground radar expert, Flying Officer Albert Glazer who, with Corporal Les Card, also RCAF, often flew in their aircraft.

Force K had been brought to Malta at Prime Minister Winston Churchill's suggestion. It comprised two small 5,700-ton cruisers, *Aurora* and *Penelope*, and two modern destroyers, *Lance* and *Lively*. It was led by a brilliant Captain W.A. 'Bill' Agnew. For the first time since Italy had entered the war, a naval strike-force – including

---

* By war's end the FAA biplanes had sunk 33 Axis vessels – a figure confirmed by Tullio Marcon. About half were hit by Swordfish and many, later, by Albacores during the closing months of the Tunisian campaign.
† Unlike the normal Wellington bombers which attacked the enemy's ports at night and occasionally bombed ships at sea.

cruisers with six 6-inch guns and destroyers with eight 4-inch guns
– was to be based in Malta. Now that the big cat of the Luftwaffe
Fliegerkorps had departed from Sicily, Churchill no doubt felt that
the mice could play.

Once the night-operating Goofingtons had searched for, and
located, enemy ships at sea (thanks to the early form of radar they
carried), methods were devised to bring the attacking forces of the
surface ships of Force K or the 'Stringbags' of 830 Squadron to the
scene. Home-made radar homing-beacons called 'Roosters', assembled by the ground radar experts, were placed on the leading cruiser
of Force K and inside one of the Goofingtons. These enabled ships,
Swordfish and Goofingtons to find one another in the dark. Just to
be able to find and, if required, to illuminate the enemy at night was
at times sufficient, and on one occasion ships which a Goofington
had found south of Messina, were first attacked by Swordfish, then
bombed by Wellingtons and finally torpedoed by a submarine
which, unknown to the others, had also been stalking the vessel.

Although it was not normal for a Goofington to join in an attack,
on the night of 8 October one piloted by the author hit the supply
ship *Amsterdam* (8,670 tons) with a stick of 250-pound bombs which
had been set with 11-second delay fuses. As the sea was calm, skip-
bombing was used. Skip-bombing is a deadly game of ducks-and-
drakes where the bombs are sent skipping across the sea towards
the vessel. When last seen, the *Amsterdam* was shrouded in smoke,
with the destroyers *Gioberti* and *Passagno* alongside. Tullio Marcon,
who has supplied some of these details, also advises that *Amsterdam*
was then towed to Naples – the attack had taken place near
Marettimo Island, west of Sicily – and was under repair for many
months.

Lieutenant 'Pancho' Pain, the ex-Petty Officer who was temporarily in command of 830 Squadron, occasionally flew in one of
the three Goofingtons, as did other pilots and observers as well as
telegraphists both from 830 Squadron and from *Aurora*, the leading
ship of Force K.

October was also a good month for the unmodified Wellingtons.
On the night of 5/6 October, 'Wimpys' dropped 34,200 tons of
bombs on Tripoli and claimed a hit on a tanker. 104 Squadron, also
with Wellingtons, claimed a number of hits on a merchant ship
during a raid on the last day of the month. At various times detach-

ments from 38, 40 and 104 Squadrons were in Malta during this month, all with normal bomb-carrying Wellingtons.

One particularly praiseworthy effort this month took place on the 10th when pilots Osborn, Coxon and Campbell, in their 830 Squadron Swordfish aircraft, operated *twice* in one night, claiming, in all, one ship sunk and two damaged. To fly for hours at night without an auto-pilot behind just one engine, to be geared up during an attack when disaster could so easily strike, to fly home dead-tired and then to do it all again, required superb courage. The crews would have even started out tired, as on a busy airfield such as Hal Far it was never possible to enjoy real rest during the day when air raids were always liable to occur.

In an ominous move, this same month, six German U-boats were reported to have arrived from the Atlantic. Clearly, the enemy was taking new steps to make life more difficult for Malta. Would the U-boats be operated against Allied convoys and submarines? Would more be arriving? Would November continue to favour the Allies now that both day and night location and shadowing of their convoys was possible? Attacks from Malta were being successful but would retribution soon follow? It was an axiom among the brilliant crypto-analysts at Bletchley Park that 'Success breeds failure, and the greater the success the greater the failure', the thinking being that, the more successfully they cracked the Enigma codes, the more certain it would be that these codes would be changed.

Overhanging everything in the Mediterranean was, as usual, the state of the land war in the Desert. When would the two armies facing one another at Sollum, on the Egypt–Libya border, break out and which would break out first? Both were building up supplies. November 1941 could well turn out to be a critical month both for Malta and the see-saw war.

5

Force K Attacks

November 1941

'In November [1941], the total tonnage fell to 37,000
tons. Of these 26,000 tons was sunk and 2,000
damaged. This was 77 per cent. The battle [Operation
Crusader] was not decided during the land fighting
but rather by those external factors.'

Vice-Admiral Weichold,
Head of the German Naval Staff in Rome,
Der Krieg der achsenmachte in Mittelmeer (1973)

NOVEMBER 1941 TURNED out to be a critical month in the
Mediterranean war and especially perhaps for Malta. During this
month aircraft, submarines and surface ships between them
severed the enemy's supply lines to Libya as never before – nor, alas,
again thereafter. Their successes brought retribution, as will appear,
and almost for the first time since Italy had declared war on the
Allies, the form of retribution provided assistance to the Allies in
two distant, but enormously significant, theatres of the war in
Europe: in the Battle of the Atlantic and on the vast Russian fronts.

November was also the month when the Eighth Army again
advanced into Libya. Launching his offensive, Operation Crusader,
a few days before the date when Rommel planned to attack Tobruk,
General Auchinleck had beaten Rommel to the first punch. The
stalemate which had existed in the Desert ever since April was
broken. The Eighth Army rapidly gained ground, Rommel was
driven back towards Benghazi and Tripoli, and Tobruk was relieved
on 28 November. Thereafter the Allied force swept forward in huge

strides, much aided by the RAF which, in Air Vice-Marshal 'Mary'* Coningham, had found itself a forceful leader and a person who, under Air Marshal Tedder's guidance, had raised the level of close co-operation with the Army to unprecedented heights. The fact that the British were in a position to attack before Rommel was because, as Vice-Admiral Weichold wrote in the book cited at the head of this chapter: 'The Battle had already been lost by the Axis months previously through the British mastery of the sea and air' – this mastery deriving from the large number of ships which had been damaged or sunk by British aircraft, submarines and the Royal Navy's Force K operating out of Malta.

Lieutenant Commander Cayley in *Utmost* began November 1941 in style when on the first day of this eventful month he sank both the supply ships *Marigola* (5,996 tons) and *Balilla* (2,463 tons); one being sunk by gunfire and the other by torpedoes. *Marigola* had been damaged by *Urge* (Lt Tomkinson) about a week earlier, and was grounded in shallow water off the Tunisian coast before being finished off by *Utmost*.

The Blenheims of 18 Squadron then hit and possibly sank the *Anna Zuppitelli* (1,015 tons). Meanwhile the Wellingtons of 104 Squadron had been active. Following upon the success they had achieved on the night of 31 October by low-level night bombing – a highly unusual role for these relatively large aircraft – a maximum effort was arranged for the night of 2 November when Wellingtons, again at low level, attacked Castel Benito airfield near Tripoli. In the words of second pilot Philip Dawson who was assisting his skipper, Pilot Officer Doherty,

the aerodrome was full of aircraft while the defences were pitiful . . . the opposition soon ceasing after being machine-gunned by the aircraft's turrets. We made four or five bombing runs at pretty low levels and had some hits on the hangars. It was quite a sight with gunners in a few aircraft all firing at targets on the 'drome at the same time. There were fires all over the place. For our last run at below 800 feet I went on the beam guns to fire at flashes coming from the palm trees. During the raid one aircraft appeared with its navigation lights on but soon disappeared

---

* Arthur Coningham was a New Zealander; hence the nickname 'Maori' which was humorously distorted to 'Mary', but with no suggestion of effeminacy.

after the gunners of two or three of our aircraft all fired at it. Quite a party!*

This excitement, however, pales into significance when compared with the magnificent feat accomplished by Force K on the night of 8/9 November 1941. An important convoy destined for Rommel and his armies in North Africa departed from Naples during the night of 7 November. Because of the heavy mauling that Tripoli-bound convoys had suffered during the preceding months, the enemy decided to route this large and important convoy, which consisted of five merchant ships and two tankers escorted by six destroyers, the long way around Malta. First it passed through the Strait of Messina which separates Sicily from Italy. Thence its route would take it eastwards or even north-eastwards, towards the Greek coast and islands. From there it would alter course to almost due south until nearing Benghazi. Then it would head west to Tripoli.

This circuitous route more than doubled the time (and precious oil expended) when compared with the direct route Palermo–Cape Bon–Tunisian coast–Tripoli, but was chosen because it seemed much less likely to be attacked. It would keep the convoy beyond the radius of action of Malta's Swordfish and, for much of the journey, beyond the range of the RAF Blenheims also. The route also added distance between itself and Malta's deadly U-class submarines of the Tenth Flotilla.

Other precautions had also been taken. The enemy convoy would pass within likely range of the Blenheims only during the hours of darkness and, to counter the threat posed by Force K in Malta, it would, when passing east of Malta, have the added protection of a formidable Italian naval force which comprised two 10,000-ton cruisers, the *Trento* and *Trieste*, and their screen of four destroyers. These big fast cruisers, with guns of 8-inch calibre, far out-gunned the British cruisers *Aurora* and *Penelope*, which carried only 6-inch guns. As a result, if the two naval forces were to meet, the Italians would have many advantages in both numbers and firepower.

As a final measure, to ensure that this vital convoy would not be molested by any British ships sallying forth from Malta, a line of Italian submarines had been stationed to the east of Malta to detect,

---

* Letter to the author, March 1995.

and if possible to intercept, any warships heading for the convoy. In an attempt to protect it from daily air attack, and to avoid possible detection by Malta-based reconnaissance aircraft, relays of aircraft, over sixty in all, flew around it. It was as well protected as any southbound Axis convoy could be.

As Ultra intercepts were by then being passed direct to Malta, it is reasonable to assume that the Navy and RAF chiefs in Malta had foreknowledge of the convoy's initial departure and destination, although not necessarily all details of the route it intended to take.

In spite of the protection which it was supposed to be receiving in the air, the convoy was first sighted by the RAF at about 4.40 in the afternoon of 8 November. By then it had passed through the Messina Strait and was on its way towards the coast of Cephalonia. The American-built Maryland reconnaissance aircraft was flown by Wing Commander Dowland GC, the CO of 69 Squadron. Within about an hour of the sighting being reported to the underground RN/RAF Ops Room at Malta, Force K, as the last light left the sky, was on its way to intercept and engage.

It is never easy to intercept at night an enemy force whose position is not precisely known, and it started to appear to the men manning the British ships that they had missed the enemy and would have to return empty-handed to Malta.* But just then the tell-tale blips of a large convoy appeared on the radar screens of Force K, followed soon after by a visual sighting.

The enemy were quickly closed by the high speed which Captain Bill Agnew, the Force's leader in *Aurora*, liked to maintain. He also liked to close and engage in a line-astern formation of *Aurora*, then *Lance*, *Penelope* then *Lively*, with each ship keeping in the wake of the one ahead. It was, as he had earlier explained to the author, 'as if we were one big ship. That way we avoid all possible confusion of firing at one's own ships; all too easily done during a night engagement.'

Neither the merchantmen nor their escorts were equipped with radar. As a result they had no warning that the four British ships

---

* Because of the proximity of enemy-based torpedo- and bomber-aircraft, it had been decided that while in Malta Force K should not normally operate in daylight hours, but a concession of one hour after dawn and another before dusk was allowed.

were bearing down on them with guns trained. They remained in blissful ignorance until being straddled and hit. Meanwhile Captain Agnew led his ships into a better position where the enemy could be more easily seen in the moonlight.

Captain Agnew was fond of remarking that he was 'a Whale Island Man', Whale Island being the Royal Navy's Gunnery School in Portsmouth harbour. Captain Dudley Nichol of *Penelope* also ran a ship which could shoot straight and the two destroyers, though armed with less deadly guns, had enough weight of shot to contribute to the decimation of the convoy.

According to a plan which had been worked out beforehand, the captains of the ships of Force K first attacked the enemy escorts. They had no wish to be torpedoed and they knew that if they could rapidly dispose of, or scatter, the escorts, then the merchant ships were at their mercy. By then they had also become aware that, a few miles behind the convoy which they were about to attack, was another presumed convoy consisting of, as those on board *Lance* described it, 'two merchant ships and one or two destroyers'. The presumption was false. This convoy was in fact the two big Italian 8-inch gun cruisers with their four destroyers. However, Captain Agnew continued with his plan to rout the enemy destroyers and then deal with the defenceless supply ships.

No action was being taken by the enemy. If they had at any time sighted the two cruisers and destroyers approaching from the west, they would naturally have assumed that these were the *Trento* and *Trieste* with their own destroyers.

The enemy destroyers *Fulmine*, *Grecale* and *Euro* were all soon hit or sunk. The lead destroyer *Maestrale* was also damaged. She and others, after trying in vain to lay a protective smokescreen, rapidly steamed clear of the area. The enemy supply ships were then picked off and, in a matter of a few minutes, were all either sinking or on fire with no hope of surviving.

The ships sunk were *Conte di Misurata*, a tanker (5,014 tons), *Minatitlan*, another tanker (7,599 tons), *Rina Corrado* (5,180 tons), *Sagitta* (5,153 tons), *Maria* (6,339 tons), as well as two German ships, the *Duisberg* (7,389 tons) and the *San Marco* (3,113 tons). *Aurora* certainly sank several but *Penelope* (Captain Dudley Nichol) helped to sink *Fulmine* and finished off the *San Marco*. *Lance* (Lt/Cdr Northcott) torpedoed one of the tankers and set her ablaze and in all fired 434 rounds from her 4-inch guns. *Lively*, under her trumpet-playing skipper Lieutenant Commander Hussey, as well as contributing to the slaughter of the merchant ships, also succeeded in jamming the enemy's W/T signals. Both *Lance* and *Lively* returned the fire which was coming from the 'destroyers' of the other presumed convoy but was in fact the 8-inch shells being fired by the big Italian cruisers.

Once assured that none of the supply ships could survive, Captain Agnew led his triumphant force back to Malta at high speed. At no time, either outwards or homewards, were the Italian submarines which were lying in wait detected, and Force K easily avoided the torpedoes which were dropped soon after dawn by four Italian aircraft, as they were released at too great a distance. However, this did not stop Rome Radio from claiming hits on the cruisers, nor could VAM resist the temptation, upon learning of this incorrect broadcast, of signalling Captain Agnew about the efficiency of the dockyard which, he noted, had immediately made good the supposed damage.

In his diary Count Ciano, Mussolini's son-in-law and Italian Foreign Minister, also noted the engagement. 'All, I mean *all* our ships were sunk and one, or maybe two or three destroyers . . . Naturally our headquarters are pushing out their usual imaginary sinking of a British cruiser but nobody believes it.' Later when someone purported to prove that a British cruiser had been damaged, since aerial photographs showed it to be docked close to the Valletta floating-dock, Ciano likened this to 'proving that a man was dying because he lived alongside a cemetery'.*

After this swift, but effective, night action, Captain Nichol commanding the other cruiser *Penelope*, in the best British Naval tradition, composed a message appropriate to the occasion, signalling *Aurora*: 'Congratulations on your magnificent borealis.' It was later remarked that the encounter had only been 99.9 per cent successful because, although no ship of Force K was hit, and there were no human casualties, five canaries aboard one of the victorious vessels died from noise, fright or shock or, as one wag suggested, 'Probably yellow!'

---

* See his *Diary 1939–1945* (London, 1947), ed. Malcolm Muggeridge.

Only after Force K had returned to harbour was it known to the men on board that there had been such a powerful cruiser force in their vicinity. It has since been assumed that because Force K had not, as it happened, approached the enemy convoy *direct* from Malta, they had unwittingly skirted around the big cruisers which, quite logically, had been positioned to the west of the convoy and on the direct track between Malta and the convoy they were protecting. Since the Italian cruisers also lacked radar, they were firing virtually blind during the battle, aiming more in hope than expectation. In all, 207 rounds of 8-inch shells had been fired by the big cruisers at Force K in the knowledge that a single hit from such a weighty shell could have crippled any of the British attackers. Conversely the 4-inch shells fired in their direction by *Lance* and *Lively* were likely to do very little harm to the big cruisers.

While the author was researching material for this book and looking for an explanation as to why neither Wing Commander Dowland nor Captain Agnew, nor apparently anyone else in Malta, seems to have known that the *Trento* and *Trieste* were also guarding this vital enemy convoy, an Air Gunner, Desmond Haynes, who often flew with him from Malta, reminded him that they had spent most of the previous night, that of 7 November 1941, in an ASV-equipped Wellington aircraft of his Special Duties Flight, shadowing a convoy 'off Greece' as Haynes had noted down. Haynes had also noted that the convoy consisted of '*two Cruisers*, eight destroyers and four Merchant ships'. Although it is thought that this unlikely combination was more probably eight merchant ships and four destroyers – recognition of ships from aircraft at night always being cloaked in uncertainty – the specific reference to 'two cruisers' is of particular interest. It is therefore postulated that the situation for the nights of 7 and 8 November may have been that the *Trieste* and *Trento*, having successfully escorted the other convoy 'off Greece' to a point where it was beyond attack from Malta, then backtracked to join the *Duisberg* convoy late on 8 November.

If such a sensible arrangement had been made before the cruisers originally departed from Taranto, it would not have required any wireless communication to Tripoli. All Tripoli was interested in knowing was what convoy was coming and approximately when it would be arriving. If information about the intended movements of the *Trieste* and *Trento* was not sent by W/T then it could not have been intercepted by Y Service and decoded by the Ultra team. This possible explanation also accounts for Wing Commander Dowland's failure to sight and report upon the cruisers when locating the convoy in the late afternoon of 8 November because they would not then have been near the convoy. If the *Trento* and *Trieste* with their destroyers had been only about 4,000 yards behind the *Duisberg* convoy, as was the case when Force K attacked, it seems inconceivable that Dowland would not have seen them from above.

The great Force K victory of 8 November 1941 was the single convoy disaster which most alarmed the Axis leaders. Yet though so significant in its effect, it was by no means the full story. Although the Axis powers were clearly upset by the loss of an entire seven-ship convoy, this was only the culmination of a series of attacks which, with growing intensity, were steadily cutting deeper into the enemy supply lines between Italy and North Africa. Ship by ship, week by week, month by month, Rommel was being denied the supplies which he needed. And most of these attacks were being made by either submarines or aircraft based in Malta.

Even if we count the convoy which Captain Mack totally destroyed on 16 April 1941, when he sank five supply ships and all three destroyers, and add the five more ships which Force K destroyed over the next three–four weeks of November/December 1941, the total number of ships sunk by Royal Navy surface ships in Malta adds up to only about twenty-eight. This pales into insignificance when compared with the several hundred that were sunk or damaged by marauding submarines and FAA and RAF strike-aircraft based in, or operating from, Malta.

Captain Agnew and Force K wrote a glorious chapter in the history of offensive operations from Malta – and the author will always be proud of the close association which existed between his small Special Duties Flight of ASV-equipped Wellingtons and those four gallant ships. Sadly, however, the Force K chapter was to be an all too brief one, as its activities were soon to be cut off in its prime.

Nonetheless, for the present the victory marked a turning point in the course of the war and was followed by swift and far-reaching consequences. Although 693 Italian seamen were rescued the next day from a watery grave, retaliation came not from the humiliated Italians but from Hitler and the OKW in Berlin, the Germans perhaps goaded into action by the loss of the two German vessels.

Hitler's reactions were dramatic. The order went out that Luftflotte II, the huge Air Army facing Moscow – one of the three German air force headquarters on his Eastern Front – was to be moved to Sicily. There, under Marshal Kesselring, the man appointed to command all Germany's Mediterranean forces, it had orders to reduce Malta by bombing to such a state of impotence that it would no longer pose the remotest threat to the Axis' African convoys. It was possible that Luftflotte II might have been moved to the area in any event, now that winter was stalling action on the Moscow front; but if Malta had not posed such a serious threat, this formidable air force might have been moved to Libya to support Axis forces in the Desert, especially as Rommel was then assembling all the supplies he could muster for an attack on Tobruk planned for later in November. In any event, this large experienced air force, one which had worked well in co-operation with the army attacking Moscow, was moved to Sicily, and not to Libya, and in the months to come Rommel would need all the air support he could get as he and his troops were forced into flight.

Nor was this all. Much to Admiral Doenitz's fury, as the ace U-boat commander Otto Kretschmer has recently confirmed to the author by letter, Hitler also ordered a large percentage of Doenitz's successful U-boats to be transferred from their Atlantic killing grounds to new Axis bases in the Mediterranean. Assuming that all the U-boats would have successfully negotiated the perilous passage through the Strait of Gibraltar, one of their duties in the Mediterranean was to ensure that Allied convoys should not be allowed to reach Malta. This British bastion, which was proving to be such a thorn in the sides of the generals fighting the British in the Libyan Desert, was to be starved out, as well as bombed out.

By 15 December 1941, approximately half the number of U-boats which had been operating in the Atlantic were either in the Mediterranean or on their way there. However, air attacks by gallant Swordfish FAA crews based in Gibraltar were already making them pay for daring to attempt to sneak their way past this famous rock, most firmly in British hands.

The decisions taken by Hitler and the OKW in Berlin to move Luftflotte II to Sicily and large numbers of U-boats to the Mediterranean were of profound psychological, as well as material, significance. Hitler, on this occasion, was reacting to an Allied success; he was taking a *counter*-move. For the first time since invading Poland on 1 September 1939, he was dancing to the Allies' tune. A faint light was appearing at the end of a long dark tunnel.

As well as the reservations expressed by Admiral Weichold in the epigraph to this chapter, Count Ciano was equally lugubrious. On 9 November his diary records: 'Since 19 September the Axis have given up trying to sail convoys through to Africa [direct ?] and the losses suffered by the merchant fleet are so high as to discourage further experiments.' Already on 6 October he had written: 'The supplies for Africa are becoming more and more difficult. Only 20 per cent of the material set aside for September has been shipped and delivered.' Written long before the great triumph which Captains Agnew and Nichol achieved on the night of 8/9 November 1941, this paragraph makes it clear that Force K's successes were only the latest in a long chain of disasters for the Axis. Malta was paying for its keep.

Other successes in November were to follow. An Italian submarine of the Perla class (853 tons) was attacked by Swordfish of 830 Squadron (Lt Coxon) and damaged. This submarine – as was the fate also of the destroyer *Libeccio*, damaged by Force K on the night of 8/9 November – was finished off by 'Wanks' in *Upholder*. Blenheims of 105/107 Squadrons on the 17th made a low-level attack off Zuara and, with Pilot Officer Ivor Broom among the attackers, left a 4,000-ton ship ablaze.

The parlous shortages of fuel available to Rommel are indicated by an Ultra intercept which, commenting upon the loss of the Italian ships *Procida* and *Maritza* on 24 November, states that between them they were carrying 'three times the total stocks of petrol then available in Cyrenaica'.* By mid-November the enemy's fear of Force K's operations from Malta was dominating their shipping movements to North Africa. *Procida* and *Maritza* had, for example, sailed from Taranto on 14 November and headed eastwards to arrive at Piraeus, the port near Athens, on the 17th. By then, the enemy were trying a new tactical approach. In their desperation to meet Rommel's constant demands for fuel, ammunition and other supplies, they were sailing relatively small groups of ships simultaneously from many

---

* Germany tended to refer to Libya and Tripolitania as 'Cyrenaica'.

different ports. If some got sunk, others would survive. Force K could not be in two places at once. The armed merchant ship, the *Adriatico*, had sailed from Reggio di Calabria, opposite Messina, and was also heading eastwards to Argostoli on the Greek island of Cephalonia. From there she hoped later to make a night-dash to Benghazi. The tanker *Berbera*, also heading for Benghazi, was first trying to get to Navarino, the Greek port on the western Pelopponese: site of the famous battle in the Greek war of independence which saw the defeat of the Ottoman navies. The supply ships, *Citta di Tunisi* and *Citta di Palermo*, were aiming to berth in Suda Bay, Crete, where the *Procida* and *Maritza* were also next planning to berth. These roundabout routes, as we know, were burning up precious oil, as well as causing lengthy delays.

With so much heading towards Greece, Force K, upon departing from Grand Harbour at dusk on the 23rd, also headed eastwards. However, the Force was detected by both a submarine which had been placed specifically to intercept her anticipated track, and later by shadowing aircraft. The enemy's reactions to the news that Force K was again at sea were dramatic. Although there were diverse ships at sea and it was clearly impossible for Force K to be threatening all of them, the Italian Admiralty ordered all their supply carriers to hasten back to port.

Signals officers on board *Lively*, however, had by then become expert at interfering with Italian Navy signals and succeeded in jamming some of these orders. *Lively's* telegraphists also made life difficult for the Italian authorities by jamming the position reports which were being made by some of the aircraft shadowing Force K. Petty Officer Griffin, on board *Lively*, found his hands almost too full and resorted to 'controlling' the enemy shadowing aircraft using their call signs. At one time he even ordered them all to maintain W/T silence, which they did. The Petty Officer Telegraphist John Mountfield, on board *Lance*, also took a hand and successfully jammed messages sent on other Italian frequencies.

Meanwhile Captain Agnew himself was adding to the enemy's confusion. Although he now had reports from one of the Malta-based Wellingtons giving the position of *Procida* and *Maritza*, he continued to head his ships as if he was making for Alexandria, rather than indicate to the enemy shadower that he was intending to attack one of the enemy convoys. Thanks to the clever tactics of the telegraphists aboard *Lance* and *Lively*, the *Procida* and *Maritza*, with their escorts, failed to receive the 'return to harbour' order. Later, when no longer observed from above, Captain Agnew knew that he still had time to alter course to intercept these two. As indeed he did.

When *Procida* and *Maritza* were duly sighted they were found to be accompanied by the torpedo-boats *Lupo* (679 tons) and *Cassiopeia* (642 tons), as well as by a circling German aircraft which, as some others had earlier done, mistook the British cruiser force for additional Italian naval vessels arriving to protect the small convoy. Accordingly, the aircraft fired off appropriately friendly recognition signals. It would seem from this that the Luftwaffe had not been warned that Force K was in the area, or even at sea.*

In the engagement which ensued, it was left to *Penelope* to deal with both *Procida* and *Maritza* as, by the time Force K opened fire, a number of hostile Ju 88s had awoken to the fact that, although the action was taking place approximately midway between Crete and Benghazi, the warships were British and not Italian. *Aurora*, *Lance* and *Lively* fought off dive-bombing attacks, as also did *Penelope*, but no hits on any of the four warships were scored.

Initially the two torpedo-boats escorting *Procida* and *Maritza* had attempted to get within range to torpedo the ships of Force K. Soon, however, both were laying smoke and retreating fast towards Crete. Captain Nichol in *Penelope* pursued the attack, and as both *Procida* and *Maritza* were carrying fuel and ammunition, with some cargo stowed on deck, it did not take many hits before they were set on fire. Fire was followed by explosions. It would appear that no sailors survived from either ship. Force K had scored another notable victory, even if the escorting torpedo-boats had escaped with only minor near-miss damage.

Italian cruisers were also at sea that month and at least two suffered major damage. On a night reconnaissance to locate targets for the FAA Swordfish, the author flying one of the SDF Goofingtons had located a vessel just south of the Messina Strait. With the crude radar on board, it was difficult to identify the kind of ship in the

---

* This seems to indicate a lack of co-operation between the Italian Navy and the German Air Force.

dark of a moonless night, especially as it was close to the Sicilian shore which showed up all too clearly on the tiny cathode-ray tube of the ASV. A 'large enemy ship' was reported to Malta by W/T.

While waiting for strike-aircraft to appear from Malta, a number of parachute flares were dropped by the aircraft in order to be able to identity the ship better. By the light of the flares, it was recognized as a cruiser and confirmation of this came when it opened up at the Wellington with what appeared to be a score or more of anti-aircraft guns. Some shells came near enough for the smell of cordite to be sensed inside the aircraft.

Soon afterwards, before any attacking aircraft from Malta could have arrived, to the complete surprise of all aboard the Wellington, the cruiser appeared to explode with a big flash, followed by clouds of smoke. This was duly reported to Malta.

During the debriefing of the Wellington crew back at base, one of the theories voiced by an over-enthusiastic gunner was that 'we must have dropped a flare down a funnel and this must have set alight some ammunition'. However unlikely this was, it had occurred to the author that the cruiser might have experienced a 'flash-back' from one of its many guns which could have detonated ammunition aboard. It was several days before the mysterious explosion was explained.

The Wellington's crew, while dropping flares, were unaware that the submarine *Utmost* (Lt/Cdr Cayley) was also in the area. He, too, had located the cruiser: the *Duca d'Egli* – a 6-inch gun ship of 9,959 tons. At first when our parachute flares descended, Cayley was not at all pleased. They illuminated his submarine, which was on the surface, far too clearly for his liking. However, when the cruiser abruptly opened fire at the Wellington with the attention of those on board concentrating upon this action, Cayley took the opportunity to close to within torpedo range and hit the cruiser. The *Duca d'Egli* did not sink but limped into Taranto where she was several months under repair.

Another cruiser, *Duca d'Abruzzi* (7,874 tons), was also damaged at much the same time, 21 November 1941, by the Swordfish of 830 Squadron when near Tripoli.

On 29 November the Blenheims of 18 Squadron claimed to have sunk one large ship and damaged a troop-ship near Tripoli, while Wellingtons, on a raid on Benghazi, sank the *Priaruggia* (1,196 tons).

Two days later, Blenheims from 18 and 107 Squadrons damaged the tanker *Volturno* (3,363 tons) during an attack which earned Flight Lieutenant Edmonds, who had taken part in the earlier attack, a well-earned DFC. The same two squadrons then sank the *Berbera*, another tanker of 2,093 tons, two days later. A memorable month for Malta closed with Blenheims sinking the *Capo Faro*, a supply ship (3,476 tons), on the last day of November.

All the strike elements in Malta had scored well during the month: the RAF Wellingtons and Blenheims; the FAA biplanes, with the Albacores of 828 Squadron now learning their trade by accompanying the Swordfish of 830 Squadron on their strikes; the submarines of the Tenth Flotilla led, as usual, by *Upholder* and, above all else, by the Royal Navy's Force K. Although playing only supporting roles, the Marylands of 69 Squadron by day and the Goofingtons of the SDF by night had, by effective air reconnaissance, also made their contributions.

It also raised the spirits of all in Malta to learn, by the end of the month, that Rommel was in full retreat in the Desert as Operation Crusader gained pace. All in Malta knew that the fortunes of the land war in the Desert, and those of the air–sea war in and over and under the waters around Malta, were irrevocably intertwined. Initially it had been reckoned in Whitehall that if the Eighth Army could advance to, and hold, Benghazi, then Malta could survive. However, by November 1941, it had come to be recognized that the reverse was true. It was realized that, for as long as Malta held firm and could strike back, then and then only could the Eighth Army triumph.

Retribution for those in Malta was soon to follow. November 1941 had constituted a watershed. Thereafter things on that lonely and now besieged, as well as bombed, outpost were never to be the same again.

6

The Tables Turned

December 1941–March 1942

'The British knew where the weakness in Rommel lay.
With aircraft, submarines and surface vessels, they
attacked the supply convoys from Italy to North
Africa. Retribution was overtaking the Italians for not
having eliminated Malta before the North African
operation began.'

Grand Admiral Karl Doenitz, *Memoirs* (1959)

DECEMBER BEGAN WHERE November left off, with Force K eliminating what was left of another convoy to North Africa. On 1 December, during a long night reconnaissance, an SDF Goofington located and reported a number of enemy ships at sea in the knowledge that a number of RN ships were out looking for them. The cruiser *Aurora* still retained the home-made 'Rooster' which Al Glazer had devised and which had become a key element in the cooperation between the Goofingtons of the SDF and the Naval surface ships based in Malta.

By then, the successes gained by Force K had led to Rear Admiral B. Rawlings being sent to Malta with additional surface ships. This enlarged strike-force, Force B, left Alexandria under the command of Admiral Rawlings on 27 November 1941 to serve as reinforcements, since it was suspected that the Italians, in order to counter Force K, would be using their big cruisers (almost twice the size of *Aurora* and *Penelope*) and battleships as escorts of their convoy. Force B consisted of the cruisers *Ajax* and *Neptune*, sister ships, of 7,000 tons with eight 6-inch guns. Two destroyers *Kimberley* and *Kingston* with six smaller guns accompanied the cruisers. Force B arrived in Malta on 28 November.

With a choice of reported targets to attack, Admiral Rawlings, who had reports of two separate Italian cruiser forces at sea, one of three cruisers and the other of a single cruiser both with their destroyer screens, came to the conclusion that the one with the reported solitary cruiser was, in fact, not a cruiser but the Italian battleship *Duilio*. He also calculated that both Italian naval forces appeared to be converging in order to rendezvous during the night. He therefore decided to position his sizeable force of four cruisers and destroyers ahead of the expected position of the enemy and there to await events. Meanwhile a sighting report from the submarine *Thunderbolt* gave a later indication of the position and speed of an unescorted supply ship steaming south at 10 knots, while VAM relayed a report, probably Ultra-based, of two merchant ships and a destroyer in a more northerly position also heading south.

In this confusion of signals, including one from the Goofington which indicated that a second enemy convoy might be at sea but in another position relative to his cruisers, Admiral Rawlings decided to split his force* and despatch *Aurora*, with *Penelope* and *Lively* – all ships of the former Force K – to intercept the lone merchantman while waiting with his remaining bigger cruisers to intercept the expected warships. Unbeknown to Admiral Rawlings at the time, he was positioning himself and his force to intercept nothing as, following upon the loss of the MV *Capo Faro* to the Blenheims, and the damage to the MV *Iseo* and engine trouble in the Italian cruiser *Garibaldi*, what remained of that convoy had, along with its heavy escorts, all turned back. The warships headed for Taranto and the damaged *Iseo* for Argostoli in Cephalonia.

However *Aurora*, *Penelope* and *Lively*, still in touch with their friendly SDF Goofington, ploughed on towards the intended merchantman, keeping in contact with the aircraft via their own

---

* As long as Admiral Rawlings was in Malta, the Naval strike-force became Force B; when he departed back to Alexandria with what was left of the ships he had brought with him, the force in Malta again became Force K. When Force B split into two, those on board *Aurora*, *Penelope*, *Lively* (and the author in the Goofington) regarded themselves as back in Force K.

private code and W/T frequency as in the past – the Goofington, thanks to *Aurora*'s Rooster, always knowing the relative position of what its captain liked to term 'their' ships below.

Originally the enemy had consisted of a supply ship escorted by a destroyer, but by the time that Force K, guided by its Goofington, had located an enemy in the area north of Benghazi, the supply ship *Adriatico* (1,976 tons) was unescorted and although its crew were given several chances to abandon ship, they decided to fight back. As well as carrying cargo including nearly 400 tons of precious air-craft petrol, *Adriatico* had troops on board and was armed with two 120-mm guns as well as lighter guns. When, instead of surrender-ing, it fired back at the British warships, it was rapidly sunk by *Lively* on orders from Captain Agnew. It went down, with its petrol causing massive explosions.

Rather than return in daylight to Malta, Captain Agnew then took his three ships westwards across the Gulf of Sirte, as reports had been picked up of other potential 'customers', including a tanker, obviously heading for Tripoli and expected to be in the region of the Kerkenah Bank that evening. During this daring daylight sortie relatively close to North Africa, Captain Agnew's Force had, not surprisingly, been detected by Italian Cant floatplanes on recon-naissance but, as before, the telegraphists aboard *Lively* took a hand in jamming their reports and causing confusion over their W/T wavelengths.

The new enemy consisted of the tanker *Iridio Mantovani* (10,400 tons) – a prime target of priceless worth – protected by the destroyer *Alvise da Mosta*. This precious load of fuel had managed to get within about seventy miles of Tripoli before it had been pounced upon and attacked by Blenheims from Malta. A 250-pound bomb had struck home and had stopped it in its tracks. However it, and its cargo, were still afloat and the destroyer *Alvise da Mosta* was doing its level best to tow it the last few miles into Tripoli.

Towards evening, Force K sighted this struggling combination and *Aurora* opened fire with her 6-inch guns at extreme range (about nine miles). Although the destroyer put up a gallant fight and endeavoured to fire back with her smaller guns which lacked the range, the fight was an unequal one. *Alvise da Mosta*'s captain also made two gallant attempts to close *Aurora* in order to torpedo her, but soon the destroyer was being ripped to pieces by the 6-inch shells of *Aurora* commanded by her master gunner, Captain W.G. Agnew who, since his *Duisberg* convoy success, could now add the CB to his other decorations.

After *Alvise da Mosta* had blown up and sunk with a series of terrific explosions as her magazine caught fire, Force K finished off the stationary *Iridio Mantovani*, with *Lively* firing the final decisive torpedo. When *Iridio Mantovani* went down, she took with her a total of over 8,699 tons of various desperately needed fuels: benzine, naphtha oil and petrol. In his diary entry for 1 December, Count Ciano had recorded: 'Of the whole convoy of five ships, two ships arrived, one was forced to beach at Suda Bay and two were sunk.' The next day he was to lament: 'Another of our ships has been sunk, almost at the entrance to Tripoli. It was the *Mantovani* loaded with 7,000 tons of petrol. It cannot be denied this is a hard blow.'

After these two further successes and the successful return of the three warships to Malta, Vice Admiral Ford sent a congratulatory signal to Captain Agnew:

> I want to compliment the engineering staff of Force K on the great efficiency of their department, without which the very successful operation carried out at a high and prolonged speed could not have been obtained.

The generous leader of Force K then signalled back that it was 'entirely due to the ASV Wellington that Force K had been able to intercept the *Adriatico*', and he mentioned 'his appreciation of the fine performance given by F/Lt Spooner. He stayed in the air long past his endurance in order to make certain that he homed me satisfactorily on the target.'

Captain Agnew was unaware that the author had devised ways of shadowing while using only minimum fuel, and at one point during this operation he had signalled the ASV Wellington in plain language 'Go home'. Unbeknown to the author, Captain Agnew had taken the trouble to ascertain that his Goofington had a normal endurance of ten and a half hours. This particular flight was over thirteen hours long with the final 200 miles entailing technical and weather difficulties. One engine was faulty and all the aerials – both W/T and ASV – were iced up. After a series of

SOS calls, the Wellington reached Malta, long after dawn, with dry tanks.*

However, life for those in Malta was also beginning to become less pleasant. After the *Duisberg* convoy disaster, Hitler was forced to realize that, if he wished to continue to help his favourite General Rommel, he had only two choices: either to invade and capture Malta, or to destroy completely all the offensive forces stationed there and thus render the island incapable of offensive operations.

There was, of course, the third choice, namely to abandon North Africa to the ineffective Italian Army and to extricate as best he could the Afrika Korps and its supporting Luftwaffe. However, Hitler's policy from 1942 onwards seems to have been to support lost causes. He was a firm believer, fortunately for the Allies, in the dictum of never yielding a yard of ground for strategic purposes nor of preserving his resources for another day, even when a campaign was clearly lost.

Malta's fight back in 1940, and especially the devastation wrought by Malta-based vessels and aircraft on Axis convoys in the Central Mediterranean in 1941, again brought the question of an invasion of Malta to the fore both in Italy and Germany. In 1942, the Axis plan was sensibly submitted for comment to the Japanese who by then had successfully seized many fortified islands in the Pacific. This final plan, known in Germany as Operation Herkules and in Italy as Operazione C3, was envisaged as taking place during a suitable night in July 1942 and was based on the presumption that air and naval supremacy would first have been achieved. It included the employment of twenty-three batteries, six groups of artillery and the gradual attrition of Malta's defences by massive air attacks from 20 March onwards. It also proposed to use famine as a weapon in the knowledge that Malta could never feed itself.

German participation was now heavily involved. New parachute units were to be formed, Italian units being trained up by the Germans: as part of the plan three waves of paratroops would

---

* At a celebratory lunch given by the VAM at Fort St Angelo to celebrate Force K's great victories, the author found himself the only junior non-Naval officer present. Captain Agnew had arranged the invitation. As he told the author: 'I regard you as a part of Force K. You are my night eyes.'

be landed in the Dingli/Zurrieq area. Landing-craft practice on the rocky coast of Tuscany was also initiated, and in various naval yards throughout Italy the required assault craft were put under construction.

As well as 16 troop-ships, 270 landing-craft and 50 other vessels, German troops would be carried in several hundred gliders. As Italy was fast becoming bereft of fuel, 40,000 tons of naphtha oil for use by the Italian Navy would be forthcoming from Germany.

In all, 900 aircraft would be involved, including 300 bombers, 180 fighters and 60 torpedo-bombers; these last were intended to prevent the Royal Navy from interfering. Hundreds of transport planes would be deployed. The gliders would land in the Kalafrana area during the evening of their D-Day, followed by the arrival of landing-craft during the night on the beaches near Krendi, on the coast of Gozo and at Marsaxlokk Bay. Dummy landings made north of Sliema and opposite Mellicha would by then, it was hoped, have drawn off many of the defenders.

With German involvement and the necessary oil supplies now assured, Italy urged that the invasion be brought forward to June 1942. However, the German OKW ruled out June on the grounds that priority had to be given to attacks being planned elsewhere, among them Rommel's plan to drive into Egypt. Some of their troops and aircraft would also be required initially for operations on the Russian fronts. The spectre of insufficient oil was also beginning to haunt many German minds. They were already finding it difficult to supply the 40,000 tons of naphtha required by the Italian Navy.*

With their other plans in mind, the Germans, after early May 1942, left it largely to the Regia Aeronautica to keep up the continuing neutralization of Malta by aerial bombardment, although the arrival of Spitfires in Malta during March–May 1942 put a different complexion on these plans. The Italian Air Force, far from continuing to neutralize Malta, soon lost the measure of air superiority over Malta which the Luftwaffe had gained during the March–April period.

---

* Italy had virtually no oil and was dependent on Germany for supplies of naphtha, a by-product of Germany's many coalfields. One reason big Italian warships seldom left port was lack of naphtha.

However, with the failure of the two Allied convoys intended for Malta in June, when only two of the seventeen ships reached Valletta (four were sunk, and eleven turned back), the Axis expected the island's powers to be greatly reduced.

With Rommel's capture of Tobruk in June 1942, and the conquest of Egypt in sight, the Germans began to send him virtually everything he wanted, including even the landing-craft which had been assembled for Operation Herkules. This last action was the final nail in the coffin for the various plans which had been made to seize Malta, in spite of the fact that, by then, both sides had come to realize that Malta was the key to the critical supply problems which the Axis forces were facing in North Africa. In other respects, the German leaders were never keen to launch the invasion. Goering, in particular, recalled the high level of damage sustained in the capture of Meleme airfield and Crete, when no less than 5,140 of the 13,000 airborne troops became casualties. Hitler also did not relish having to rely upon the Italian Navy.

Bombardment and siege were now seen as alternatives to invasion. If Malta could not be supplied, then the defenders of the besieged island would have to surrender due to lack of food, as well as shortages of the various implements of war. With Malta out of the war, there would be little to prevent supplies reaching Tripoli and other North African ports. On the other hand, if Malta were to be sustained to the point where successful offensive operations could be maintained by the Allies, then the Axis forces in the Desert could never be assured of receiving the supplies they needed to overcome the British Eighth Army which opposed them. Either way, Malta was the key.

Ironically two German *victories* were indirectly responsible for the decision not to invade Malta. The heavy losses in capturing Crete caused Goering to hold back. More significantly, Rommel's capture of Tobruk, and his advance to within seventy miles of Alexandria, appeared to make the invasion unnecessary.

It soon became apparent that Hitler's first move to prevent his favourite General from being swept out of Africa by the combination of Crusader on land, and the loss of fuel and other supplies by sea, was to try to pound Malta into some form of impotence. Whether or not this assault by bombs was a prelude to a forthcoming invasion of Malta was, at that time, anyone's guess.

Most people on the island reckoned that an invasion was more than likely and, as the blitz increased in fury, many in the Royal Navy and RAF, and at the dockyards, were given the rudiments of man-to-man combat training by those in the Army who were expert in these brutal arts. Rifles and hand-guns, to the extent available, began to be given to those at the airfields who were thought capable of using them.

For fear of invasion, a number of unofficial home-made light AA gun-posts were established at the airfields, using machine-guns taken from bombers destroyed on the ground. These were manned by a strange but enthusiastic collection of RAF personnel from decorated Wing Commander pilots to humble Airmen Second Class. The airfields were also heavily mined so that, in the event of an invasion and the likelihood of the airfields falling into the hands of the enemy, they could be self-destructed. Everyone in Malta knew that Crete had fallen to airborne troops and that possession of an airfield would be a prime objective of any invaders.

The number of air alerts had increased alarmingly: there were 31 in September; 57 in October; 76 in November, and now 169 in December. Moreover, it seemed certain that there would have been many more but for the appalling December weather when rain, low cloud and storms prevented virtually all flying from taking place, on both sides, for several days at a time. There also seemed to be a twenty-four-hour Christmas truce, using the weather as an excuse.

It was not just the number of air raids that was perturbing but the determination with which they were carried out. The Luftwaffe had again taken over the airfields in Sicily. The raids of the previous three months had been largely ineffective. The Regia Aeronautica were peculiarly unpredictable. Some formations turned back almost as soon as the first of the island's now-weary Hurricanes appeared. Others dropped their bombs, deliberately so it seemed, way out to sea, whilst other Italian bombers flew over the island at considerable height in airshow formation of three or five and dropped their bombs with considerable precision. Even when under fierce attack by Hurricanes, and with anti-aircraft fire bursting all around them, they never wavered or broke tight formation. To see one of these aircraft knocked down and to see the others carry on without altering formation was a strange and wondrous sight.

Regardless of whether any bombs had been dropped or not, Rome Radio invariably claimed damage to a number of fictitious Malta targets, once mentioning the isolated, uninhabited rock of Filfla. On another occasion, Rome Radio claimed damage to Valletta's marshalling yards: a surprising claim for an island with no rail system.

The December raids were very different in character. The bombers were either the near vertically diving Ju 87 Stuka or the less spectacular Ju 88s which dived at an angle of about forty-five degrees from the vertical. The pilots of both appeared to be quite fearless and dived almost exclusively at targets either in the harbours or on the three airfields.

Strange as it may seem, it was preferable to be attacked by the diving Junkers rather than by the unpredictable Italians. Dive-bombing is quite tolerable because it is obvious, to those watching on the ground, approximately where the bombs will fall and 99 times out of 100 it can be seen with experience – and all in Malta gained plenty of that – that the target is elsewhere. High-level bombing from (say) 15,000–19,000 feet is different. Observers on the ground have no idea when the bombs will be released or have been released. Even if bombs could be seen when leaving the aircraft, observers would only have the haziest idea where they were likely to fall.

It was to the advantage of all in Malta that buildings were made of stout stone blocks, that there was virtually no wood to burn in any of them and, above all, that the ground was mainly soft limestone. This last meant that slit trenches could easily be hacked or even sawn out and that each bomb merely made a relatively small crater. Private slit trenches were dug everywhere around the airfields (the handful of SDF aircrews dug their own, using axes and adzes) and many, if not most airmen preferred to watch the dive-bombers rather than spend prolonged periods beset with anxiety in evil-smelling damp and dark shelters, not knowing what was happening above.

In any event, the rule at airfields was for airmen to ignore the persistent air-raid sirens and to carry on working until a local airfield alarm or signal was given. Had this not been so, little work would have been done during December 1941 and the months that followed, since alerts could sometimes last for up to six hours or more. On average, there were about seven alerts each day.

The most persistent, annoying and damaging consequence of the frequent air raids was that, until the AA ammunition ran short (as it started to by about March 1942), the vast amount of shells fired upwards later came raining down as a steady stream of hot and jagged shrapnel. Soon everyone on the airfields had obtained a British Army-issue 'tin hat' from the hundreds of Army personnel now permanently stationed nearby with the job of filling in the craters.* Moreover, we got in to the habit of wearing this protective helmet at all times.[†]

The effect of the incessant bombardment was to make it increasingly difficult for the aircraft and submarines to strike back. Ground facilities were destroyed and routine maintenance of aircraft and submarines became an arduous struggle.

One notable exception to the reduction of successes at sea achieved by Malta-based attackers, came on 13 December when the submarine *Upright* (Lt Wraith) hit and sank two brand-new 6,835-ton supply ships, the *Fabio Filizi* and her sister ship, the *Carlo de Greco*. Both were on their maiden voyage and the loss of these two ships, which had taken so much time and materials to build during wartime, was a bitter blow to the enemy. It further reduced the fast disappearing numbers of merchant ships available for the North Africa-bound convoys.

Notwithstanding Malta's difficulties, 13 December 1941 was a date of major disaster for the Axis powers. From Ultra intercepts, it was known that Rommel – then in fast retreat back to Benghazi and beyond as Auchinleck's Operation Crusader gained pace – was in dire need of petrol. On 10 December he had signalled that he had only one day's supply. In response to Rommel's pleas, two 5,069-ton Italian cruisers were loaded with petrol and other emergency supplies and were rushed towards Tripoli.[‡] The *Alberico da Barbiano* and *Alberto di Giussano*, with an Italian admiral in command, were however sent to the bottom on this unlucky 13th.

By chance, a force of Royal Navy destroyers, led by Commander

---

* The Army allocated 500 men per day to each airfield, and all airmen not otherwise employed pitched in, as did aircrews.
† So much so that a bald patch appeared. The poor diet may have contributed.
‡ By coincidence, two fast RN minelayers *Weshman* and *Manxman* were at the same time being rushed with supplies to Malta.

Stokes and consisting of *Sikh*, *Legion*, *Maori* and the Dutch destroyer *Isaac Sveers*, while on their way from Gibraltar to Alexandria via Malta, had happened to run into these Italian cruisers just as the latter were rounding Cape Bon. An SDF Goofington, flown by the author's former co-pilot Flight Sergeant Denis Reason, just promoted to command, had also been sent to that area with orders to look for possible shipping targets; as usual, the Swordfish of 830 Squadron and the Albacores of 828 Squadron were standing by in readiness at Hal Far awaiting a positive sighting report from the aircraft. The SDF crew did not know that Commander Stokes and his four destroyers were *en route* to Malta from Gibraltar and it seems unlikely that Stokes knew of any ASV-equipped aircraft operating in the area at that time. With more certainty, it can be assumed that neither Commander Stokes, and most certainly not Flight Sergeant Reason, knew anything about Ultra.

The two Italian cruisers, however, were well known to Malta. In response to an earlier SOS for fuel, they had originally set forth from Palermo for Tripoli on 9 December but were attacked during the night by Malta-based Swordfish and Albacores. Although undamaged, the Italians bolted back to Palermo and tried again next day. That night they were again attacked by the FAA biplanes. Again they escaped unharmed and hastened back to Palermo.

For a third time, this time escorted by the torpedo-boat *Cigno* (652 tons), they set forth on 12 December from Palermo and reached Cape Bon at 02.00 hours on that fateful 13th. They had orders, as before, to return to Palermo if discovered or attacked by Allied aircraft.

Force K was by then running short of oil (Malta's problems seem almost always to have echoed Rommel's). Accordingly it was left to the Swordfish/Albacores to try to attack these petrol-carrying cruisers. However Commander Stokes, on the 12th, was also advised that the two cruisers were again at sea. (If they had not been attacked during the nights of 9/10 and 10/11 December and had not returned each time to Palermo, there would have been no chance of a confrontation between the Allied destroyers and their cruisers.) He was urged to make maximum speed in the hope of a possible interception. However it was not a realistic hope as the Italian cruisers, by rights, should have been well past Cape Bon before the Allied destroyers could reach that area.

To avoid the thickly sown minefields known to be in the channel between Cape Bon and Sicily, and to 'cut the corner' off Cape Bon in the hope of a possible late interception, Stokes led his ships as close as he dared to the Tunisian coast, well within the neutral three-mile limit of that French colony (where mines should never have been sown). While still perilously close to the Tunisian shore, Commander Stokes was astonished to be almost run down by the two Italian cruisers which were proceeding *northwards* and signalling one another by lights. The two forces, both taking advantage of the unmined waters of neutral Tunisia, nearly collided.

Although the destroyer look-outs saw the Italians, the Italian sailors never saw the destroyers. As a result, a veritable school of torpedoes from the four Allied destroyers soon hit both Italian cruisers and caused their deck cargoes of petrol to erupt. The destroyers also opened fire with their guns, scoring several hits.

Although the torpedo-boat *Cigno* escaped in the dark, the fate of both cruisers was sealed. Before being sunk the Italians, taken completely by surprise, managed to fire off a few rounds at the only light they could see, namely the Cape Bon lighthouse, and successfully dowsed it.*

Later the *Cigno*, accompanied by other vessels, helped to pick up 645 survivors from the 1,665 aboard the two Italian cruisers but the admiral, and over a thousand others, perished. Why were the *Alberico* and the *Alberto* heading *north* and why had they run straight into the Allied destroyers?

Desmond Haynes, one of the SDF's Wireless Operator/Air Gunners, was flying that night in the SDF aircraft commanded by Flight Sergeant Reason. He remembers the evening well. After the long night hours of searching, the Goofington crew eventually located, by ASV, what they thought might well be some enemy ships. It had taken several hours to pick up the enemy cruisers because they were not where they were expected to be and were well behind the scheduled position. As Desmond Haynes has explained: 'As it happened, it was about two hours before we made contact with the cruisers as they had made a wide sweep westwards instead of taking the direct crossing [from Marettimo Island] to Cape Bon.'

---

* This was a navigational loss to our air forces, as its light had constituted the only visible beacon south of Italy.

Clearly the cruisers were keeping as far away from Malta as possible for fear of being within range of the Swordfish and Albacore torpedo-bombers. Ironically, if they had made the direct crossing to Cape Bon, they would have been clear and away down the Tunisian coast long before Commander Stokes and his destroyers could have intercepted them. However, as the ships were hugging the shore just south of Cape Bon and, because shore-lines on those primitive ASV-radar screens showed up all too clearly, it was never certain if the additional smaller and adjacent 'blips' on the ASV screen were ships, off-shore rocks or just more of the incessant radio interference lines which, along with the sea returns, tended to clutter up these tiny screens with unwanted information.

To make sure that he had located a worthwhile target for the Swordfish/Albacores standing by at Hal Far, and in order to be able to provide Malta with a better description of what his ASV had located, Flight Sergeant Reason, as was normal, flew low over the ships. Having checked that he had located the two cruisers, the appropriate sighting report was then sent immediately to Malta so that the Swordfish/Albacores could take off.

The men on board the Italian cruisers either heard or saw the aircraft. This was enough for the Italian sailors. Twice before they had been attacked at night and had managed to escape unharmed. They were disinclined to risk a third encounter, especially with their vulnerable deck cargo of petrol. Mindful of their orders, they turned around rapidly and had barely settled down to their new heading when they were hit by a wave of torpedoes, fired at almost point-blank range. As Desmond Haynes and others in the Goofington observed, one cruiser was soon ablaze from stem to stern and the other had a raging fire amidships.

A first-hand account of the sea battle is provided by Walter Arpino, a young sailor who was on the bridge of *Maori* as one of the destroyer's look-outs. Although he had never before been in a battle, his feeling was one of electric excitement rather than fear. The ships were so close that, even in the darkness of a night in which the moon had scarcely risen, he could see men running across the deck of one of the Italian cruisers 'as if in confusion and total surprise'. As he remarked, 'It all passed so quickly that I never really had time to think.'

Both Italian cruisers were set on fire and sunk within less than five

minutes. In point of fact, although Commander Stokes was proceeding at 30 knots in an effort to intercept, he was nevertheless
under orders 'to stay out of trouble and on no account to become
involved with superior forces'.* One reason for this was that each of
the destroyers was carrying, as passengers, a number of RAF and
other key personnel to be off-loaded in Malta – this by now being
almost the only means of transporting much wanted men to the
besieged island.

The action had been so sudden and swift that, next morning, one
of the passengers on board *Legion* appeared at breakfast. Buttering
his toast, he said suddenly to the wardroom at large, 'Did anything
happen last night? I thought I heard gunfire!'*

It comes as no surprise to learn that, according to an Ultra intercept of 23 December, Rommel was signalling Berlin that he now had
no petrol remaining.

On the day after the sinking of the two cruisers, another Italian
naval disaster occurred. *Urge*, with Tommo still in charge, hit the
Italian battleship *Vittorio Venuto* and put it out of action for a couple
of months. By then, the enemy had deployed almost their entire
navy in trying to force through separate convoys. At one time, in
addition to the *Vittorio Venuto*, they had both the *Littorio* and *Duilio*,
their other serviceable battleships, escorting convoys to North
Africa, as well as many cruisers and destroyers, in order to try to get
a number of merchant ships through more or less simultaneously.
This brought forth the sarcastic comment in Count Ciano's well-
kept, but private, diary: 'All the [big] ships and all the Admirals are
at sea. God help us!'

In spite of the aforementioned successes, December 1941 turned
out to be a disastrous month both for the British Navy in general,
and for Force K in particular. In Alexandria harbour daring Italian
frogmen, riding astride modified torpedoes, managed to hit the two
British battleships there, *Queen Elizabeth* and *Valiant*, leaving both
resting on their bottoms in the mud. The introduction of Admiral
Doenitz's submarines from the Atlantic was also making itself felt.
Stung into action by the Italian and German shipping losses in the
Mediterranean, Hitler was determined to remedy the situation:

---

* As reported in the *Illustrated London News*, December 1981.

both to prevent cut-off Tobruk from being supplied from Alexandria by sea, and to inflict casualties on the submarines and surface ships which were disrupting the flow of Axis supplies to North Africa. U-boat activity was also to prevent Malta from being supplied.

During November, the few German U-boats already in the Mediterranean had sunk the aircraft-carrier *Ark Royal* and the battleship *Barham*, the latter with the loss of 868 men. In December, they damaged one of the last remaining British battleships in the Mediterranean, *Malaya*, as well as the cruiser *Galatea*.

The loss of the *Ark Royal* was keenly felt in Malta as many of the Hurricanes, which alone in November 1941 were defending Malta in the air, had arrived at Ta Kali via that carrier's flight-deck and, with the Luftwaffe dominating overhead, there was need for a constant supply of replacement fighters. The later Hurricanes with cannons, though still outmoded, were more of a match for the superior Me 109s.

From mid-December 1941 to the end of that month, apart from the success of the Swordfish of 830 Squadron in sinking the small tanker *Lina* (1,235 tons), neither submarine nor aircraft managed to score a single hit. On the other hand, at least four supply ships, including the German *Ankara*, were able to bring much needed relief to the retreating Rommel who had come to a halt near El Agheila, about half-way between Benghazi, now in British hands again, and Tripoli.

The balance of naval power swung further in the direction of the Axis when, on the night of 18/19 December 1941, the ships of Force B – the former Force K strengthened by the bigger 7,000-ton cruiser *Neptune* and with its usual *Lance* and *Lively* reinforced by the destroyers *Kandahar* and *Havock* – again put to sea only to run into disaster. *Neptune* and *Ajax* – the latter being unserviceable – had been brought to Malta in the knowledge that the enemy had, by late November, resorted to using their battleships and big cruisers as escorts of their convoys.

Much has been written as to why *Neptune* (Captain 'Rory' O'Conor), which was in the lead on the night of 18/19 December, led the force into a newly laid minefield when within less than twenty miles from Tripoli. What can be said with certainty, because the author was in the air looking for the enemy when it happened (although unaware of the tragedy below), is that Al Glazer's Rooster was not functioning from *Aurora*, making it impossible for our ships to be located at long range on the Wellington's tiny ASV screen. Regular Royal Navy codes and frequencies were also in use and not the private ones previously agreed between the leaders of Force K and the SDF; these Naval codes were not available to the SDF.* We could therefore not communicate direct with our ships. From David Beaty's Log Book entries (David was the author's second pilot that night) it would seem that we advised Malta that we had located the Italian battlefleet.

The result of Force B running into this hitherto unrecorded German-laid minefield was that *Neptune* sank within a very few minutes after having touched off at least four mines; that *Kandahar*, which had gone to her aid, had forty-two feet of her stern blown off but, miraculously, remained afloat; and that both *Aurora* and *Penelope*, which were trailing paravanes, were also damaged but to a much lesser extent, although *Aurora*'s damage at first limited her to a maximum speed of 10 knots.

Although *Lively* made a request to go to the aid of the stricken ships, this had to be refused. Captain Agnew, now back in command after the loss of Captain O'Conor who was his senior, was meanwhile doing his best to get *Aurora*, accompanied by *Havock* and *Lance*, back to Malta before daylight. He had left Captain Nichol, in the less-damaged *Penelope*, in charge of the disaster area with the aim of making arrangements to take *Neptune* in tow. But before this could happen Captain O'Conor and all his crew, bar one, went to their doom below the waves when *Neptune* hit her fourth mine.

With damage to *Penelope* and *Aurora*, and the former ship suffering further damage[†] while under repair in Malta from a number of bomb near-misses, this action signalled the end of the small but gallant Force K. Not until the end of the Tunisian campaign, a year

---

* The author's Log Book reads: 'Search for enemy fleet and convoy 8+ and 11+ sighted but no contact with our forces. S.O.S. sent,' indicating that the enemy ships had been found – well to the east of Tripoli as it happened – but no contact by ASV Rooster or W/T with our Naval Force could be made. The SOS refers solely to the aircraft's faulty engine and icing-up problems.

† Her sides were so pock-marked by near-misses that, before she managed to depart under her own steam, *Penelope* had been dubbed 'Pepperpot'.

or more ahead, was an effective Royal Navy Force to be based in Malta. The other ships of Forces B and K all managed sooner or later to get away from Malta, except for the destroyers *Kingston* and *Lance* which were sunk by bombs in harbour. All, except *Aurora*, were employed early in 1942 as escorts of merchant ships to and from Malta. *Lively* was sunk off Crete in May 1942.

The sequel to this sorry tale of the night 18/19 December 1941 is slightly less depressing. The next night, the destroyer *Jaguar* was led to the stationary and powerless *Kandahar* by an SDF Goofington piloted by Flight Sergeant Reason. *Jaguar* managed to bring back most of *Kandahar*'s crew to Malta just before she finally sank. Why *Kandahar* was not finished off during daylight on the 19th when immobile and so close to Tripoli, remains a mystery. Without power, she was a sitting target. Before locating *Kandahar*, Denis Reason had detected what could have been either E-boats, as he thought, or destroyers as the Navy thought more probable, coming from Tripoli apparently to attack the stricken ship. However he skilfully diverted their attention away from *Kandahar* before leading *Jaguar* to where the stationary destroyer lay, by now submerged from her funnel aft. In all 168 men, including *Kandahar*'s captain Commander Robson, were rescued and brought back safely to Malta by *Jaguar*.

Lieutenant Commander Hine, *Jaguar*'s captain, later mentioned, and praised, the Wellington crew. 'The work on the part of the aircraft [Reason's] is deserving of the highest praise and the fact that *Kandahar* was found was entirely due to the skill and perseverance displayed by the crew.' Sadly, within a week, Flight Sergeant Denis Reason and all his crew were also lost to the waters of the Mediterranean. Like others before and after them, they simply went out in a Wellington at night, in the foul weather which persisted that month, and never came back – whether as a result of weather, enemy action, ice, engine or other mechanical trouble will never be known. The decoration for which he had been recommended had not had time to be processed.

A month which had started in triumph was ending in disaster and, as the bombing increased, the signs were that more blows were likely to fall.

By January 1942 various changes were afoot. Rommel, although having received only minimal reinforcements, including one ship-load of new and more modern tanks, took advantage of British mistakes and the problems which they now faced as a result of having their main supply bases in Egypt nearly 1,000 miles behind them, and began to hit back with startling success. For a second time the enemy had been driven almost to Tripoli only to bounce back. It was like compressing a powerfully coiled spring. Whichever side swept forward at a pace in the Desert, their rapid success added enormously to their supply problems; and the more rapid their success, the greater these became.

In Malta, the 169 enemy air alerts of December seemed light compared with the 263 times when the sirens wailed over the island in January. Flown by experienced German pilots, the more modern aircraft of Luftflotte II, which had been sent in from Russia, were inflicting massive damage on Malta. The obsolescent Hurricanes could put up little resistance against the efficient bombing of the Ju 88s, supported by large numbers of Me 109 fighters.

The Blenheims, apart from the damage caused to their aircraft on the ground, were finding the few ships they located even more heavily protected than before and, before January was out, the decision had been made to withdraw what remained of them and never to replace them. The last squadron to arrive, No. 21, was effectively reduced, by heavy air and ground losses, to a state of near uselessness within a week or two. By then, the Blenheims were also without their brave and successful leader, Pilot Officer Ivor Broom, who, having flown a dozen more operational flights than was required before being able to claim a well-earned 'rest' from operations, had been posted away to the Cairo area, *en route* to the UK.*

Before he left, Ivor Broom led a raid upon ships which had been sheltering in Argostoli, Cephalonia. As the last two of the six attackers had been shot down – and the others were not going to circle back into the hail of gunfire in order to see what had been accomplished – no positive claim could be made of any hits in that well-defended harbour. Only in recent years, thanks to a Greek Makis Panas, then a boy in school at Argostoli, has it become known that two enemy ships were both hit and sunk. How many other ships, it is wondered, were hit in enemy ports by aircraft on similar raids,

---

* Ivor Broom had miraculously survived forty-five operations while operating Blenheims, including thirty-one from Malta.

especially during the almost ceaseless pounding that Tripoli and other enemy harbours received by night from the Wellington squadrons based in Malta?*

The big Wellingtons were, alas, always the most conspicuous aircraft in Malta, and although every effort was made to disperse them in pens in far distant corners on, or away from Luqa, their losses on the ground mounted alarmingly. Generally, air operations from Malta had become few in number and precarious in nature. These anti-blast pens – three-walled enclosures into which the aircraft could taxi direct – had been built, largely by Army personnel, to shelter aircraft, as well as petrol-bowsers, road-rollers and the like. With no mechanical aids or cranes available, in the early days of the siege, they were neatly built of cut stone. Thereafter sandbags were used, but most were built by hand, by soldiers and airmen using empty four-gallon petrol tins filled with rubble.† It took 60,000 such tins piled over 10 feet high to make a Wimpy pen. There was no shortage of rubble, as the pounding continued.

All too soon, ammunition for the light and heavy AA guns began to run short and before long the order had to be given that only bombers were to be shot at. Me 109 pilots – who always had ample speed to get away from Hurricanes – were not slow to realize this and those on the ground had to endure the humiliation of seeing Me 109s patrolling low around their airfields. The German pilots added to the indignation of the airmen by openly strafing the airfields before departing back to Sicily. It was difficult to bear. Even some of the Ju 88 bombers seemed able to outrun the few worn-out Hurricanes which remained.

Some successes at sea were still being scored. *Sirio*, a tanker of 5,300 tons, was hit by *Upholder*, and *Saint Bon*, an Italian submarine, was also sunk by the ever efficient Wanklyn VC. The Albacores of 828 Squadron had by then learned how to score at night and on the night of 7/8 January sank the *Perla* (5,740 tons). Lieutenant Woodward in *Unbeaten* sank *U374* and *Umbra* sank the 301-ton salvage vessel *Rampino* off Sousse, Tunisia.

Although Blenheims hit the *Brook* (1,325 tons) it cost them three of the four attacking aircraft. Such heavy losses could not be justi-

---

* Appendix II gives some of the answers.
† Sailors from Force K helped to build the pens round the SDF Goofingtons.

fied. *P34*, *Ultimatum*, sank another Italian submarine, the *Dalmatia*, and the *Pistoia* (2,448 tons) was damaged by Wellingtons.

However, the major triumph of what was otherwise a rather lean month for the aircraft and submarines based in Malta was the sinking of the big 13,089-ton *Victoria*, a splendid merchant ship which was regarded by the Italians as the pearl of her merchant fleet, and probably the fastest supply ship then afloat. In the end she was sunk by torpedo hits dropped by Lieutenant (A) Baxter Ellis, known as 'Ferret', flying Albacore '4K' of 826 Squadron on the night of 23 January 1942 operating from Berka, near Benghazi. His observer was Sub Lieutenant (A) Jeff Powell, later Commander Powell DSC, and many of the details which follow have been supplied by him. However, some authors have attributed the sinking of the *Victoria* to either, or both, 830 Squadron Swordfish and 39 Squadron Bristol Beaufort daylight torpedo-bombers. Both, at different times, were attempting to find and sink this prize target. As Goofingtons of the SDF and Wellingtons and Blenheims from Malta also played useful roles, and as the *Victoria* was as big a prize as almost any other in the war against Rommel's supply lines, a full account is given.

Only a day or two before the sinking of the *Victoria* on 23 January Rommel, spurred on by fresh fuel supplies and a delivery of Mark IV tanks, had taken the advance guard of the Eighth Army near El Agheila by surprise. Owing to errors on the British side, which cost Major General Ritchie his command of the Army, and resulted in Auchinleck, as GOC-in-C Middle East, personally taking charge of the army in the field, Rommel had been able to seize British petrol stocks and was suddenly advancing as fast as, for the past two months, he had been retreating.

Victoria had sailed from Taranto on 22 January and, as she was carrying vital supplies and part of a Panzer division with appropriate equipment, she and other ships with which she was to join up later were to form a convoy, code-named T18. This would be protected by the battleship *Duilio*, three *Aosta* cruisers and over a dozen destroyers. Now that the British battleships in Alexandria had been immobilized and Force K in Malta was no longer a threat, the Italian Navy was sending more of her big ships to sea, although such operations continued to be limited by the amount of naphtha that Hitler and Germany allocated to Italy.

Victoria's departure from Taranto was in all probability well known to the Allies through Ultra intercepts, but first she had to be officially located by means more obvious to the enemy. Accordingly, an SDF Goofington with the author in command was despatched to find her in atrocious weather which caused the ASV aerials of his aircraft, and much else, to ice up. Eventually we located what was reported as 'one battleship, one liner, three destroyers and two or more unknown ships' heading southwards. Flares* were dropped to try to get further information. These caused the convoy to alter course eastwards.†

Now that a convoy which included *Victoria* – a vessel which could make over 23 knots – had been detected, every effort was made on the 23rd to follow its progress and to attack it as it headed southwards from Taranto. A few Blenheims of 21 Squadron remained in Malta and one was sent on a reconnaissance mission to locate again, but not to attack, this important convoy. The Blenheim duly discovered *Victoria*, the other merchant ships and their battleship escort, as well as the *Aosta* cruiser group just as the two groups were about to join forces to form convoy T18. Fearing an attack, the Luftwaffe sent twelve Ju 88s to supplement the formidable sea escorts. Both sides were pulling out all their stops: one to attack and the other to defend their precious convoy.

Meanwhile, six Blenheims from 11 Squadron based in the Middle East had been sent to attack but, with one shot down, the others either missed or failed to get within range. With over a dozen Italian warships as well as the Ju 88s around T18, it was akin to murder to attempt a low-level bombing strike. One Blenheim at least dropped bombs at the battleship *Duilio* from 10,000 feet but without scoring a hit. Two Blenheims of 21 Squadron were also sent from Malta to attack but, owing to a clearing in the weather, they failed to get close enough.

Along with the Blenheims, or soon thereafter, three Beauforts of 39 Squadron from the Middle East attacked and, possibly because the enemy was concentrating on driving off the Blenheims, one

---

* The flares also made it legitimate, according to Ultra security rules, for the convoy to be attacked, although these rules were unknown, at the time, to those operating from Malta.

† Appendix III charts *Victoria*'s passage and the attacks made upon her.

obtained the all-important torpedo-hit on the *Victoria*. This handsome ship was not sunk or stopped but her speed was greatly reduced and she fell behind the other ships of the convoy.

This strike was a magnificent achievement as the twelve Ju 88s were now patrolling the mass of ships and the convoy was protected by firepower from the Italian destroyers *Vivaldi*, *Da Noli*, *Malocello*, *Aviere*, *Camacia Nera*, *Geneide*, *Alpino*, *Bersagliero*, *Carabiniere*, *Fusiliere*, *Orsa* and *Castore*, together with that from the three cruisers, the battleship *Duilio* and from five well-armed supply ships. It was enough to daunt any but the bravest.

The Swordfish from Malta had also been alerted to the presence of the *Victoria*, the *Duilio*, the three cruisers and the four other merchant ships, which themselves were prize targets: *Monviso* (5,322 tons), *Ravello* (6,142 tons), *Monginevro* (5,324 tons) and *Pisani* (6,339 tons). Reports had it that an entire Panzer Division was being sent to Rommel via the convoy T18.

On the night of 23/24 January Lieutenant Commander Hopkins,* another observer who had taken command of 830 Squadron, led a formation consisting of four Swordfish and two Albacores of 828 Squadron. The weather was vicious and the single-engined Swordfish following him and one Albacore soon turned back either with mechanical or engine defects or because they had lost sight in the rainstorms of their leader who alone had the ASV equipment with which to find the enemy. By then, a second Goofington, flown by Flying Officer David Beaty, had been sent out. This crew also located T18 and, while shadowing during most of the night of 23/24 January, dropped flares at 5–10 minute intervals in order to guide attackers to the scene. These included a force of Wellingtons of 40 Squadron which had departed from Luqa. Although they sighted the convoy and dropped bombs, they did not seem to hit or stop the convoy. Wellingtons from 38 Squadron based in Egypt also attacked, having been guided to the scene by Beaty's flares.

Hopkins, with his ASV on board, eventually located the convoy which by then was many miles east of its original track, but decided that, since he now had only one torpedo-carrying aircraft with him – the surviving Albacore – and barely enough fuel to get back to

---

* Later Admiral Sir Frank Hopkins.

Malta, he would return and collect another strike-force. The wind and rain persisted but after a muddy refuelling at Hal Far, this determined leader again departed in his open Swordfish and managed to lead three torpedo-carrying aircraft through the blustering gregale (a nasty kind of Mediterranean storm) back to where the convoy should have been.

By then, unknown to Hopkins and his gallant followers, *Victoria* had already been sunk by Lieutenant 'Ferret' Ellis* in his Albacore of 826 Squadron† but Frank Hopkins successfully located the rest of the convoy and, almost as morning light began to appear in the east, possible torpedo hits were claimed on two of the remaining supply ships. With the last drop of petrol in their tanks, the biplanes got back to Malta in daylight. The Swordfish had been airborne almost a whole hour beyond their normal endurance. It was an astonishing feat of determination and Lieutenant Commander Hopkins, who had spent nearly twelve hours in the air, in an open cockpit exposed to every form of violent weather – turbulence, ice, hail, wind and rain – rightly deserved his immediate award of the DSO.

Malta could not directly claim the sinking of the *Victoria* – that credit belongs to the RAF Beauforts and FAA Albacores based elsewhere – but various aircraft from Malta had played a part: the Goofingtons, which located and shadowed her, the Blenheims which relocated the enemy ships in daylight and the two gallant FAA sorties led by Frank Hopkins DSO.

The operation to stop *Victoria* and the rest of convoy T18 was typical of others. Now that Malta-based ships, submarines and aircraft had driven the enemy into taking the Greek-coast route to Tripoli (which in January 1941 was the only port open to the enemy

---

* Ellis was awarded the RAF's DFC but as the Navy did not then allow its personnel to display RAF awards he was duly told to take down his DFC ribbon. Later Ellis was awarded a DSC and when King George VI came to pin it on him, he was asked why he was not wearing the ribbon of his DFC which the King had personally awarded him. When he advised His Majesty that he had been told to take it down, the monarch responded: 'You can bloody well put it up again.'

† It seems likely that the leader of the 826 Squadron Albacore strike-force, Lieutenant Commander Corbett, also scored a torpedo hit on the *Victoria* as those on board mentioned two torpedo strikes. Corbett, however, was shot down, rescued by the Italians and became a POW.

until Rommel recaptured Benghazi), close co-operation between Malta and the Middle East was essential.

Only aircraft or submarines from Malta could sight and attack enemy ships in the early stages of their journeys southwards. This detection was essential even if the final assault was later to be made by ships, submarines or aircraft based in North Africa. If only for Ultra security reasons, it was essential that Malta should first find – and be seen to have found – the enemy ships at sea.

As ever, events at sea were being shaped by what was taking place in the see-saw Desert War. All too soon, Libyan bases would be denied to the Allies. In an alarmingly swift onrush, Rommel, by February 1942, had advanced half-way to Alexandria, and Benghazi had changed hands for the fourth, but not for the last, time. To save the situation, Auchinleck, the GOC Cairo, now personally took charge of the Eighth Army and the two forces came to a halt, facing one another at Gazala fifty or so miles west of Tobruk.

February and early March 1942 was a period when almost every-thing in the Mediterranean war became finely balanced. Both armies were poised at the half-way point between Alexandria and Tripoli. Malta was still being bombed several times daily. The FAA and the submarines based in Malta were scoring but not with the same rate of success as had been achieved in the last months of 1941. Hitler's counter-measures against Malta had largely paid off.

By then, the enemy had at last discovered that the submarines were based at Manoel Island and not in Grand Harbour. Attacks on the base there intensified, causing the submarines to spend most of the daylight hours submerged. The flats and residences where the crews had enjoyed their brief rest periods had largely to be aban-doned. Belts also had to be tightened.

The Swordfish sank the *San Giovanni* (5,628 tons) on 1 February. *Umbra*, commanded by Lieutenant Maydon, sank the *Napoli* (6,142 tons), on the 3rd after Albacores of 828 Squadron had earlier attacked and damaged that supply ship. On 6 February the Polish submarine *Sokol* (Cdr Karnicki) accounted for a schooner. The destroyers *Zulu* and *Legion*, aided by an SDF Wellington, sank both the coaster *Gringo* and a 500-ton supply ship loaded with paraffin during the night of 6/7 February. *Upholder*, never to be outdone, sank the *Salpi* (2,710 tons) and damaged the *Duino* on the 8th. *P38* (Lt Hemmingway), with assistance from the Swordfish of 830

Squadron, sank the *Aristo* (4,116 tons) on the 19th, but this was to be their only success before one of the efficient Italian torpedo-boats sank her four days later.

P36, another U-class submarine, was also soon to be lost, although she damaged the destroyer *Carabiniere* on the 16th. Two days later, 828 Squadron Albacores damaged another vessel. Wanklyn in *Upholder* closed the score for what had been an average month by sinking the *Tembien*, a supply vessel of 5,585 tons, on 27 February.

The losses of Allied submarines at sea were mounting all too steadily for the liking of Captain Simpson. *P32* and *P33* had already gone down in August 1941, presumably mined off Tripoli even before *Neptune* suffered the same fate. Over and above this, submarines such as *P39* were also being damaged, if not destroyed, in and around his base by enemy bombing.

Life for the survivors of the Tenth Flotilla was becoming daily more grim, with minefields laid by enemy aircraft now only just outside Malta. From 1941 onwards Germany had been assisting the Italians with the laying of mines, and many of those outside Malta had been dropped from low-flying Luftwaffe aircraft operating from Sicily. These mines were apt to be of sophisticated design and were very difficult to sweep, especially given the island's lack of modern minesweepers. The sea lanes outside Valletta, Sliema and the main channel to Grand Harbour were so perilous during 1942 that, until modern minesweepers could be brought in, mines threatened to bring submarine activity to a halt.

As if this were not enough for the hard-pressed submarine crews, between patrols food was short, rest and recreation virtually nonexistent.* Furthermore, in such a small tight-knit community, every loss of a submarine was keenly felt by those remaining.

The Wellington squadrons continued to bomb the enemy ports at night but with greatly reduced numbers as their losses on the

---

* Most submarine commanders arrived in port in need of rest but one, to quote from Captain Simpson's memoirs *Periscope View*, 'set a pace in Malta that would have put lesser men in hospital'. He would arrive back for his next patrol looking pale and worn out. After letting his No. 1 take the submarine to their patrol area while he recuperated, he would emerge 'as fresh as a daisy', delighted to have exchanged the dangers of shore leave for the relative safety of a patrol. Moreover, he proved to be a successful submarine commander and survives to this day.

ground mounted. The RAF Official History of the war singles out a successful raid on the night of 2/3 March, when sixteen of these twin-engined bombers, many of them replacement aircraft flown in from the UK, were assembled for a raid on Palermo. A large supply ship estimated at 9,000 tons – part of a convoy which was assembling for a forthcoming journey to Benghazi – received a direct hit and was set on fire. Prints taken on a photo-reconnaissance flight next day by the indefatigable 69 Squadron showed the cargo being transferred to another ship and two other ships – one estimated at 6,000 tons and another at 2,000 tons – sunk and lying on the bottom. This was cheerful news to the Wellington bomber crews whose relentless pounding of Naples, Palermo, Tripoli, Benghazi and other ports seldom attracted this kind of positive confirmation of their results. The ships sunk were believed to be a German vessel, the *Cuma* (6,652 tons), the *Securitas* (5,366 tons) and the *Le Tre Marie* (1,026 tons). Another German ship, the *Marin Sanudo* (5,081 tons), was sunk by *Uproar* on 5 March (Lt Kershaw) in a brilliant attack using Asdic to locate the enemy's position.

Una (Lt Norman) sank another three-masted schooner and Lieutenant Harrison, in *P34*, sank an Italian submarine, the *Ammigalio Millo*, on the 14th. At 1,461 tons she was over twice the size of the attacker. *Unbeaten*, with Lieutenant Woodward still in charge, sank a smaller submarine, the *Guglielmotti*, and damaged the *Pisani* (6,338 tons) on the 16th.

Swordfish, now combined with the Albacores to form the Royal Navy Air Squadron, were also used to lay mines and it is thought that one of these sent the German ship *Achaja* (1,718 tons) to the bottom on 17 March. Wanklyn in *Upholder*, never for long out of the news, sank the Italian submarine *Tricheco* (810 tons) on 18 March but missed hitting the huge Italian battleship *Littorio* at long range.

By then, this remarkable VC-decorated submarine commander, who had so nearly been removed from command of *Upholder* by 'Shrimp' Simpson after his early unsuccessful torpedo attacks, had accounted for fifteen enemy vessels sunk and another five damaged. *Upholder* by then was on her twenty-third patrol from Malta – another record achievement.

For the rest of the month of March, however, neither the RN, FAA nor the RAF in Malta could add to their score. And on 20 March

Kesselring let loose all his Sicily-based aircraft in a massive sustained blitz which was nearly to succeed in reducing Malta to rubble.

Given the loss rate of submarines, as well as aircraft, Captain Simpson was now having to discuss with his superiors in Alexandria whether or not the Tenth Flotilla could remain at Manoel Island. By the end of March, the Tenth had lost, either on patrol or while in or around Malta, *P32, P33, P36, P38, P39, Undaunted, Union* and *Usk*. On missions from or to Malta, other Allied submarines had also been lost: *Cachalot* (a large vessel which had made successful supply runs to Malta), *Narwhal* (a big Free French minelayer), *Odin, Orpheus, Oswald, Perseus, Rainbow, Regulus, Tempest, Triad* and *Triton*.*

As many of these underwater craft were victims of enemy-laid mines, those sunk by this insidious weapon inevitably lost almost all on board. Moreover all the O, P, R and T-class boats lost were considerably larger than the Unity-class boats, which officially constituted the Tenth Flotilla, and had crew complements in excess of the thirty or so men who made up the crews of the smaller boats. Submarines ex-Malta were also apt to be carrying up to forty passengers. *Olympus*, for example, which sank on 8 May 1942, went down with ninety-eight on board.

Even the arrival towards the end of March of a few Spitfires via the decks of an aircraft-carrier which had advanced half-way from Gibraltar was to bring no relief. To the chagrin of all on the island, their presence made little or no difference to the ever-increasing intensity of air attacks. By then, the Luftwaffe had become even bolder, seeming to know or deduce that the island had become chronically short of AA ammunition, and that its few outmoded Hurricanes were all but worn-out, as were the barrels of many of its AA guns.

Could conditions get worse? Could the island survive? Would Rommel, halted at Gazala, advance and further isolate Malta? Force K was finished. Would the submarines also have to depart? Under the almost continuous rain of bombs, could the RAF and FAA commands succeed in keeping any aircraft operational on the three harassed, pockmarked airfields?

A crisis point was clearly being reached.

---

* For details see E.A.S. Bailey, *Malta Defiant and Triumphant* (1992).

7

Darkest Days

April–10 May 1942

'It was held in London that it was essential to
launch the Libyan offensive in order to relieve Malta.
The truth was that it was essential to hold Malta in
order to make it possible to launch the Libyan
offensive.'

John Terraine, *The Right of the Line* (1985)

IT DID NOT seem possible for conditions in Malta to get worse,
but they did. Firstly, the convoy to relieve the now chronic shortages
of fuel, food, ammunition and much else – a convoy from
Alexandria with the code name MW10 – narrowly failed. The MV
Clan Campbell was sunk *en route* and the *Breconshire*, the RN supply
and oil-carrier which had done more than any other vessel to bring
relief to Malta on several previous occasions, was hit when only ten
miles short of her destination. Towed into Marsaxlokk Bay in a
sinking state, she rolled over on to her side; only a small amount of
cargo, including some oil, was eventually recovered. The two ships
which succeeded in reaching Malta, the *Pampas* and the Norwegian
Talabot, were both set on fire and sunk by German dive-bombers
with only a fraction of their cargoes unloaded. These were bitter
blows.

By this time, enemy forces on the Sicilian airfields were at their
main strength. According to statistics furnished by the Air
Historical Department of the MOD, there were now 172 Ju 88s
divided between Catania and Comiso airfields; 137 Me 109s at
Comiso, Gela and San Pietro; 21 night-fighting Ju 88s of 1/NJG 2 at

Catania; 32 Ju 87s at San Pietro and 27 Ju 88s used for reconnaissance, at Trapani. As the proximity of Sicily to Malta enabled each aircraft to make several raids per day, Malta's position – pending the arrival of hoped-for Spitfires – was untenable.

An even greater blow to Maltese personnel, Servicemen and local inhabitants alike, was to follow. When the Spitfires finally arrived in satisfactory numbers – over sixty in all – they were nearly all rapidly destroyed – most of them on the ground but some in the air – by the confident and more experienced Me 109 pilots of JG 53. For months, everyone on the island down to the smallest child had believed that Spitfires, and only Spitfires, could save it from the non-stop pounding it was receiving. But these Spitfires, the first nine of which arrived on 21 March 1942 followed by seven eight days later, had been flown off aircraft-carriers by largely inexperienced pilots, none of whom had ever before been on an aircraft-carrier; were by no means in fighting trim, and were soon destroyed. For all in Malta, for perhaps the first time, the light at the end of the tunnel could hardly be seen. It was a depressing period.

Although it seemed almost impossible to bomb Malta's harbours and airfields more than they had already been bombed in March, the weight of bombs which were dropped in April 1942 was nearly four times that of the previous month, itself the heaviest month of bombing so far. In that month more bombs were dropped on tiny Malta – an area, remember, smaller than the Isle of Wight – than were dropped on the whole of Britain during any month of the war. Practically every Serviceman in Malta who was still capable of rational deduction, was convinced that the furious blitz which had started on 20 March was a prelude to a forthcoming invasion: as indeed it was intended to be, according to the Italian invasion plan, Operazione C3.

Although, in the weeks following, the men on the three airfields, and those around the dockyards, were bombed more incessantly, and with more devastating results, than other British Servicemen were bombed throughout the war, they did not lose their sense of humour. From out of the ruins which surrounded these vital installations, and during a period when the Luftwaffe paid no respect to the Easter Holy Week, came a new version of the great Easter hymn (Luftwaffe version).

'Tis Holy Thursday, let us snooker
All the bloody planes at Luqa.
Forward Messerschmitt and Stuka,
   Hallelujah!

Good Friday; 'tis now Hal Far's turn.
Bomb the crews. Make aircraft burn.
Will the blighters never learn?
   Hallelujah!

Christ the Lord is risen today.
Let's bomb the harbour, bomb the Bay.
Bombing the effing place all day.
   Hallelujah!

Easter Monday, let it rip,
Smite the island, thigh and hip,
Tear it off a Safi* strip.
   Hallelujah!

Bill Metcalfe, an airman who worked day and night at Ta Kali, has described how this sustained blitz began. His diary entry for 20 March reads:

Pay Day. It is now 9.05 p.m. and I've just come through the worst blitz that's ever been known in England, Germany or Malta and all of it on Ta Kali. It is estimated that at least 250 kites of various makes took part and the 800-odd bombs that were dropped on the 'drome were made up of all shapes and sizes. Huddled in that slit trench with poor little Cherry [a stray dog which he was befriending] and four other chaps, I thought the end had come. Billets were blown up right and left. Two more petrol bowsers on fire. Spitfires, Hurricanes, Beaus, Blenheims and the odd Maryland all lying wrecked and smouldering. The smell of cordite and the crash of falling bombs added to the hellish row of the ack-ack barrage, has sent me more or less stone deaf.

Next day Bill's mate was killed two minutes after he left him; the Officers' Mess, at Point de Vue, was also hit and six inside, most of them pilots, were killed instantly.

By 23 March Bill Metcalfe mentions in his diary that he has not

---

* Safi strip was one of the main dispersal areas for aircraft. It was about half-way along the tortuous taxi-track which had been built to link Luqa to Hal Far. It became a favourite target.

eaten or washed for three days, so he raids the food store. After this he walks the several miles to Luqa to 'help with the Spits there'. So it goes on for the next seven weeks.

For a while Ta Kali, the fighter airfield, was so obliterated that fighters could not operate. This meant that the AA guns, in spite of their worn-out barrels and their shortage of ammunition, and aided only by the home-made light machine-gun posts that had sprung up, were all that the island possessed to repulse raids of over 100 bombers at a time. But for that month of the war the AA guns, many of which were manned by Maltese of the Royal Malta Artillery, could claim more enemy aircraft shot down than could the RAF fighters. Over 150,000 rounds were fired aloft with gunners claiming about 120 aircraft destroyed. Even so the numbers coming over seemed not to diminish.

Under this bombardment, and given the increased mining of surrounding seas, Admiral Cunningham decided with great reluctance that the Manoel submarine base was no longer tenable, and the vessels of the Tenth Flotilla – what was left of them – headed eastwards to Alexandria and Beirut. This tale of woe was aggravated when *Upholder*, with Lieutenant Commander Wanklyn VC, failed to return from a patrol, sunk by an enemy torpedo-boat.

Before departing for safer bases eastwards, Malta-based submarines scored a few successes, which constituted Malta's total offensive that month as the RAF and FAA sank nothing. Pride of place went to Lieutenant Commander Tomkinson in *Urge*, who sank the 5,069-ton Italian cruiser *Della Bande Nere* north of Sicily on 1 April. *Una* (Lt Norman) then sank the *Ninetto** (5,335 tons) on 5 April. Otherwise the only other success during the month was that of *Umbra* (Lt Maydon) who sank the *Assunta de Gregori* (4,220 tons) on the 19th. This, sadly, was to be the last ship of any kind sunk by a Malta-based submarine for many months and the much bombed Lazaretto buildings were left empty with only a skeleton maintenance staff.

It was an indication of the effectiveness of the Luftwaffe attacks that Lieutenant Norman, during his final Malta-based patrol down the Tunisian coast in the Lampedusa area – which had once been

---

* Described by him as the *Palestrina*.

such a happy hunting-ground for Captain Simpson's gallant band – could lament in his patrol report of 19–30 April: 'Three convoys escaped because no RAF recce, due to Malta bombing.' This remark also emphasizes how useful the day and night aerial reconnaissance flights had been to the submarines of the Tenth Flotilla.

Notwithstanding this comment, and in spite of almost non-stop bombing, the only two RAF units remaining in Malta, other than the over-worked and outmoded fighters, were 69 Squadron, the indefatigable daylight PR squadron used for day reconnaissances, and the SDF, now handed over to Flying Officer Peter Rothwell,* for similar night duties. It was only thanks to heroic efforts, including much cannabalizing of damaged aircraft, that any Marylands, Goofingtons or other aircraft capable of reconnaissance duties could be made available. However, as Lieutenant Norman comments, they were all too few.

With the Allied sea and air offensive stalled in the Central Mediterranean, Axis convoys now sailed largely unmolested to North Africa. According to the official post-war Italian figures,† out of the 151,578 tons of supplies sent by sea to North Africa that April, 150,389 tons duly arrived. Moreover every one of the 1,349 personnel scheduled to join those in the Desert reached their destination.

The 150,389 tons of supplies arriving to aid Rommel and his Axis armies in North Africa was a total never before reached, and never afterwards surpassed. Rommel, temporarily halted at Gazala, some 250 miles east of Benghazi and only about 400 miles from Alexandria,‡ welcomed every ton. Like his opponent, he was building up supplies for the next push forwards.

Hitler's policy of neutralizing Malta by bombing was succeeding. The FAA biplanes, Swordfish and Albacores were virtually wiped out. The bomber Wellingtons were either destroyed on the ground or flown away to Middle East bases for greater safety and

---

* The AOC ordered the author to 'steal' an incoming transit Wellington bomber and fly himself and Beaty's equally exhausted Goofington crew to Cairo. The incoming crew, left in Malta without an aircraft, were not amused.
† See Appendix IV.
‡ And, unfortunately for Rommel, about 800 miles by road from Tripoli, his main port.

the Tenth Flotilla was on its way to bases in the Eastern Mediterranean. Bereft of submarines and bombers, Malta was left with nothing with which to strike back. The April arrival in Africa of 99.2 per cent of the supplies despatched clearly shows that, with Malta out of action as an offensive base and with Benghazi again in Rommel's hands, the large RN and RAF forces available in Egypt were almost totally ineffective in stopping supplies reaching the enemy in the Desert.

To compound Malta's plight, the failure of convoy MW10 had added enormously to the island's already grim subsistence problem. Hunger, as much as bombing, was worrying the inhabitants. How could the island survive?

Not for the first time in the war, Prime Minister Winston Churchill personally took a hand. With his experience at the Admiralty, he had appreciated from the outset the value of Malta better than most politicians. He was among those whose instincts told them that Spitfires, and only Spitfires, could save the island, despite the failure of the first batches of these aircraft to defeat the enemy. By May, an analysis had been undertaken of the reasons for this failure and for the continuing success of the Ju 88s and Me 109s of Fliegerkorps II which, operating from their Sicilian airfields, were reducing Malta to impotence. In other theatres the Spitfire was still proving as good as, or in some respects better than, the excellent Me 109 Fs – a recent and effective version of the Messerschmitt fighter – which were protecting the German bombers so well over Malta.

This analysis showed that the Spitfires had not arrived in fighting condition: they were burdened with additional long-range fuel tanks that had to be removed; they needed to have their voice radio sets adjusted to local frequencies and to have filters added to protect their engines against the dust, as well as having to be refuelled and armed. Since it had been impossible to conceal the aircraft-carrier's departure from Gibraltar or the aircrafts' arrival at Ta Kali, which was being raided and photographed several times a day, most of the aircraft were destroyed on the ground. The delivery pilots were largely inexperienced, about half having no battle experience at all; the island also lacked a first-class air controller, one with experience of controlling RAF fighters against incoming aircraft. Moreover, it was deemed essential that the aircraft should arrive together in Malta in adequate numbers, as happened on 20 April, when forty-seven Spitfires flew in from the large US aircraft-carrier *Wasp*, which had been loaned to Britain for the purpose.

Measures were put in hand to correct these faults and, in particular, to see that as many Spitfires as possible should arrive at the same time in good fighting trim so as to give the RAF a fair chance against the Luftwaffe's greater numbers. This meant also that, in order to ensure the rapid take-off of aircraft after arrival, skilled Spitfire pilots had to be available to take over the aircraft as soon as they reached Malta.

Churchill personally telephoned the American President F.D. Roosevelt and again requested to borrow their aircraft-carrier *Wasp*. With the President's immediate agreement, arrangements were made for *Wasp* and the Royal Navy aircraft-carrier *Eagle* to sail together towards Malta with a total of sixty-four Spitfires either packed inside or crowding their decks. Great efforts were made this time to send Spitfires which were in good fighting trim and, most importantly, to make arrangements in Malta for the swift removal of their overload tanks, a rapid recalibration of radio frequencies, and to ensure that they should be swiftly refuelled and armed, with experienced Spitfire pilots standing by to take over.

The air control problem was solved by sending to Malta the outstanding fighter-controller of the war: the former First World War pilot Group Captain A.B. Woodhall who had gained the confidence of all fighter pilots during the Battle of Britain. He was known to all as 'Woody'. Only a first-class ground controller had the ability successfully to vector the fighters towards the approaching bombers; it required great skill and experience to make the best use of the radar plots of the approaching enemy formations. Woody was an expert at getting his fighters into the ideal position above the enemy and up sun of them, and he managed to direct the Spitfires into these attacking positions before the enemy bombers, with their fighter escorts, could reach their island targets.

Another innovation was to split the arrival of the Spitfires between the three airfields, and also to stage their arrival so that when the second batch arrived, the first batch would already be in the air to protect them, and so on with subsequent batches. With the life of the island at stake, no slips could be tolerated and, to the credit of all, there were none when on 9 May the next batch of Spitfires arrived. Some, after landing in Malta, were in the air, refuelled, rearmed and ready for battle with an experienced fresh pilot at the controls, in as little as nine minutes.

This date, 9 May 1942, is remembered by the Maltese to this day. So, more especially, is the next one, 'The Glorious Tenth of May', when the Spitfires routed the attackers with up to sixty-three enemy aircraft destroyed.*

The task of the defenders was made easier by an extraordinary coincidence. On the same day, 10 May 1942, Kesselring reported to the OKW and Hitler that his task of neutralizing Malta was complete: 'There is nothing left to bomb.'† Malta, he indicated, had been eliminated as a base from which to threaten the Axis' supply route to North Africa. Accordingly, he began to withdraw Fliegerkorps II from Sicily and, in response to urgent pleas from Rommel, to send most of it to the Desert where its highly experienced pilots, as well as their up-to-date aircraft, were much wanted.

On this glorious tenth of May 1942, the spirits of all in Malta were almost magically lifted. Everyone in the island sensed that a change was taking place. The inhabitants, who had lived like troglodytes for so long, came out of their rock shelters and gazed upwards as formation after formation of Spitfires tore into the German and Italian aircraft. With Woody's superb controlling, many of the attackers were pounced upon before reaching the island. One who was there has well described the scene: 'It was like a Henley regatta; with shot-down Germans in their dinghies all rowing like mad to try to get back to Sicily, while the RAF Air–Sea Rescue launches moved among them to pick up as many as possible.'

Abruptly, air superiority over Malta had been regained, and henceforth was never to be lost. Malta could breathe again. It would not be long before Malta would be back on the attack. As Admiral of the Fleet Lord Lewin has remarked, with irrefutable logic: 'There wasn't much point in saving Malta unless it could strike at the enemy.'

---

* Even Rome Radio, notoriously incorrect, admitted to the loss of forty-seven aircraft.

† But one beautiful palace on a headland was spared. Kesselring had decided that it would later be his.

8

Wellingtons to the Fore

'The fall of Malta would, for the Italians, be like the
healing of a creeping disease. It would make Italy safe
from invasion by the Allies and its fall would have far-
reaching results on the strategic plans of the whole war.'
Vice-Admiral Weichold, 'Axis Policy and
Operations in the Mediterranean'

ALTHOUGH THE TWIN-ENGINED Vickers Wellington bomber served
RAF Bomber Command throughout the war, and was the only type
to do so in the UK, by 1941 it had become secondary to the bigger
four-engined Halifax and Lancaster bombers in operations over
Europe. In the Middle East, however, and especially perhaps in
Malta, it was a different story. There the Wellington became the
Allies' most effective bomber until the arrival of the B-24 Liberators
in 1943, but even then these US-built four-engined bombers did not
normally operate from Malta.

Although the Wellington, or 'Wimpy' as it was affectionately
called in the RAF,* was the largest type to operate regularly from
Malta, it could, in experienced hands, successfully take off with a
full bomb-load from Luqa's main runway even during the hottest
of summer evenings when reduced air density meant loss of engine
power and less wing-lift, although on such occasions the runway
was only just long enough. Sadly, however, 'experienced hands'
were not always available and a number of heavily laden Wimpys
crashed immediately after take-off with tragic results. A number of

---

* After the strip cartoon character 'Wellington J. Wimpy', well known in both the
USA and the UK.

other Wimpys landing at night without normal, or at times without any, runway lighting – not an unusual condition on Luqa's down-hill and often bomb-poxed runway – also came to grief. Human nature being what it is, it was seldom that aircraft on delivery to Malta were being flown by experienced crews. Apart from the natural tendency of operational squadrons in the UK to avoid sending their best crews to far-distant Malta, delivery crews, on the whole, were apt to be 'new boys' with little, if any, operational experience.

It was asking much of relatively inexperienced pilots to have to land on a Malta airfield – usually blacked out because of air alerts – after a ten-hour flight from Gibraltar which, in virtually every case, was the longest flight they had ever undertaken. Some crews were also unsettled by the fear that they might be landing in Sicily, not Malta, as the enemy had developed the cunning habit of contacting the delivery aircraft by W/T and giving them false directions in attempts to lure them to land at an airfield on that island. Delivery crews were warned about this, so always had it in mind. However, some still fell into the trap. Nor did it help the peace of mind of the delivery pilots that the long Gibraltar–Malta flight consumed much of the petrol on board and made the crews anxious to land as soon as possible, whether or not an air raid was in progress. To cap it all, some of the 'new boy' crews had hardly ever before landed a Wellington at night.

All Wellingtons in Malta operated normally only at night. Although the aircraft had both a front and rear turret with twin machine-guns in each, its lack of speed, its large size and lack of manoeuvrability made it no match against even an Italian biplane fighter in daylight. Against a German Messerschmitt 109 or 110, it stood almost no chance in combat.

At first, for nearly a year, Wellingtons based at Luqa were used only as bombers – their pre-war designed role. The first squadron to arrive there, in November 1940, was 148 Squadron of Bomber Command. At that time the airfield at Gibraltar had not been sufficiently developed to handle Wellingtons. Consequently, 148 Squadron had to fly direct from the UK over German-dominated Europe. Not surprisingly, two of the dozen aircraft failed to accom-plish this feat.

Within a few days, the surviving ten aircraft of 148 Squadron had raided Naples and, until quite late in 1941, 148 Squadron operated from Luqa with considerable success, bombing targets in Sicily, Italy and North Africa. The first CO of 148 Squadron was Squadron Leader, soon to be promoted to Wing Commander, Patrick Foss.

Initially the Luqa runway was not long enough even for a winter take-off and, after two heavily loaded aircraft had crashed on take-off with fatal results, steps were taken to make this manoeuvre less dangerous. The armour-plate was removed from the aircraft, less fuel was carried and the Luqa village church, near the end of the runway, was demolished.*

Foss's clearest recollection is of the occasion in December 1940 when he, and others from 148 Squadron, were required for once to operate in daylight. A report had been received that Castel Benito airfield, near Tripoli, was crowded with about 200 aircraft lined up in rows. Three aircraft of 37 Squadron, which also operated Wellingtons and which were in Malta on their way to Egypt, joined nine of 148: six operated in daylight, near dusk, with the other six following up at night.

The aircraft flown by Patrick Foss, who took off in daylight, became a near casualty. Over Castel Benito airfield it was attacked by a CR 42 Italian fighter which fired several bursts into it. Foss only just managed to get back to Malta with a wounded gunner but the aircraft was so badly damaged that next day it was declared a write-off. At times during this attack, Foss's Wellington, in its efforts to evade the Italian fighter, flew so low over the enemy airfield that it created a dust storm which, as much as anything else, probably caused the fighter chasing the Wellington to miss more often than hit. Another Wimpy on this raid was also damaged and had to crash-land in the dark at Malta. Wing Commander Foss, in his book *Climbing Turns*, reports that 'next day our HQ told us that 109 Italian bombers had been either destroyed or damaged. [This constituted] more than half the bomber force which the Italians planned to send to the desert to support the attack being made by General Graziani.'

Two days later, Generals Wavell and O'Connor with the Desert Rats, as the troops of the Eighth Army were known, counter-attacked and soon had the entire Italian army on the run. 148

---

* Its stones were kept and numbered. This enabled it to be rebuilt post-war.

Squadron, aided by 37 Squadron, had made a notable contribution to this great 1940/41 Allied victory which drove the Italians all the way back to El Agheila, 600 miles from the Libya–Egypt border.

Foss and his crews were also the first to discover that the Italian AA fire at night was more colourful than deadly. He was also the first, later, to warn Malta that the Germans had set up some AA batteries and must therefore have arrived at Naples. 'How did he know?' he was asked. 'Because the AA fire was accurate!' Photographs of Naples were taken by 69 Squadron the next day. They showed stores marshalled along the dockside in neat orderly rows, nothing like the usual higgledy-piggledy fashion of the Italians. This confirmed that the Germans had indeed arrived.

Patrick Foss, who was originally advised that he would be in Malta 'for about ten days',* spent nearly nine months there. He estimates that in that period about fifty Wellington aircraft were lost at Luqa on the ground, although losses in the air were remarkably few. Some of the ground losses were due to crashes and to inexperienced transit crews arriving at night, but most were caused by Luftwaffe bombing and strafing both by day and night. The Italian Air Force also raided the airport at higher levels. Fortunately, replacement Wellingtons from the UK were fairly plentiful.

These losses first began to be severe during January 1941 when the dive-bombing Ju 87s and 88s of the Luftwaffe were plastering both the harbour, where Britain's newest and biggest aircraft-carrier *Illustrious* lay damaged,† and the airfields from which it was thought the Hurricanes were rising to meet them.‡

Almost unannounced during this '*Illustrious* blitz' period, large bodies of soldiers arrived daily at Luqa, and at the other two Malta airfields, to fill in the bomb craters immediately after they were made. This was the beginning of the superb Army–RAF co-operation which enabled the three Malta airfields to remain open for virtually the entire war, except for an occasional day or two during the heavy blitz of March–April 1942.

---

* He was not the last airman to become the victim of this joke.
† Hit by Ju 87s and 88s with great damage and 126 dead when escorting two merchant ships to Malta.
‡ Hurricanes were not normally kept at Luqa at that time but the Germans were taking no chances.

In September 1941, three ASV-equipped Pegasus-powered Wellington VIII aircraft arrived at Luqa. They were normal Mark Ic versions,* apart from the addition of ASV radar equipment. They carried rows of extra aerials along each side and under their wings, together with a very prominent display on top of the fuselage. They also had a small bulge under the front turret. Initially dubbed 'Sticklebacks' these Wellingtons, for no particular reason, became more generally known as 'Goofingtons'.

The ASV was at this time still a Top Secret device.† No reference could be made to it in signals or in official reports, nor could the crews explain to others what it was or what it did, although these odd-looking aircraft attracted much curiosity and many questions.

The three Goofington crews had come from 221 Squadron which, operating from a base in Northern Ireland, had been attempting without much success to use the ASV to detect U-boats over the waters of the Atlantic. However, this early form of airborne radar largely lacked the required sensitivity for such a task.

In the calmer waters of the Mediterranean, the ASV worked more efficiently and could detect small ships at a range of ten miles or so. Liners and battleships, under favourable conditions, could be picked up at distances of up to nearly thirty miles. It was also a useful guide to the crews of these Goofingtons, when operating in the Central Mediterranean, that the island of Malta would appear on the small cathode-ray tube, at the heart of the device, at about eighty miles. However, in conditions of cloud and rain, effective distances were considerably less.

Officially named the SDF (Special Duties Flight – Luqa) these three Goofingtons had been sent to Malta to provide the same kind of aerial reconnaissance, at night, as was being provided in daylight hours by the Marylands of 69 Squadron. Enemy ships could thereafter, in theory, be located and shadowed throughout the entire

---

* Initially the Wellingtons had Bristol Pegasus engines, and were styled Mark Ia–Ic. Some later versions had slightly more powerful Rolls-Royce Merlin engines, and were styled Mark II. Much later the powerful Bristol Hercules engines were fitted; they became Mark III.

† The AOC Malta once sent a signal which mentioned 'ASV'. Tactfully, the author, then leader of the flight, reminded his AOC that these initials were not to be used openly. The AOC's next signal to the author referred to the device as 'your bloody instrument'.

twenty-four-hour period, if so required, although when bad weather arrived, theory and practice hardly matched.

However, thanks to the enterprise of the AOC Air Vice-Marshal Lloyd, the leader of Navy Force K in Malta Captain W.G. Agnew and that of the Goofington crews, the process of night reconnaissance and shadowing was soon to be taken a step further. In Malta, a young RCAF ground radar expert had arrived, Flying Officer Albert (call me 'Al') Glazer. He and his assistant, another Canadian, Corporal Les Card, knew more about radar than most at that time. Both also had fertile imaginations and, in Malta, novel ideas were always given encouragement both by the Royal Navy and the RAF.

In discussions between Captain Agnew of HMS *Aurora*, his Chief Radio Officer, Al Glazer and the author (who from November 1941 had been put in charge of the Wellingtons of the SDF), a unique form of air–sea co-operation was devised. In brief, the ASV-equipped Wellington, heavily loaded with fuel and flares, would hunt all night, if needs be, for the expected enemy ships. Meanwhile RN Force K – which comprised two cruisers and two destroyers, and which, because of the proximity of enemy dive-bombers, normally operated only at night – would have put to sea from Grand Harbour an hour before nightfall and would be proceeding at 28 knots in the direction where Intelligence signals showed the enemy ships were likely to be found. If the searching Goofington (the author himself normally operated with Force K) located a target, then, by employing a code which had been invented exclusively for use between the ships of Force K and the aircraft of the SDF, and using a W/T frequency which had also been privately agreed between the two units, the Wellington's crew would direct Force K towards its quarry.*

The directing process was made simple because Al Glazer had constructed an ASV homing beacon, known as a 'Rooster', and had it placed on one of *Aurora*'s masts: *Aurora* being the lead ship of Force K. Al Glazer had made the Rooster from a spare IFF set and it enabled the hunting/shadowing Goofington to pick up Force K by

---

* This was known as the SAIR (Sea to Air) code and was condensed to a mere half dozen signals. The W/T frequency of 8888 cycles was used, the number being easy to remember and that frequency band working well in the Central Mediterranean. For further details see A. Spooner, *In Full Flight* (1965).

ASV at about 100 miles. The 'blip' made by the Rooster on *Aurora*'s mast appeared on the aircraft's tiny radar screen in a distinctive form and shape. It could never be mistaken for anything else.

After many hours of searching over a featureless sea, in an area where forecasts of upper winds were little more than guesswork as the nearest Allied meteorological stations were nearly 1,000 miles away at Gibraltar and Alexandria, the Wellington crew, although finding the enemy ships, would not, by then, know their position within an accuracy of about fifty miles. The Force K navigators also admitted, in pre-operational discussions, that, unless the stars were visible, they were also liable to be a few miles off course. It was therefore agreed that, rather than have the Goofington provide the on-rushing ships of Force K with an estimated position of the enemy in latitude and longitude which could be far from accurate, the aircraft would simply pass to Force K, via their private communication radio link, the relative course to steer and the distance to travel from its prey. This was only made possible by being able to 'see' Force K at 100 miles thanks to the aircraft's ASV and Glazer's home-made Rooster.

This bearing and distance to the enemy was all that Captain Agnew needed. Again and again, this information would be passed to him, as the Goofington shuttled between friend and foe. As Force K drew closer to its enemy, the ASV aircraft could get one, then the other, on its radar screen simply by turning rapidly through 180 degrees. At the same time the Goofington would have been shadowing the enemy on its ASV set at a distance of about five to ten miles from the ships in order to remain both unseen and unheard. Thus, when Force K was close enough to 'see' the enemy ships on its own radar sets, and/or visually in the moonlight and opened fire at an appropriate moment, the enemy were taken completely by surprise.

The only time during the night when the enemy were made aware of the Goofington was when, after initially sighting the ships, the aircraft swept low overhead in a quick pass or two in order to report upon the composition, course and estimated speed of the supply ships and to gain information about the number and type of escorts which appeared to be accompanying them.

This co-operation was further enhanced by having officers and signalmen from Force K fly in the aircraft and by Al Glazer and the author paying visits to Captain Agnew and his specialists in *Aurora*. Both Al Glazer and Les Card also flew, at times, with the author. We became *their* aircraft and those in Force K became *our* ships. A posse of their naval ratings even came up to Luqa to help build a protective pen around 'their' aircraft.

The Goofingtons also carried out a similar form of co-operation with the Swordfish of 830 Squadron. These ancient aircraft lacked the fuel to search for ships at night, as the enemy soon took care not to come close when passing Malta. Consequently, the SDF aircraft, when operating with 830 Squadron, went ahead, searched the area where ships were likely to be and, if finding them, reported their position by W/T to Malta.

The Swordfish crews at Hal Far stood at immediate readiness awaiting this signal and, upon receiving it, took off at once in the appropriate direction. On those occasions when one of the 'Stringbags' also had its own ASV Mark I on board, Al Glazer again rose to the occasion. He made another Rooster but this time it was fitted inside the Goofington. This enabled the Swordfish leader to home on to the shadowing Wellington which, while remaining out of sight and earshot of the enemy, maintained a position of about five to ten miles between them and Malta.

These operations were typical of the way the Services in Malta co-operated. Three different Services, the Royal Navy, the Fleet Air Arm and the RAF, simply got together to resolve a common problem and, regardless of differences in rank and established procedures, the leaders involved worked out how best a job might be done and duly 'invented' both the tactics and the means of doing it.

On other occasions, SDF aircraft went out at night simply to locate and shadow enemy ships, the purpose being to confirm Intelligence reports which it is now known came from Ultra intercepts. Once located, daylight reconnaissances and strikes would follow.

For night operations, a supply of parachute flares was carried in the Goofingtons in case illumination was requested by an attacker but, as often as not, the bright Mediterranean moonlight was sufficient. On rare occasions, bomber Wellingtons were also despatched to attack the ships which the SDF aircraft was shadowing, but the chances of hitting a moving ship at night by high-level bombing, even when the ships were illuminated by flares dropped by the SDF aircraft were slight although, as was usual, the ships gave away their position to the bombers by firing at the flares. This last was an utterly futile action by the Italian Navy since, by the time the flare had fallen free from the aircraft and its parachute had opened, the aircraft which had dropped it was already some distance away.

Notwithstanding the difficulties of using Wellington bombers to attack ships at night, a success was scored on the night of 31 October 1941 by crews of 104 Squadron.* Two accounts of this attack have been received from crew members who took part.

A Goofington was first sent to find the enemy at sea and a successful sighting report was transmitted back to Malta using normal RAF codes and W/T procedures. A pilot, Percy Huggins, who was captain of a 104 Squadron Wellington during that night attack, takes up the story.† Huggins' account tells much about how brilliant the Mediterranean moonlight could be.‡

We had been outward bound for some time when we intercepted a message on W/T that the search aircraft had located the convoy. As we got close, the recce aircraft brought us to the spot by pre-arranged firing of Verey lights. The arrangements worked like clockwork.

It was amazing how clearly we could see everything. The beam cast by a three-quarters moon showed up the ships distinctly and we did our attack from between 2,000–3,000 feet. Our targets were the merchant ships and, in particular, the largest one. I decided to drop four sticks each of 4 × 250 lbs bombs on four different bombing runs. The first two sticks overshot but someone else in our quartet of attackers got a hit, for the vessel slowed and appeared in trouble. All the time the destroyers were pumping up considerable quantities of light flak at us: red and green stuff which spiralled swiftly upwards and often lit up the cockpit as the shells passed.

After our third attack we could see that the ship was badly damaged and possibly sinking, so I decided to let our last stick go on one of the smaller vessels.

---

* Wellington squadrons or part-squadrons 37, 38, 40, 104 and 148 arrived and departed from the Middle East as and when required; and also, as and when petrol was available in Malta. 104 first arrived during October 1941, Wing Commander 'Teddy' Beare i/c. By then 148 Squadron had departed. By October 37 Squadron was also largely at Luqa, Wing Commander R.C.M. Collard i/c.

† The three other skippers were Pilot Officers Ferry, Goodwin and Doherty.

‡ Percy Huggins' account is included in Robert Ginn's history of 104 Squadron, *Strike Hard*.

At the end of this eventful sortie, Percy Huggins had to spend a frustrating two and a half hours circling around the rock Filfla, a few miles south-west of Malta, awaiting permission to land as an air raid was in progress at Luqa. Philip Dawson was in the crew of Pilot Officer Doherty, one of the other aircraft engaged in this attack, and he reports that it was his skipper's third run, made at only 200 feet, which hit and stopped the large merchant vessel.

Pilot Officer Huggins also comments on the nuisance raids undertaken by Wellingtons over enemy ports.

> They were intended to keep the Axis defenders busy and to impede the work of unloading shipping. Each aircraft carried sixteen 250-pounders and we were detailed to drop one bomb at a time over a period of two hours when we would be relieved by the next aircraft. We were guided to Tripoli by the flak being fired at Squadron Leader 'Dinghy' Young.* When we arrived, he departed.
>
> It was quite fun dodging in and out from the sea, trying to fox the defences, which were plentiful but not very accurate. When we dropped a flare over the harbour we could see the light-flak guns popping furiously at it in an effort to put it out. Frequently, the searchlights flicked over our aircraft, but in the whole two hours, they only once held us . . . and that was not for long. In the end it got a bit monotonous.

Like other pilots on one of the big raids on Castel Benito airfield which, as when Pat Foss had attacked it, was crowded with enemy aircraft, Percy Huggins remembers such an occasion well. It was the night of 2 November 1941 when 'Squadron Leader Dinghy Young and I were to attack the aircraft in the southern dispersal area of the big airfield. I streaked across the southern end looking for aircraft. The bomb-aimer called out, "Lots of aircraft below, Captain – dozens of them!"'

Huggins then released flares and a dazzling arc of light appeared all over the southern end of the aerodrome. Other flares appeared. It was a floodlit performance. Pilot Officer Huggins' bomb-aimer first dropped a stick of four high-explosive bombs,

> right among a bunch of machines. It was impossible to miss . . . I saw one of Dinghy Young's sticks go down. Between us, we already had several

---

* Later a sub-leader of the famous Dam-Busting raid. The 'Dinghy' came about as a result of his having been shot down over the sea (twice, it is thought) and having to take to his aircraft's dinghy.

aircraft blazing on our section of the target. The same thing was happening at other points. I tried to count the number of blazing machines but gave up. A mighty explosion occurred beside the hangars, to be followed by a large fire which raged furiously belching out thick black smoke.

After Huggins had dropped all his bombs, which included a large number of smaller incendiary bombs and a number of splinter bombs to cause ancillary damage, he manoeuvred his Wimpy so as to give his air-gunners a chance to join the other gunners who were already sweeping low over the airfield shooting at everything. Thousands of rounds were expended as, with the smell of cordite inside the aircraft, the attack continued.

Later, it was learned that, at the time of the attack on the airfield, many of the top Italian Air Force commanders were about to commence a special dinner. No doubt they also will remember the occasion well!

Philip Dawson, again flying as second pilot to Pilot Officer Doherty, also remembers the same raid on Castel Benito airfield.

All aircraft were on this one. The moon was nearly full. The aerodrome was full of aircraft while the defences were pitiful, only a few light flak guns whose gunners were machine-gunned by the aircraft, the opposition soon ceasing.

We made four or five bombing runs all at pretty low levels and had some hits on a hangar. It was quite a sight with gunners in a few aircraft all firing at targets on the 'drome at the same time. There were fires all over the place. For our last run at under 800 feet, I went on the beam guns to fire at flashes coming from the palm trees – obviously rifles etc.

During the raid an aircraft appeared with its navigation lights on but soon disappeared after the gunners in two or three of our aircraft all fired at it. Quite a party!

Albacores, another slightly more modern FAA single-engined torpedo-carrying biplane of 828 Squadron, which had arrived in Malta in October/November 1941, also took part in some of the attacks upon ships which were being shadowed by the crews of the SDF. However no Albacore was then fitted with any form of airborne radar and, initially, their successes were less than those accomplished by the Swordfish of 830 Squadron.

One of the three SDF Goofingtons was lost on operations with all its crew, and SDF aircraft also suffered the inevitable losses on the ground. Fortunately, however, other Goofingtons belonging to 221 Squadron were being sent to Egypt: these had to land in Malta to refuel and, with permission from the AOC, several of these were waylaid in order to make good the losses.* As a result Malta, even at the height of the 1942 blitz, was rarely without a radar-equipped Wellington for night reconnaissance operations. The policy of keeping the Goofington in 14-foot anti-blast pens a long way from the runway, helped to keep them to keep in service longer than some other Wellingtons.

From time to time, Wellingtons of the bomber squadrons were used to drop magnetic, and then other types, of mines. These operations in the RAF were always called 'gardening', the long thin mines in the bomb racks having been dubbed 'cucumbers'. In order to distinguish those Wellingtons which were carrying bombs – as most were – from those which were mine-laying, the latter type became known as 'Miningtons'. Con Rutter, an airman stationed in Luqa, remembers seeing an official Operations Order which referred to Goofingtons, Miningtons, Flashingtons (Wellingtons which carried only flares) and Fishingtons (those with torpedoes).

The Fishingtons were to appear first in Malta during the late summer of 1942. These were Wellingtons modified to carry in their bomb bays two torpedoes of the 18-inch diameter Mark XII type. This was an idea initially devised by 38 Squadron (Wellingtons) when based in Egypt, and was promoted by the enterprise and energy of Wing Commander Chaplin, the squadron CO. The big RAF maintenance Middle East Unit near Cairo carried out necessary modifications late in 1941 and, in due course, Chaplin and others began to use these aircraft, mainly at night, to help protect the convoys which, operating from Alexandria, were supplying beleaguered Tobruk by sea.

One 38 Squadron Wellington, modified to drop torpedoes, came to Malta on an experimental night operation with the author's Goofington. Having no ASV, the Fishington had to be led by the Goofington in formation towards the target in mid-Mediterranean, but an unexpected total eclipse of the moon at the critical period of

---

* In all, during the first few months of 1942, the author used eight different Goofingtons so at least five must have been added.

1. The author, Squadron Leader Tony Spooner DSO DFC, who commanded the SDF (Special Duties Flight) at Luqa October 1941–March 1942.

2. FAA Swordfish with 1,600-pound torpedo. This open-cockpit biplane, with
xed undercarriage and fixed-pitch propeller, looked as if it had strayed from the
First World War by some time-warp. In the hands of the crews of 830 Squadron
FAA, it was highly successful in night torpedo attacks from Malta.

3. Adrian Warburton who arrived in Malta as a navigator but rapidly established himself as an outstanding pilot. His photographs of Taranto in November 1940 helped to make that raid a success. By the time he left Malta he had been awarded two DSOs and four DFCs. Never one to conform, he is here about to fly a USAAF aircraft in carpet slippers, scarf and civilian trousers.

4. One of the Glen-Martin Maryland US-built fighter-bombers in which Adrian Warburton carried out many of his photographic reconnaissance missions. It may have been taken in Greece when 'Warby' deliberately landed in enemy-held territory to collect 'booze' for the mess and a girl-friend.

5. Two great submariners, Admiral Max Horton and Captain 'Shrimp' Simpson.

6. Lieutenant Commander Wanklyn – the most successful British submariner of the war and Malta's first VC. The tonnage he sank in *Upholder* was never exceeded.

7. Two of the most successful U-class submarines, *Upholder* (Lt/Cdr Wanklyn VC
with earlier-designed bulge and *Urge* (Lt/Cdr Tomkinson),
a later modified example.

8. Air Vice Marshal Hugh Pughe Lloyd and Vice Admiral Wilbraham Ford.
These dynamic leaders were probably the only two persons in Malta who were
privy to Ultra information, as decoded by the experts at Bletchley Park.

9. Bristol Blenheim dropping bombs. Insufficiently armed and protected, the Blenheims suffered calamitous casualties in Malta. Ivor Broom who flew this type as a Sergeant Pilot in Malta, later became a distinguished Air Marshal with a DSO, three DFCs and an AFC.

10. Captain 'Bill' Agnew, the exceptional leader of Force K. Their sinking of the entire *Duisberg* convoy had far-reaching repercussions.

11. HMS *Aurora*, the leading cruiser of Force K, outside Grand Harbour, Valletta. Although only a light cruiser *Aurora* and her sister ship HMS *Penelope* inflicted enormous damage on enemy ships.

12. HMS *Lively*, one of the destroyers of Force K. Her commander, Lieutenant Commander Hussey, was an expert jazz trumpeter. She and her sister ship HMS *Lance* contributed to the success of Force K.

13. Lieutenant Commander Dick Cayley with the crew of HMS *Utmost*. Later this splendid submarine commander returned to Malta as commander of the submarine *P311*.

14. FAA Albacores with torpedoes. This FAA biplane with fixed undercarriage performed miracles from Malta despite its obsolete design, especially during the Tunisian campaign. An Albacore also sank the *Victoria*, 'the pearl of the Italian merchant fleet'.

15. A Spitfire being refuelled and rearmed in Malta by soldiers, sailors and airmen working together. Note the protective anti-blast pen built from empty petrol tins filled with rubble, of which there was no shortage. On 'The Glorious Tenth of May' 1942, Spitfires saved Malta. Later, Spitfires also carried bombs.

16. A Wellington of 104 Squadron photographed in Egypt. Wellingtons of 104 an other squadrons in Egypt operated from Malta whenever required, always provided that fuel was available on the island. 104 Squadron operated the Mark variant with Rolls Royce Merlin engines.

17. This shot-up 'Goofington' (an ASV-equipped Wellington) had to raise its wheels to avoid ending up in the quarry at the end of Luqa's downhill runway. It had no brakes due to hydraulic damage. Note the ASV aerials on top of the fuselage, under wings and down sides. The author's SDF flew similar aircraft.

18. Bristol Beauforts, torpedo-carrying aircraft which were led in Malta by Patrick Gibbs. The leading aircraft has been modified to include a rearwards firing machine-gun.

19. Flying Officer Arthur Aldridge DFC and bar. He both torpedoed a large Italian cruiser, *Trento*, and sank a major German cargo ship, the *Reichenfels*.

20. Lieutenant Maydon who in HMS *Umbra* applied the *coup de grâce* to the 10,000-ton Italian cruiser *Trento*, after Arthur Aldridge had stopped it and set it on fire.

21. Squadron Leader Patrick Gibbs, the inspired leader of the Malta-based Beaufort torpedo-bombers. No officer gave more of himself than did this master strategist and tactician.

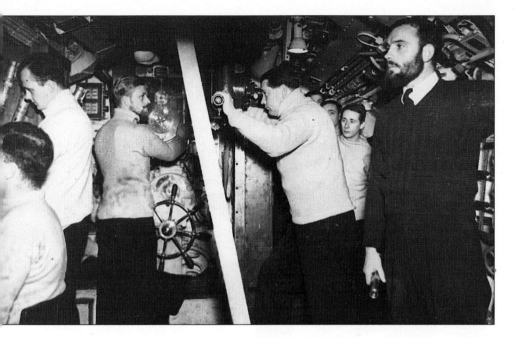

22. The crowded control room of *Utmost*. Lieutenant Boyd is at the 'fruit-machine' (the Director Attack computer) on the left. Lieutenant Commander Cayley is at the periscope. Lieutenant Oxborrow is on the right. Note the cramped conditions.

23. Crowded torpedo-room with 'tin-fish' in place. Space was always limited, especially in the small U-class type of submarine.

24. *Rorqual*, a large mine-laying submarine, departs Malta. Apart from her size, her silhouette was similar to that of an aircraft-carrier; and a U-boat commander once mistook her for one. *Rorqual* also brought desperately needed supplies to Malta.

25. Lieutenant 'Rufus' Mackenzie whose sinking of Mussolini's cargo-carrying yacht *Diana* was a notable success. Now Vice Admiral Sir Hugh Mackenzie, he is one of several young Malta submarine commanders who later rose to Admiral rank.

26. Charioteers at sea. All brave volunteers, they were Britain's answer to the successful Italian 'one-man submarines'.

27. 'Anybody in there?' HM King George VI inspecting charioteers. On one sortie from Malta, an Italian light cruiser was sunk.

28. A typically battered Beaufighter alongside Malta.
Both a day- and night-fighter, bomber and later in the war,
torpedo-bomber, it was as powerful as it looked. The type served Malta well.

29. Canadian Flight Lieutenant Dallas Schmidt DFC and bar. Malta's outstanding daytime Beaufighter pilot, he became an Alberta cabinet-minister. His final Malta mission included two bale-outs.

30. The wake reveals the fate of an enemy merchant ship, the *Ringulv*, sunk by a torpedo fired by Lieutenant John Roxburgh in his submarine *United*. Note that an enemy aircraft has dropped a bomb close to where the submarine is or was: also that some of the torpedoes have missed their mark. A PRU Spitfire flown by Keith Durbidge took this unique photograph.

31. Lieutenant John Roxburgh, then our youngest submarine commander, now Vice Admiral Sir John Roxburgh.

32. HMS *Safari*'s officers. Under Commander Ben Bryant, this submarine operating from Malta made a splendid contribution to Allied victory. Many of her successes were scored by her effective gun. Admiral Sir Ben Bryant later became RN's Flag Officer, Submarines.

33. *Safari* sinking the *Entella* (2,691 tons) – a rare wartime shot (in both senses of the word), March 1943. In all *Safari* fired 91 torpedoes and over 1,000 rounds of her 3-inch gun. These sank 39 ships and damaged about a dozen others. Commander Ben Bryant was one of her notable commanders.

34. *Ultor's* pennant showing their many successes. The dark bars indicate warships torpedoed. The stars each represent a sinking by gunfire. As well as the cloak and dagger emblem, note the lighthouse symbol signifying a beach-marker sortie. Lieutenant George Hunt DSO and bar, DSC and bar, was her outstanding commander.

approach put paid to the experiment. We should have consulted an almanac.

Later, Wellingtons in the UK were similarly converted into Fishingtons and, by 1942, Coastal Command crews were being specifically trained in the difficult art of dropping torpedoes by night from Wellingtons which were also equipped with ASV: an obvious development. Three or four of the first UK-trained Fishington crews on their way to the Middle East were stopped (waylaid?) at Malta and began to operate there from September 1942.

While a relatively large number of Wellingtons were generally available in Egypt to work closely with both Army and Navy, principally by bombing those ports in North Africa which were being used by the enemy to unload their supplies, the smaller number of Wellington bombers in Malta concentrated upon attacking enemy ships in their ports of embarkation, such as Naples and Palermo, and in the enemy's principal North African port of Tripoli, which was generally beyond the range of the Middle East Air Force's Wimpys.

Although large numbers of Wellingtons of all variants were destroyed on the ground in Malta, relatively few were lost on operations until the arrival of the Fishingtons. Then, as with other aircraft used to attack ships at low levels, the casualty rate rose sharply. Also, by then, enemy night-fighters were more active.

On the whole, the Wellington was a type which served Malta well, although only towards the end of Malta's war did any Wellingtons appear on the island powered by the two 1,450-hp* Bristol Hercules engines. These transformed this hitherto underpowered aircraft into a much more formidable machine. The 1,000-hp Pegasus-powered Wellington could only just maintain height on one engine. When equipped with all the additional ASV aerials, the performance was so degraded that any chance of operating on a single engine became extremely doubtful.

The deficiencies of power of the Pegasus-powered Wellington – especially those encumbered by ASV aerials – is well illustrated by Eric Cameron, a Canadian Wireless Operator/Air Gunner who

---

* Later 1,600 hp.

arrived in Malta as a crew member of an SDF Wellington during 1942. He writes:

> The German jamming station tricked our crew (Flying Officer Fanshawe in command) when we were flying around the north-east tip of Sicily and the starboard engine conked out. To lighten the aircraft, we jetti- soned bombs and flares and, unintentionally, panicked half a dozen E- boats who thought they were being attacked.
>
> The aircraft was still losing height as we hastily threw overboard everything that wasn't bolted down, including two beam-guns, ammunition belts and even the Elsan toilet. The wireless operator sent out an SOS and requested a magnetic course to steer to reach Malta [they were over 200 miles away between Sardinia and Tunisia]. A radio signal loud and clear came through. Fanshawe headed on that course and we continued to lose height. Next thing we knew searchlights blazed around us and ack-ack batteries opened up. We were heading into Tunis harbour at about 3,500 feet. We managed to turn away without getting hit. By then the navigator had got the map straightened out and we headed for Malta, barely maintaining 2,300 feet.

Eric Cameron has also retained a copy of a congratulatory signal sent from the AOC to 69 Squadron in which, it is interesting to note, even the AOC referred to the torpedo-carrying Wellingtons as 'Fishingtons'.

Very little has been written about the hard-slogging and often unspectacular operations flown by bomber Wellingtons operating from Malta. But thanks to David Gunby's splendid first-hand account of his experiences in Malta with 40 Squadron a clearer picture is now available.*

Like other Wellington squadrons, 40 Squadron was in and out of Malta on more than one occasion, depending often on whether there was fuel available for these bombers, or whether their presence was especially desirable, perhaps because a Malta-bound convoy was heading for the island. On such occasions Wellingtons would be flown in from Egypt specifically to attack the airfields in Sicily and Sardinia where the Italian and German dive- and torpedo-bombers would be based awaiting their chance to attack the Malta-bound convoy.

---

* See his history of 40 Squadron, *Sweeping the Skies*. Similar accounts could also have been written by those who flew from Malta with 37, 38, 104 and 148 Squadrons.

On Gunby's first arrival on the island with 40 Squadron in October 1941, one aircraft – as was not unusual on the long flight direct from the UK – failed to arrive and two others nearly ran out of fuel. Night navigation over a blacked-out, well-defended Europe was never easy and one of the Wellingtons *en route* to Malta, with the petrol gauge low, had to fly direct over Sicily, in the clear light of dawn, before landing at Luqa with only a few minutes of fuel remaining.

In October 1941, living conditions in Malta were just tolerable. The food was limited and monotonous but at least there were none of the stark shortages which were soon to follow. Nor was there a water shortage, and a passable version of beer was being locally made. The Luftwaffe had not then returned to Sicily and the raids, which were carried out on most days by the Regia Aeronautica, were annoying and disruptive rather than highly alarming. Generally the Hurricanes at Ta Kali airfield had the measure of the Italians in the air by day, and Beaufighters took care of Italian night raids.

Accommodation even for aircrews, who were generally given the best of everything available, was poor. The NCO aircrews, who constituted the bulk of the Wellington crews of 40 Squadron, were lodged in the notorious Poor House-cum-Leper colony on the outskirts of Luqa. This was a huge stone-built institution-like structure, bare of every comfort and, by 1942, without heat or light,* where the men were obliged to sleep on temporary palliasses spread on the terrazzo floor. It shared the area with the Malta leper colony whose victims 'hung around the fringes of the Mess and our quarters to beg for cigarettes. They were a pitiful sight with their bandaged extremities,' Eric Cameron recalled.

---

* When the author's NCO crew were billeted in the Poor House, they found some unoccupied upper rooms and, led by Desmond Haynes, made themselves comfortable in a pent-house flat. Unofficially, using wiring from wrecked aircraft and switches from a bombed building, they connected themselves to the main electricity power cable so were able to enjoy the luxury of both light and heat. However power cuts were fairly frequent. The author, after twice being bombed out at Luqa and, having obeyed the AOC's instructions to 'find yourself a car', chose to live in some comfort at a former Navy Officers' Mess at relatively unbombed Kalafrana. However, even here, he once awoke to find glass all over his bed as a bomb had fallen just outside his window. Generally, by then, falling bombs no longer disturbed sound sleepers.

Operations began for 40 Squadron with a nuisance raid over Tripoli on 28 October 1941 by six Wellingtons dropping bombs one at a time while lingering for two hours over the target. As David Gunby remarks, 'the defences were not as concentrated as they were over Europe but we were in the danger zone quite a long time.' Similar nuisance raids over Naples and Palermo followed.

A change came when, on 2 November 1941, a dozen Wellingtons from Luqa drawn from 40 and 104 Squadrons attacked the big airfield of Castel Benito near Tripoli, in the raid earlier described by Percy Huggins and Philip Dawson. With poor defences at the airfield, the bombers swept in low, strafing as well as bombing. It was an invigorating operation, although fraught with additional dangers, and it was no surprise that one crew failed to return. In all, five raids were made by 40 Squadron that week, including one to drop bombs on Benghazi.

On Armistice Day, 11 November 1941, a maximum effort of nineteen aircraft from 40 and 104 Squadrons were despatched to bomb the Royal Dockyard at Naples which they left in flames, at the cost of one crew of an aircraft which was flying on only one engine and which had to ditch on the return when only thirty miles from Malta. Some of the crew were killed during the ditching but, with the dinghy being blown steadily towards Sicily, three survived to become POWs after spending four and half days in their tiny rubber craft.

Already AOC Lloyd was bringing 40 Squadron nearer to its intended strength by 'waylaying' transit Wellingtons, which had landed at Luqa only to refuel on their way to the Middle East. With aircraft being destroyed on the ground, this became almost the only way to replace losses.

Other raids with ten aircraft were made upon Brindisi, Tripoli and Naples and on 21 November an effort was made to bomb an enemy convoy south of the Strait of Messina which a Goofington had found and was illuminating. Swordfish were also despatched, and the Goofington crew overhead noted, with some relief, that the enemy flak was concentrated upon the low-level torpedo-droppers. David Gunby comments, as did all who had to fly during those 1941 winter nights, upon the appalling weather with 'the aircraft being thrown about all over the place to such an extent that on one occasion we all honestly thought our end had come'. Another aircraft had to ditch after further raids on Benghazi. This time only two of the six crewmen survived.

Navigation to Naples, raided by twelve aircraft on 27 November 1941, was made easy by the glowing beacons of the volcanoes Stromboli, *en route*, and Vesuvius, close to the target. In raids on Catania in Sicily, the Mount Etna beacon was similarly invaluable. The vile weather on the next night, the 28th, caused many to turn back on their way to Benghazi, when stronger German AA defences were also encountered. However, three ships were sunk in that harbour on that night.

The Royal Arsenal at Naples was the target for another major attack on 5 December. CR 42 fighters were encountered under brilliant Mediterranean moonlight and, after a long battle, one of these shot down the crew of Pilot Officer Hutt, only he and his co-pilot surviving. Fortunately such conditions were rare at this period and enemy fighters were not usually encountered at night.

A switch was made when twelve crews flew east to bomb the Greek harbour of Patras where, as Gunby has written, the aircraft, bombing from only 3,000 feet, 'came under fairly hectic AA gunfire before escaping into the low clouds'. Flying at this low level, the crews were also acutely conscious of the proximity of the mountains in the Gulf of Corinth.

During this period, when the Eighth Army advance was fast approaching Benghazi, that port seems to have been attacked as often as Tripoli. Since the Germans provided the AA guns here, Benghazi was defended better than other places and the crews did not relish the job they were given, on 13 December 1941, to lay mines inside the well-defended harbour. The task, which they had never before attempted, was one which required dangerous night-flying as the mines had to be dropped at only 500 feet. Gunby himself made three low-level runs over the target. The task was assisted by four other Wellingtons who flew low over the harbour to draw the searchlights away from the mine-droppers. Fierce AA fire shot down one of the aircraft, flown by one of the sergeant pilots who was billeted in the Poor House. As another crew member recorded, 'To see those empty beds, gives me the creeps.'

It was not all beer and skittles for these Wellington crews. Taranto, and its oil storage tanks, were the targets on the nights of 15 and 16 December but three nights later when the crews were going out to their aircraft prior to departure, a bomb landed among them. 'Single-handedly the intruder had destroyed three Wellingtons and put many more out of action,' Gunby writes. 'The Luftwaffe had arrived back in Sicily.'

When it came to 40 Squadron's turn to attack, once again, the Tripoli airfield of Castel Benito they could now only muster three aircraft but, thanks to good work by the ground crews, it had risen to five for their next attack. By 27 December, thanks to the AOC's sleight of hand in replacing lost aircraft, as well as the valiant work by the dedicated, often-bombed ground crews, eleven Wellingtons were available to attack Tripoli.

Malta had become adroit at making the most of difficult conditions. Rules and regulations became secondary to getting a job done, often by any means possible. Robert Ginn, a member of 104 Squadron, provides a graphic example in his squadron history. When an incoming Wellington crashed, writing off its under-carriage and arriving in a flurry of dust with smoke pouring out of it ominously, the ground crew of the squadron, in their one and only truck, rushed to the scene and, in a trice, removed a wing-tip from the damaged machine. This item was wanted for one of their damaged Wellingtons, and they had their prize off and were away before even the ambulance or the fire tender had arrived. Enterprise ruled.

Retribution for the Tripoli airfield attack of the night of 27/28 December 1941 came the next day when the Poor House was hit. A more damaging attack came in the afternoon of 29 December, when Ju 88s, accompanied by Me 109s, blasted Luqa and destroyed nine Wellingtons, three of which belonged to 40 Squadron. But that was not all: 'the bang [which followed] seemed to lift us up and bash us down again and we were almost a mile away in the crew room,' one airman recorded. A direct hit on an aircraft already bombed up had set up a chain reaction. 'As bombs went off and petrol tanks exploded, other machines were set alight and the whole dispersal area seemed ablaze. The fire had reached the bomb dump and we were all awaiting this explosion. It came all right and shook the whole island.'* The bomb dump 'left a crater 30 feet deep and 60 feet

---

* The author was Luqa at the time and remembers it well.

wide. On either side of the road the place was littered with burnt out aircraft. For about one square mile the place was absolutely littered with debris, engines, bits of propellers and other parts of aircraft.'

Yet that same night 40 and 104 Squadrons between them mustered seven aircraft for an attack on motor transport yards and petrol dumps at Misurata, east of Tripoli, and one aircraft scored a direct hit on what was thought to be the sleeping quarters of enemy airmen. The Wellingtons, in the moonlight, then strafed vehicles on the Tripoli–Benghazi road. 'This was damned good fun,' so one front-gunner, Bruce Holloway, recalled, 'with a roar of the engines and all guns blazing on to the road. We were at 200 feet and I could see the transports stop and men running . . . I was sorry to leave.'

As before, the ground crew performed near miracles in patching up damaged aircraft and, by January, nuisance raids, although carried out by depleted numbers of Wellingtons, were again resumed.

The Luftwaffe was also an Air Force that never gave up and, as an airman records:* 'two sticks of bombs from a Ju 88 caught the neighbouring kite, "U for Uncle", [and set it] on fire and I shan't forget the feeling of hopelessness when the dirt and cordite fumes had passed and the shrapnel began to fall.' It was heart-breaking: as soon as the ground crews patched up a 'wounded' aircraft, the Luftwaffe again inflicted damage.

Air Vice Marshal Hugh Pughe Lloyd, the AOC who did so much to harass the enemy during his tenure of office June 1941–July 1942, was a fighter. He went to Luqa and personally addressed the crews. He impressed upon them the importance of continuing their attacks and, on discovering that a large collection of aircraft had been assembled at Castel Vetrano airfield in the south-west of Sicily as a result of other airfields there having become waterlogged,† he arranged a daring daylight strike using every serviceable Blenheim, ten in all, from the remains of the two squadrons then still at Luqa. This raid, led by Squadron Leader George Lerwill, was a success and, in its turn, destroyed about a dozen Axis aircraft on the ground.

The same night AOC Lloyd sent every available Wellington – a

* Martin Johnson, quoted in David Gunby, *Sweeping the Skies*.
† The same was fast happening at Hal Far and Ta Kali.

bare five only – to stoke up the fires still burning at Castel Vetrano and when they came back he had them refuelled and re-armed to go out again and repeat the dose. 'As well as the 12 enemy aircraft destroyed,' writes David Gunby, '42 others were damaged and 500 drums of aviation fuel lost. The RAF casualties were one crew shot down over the target with no survivors.'

Air Vice Marshal Lloyd, AOC Malta – known to all as 'Hugh Pughe' – like Captain 'Shrimp' Simpson who was in charge of the Malta submarines, was of the bulldog breed. He never gave up; he never let go. He even arranged for his few undamaged or reconditioned Wellingtons to make occasional triple attacks on Sicilian airfields, with aircraft being twice refuelled on the runways, in the course of the same night.

The AOC's other forte – apart from his ability to waylay transit aircraft – was his keen eye for the right men to lead his few units. In an island where losses of aircraft on the ground were so frequent, and where it was almost impossible to get a passage away from it, there were always many more crews than aircraft. Hugh Pughe Lloyd knew whom he wanted to fly those few aircraft and made his own rules, if necessary, to get them. His elevation of Sergeant Pilot Ivor Broom from the ranks to lead the Blenheims was an inspired move. His encouragement of Patrick Gibbs to lead, and later command, the Beauforts (as will be seen) did much to keep Malta on the offensive during the otherwise 'sterile' period of summer 1942 when even the submarines had been forced to depart. His trust in the formerly disgraced Adrian Warburton was indispensable in keeping the island informed of enemy movements. Nor was his trust abused as Warburton's two DSOs and four DFCs, all earned in Malta, clearly testify.

Admiration for the AOC was not confined to the aircrew who had the privilege of seeing him during his many visits to the Ops Room where he gave up time and sleep to see his crews depart and arrive. The author's initial meeting with his AOC took place at about 4.30 a.m. on a late October night full of wind and rain. The Air Vice-Marshal had come to see him, still a humble Pilot Officer, arrive back from a long Goofington night sortie. 'I was worried', he said, 'about how on earth you were going to land back in such lousy weather conditions.'

Later Lloyd acted more as a wise father and friend than as an

AOC. Lowly ground crew were equally inspired by him, just as lowly submariners were inspired by the human touches of Captain Simpson. One ground crew man has put it in these terms:

> The whole of Malta's efforts were utterly dedicated to being a major thorn in Rommel's foot. The pinnacle of this defiance was one man: Air Vice-Marshal Hugh P. Lloyd, a magnificent Welshman. His memoirs of Malta are, in my view, the best of all literature dealing with this place at this time. His title *Briefed to Attack* is an accurate reflection of the spirit of the man and the way he communicated to all his troops. Not for him the safe deep underground HQ; more often than not he would appear in his car, amidst the virtually incessant attacks, popping up in all sorts of places . . . he was essentially the man for the hour.

At the other end of the scale, no one thought more highly of the AOC Malta than the calm, thoughtful AOC Middle East, Air Marshal (Sir) Arthur Tedder, Hugh Pughe Lloyd's superior in Cairo. Tedder had every reason to be angry at Lloyd's constant waylaying of aircraft destined for Tedder's own Desert Air Force but, with remarkable tolerance and intelligence, he understood the problems which his underling in Malta was daily having to face. Far from being put out by the AOC Malta, his admiration for his fighting qualities was such that, when it became obvious that Major General Dobbie, the Governor of Malta, had to be replaced, he opposed General Auchinleck's amazing suggestion that Air Vice Marshal Lloyd be appointed as Governor and Commander-in-Chief in Malta only on the grounds that Lloyd's energies should not be diverted to civil administration matters. As he wrote in his book *With Prejudice*: 'The air was the key to Malta. All Lloyd's attention was needed for the battle. Lloyd, if he became that Governor, would be obliged to leave much of the air operations to sub-ordinates.' Of Lloyd himself Tedder wrote: 'His personal bravery and dynamic energy have widespread effect and, more than anyone else, he is the personification of Malta. To see the morale of RAF personnel is one of the most stimulating experiences I have ever met.'

Throughout January 1942, 40 Squadron kept up its nuisance raids on enemy ports, despite atrocious weather. In between these raids on Tripoli, Catania and Paltermo, it was deployed to attack the coastal road east of Tripoli, with instructions to knock out anything that moved. The gunners in particular enjoyed these operations,

and up to an hour was spent over the road, both bombing and strafing, Mediterranean moonlight providing near daylight conditions
for these exciting low-level sorties. The aircraft's designers would
have been astonished to learn that their heavy bomber was being
used at night on low-level strafing operations.

Landing back at Luqa could be a problem, even without the assistance of the Luftwaffe. As one pilot has described it,

> As we came in, my rear-gunner who had spotted a Ju 88 on our tail called
> out, 'The bugger's right behind you: coming in right behind you!' We
> were 20 feet off the ground when they switched off the flare path, leaving
> us to touch down in the dark. I swung off the runway just as the Ju 88
> dropped a stick of bombs right the way down the runway. The crew and
> I spent the next hour in a goat cave.

During that month, according to Gunby, over fifty aircraft were
lost on the ground. But for the flow of transit aircraft which had to
land to refuel at Luqa, and were retained in Malta, there would have
been almost none of any type on the island before the major
Luftwaffe blitz, which began on 20 March 1942.

40 Squadron flew its last raid of this visit from Malta on 14
February 1942. It was typical of the conditions that the crew of the
last aircraft to depart that night had twice to dive for shelter prior
to take-off, while awaiting a period when Luqa was not under
attack, and that, on their return, they had to land during yet another
raid. They were envious of the ability of the submarines to sub-
merge so as to remain unseen during daylight hours. Even next day,
when some aircraft of 40 Squadron were already leaving for the
Middle East, one Wellington with engines running received a direct
hit resulting in several casualties.

The difficulties of trying to operate out of Malta during April
1942, at the height of the blitz, are well described by Stan
Thorogood. He writes:

> My next visit to Malta was on 20 April 1942 when a detachment of eight
> aircraft and fourteen crews of 148 Squadron flew in to Luqa from Kabrit,
> Egypt. We arrived about 5 in the morning to be greeted with 'get out of
> the aircraft as quick as you can, an air raid is about to start.' I, and the
> rest of the crew, grabbed a bag and were led to a nearby shelter. On our
> way I noted that Luqa and the airfield had been badly hit, the runway
> was a mass of filled-in bomb holes and every building had been hit, or

was damaged, from a near-miss. After the raid, we went back to our air-craft [which had been reduced to] burnt-out engines and a few puddles of aluminium and our kit had gone with it. After this, we went to our billet at Naxxar where we learnt that the [first delivery of] Spitfires from the USS *Wasp* had been virtually wiped out having been caught as they landed, virtually out of fuel.

My crew was immediately allocated another aircraft for operating that night. We were to do two or three operations under the cover of dark-ness but, when we went back to the airfield, our craft had [again] been destroyed. The same thing happened the next day. We had better luck on 23 April. The unit was down to three aircraft and our first target was Comiso airfield in Sicily. We evaded the enemy fighter-bombers circling Luqa and went straight to our target. This was bombed but we were immediately hit in our open bomb-bay by an AA shell causing consid-erable damage to the aircraft but no casualties. This precluded our observation of the bombing. On landing back at Luqa, we cut the engines for fear of fire from our leaking petrol tanks and pushed the air-craft off the runway to allow the other aircraft to land. Their crews informed us that we had destroyed about thirty enemy aircraft. The two other crews operated again that night. The target was Palermo. One air-craft was shot down over the target and my crew were elected to take the one remaining aircraft back to Egypt.

It was six days that Stan Thorogood is unlikely to forget.

Flight Sergeant Reg Thackeray was a pilot of 40 Squadron when it returned to Malta in October 1942. Conditions had changed. The RAF, which by the end of October 1942 had received in all 367 Spitfires* at various times, mainly from the flight decks of the car-riers *Eagle* and *Furious*, was now well defended. On the other hand, the food situation had worsened. Although nine supply ships had been sunk *en route*, five others of Operation Pedestal had reached the island in August 1942. They were far too few and, by then, the ground crews and AA gunners, who had no way of leaving the island, were already half starved. They had been on short rations for a year or longer. On average, they had lost between two or three stones in weight and the complete lack of petrol for non-essential duties, coupled with the need for the ground crews to live away from the targeted airfields, meant that the airmen had to walk

---

* Of the 385 despatched, including the 94 earlier flown off USS *Wasp*.

considerable distances on near empty stomachs twice a day in addition to their long hours of daily duties at the airfields.

40 Squadron had soon been disbanded after its sad remnants had been flown to Egypt in February 1942 but, with a full complement of twenty new aircraft, the squadron had later been re-formed there. This time they operated the earlier, lower-powered Wellington Ic aircraft with Bristol Pegasus engines as this type of engine was regarded as being better suited to withstand the sand and dust of the desert than was the Rolls-Royce Merlin engine.

40 Squadron flew back to Malta in two Flights, with about a month's interval in between. Flight Sergeant Thackeray, who had only just been promoted to command and had been assigned his first ever crew, was part of the second Flight. He writes: 'We were delighted to meet up with our "other half" but we were staggered at their appearances – non-stop operations and the starvation diet had wreaked havoc. We were to learn all about it very soon.' Their other half had been in Malta a bare three weeks.

Unlike Bomber Command when operating over Germany, the crews did not use oxygen and generally operated at just over 10,000 feet; but Sfax, a south Tunisian port, was once bombed by Reg Thackeray from only 6,000 feet.

On a few occasions, double sorties were flown, with the aircraft being refuelled and rearmed close to the runway. Reg Thackeray comments upon the joy of being 'rewarded' for a successful operation with a piece of chocolate. On double operations, crews were rewarded between sorties with a sandwich and a cup of coffee. Any extra allowance on the sparse food ration was a bonus to be savoured, although a few cafés still managed to operate in Valletta where Reg remembers once enjoying, in a much damaged one, a solitary sardine on toast. As was inevitable with such acute shortages, a black market sprang up. This was almost encouraged by the AOC in the knowledge that the Maltese favoured his aircrews.

Wellington opposition varied. On a raid of the airfield at Trapani near Palermo, the enemy AA gunners were disturbingly accurate and, after sighting some black puffs in the sky and experiencing the always disturbing smell of enemy cordite inside the aircraft as shells exploded nearby, the aircraft was dived at over 300 m.p.h. (above twice its normal cruising speed) to escape further near-misses.

However, in general, ack-ack fire was not accurate. More feared were German night-fighter aircraft. Reg Thackeray was lucky in that he only once caught sight of a German night-fighter; others saw them more often. They gave away their presence by having a dull red light permanently glowing in their nose, thought to be either part of their radar or an infra-red tracking device.

Bomber crews, with little to fear over most targets, did their best to bomb accurately. In one raid on La Goulette – the port near Tunis – Thackeray made three runs in order to distribute his bomb load between the electricity generator station, the oil tanks and finally an estimated 2,000-ton ship which was also hit.* Explosions from the ship were seen by the rear-gunner when forty miles away. Bombs, like everything else in Malta, were never in plentiful supply.

Both aircraft and aircrew suffered in besieged Malta. The lack of spare parts, the inclement weather (no aircraft in Malta ever saw the inside of a hangar after the 1940 bombing of the airfields), the overworked, underfed ground crews, all combined to make it a Herculean task to keep aircraft serviceable.

Before Thackeray arrived, 40 Squadron had played a helping role during Operation Torch – the Anglo-American invasion of French North-west Africa which had commenced early in November 1942. They had attacked targets in Tunis and Bizerta, the Tunisian ports through which the Germans were bringing in troops, tanks and other supplies in an effort to counter the Allied forces which had landed in Algiers, Oran and other places farther west with the object of seizing Tunisia, as well as Algeria. In a period of intensive operations against these new targets, the squadron had already lost two aircraft and crews.

Flight Sergeant Thackeray's baptism in operations from Malta – indeed his first ever sortie in command of his aircrew – began the night after he arrived there when on 27 November 1942 he was detailed for a double sortie† to bomb the Bizerta docks. He carried eight 500-pound bombs and sixteen 250-pounders. The target was duly located and the bombs dropped, causing fires which the crew could still see fifteen minutes later on their way back to Luqa. As a

---

* It may have been the *St Fernand* or the *St Bernadette*.
† He was to fly to the target, return, refuel and take off to bomb the same target again.

flat battery had delayed their departure by ninety minutes, their second sortie was cancelled.

In late 1942, 40 Squadron was carrying out the same kind of operations as it had earlier, except that the principal African targets were now in Tunisia and not in Tripolitania or Libya. Tripoli was soon to fall to the victorious Eighth Army early in January 1943. Thereafter the main Allied objective was to seize Tunisia before the Germans could react and before winter arrived. Raids upon Sicilian airfields and the port of Palermo were also carried out, much as they had been in 1941.

Before Reg Thackeray departed from Malta he and his crew, usually in their 'own' aircraft L (for Leather), had attacked Sicily seven times and Tunisia twelve times; they had also raided Tripoli three times before that vital enemy port fell, at long last, to General Montgomery and the victorious Eighth Army.

Winter weather – bad but not as severe as that of the previous winter – at times prevented the targets from being seen and although, in all, the crew dropped 73,330 pounds of bombs, they brought back over 11,000 pounds. Bombing by 40 Squadron was never indiscriminate; and since bombs, like everything else in Malta, were known to be in short supply, if a target could not be identified or if clouds obscured it, a return with the bombs was then made.

The lack of food, poor hygiene – the aircrews were again housed in unbombed parts of the huge unlit and unheated Poor House* – the inevitable 'Malta Dog' (a local version of 'Gippy Tum'), diarrhoea and sand-fly fever, all took their toll. During his twenty-two operational trips, Reg found himself crewed with no less than seven different second pilots, three navigators, two wireless operators and eight different gunners, although the policy was to keep to a standard crew. It was hardly a formula for success but he appears to have taken it in his stride and only once failed to reach the area of his objective. The one occasion when he had to turn back as the result of a defective hydraulic system gave him his worst half-hour in the air, before he was able to land with near full tanks and bomb load intact. This was no mean feat since maximum-weight landings

---

* On arrival there Reg and his crew were allocated a cold area of bare concrete. 'That is your quarters,' they were told.

are never practised in training. Maximum permissible landing-weight was officially many tons less than maximum take-off weight.

In Egypt and the UK, before departing for a night sortie an aircraft was always given a short air-test to check that its systems were operating; those not functioning were replaced or repaired. But, although the RAF had gained air superiority over Malta, there were still daily air raids which, along with an urgent need to preserve petrol, ruled out this sensible measure. Petrol indeed became so short that aircraft were manhandled to a take-off position and man-handled back to their place after landing, so as to avoid wasting fuel taxiing.

History repeated itself when, on a planned double raid on a Tunisian target with several aircraft lined up for rapid refuelling, a heavy night raid on Luqa occurred. Reg Thackeray writes: 'All ground and air crew scattered. I spent several hours in a deep slit trench and was glad to be told, at the "all clear", that the second trip had been scrubbed.' Although there were no casualties, all the aircraft were damaged by bomb splinters and one was a total write-off.

A personal blow to Reg and his crew was that, when the crew returned to their aircraft, most of their kit was missing. In a half-starved island it was folly to leave anything unguarded and it was widely known that, apart from scarce personal items, crews carried a few sandwiches and drinks on their flights as well as possessions which could later be exchanged for food on the black market.* Reg recalls that, with bad weather cancelling all operations over the Christmas period, his treat for Christmas lunch was half a tin of stewed steak from the USA, not the usual thin and monotonous Maconochies M&V stew.† He was told that he could have the other half as a treat on New Year's Day.

Apart from the flak around Tunis, which the Germans were then protecting fiercely, post-Christmas hazards in the air were com-pounded by hail, sleet, icing (the island lacked all aircraft de-icing and anti-icing ingredients) and wet clinging clouds. 'To think',

---

* A single small egg cost 2s 6d (about £5, or more, in 1996 currency).

† This was served so often that, when one pilot returned to the UK and met his girl friend again, his proposal of marriage included the caveat that she was never to serve him this stew.

muses Reg Thackeray, a wartime volunteer, 'that the year before, I was trying to balance ledgers at a small Branch Bank in Yorkshire.'

When Montgomery began to advance northwards from Tripolitania into Tunisia, in early 1943, Wellington bombing attacks were shifted to a specific major road junction regarded as essential to the Axis armies opposing him. 'The first stick [of bombs] put across the road raised smoke and dust and a second stick put the last bomb right in the centre of the crossroads,' writes Thackeray.

Losses of Wellington bombers on raids were few but nevertheless mounted up. On this crossroads operation by Wellingtons, for example, one had to ditch on the way home, although the efficient Malta Air–Sea Rescue boats and crews saved its crew, as they saved many others, Allied, German and Italian.

Flight Sergeant Thackeray's last trip from Malta was on 19 January 1943 and, although his starboard engine was faulty and leaking oil, he found that he could coax some power from it. Perhaps rashly, he pressed on regardless, successfully bombed his road target and set course back to Malta after having made all necessary preparations for an emergency ditching. However, they just scraped home safely.

On the way back with his crew to the relative safety of the Middle East, his port engine failed, but again this cool and determined pilot managed a safe emergency landing at El Adem airfield, near Tobruk. The citation for the DFM which was awarded to Flight Sergeant (soon to become Pilot Officer) Thackeray for his Malta offensive operations says much about him: 'He has behaved with cool determination, continuing his search for targets until satisfied that the correct objective has been reached . . . Throughout all his operations, Flight Sergeant Thackeray has displayed great determination and courage.' Much the same could be said for other pilots and crew members of all the Wellington squadrons which operated from Malta. Although their work lacked the glamour associated with fighter and torpedo aircraft it made an indispensable contribution to Malta's war effort.

A similar tale could have been recorded about all the Wellington bomber squadrons which came and went at Luqa during hostilities. All did valiant work in aircraft which, for the most part, were being flown by pre-war bank clerks, school teachers, garage hands and even men who were only schoolboys when war broke out in September 1939.

All praise must also be given to the harassed ground crews who daily, in the face of every privation, had to perform near-miracles of improvisation to keep the aircraft flying. Though many, both in the air and on the ground, perished in the effort, their work, too, was indispensable.

The nightly Wellington bomber raids on enemy ports, whether situated in Libya, Tripolitania, Sicily, Italy, Sardinia or Tunisia, struck many deadly blows upon the enemy. Obviously, if ships were hit and sunk, then a prime Allied objective was achieved.* Likewise, many ships were damaged but not sunk by bombs. Even if ships were not hit, the damage caused to harbour and wharf installations could be almost as devastating. As was seen in Malta during the period when the island's harbours were being constantly raided, the loss of cranes, warehouses, oil storage tanks, damage to wharfs and floating docks, the destruction of lighters and barges, could all combine to reduce a harbour's unloading capacity to near zero.†

It has to be remembered that, in all that 2,000 mile-long North African coast, there were no minerals or any major industrial facilities to which the Axis powers could have recourse. If a derrick, lorry, steel girder, tin roof, bollard or even a heavy nut and bolt was destroyed by a near-miss upon a docked ship, their replacements would have to be brought by sea, or air, from Italy.

Even if all the bombs fell in harbours hitting nothing, the very duration of night nuisance raids – and they were deliberately kept long – meant that unloading would be suspended until an all-clear could be sounded. If night unloading could be suspended, then the enemy's slender shipping capacity would be further reduced, just as it was dramatically reduced by the presence of air and naval strike-forces in Malta, which by December 1941 had compelled the enemy to re-route supply ships – and to make night stops *en route* – down the Greek coast, rather than risk the direct shorter passage

---

* See Appendices II and V for details of sinkings.
† If the merchant ships *Talabot* and *Pampas* which arrived safely in Malta on 23 March 1942 could have been rapidly unloaded, Malta's plight later that year would have been far less worrying. As it was, both were sunk by bombers in Grand Harbour three days after arrival, still largely unloaded.

down the Tunisian coast from Naples or Palermo to Tripoli. The lack of ship repair facilities in North African ports further complicated life for the enemy; ships which were hit but repairable were often sent from there under tow, as far away as Naples.

Another devastating drain upon the enemy's resources, caused by the many attacks launched on their convoys *en route* to Africa, was the ever-increasing numbers of escort vessels which were deemed necessary to protect those convoys. Originally, a convoy of (say) three or four supply ships would be escorted by a single destroyer and perhaps a torpedo-boat. As the enemy losses at sea mounted, so also did the number of escorts increase until, by late 1942, it was common to find two or more escorts for each merchant vessel of a convoy. These escorts used up oil, and oil was a commodity Italy, for one, badly lacked and for which the Italian Navy remained largely dependent upon the variable supplies allotted by her German ally.

The fact that, after mid-1942, the Italian Navy made no major forays into the Mediterranean was, as we now know, mainly because Hitler – never Navy-minded – denied Mussolini the oil required to do so. What allocation of oil was made available for the Italian Navy, was, after 1941, consumed at an increasingly rapid rate by the destroyers and torpedo-boats that were deployed, in large numbers, around the supply ships that were endeavouring to find a way past Malta. As is recorded in the next chapter, there were instances where a single tanker was protected by six Italian Navy vessels.

Even the enemy's tactic of breaking up the journey by laying up ships for a night at ports such as Argostoli in Cephalonia, further reduced the enemy's already slender sea supply resources. The extra day in port meant, in effect, less shipping available. As strategists on both sides, including Rommel, had come to realize, the side which would win the Desert War would be the one which could better supply its army, in that arid unproductive desert battleground.

9

The RAF Steps In

June–September 1942

'The torpedoing of the tanker *Pozerica* on 23 August
reduced all three Italian Corps to such serious straits
that they were compelled to borrow petrol from their
ally.'

> Ralph Bennett, *Ultra and Mediterranean Strategy,*
> *1941–1945* (1989)

AFTER 10 MAY 1942 – the day when the Spitfires from the carriers
USS *Wasp* and *Eagle* routed the Luftwaffe and Regia Aeronautica,
and so regained air superiority over Malta – a paradoxical situation
ensued. For the first time for months, the island was relatively free
from non-stop bombing and impudent patrolling by low-flying
Messerschmitt fighters but it lacked the weapons with which to
strike back. Virtually all bomber aircraft had been removed. Force K
had long ago ceased to function and even the submarines of the
Tenth Flotilla had been forced to beat a retreat to safer harbours in
the Middle East.

The intense bombing campaign during March and April by
Kesselring's Luftwaffe had paid off. The island had almost ceased
to be a threat to Rommel's supply life-line. Convoys from Italy to
North Africa steamed past unobstructed. Scarcely a single ship had
been sunk for months by anything emanating from Malta; the only
score had been made by Peter Rothwell, who had taken over the
SDF. On the night of 5 June, his bomb-carrying Wellington hit a ship
which may have been the *Reginaldo Giuliani*, estimated at 5,000 tons.
The island for once was not justifying its existence.

Kesselring had reported that there was nothing in Malta left to bomb, that he had successfully neutralized the island. As a result, the huge German air corps which had been based in Sicily was largely dispersed to Middle East bases. By the end of May, Luftwaffe forces in Sicily were down to 13 serviceable long-range reconnaissance aircraft, 30 Me 109s, 6 Me 110s, and 34 bombers: a total of 83 compared with the 410 of two months earlier.

The Desert War itself hung in the balance. Rommel had been halted at the Gazala line and both sides were preparing to renew the battle. Rommel was building up supplies and was eager to advance before the effects of American aid could benefit the British. Correctly calculating that the Eighth Army would not be in a position to attack until September, he was determined to strike first. With Malta temporarily 'out of business' Rommel now held most of the aces. He also had the full services of the Luftwaffe forces in the Mediterranean now that they were no longer required to bomb Malta.

By 27 May, the German general was on the move. After some probing of the Allies' defences and securing, after a heroic fight by some gallant French troops, the desert outpost of Bir Hackeim, he pushed north from that area and, by 20 June, had taken Tobruk. This was a serious blow to the Eighth Army as, for the first time, Rommel now had a port reasonably close to the battle front-line.

Tobruk was not a big port but it could provide many of the supplies which had hitherto been moved forward laboriously from Benghazi, many hundreds of miles behind his Gazala position. By capturing the port in a swift attack, the enemy had also gained the bonus of British supplies which the Allies had been too slow to destroy.

It was at this critical juncture of the Desert War that RAF Bristol Beaufort twin-engined torpedo-bombers first appeared in Malta, albeit only on a temporary assignment. The purpose which brought 217 Squadron with their Beauforts in to Malta was the desperate need to bring supplies to the besieged island.

By June 1942, Malta had all but run out of essential commodities. In an attempt to replenish the island, it was decided to run two convoys to Malta simultaneously. One convoy, code-named Operation Vigorous, would come from Egypt: it would comprise eleven merchant ships defended by almost everything that the

Navy could muster in Alexandria. The other, code-named Operation Harpoon, would depart from Gibralter and consist of six supply ships. It was intended, by this means, to split the Italian naval defences. If they went for one, then the other might escape attention.

This concern over the Italian fleet was very real. Although Admiral Sir Andrew Cunningham had consistently drubbed the Italian Navy in sea battles, the situation had changed dramatically since 19 December 1941, when Italian frogmen had seriously immobilized the British battleships *Queen Elizabeth* and *Valiant*, at anchor in Alexandria harbour. By now, the big new Italian battleship *Littorio* had also been repaired and, along with her sister ship *Vittorio Venuto*, was ready for sea again. Both were about 40,000 tons, fast and modern. Against these, the British could only raise cruisers, although they tried to bluff the enemy by including, among the escorts for Operation Vigorous, the ancient monitor *Centurion*, disguised as a battleship. On top of the naval disaster at Alexandria, in the course of November 1941 German U-boats in the Mediterranean had sunk both the aircraft-carrier *Ark Royal* and the battleship *Barham*.

In order to counter the probable intervention of the Italian battlefleet against Operation Vigorous, it had been decided to fly 217 Beaufort Squadron from the UK to Malta. Though destined ultimately for Ceylon (now Sri Lanka) to assist in defending that island from attack by the Japanese fleet, it had orders to remain in Malta until Operation Vigorous was completed. Its role was to attack the Italian battlefleet as soon as it was seen to have left Taranto and be heading for the ships of Operation Vigorous. Petrol for the Beauforts had been brought to the island at great hazard by submarines acting as cargo carriers – the so called 'Magic Carpet Supply Service'.

However, this was only half the Beaufort story. The other half concerned a far-sighted young Squadron Leader, Patrick Gibbs. This pre-war Regular officer was experiencing a frustrating war. Although a pilot of 22 Squadron, which was one of the first RAF Beaufort squadrons, he had spent a long period in hospital during 1941, recovering from injuries sustained in a serious aircraft accident. After being passed fit, he found himself incarcerated in a Group HQ office, far removed from squadron operations. A person with firm ideas about how torpedo-bombers should be used, he aired these views vociferously although they were at variance with official policy. It did not make him popular at his Group HQ.

Partly to get him off their backs, the RAF in London had posted this outspoken Irishman early in 1942 to RAF Middle East Command HQ in Cairo, with a verbal assurance that he would see plenty of action there. However, with nothing in writing, Patrick Gibbs found himself in a top-heavy Command headquarters, holding down an office job with scarcely anything to do.

However, Gibbs' experience in Middle East Command, with access to Army and Navy Staffs, did afford him the opportunity to make himself fully conversant with the military situation in the Mediterranean. He soon started to agitate to be sent to an operational squadron, and was again airing his views about how Beauforts could best be used.

In Egypt there was one Beaufort squadron, 39 Squadron, which had been formed there. However, it was seeing little action and it had no vacancies for one of Squadron Leader Patrick Gibbs' relatively high seniority. Torpedo squadrons have only rare spasmodic bursts of activity. They were held at readiness in case enemy targets worth attacking should appear within their range. With losses on low-level daylight torpedo attacks liable to be as high as one in three, only worthwhile targets could justify such risks.

Eventually, in April 1942, 39 Squadron found a worthwhile target within its range of action and duly attacked. Not surprisingly, it lost a Flight Commander during this attack, and this opened the way for Squadron Leader Gibbs' request to be granted. By June, he was well established with this unit and had been able to bring his flying, long out of practice, up to the high standards which he set himself and others. His determination overcame considerable personal physical problems. He was never of robust constitution and the heat, along with the monotonous rations which he could seldom keep down, sapped his strength but never his resolve.

The running of the two June convoys, Operations Vigorous and Harpoon, to Malta had become a focal point for the RAF as well as for the Navy. Priorities in Egypt were being given to defending Operation Vigorous, although by then Rommel was pressing his advance rapidly beyond Gazala, had already taken Bir Hackeim and was well on his way to Tobruk.

Ultra intercepts confirmed that the main Italian battlefleet was expected to sally forth to tackle Operation Vigorous as soon as that convoy had passed through the notorious Ju 87 and Ju 88 Bomb Alley between Crete, where the Luftwaffe kept their most formidable dive-bombers, and North Africa. The enemy knew how desperate Malta was for supplies and meant to ensure that none should reach her. With the Luftwaffe strength in the Bomb Alley area now more than doubled by the additions from Sicily, the prospects were grim.

To oppose them it was decided that, as soon as there was positive information that the Italian fleet was at sea and was heading south, the Beauforts of 39 Squadron in North Africa would fly northwards to attack it. In order to get in this attack before the enemy big ships reached a point of interception with the convoy, the plan was for the Beauforts to take off from the most forward westerly RAF landing ground available – Bir Amud – locate the enemy, attack it and then carry on to land at Luqa, Malta.

To protect the 39 Squadron torpedo-bombers, it was also arranged for some long-range fighter Beaufighters to accompany them to a point where, it was hoped, they would be beyond the range of the enemy Me 109s and Macchi 202 fighters based near Gazala.

In the event, the Beaufighters were diverted to oppose the rapidly advancing Rommel and were not available to 39 Squadron. To make matters worse, the squadron's torpedo-carrying Beauforts ran into a horde of enemy fighters and, long before they could start the hunt for the Italian fleet, their numbers had been reduced from twelve to five.

Although the odds were very long against success, the five continued ahead. The Squadron Commander now led three aircraft and Patrick Gibbs the other two. By excellent navigation they intercepted the *Littorio*, the other battleship *Vittorio Venuto*, and their destroyer escorts. Flying through a hail of flak, they carried out their torpedo attacks. Every aircraft was hit but, although they dropped their torpedoes and seemed to have scored a hit on the *Littorio*, postwar records show otherwise.

Miraculously, every one of the five Beauforts, although damaged, survived the attack. Some also had wounded men on board. Equally miraculously, they all managed to reach Malta although at least two, including Gibbs, had to crash-land. Crash-landings were, by then, so commonplace in Malta that the first words which the exhausted Squadron Leader Gibbs heard, upon stepping out of the remains of his aircraft on the runway, were the admonition: 'We usually do this sort of thing *off* the runway!' It had been a nerve-racking experience. He had survived the Me 109s; he had survived the murderous flak; he thought he had torpedoed a battleship; his aircraft had been seriously damaged and he had crash-landed in a strange island. Although a non-smoker, he took to smoking cigarette after cigarette during the debriefing.

On Malta Patrick Gibbs now found himself in a unique RAF Command. Airmen and officers wore all sorts of battered uniforms. There were soldiers all over the airfield. There was no spit or polish. Pay and other parades had long ago ceased. Everyone pitched in to help everyone else. Ranks barely existed but a wonderful spirit dominated everything in what had become a do-it-yourself Air Force which operated according to its own set of rules. When the exhausted crewmen, hungry and in desperate need of a strong drink, looked for something to satisfy them, all that was available was one slice of bully beef, on what appeared to be a dog biscuit – and no strong drink at all. The crews now saw for themselves why it was deemed vital to replenish Malta.

Although Patrick Gibbs was only in Malta for two days, and was in need of a rest before being flown back to Egypt in a passing airliner, he had discovered that there were persons in authority on the island who were receptive to original ideas. To his astonishment, the weary Gibbs soon found himself expressing his long-felt and well-considered ideas to no less a person than the AOC Malta – the remarkable Air Vice-Marshal Hugh Pughe Lloyd. After so many months of frustration, Patrick Gibbs poured out his heart. He explained how he saw the War in the Desert: how success or failure depended on which side could be best supplied; how he felt that Malta held the strategic key to the situation, and how Beauforts, properly used, could help turn that key. He explained the potential and limitations of the Beauforts and stressed that, in his opinion, they could be better used from Malta than from Egyptian bases.

Squadron Leader Gibbs was, of course, preaching to the converted. Hugh Pughe Lloyd held exactly the same views but it was music to his ears to listen to the enthusiastic young officer before him.

The AOC acted with his accustomed speed of decision. He at once sent a signal to Air Marshal Arthur Tedder in Cairo to request that what remained of 39 Squadron should henceforth be based in Malta. He also decided to retain 217 Squadron, the other Beaufort squadron, and soon had the backing, once again, of his splendid AOC Middle East. London, sometime later, also concurred. Hugh Pughe Lloyd also sent Gibbs back to Cairo that same night, in order to help persuade those in Command HQ there of the merits of these suggestions – a task which Gibbs proceeded to do with his usual eloquence and determination.

Within a week, 39 Squadron, although possessing only about six fully restored aircraft, flew back to Malta with the approval of all in Cairo. Rommel in his rapid progress eastwards had already overrun the advanced landing grounds which had been available to the RAF in the desert, thereby putting Benghazi and other ports far beyond the range of Beauforts operating from Egypt. If enemy convoys to Benghazi had to be stopped by Beauforts, only Malta-based ones could now do the job.

By then the crisis which had centred around Operation Vigorous was over. Sadly, the Axis had won hands down. Although the Italian battlefleet, for a number of obscure reasons, turned back before intercepting Operation Vigorous, the Luftwaffe by itself had already won the day.

Bomb Alley had proved to be a nightmare for the convoy. Although only two of the eleven merchant ships were sunk, the escorting warships had fared badly. The cruiser *Hermione* was sunk, and three other cruisers, a corvette and another merchant ship were damaged. The final decision to turn back to Alexandria evoked some acid comments, in view of the known retreat to Taranto of the Italian battlefleet, but given that the escorts had already expended nearly all their AA ammunition though less than half the journey had been accomplished, it would have been foolish to go on. Even the phoney British battleship *Centurion* had been hit.

With *Vigorous* turning back, Malta would have been lost had not Operation Harpoon persevered. Although this Gibraltar–Malta convoy lost four of its six ships, it struggled on gallantly and, to the wild cheering of the inhabitants who surrounded Grand Harbour, the merchant ships *Orari* and *Troilus* landed nearly 25,000 tons of supplies.* These, it was reckoned, would be enough, with strict rationing, to keep Malta in business for another two months. Malta's siege had not been lifted. Its inhabitants had been granted only a stay of execution.

Even before Patrick Gibbs and the reconstituted 39 Squadron flew its Beauforts back to Malta, 217 Squadron was fast justifying the decision to allow it, first to tarry, then to remain, in Malta. Part of the Italian battlefleet which had sailed south from Taranto to intercept Operation Vigorous was a force of big 10,000-ton 8-inch gun cruisers, which were maintaining station a few miles ahead of the big battle wagons. The whole fleet had been detected at sea and was being shadowed by Malta's ever-vigilant 69 Reconnaissance Squadron.[†]

A torpedo-strike by the Beauforts of 217 Squadron had at once been laid on. This required a pre-dawn take-off in order to strike at first light. The principal targets were the same battleships *Littorio* and *Vittorio Venuto* which 39 Squadron, later that day, tried to torpedo from its North African advanced landing ground. The concept for all RAF torpedo attacks from the air was that the aircraft should attack *en masse* and from many different directions, endeavouring to get round their target so as to come in from every point of the compass. If a ship then happened to detect the tell-tale line of bubbles from a running torpedo, as was often the case, it would, in turning to 'feather' the torpedo tracks, expose itself to one running in from a different direction. Under the stress and mayhem of withering fire, it generally took several torpedoes to secure a hit. There was, it was reckoned, strength in numbers.

By one of those strange but fortunate quirks which often seem to happen in wartime, one of the Beauforts was delayed in taking off. It also happened to be the one flown by 217 Squadron's most experienced torpedo pilot, Flying Officer Arthur Aldridge, a pilot who had once dropped a torpedo at the German battleship *Gneisenau* –

---

* Although at first they cheered, when the inhabitants realized that only two of the six ships were entering, the thousands lining the harbour entrance spontaneously bared their heads in silent tribute.

† To be more accurate, their presence at sea, already known to the Allies via Ultra intercepts, was being confirmed by 69 Squadron.

and lived to tell the tale. That experience was now about to stand him in good stead.

The taxi-track between Arthur Aldridge's distant pen and the runway was blocked by another aircraft. Obliged to take off about fifteen minutes after the main force, Arthur realized that he could not hope to catch up. Instead of proceeding to the agreed point from which the others hoped to find the Italian ships by flying behind and then along their expected track, he proceeded direct to where he considered the enemy battlefleet might be. After a long flight over the sea, he came upon the advanced cruiser section of the Italian battlefleet as dawn was about to break.

It was to his advantage that 217 Squadron's Beauforts were the first to operate in that part of the Mediterranean and that the enemy sailors had never before seen their silhouette: to the uninitiated, the Beaufort bore a vague resemblance to the well-known German Ju 88, a type which often escorted enemy convoys at sea. Both types are similar in size; both have two engines and one tail. It was also to Aldridge's advantage that he was coming from out of the dark part of the night sky and flying into the rising sun.

With no AA fire from the cruiser force, Flying Officer Aldridge flew calmly past and ahead of the big ships, weighing up what to do next. Some of his crew members advocated delaying any solo attack, as mass attacks were both customary and, in this case, had been planned. However, Arthur had other ideas. It impressed him that he had not been fired upon. This meant either that he had not been seen in the half light of dawn or that he had been mistaken for a German aircraft which had come out at first light to patrol around the Italian warships.

Meanwhile he had circled back so that he was largely hidden again in the dark part of the western sky, while also being ideally placed for a torpedo run from the good 45-degree bow position ahead of the cruiser force. It all seemed too good an opportunity to miss. With the experience of attacking the *Gneisenau*, which was similar in length to this cruiser (the 10,000-ton 8-inch gun *Trento*), Arthur Aldridge released his 'tin-fish' at almost exactly the correct range of about 800 yards. By then, he had made sure that his height was right (80 feet), that his air speed was correct (140 knots), that he was flying on a straight track with wings held rock-steady so as not to induce any unwanted spin or bias upon the falling torpedo. By all the rules of the game, the torpedo had to hit. And it did.*

If was only after the torpedo was well on its way to its deadly strike that the Italians woke up to the fact that they were being attacked. By then, the Beaufort had flashed past the destroyer *Geniere* which was guarding the cruisers on *Trento*'s starboard bow. The aircraft passed so close that the gunner in the rear turret later claimed: 'I could have dropped a bottle onto its deck.'

When enemy fire finally commenced, Aldridge, directed by his navigator who had a good rearwards view, successfully avoided it by making skidding turns low down on the water, taking care never to expose his aircraft's silhouette by climbing high. On his way to safety, the Beaufort also had to fly close to the destroyer on the other wing, the *Aviere*.

Before long, the exclamation he most wanted to hear came from an ecstatic Bill Carroll in the rear turret, who alone had a good view of the cruiser, now well behind the aircraft. 'You hit it! We got it! You've blown her ruddy bows off!!!' It was a slight exaggeration but it was music to the ears of the rest of the crew. The *Trento* was stopped with smoke billowing from her bows: she was clearly on fire. But it was not that which was soon to astound the rear-gunner. The main Italian battlefleet had caught up and, in a bewildering series of manoeuvres, they all began to open fire – apparently, as Carroll saw it, at one another.

What had happened was that the main Beaufort formation, probably brought to the area by the sight of the *Trento*'s smoke and/or the belated tracer-fire from her Italian destroyers, had located the Italians, who were now in one vaguely homogeneous group. The Beauforts had then launched their torpedoes, according to their briefing, from several different directions, having first split up to do so.

The Italian ships – which now numbered twelve destroyers, the three remaining undamaged cruisers and the two huge battleships *Littorio* and *Vittorio Venuto* – were all violently altering course in

---

* The length of the Italian 8-inch gun cruisers was 635 feet; of the *Gneisenau* 727 feet. There was no torpedo-sight or aiming aid: Beaufort pilots had to drop their torpedoes by eye alone, using judgement to determine how far ahead of the moving ship they should aim, having first estimated the enemy's speed.

order to feather the torpedoes of the Beauforts running towards them. And while still turning in all directions, every ship was firing almost at random. In the half-light of morning they seemed to be uncertain whether they were being attacked from above as well as from sea level. Their AA fire was thus going upwards, as well as threatening their own ships when firing at sea level.

Bill Carroll was not the only spectator of this colourful display. One of the Malta-based U-class submarines was in the area: this was *P35* which had recently been given the name of *Umbra*. Commanded by Lieutenant Lynch Maydon, she had positioned herself astride the route which the Italian fleet was expected to take and had done so with great precision. In the report later submitted by Lynch Maydon, he wrote:

> 0611 hours. Aircraft started bombing attack [apparently he too thought that bombs, and not torpedoes, were being dropped]. The confusion which ensued is very difficult to describe. *P35* was in the unenviable position of being in the centre of a fantastic circle of wildly careering capital ships, cruisers and destroyers, of bomb splashes, none of which, fortunately, came close, of tracer streaks and anti-aircraft bursts.
>
> At one period there was not a quadrant of the compass unoccupied by enemy vessels weaving continuously to and fro. It was only possible to count the big ships: destroyers seemed to be everywhere. It was essential to remain at periscope depth, for an opportunity to fire might come at any moment. One was, in fact, tempted to stand with periscope up and gaze in utter amazement.

Umbra, after first attempting to torpedo the battleships without success, then reloaded with torpedoes while observing the battleships disappearing southwards heading for their planned interception of the ships of Operation Vigorous and (unbeknown to them at that time) an attack by 39 Squadron Beauforts from Bir Amud, later that morning.

The *Trento*, however, remained an excellent stationary target, although she now had two destroyers alongside. They were busy taking off the casualties and endeavouring to put out the fire still raging in the cruiser's bow, while protecting the cruiser, as best they could, with a smokescreen. The chance of the *Trento* being saved and being nursed back to Taranto was still a distinct possibility.

The two destroyers soon caught the scent of *Umbra* and sought to attack her. However Lynch Maydon outwitted their best efforts and eventually, at 1006 hours – some four hours after Arthur Aldridge had crippled the big cruiser – he manoeuvred his submarine into a good firing position and sent the *Trento* rapidly to the bottom with some well-aimed torpedoes. The cruiser sank with many of her 723 men still on board, including her captain.

Umbra's commander then skilfully eluded the expected counter-attack with depth-charges and, like Aldridge's Bristol Beaufort which had first stopped the big ship, he returned safely to Malta none the worse for the encounter. Those privileged to have looked through her periscope had also been richly entertained by the enemy's early morning pyrotechnic displays.

The citation which accompanied Arthur Aldridge's well-deserved DFC reads: 'Flying Officer Aldridge has attacked shipping on several occasions and in spite of heavy anti-aircraft fire, he has achieved much success. During three attacks in June [1942] in the Mediterranean, he hit an enemy warship, an enemy ship which later sank and disabled another. On the last occasion, Flying Officer Aldridge defied an extremely heavy barrage.'

Although his attack on *Trento* of 15 June 1942 will go down as the first action by a Beaufort to stop a cruiser, it was not, perhaps, the most devastating blow which Flying Officer Aldridge delivered that month. Merchant ships were Malta's prime targets, and big German vessels especially so. It was known that German merchant ships were certain to be loaded with top-priority war material for Rommel in the Desert; by contrast, an Italian merchantman might be transporting commercial goods to satisfy the wants of the Italian civilian population in Tripoli or Benghazi. Considerable numbers of Italians had their homes in both these African ports and, like the officers of the Italian forces in general, they were still maintaining the standard of living to which they had become accustomed as Fascist colonial overlords.

To an astonishing degree, the two Axis allies were continuing to follow a completely independent course. In the opinion of Field Marshal Kesselring, the Italians had never dedicated their total energies towards the promotion of the war, as had the Germans. He had noted, for example, the big difference in the messing arrangements of their armies. Whereas the Germans – officers and men – were given much the same food from their efficient but basic field kitchens, the Italian officers ate and drank extremely well, whilst their humble soldiers fared far worse than their German brothers. Count Ciano had also noted this. With caustic wit he once observed that, owing to lack of oil, the Italian fleet was seldom able to leave port; had they done so, 'this might have meant less fuel for the taxis in Rome'.

Flying Officer Aldridge's second great achievement took place only a few days later, on 21 June 1942. From Ultra-gained information, backed up by aerial photo-reconnaissance sources, it was known that a convoy of two big merchant ships destined for Tripoli was attempting to steam past Malta to the west of the island, by the direct route close to the coast of Tunisia. Not for many months had this relatively short passage been attempted. The two ships were prime targets. One was the 7,744-ton German ship *Reichenfels* and the other a big Italian tanker, the *Rosolino Pilo* of 8,326 tons. Both were transporting vital cargoes. In addition to the fuel aboard the tanker, the *Reichenfels* was carrying vehicles and men for one of Rommel's Panzer divisions. The two vessels were accompanied by two destroyers and a torpedo-boat.

In order to give Malta as wide a berth as possible, the enemy convoy headed out west of Cape Bon before turning east to round the north-eastern corner of Tunisia and thence proceed southwards. This extra precaution failed to pay off as one of the destroyers, the *Starke*, ran itself aground near the small island of Zembra, west of Cape Bon. The torpedo-boat went to its aid. This left only the destroyer *Da Rocco* with the two merchantmen. However, the ships also had the protection of three Ju 88 fighter-bombers, an Italian SM 79 and a Cant flying-boat.

Nine Beauforts of 217 Squadron took off to attack, led by Squadron Leader Lynn in the usual three groups of three aircraft, with Arthur Aldridge heading the V formation on his leader's port side. AOC Hugh Pughe Lloyd had delivered one of his fighting pep-talks prior to their departure from Luqa. Although these talks inspired many of the crews – especially perhaps the raw recruits* –

---

* The AOC once put his arm around the author's shoulders and declared impressively, 'Spooner [pause] the fate of the British Empire tonight [pause] may well rest on your shoulders.' After this the author was prepared, if necessary, to dive-bomb his Wellington down the funnels of an enemy battleship. When Hugh Pughe Lloyd spoke, it was with a Churchillian ring.

they only filled the experienced Arthur Aldridge with a feeling akin to dread. He knew what he had to do and did not need to be reminded of the dangers to be faced. More practically, AOC Lloyd had also arranged for the formation of torpedo-bombers to be accompanied by a number of Beaufighters. This was very necessary as the sky was clear, with no hope of any cloud cover being available for the attackers.

The *Reichenfels* had been hit and damaged by Malta-based Blenheims in December 1941. Could the more advanced Bristol Aero Company aircraft complete what the Blenheims had narrowly failed to do?

The Malta-based formation flew south of the expected position of the enemy and began to work their way northwards, with the Beaufighters keeping a sharp eye upon them and the Italian island of Lampedusa, with its small airfield. The three ships were first sighted by their smoke and soon the Beauforts were manoeuvring to attack. Squadron Leader Lynn and the two Beauforts accompanying him were all shot down and one of these, when careering out of control, also very nearly brought down Aldridge's Beaufort with it. It missed him by inches, skidding underneath before plunging into the waters below.

This attack was quite different from the one in which Arthur Aldridge had surprised the *Trento*. Then he had approached undisturbed. Now flak came at him in a burst like hail and both he and his navigator, as well as their aircraft, were hit; but not before he had pressed the button to launch another deadly torpedo. This was aimed at the *Riechenfels*, and though the ship turned hastily away, it could not turn completely for fear of hitting the *Rosolino Pilo* which was following on its starboard side. Arthur Aldridge reckons that he dropped his torpedo at a range of only 750 yards, this being almost the minimum required for a hit.

Four cannon shells had hit Arthur's Beaufort and for a moment all aileron control seemed lost. With the aircraft only at 80 feet an immediate ditching seemed the only possibility, but as the aircraft skimmed over the flat sea Aldridge found it to be just controllable. The injuries to both himself and his navigator were not too serious and soon Aldridge and his crew, with their wounds patched up by the uninjured gunners, were on their way back from another triumph. The *Reichenfels* had been well and truly struck, perhaps even by two torpedoes. A claim was also made for a hit upon the Italian tanker.

Their relief at having escaped relatively unscathed was soon shattered. Aldridge had spied a fellow Beaufort on his starboard side flying straight with a Ju 88 on its tail. It was obvious that its pilot was either dead or wounded and unable to take avoiding action. Although only able to manoeuvre slightly and with considerable difficulty, Aldridge edged his aircraft towards that of his wounded colleague, planning to get alongside the Ju 88, so that his gunners could attack it from the side. The ruse worked and, after a burst of fire from his gunners, the port engine of the Junkers began to smoke. As it turned away from its quarry, Bill Carroll, Aldridge's gunner, was about to deliver a hail of bullets into its exposed underbelly when a Beaufighter appeared from nowhere and shot the German straight into the sea below. In all, the Beaufighters shot down three of the convoy's protecting aircraft.

The other more seriously damaged Beaufort managed to get back to Malta and the badly wounded pilot, Pilot Officer McSharry, despite a severe wound in his throat where an artery had been severed, landed it successfully before passing out from loss of blood.

Arthur Aldridge himself had problems to master. His instruments had been put out of action and his navigator was dazed from his wound, but with his airspeed being called out to him by a crew member using the navigator's instrument panel, Arthur also landed back safely in his Beaufort DD 958.*

The *Rosolino Pilo* survived, and a day later landed her precious cargo of fuel. As one-third of the attacking Beauforts had been lost and others damaged, it was hardly a great triumph. These losses, added to those which had already taken place, much reduced 217 Squadron's striking power. Of the twenty-eight crew members of 217 Squadron who had been sharing a dormitory in Malta's usual makeshift fashion a week before, only ten remained; the others had either been lost in action, or were confined to hospital. Life for Beaufort crews was never easy and, in Malta, was apt to be cruelly short.

---

* It was a Mark I with Bristol engines. The Mark II, with American Pratt and Whitney engines, was a later and better model but there was no one in Malta with the experience and tools to service this type of engine.

However, the attack upon the two enemy merchant ships had produced one great victory for the Allies. Not for a long time did the enemy attempt to use the short route to North Africa. A convoy which had already been prepared for sailing from Palermo down that route was now re-routed towards Taranto, from whence it had first come, in order to attempt a passage via the Greek-coast route. This dithering, as the enemy wondered how best to try to get supplies to Africa past Malta, was costing them precious oil as well as unacceptable delays.

The war diary of the Luftwaffe's JG 27, based in North Africa, shows the almost desperate supply situation in which the enemy Air Forces there found themselves. The entry for 26 June 1942 – five days after Rommel had taken Tobruk – reads: 'On 26 June, the fighters sent forward to Sidi Barani were kept busy but, apart from a single petrol bowser, the *Gerschwader* [a group of about 100–120 aircraft] had nothing on the spot. The pilots had to fly their missions on empty stomachs . . . two days later the whole *Gruppen* were grounded for fuel shortage.'

In a way, Arthur Aldridge had induced the enemy to switch tactics *twice* as, after his torpedoing of the *Trento*, the Italian battlefleet never again ventured forth to dispute the ownership of the Mediterranean. By June 1942 their claim that the Mediterranean was *mare nostrum*, as Mussolini had been fond of boasting, had become a source of embarrassment to the Italians and a joke to the Allies.

As Arthur Aldridge left the spotlight, so Patrick Gibbs began to dominate Beaufort operations from Malta. Initially, others with higher seniority were to command the units there. Although Gibbs' ideas had, by late June 1942, come to be accepted by all concerned – by the AOC Malta, by Air Marshal Tedder in the Middle East and by the Air Ministry in London – Gibbs was nevertheless junior in rank to Wing Commander Willie Davies, who was in command of 39 Squadron, and to the Commanding Officer of 217 Squadron. But even with others in command, Gibbs was invariably present when operations were planned and tactics discussed. With his drive and initiative he was not the type of man to be overlooked; nor, in Malta, were people likely to let this happen.

Thanks to the arrival of *Troilus* and *Orari* and the Magic Carpet

Service operated by HM Submarines, petrol for aircraft strikes during the months of June–September was more readily available than it had been previously. As a result, whenever the torpedo-carrying Beauforts went in search of a worthwhile quarry – and between them 39 and 217 Squadrons could muster as many as a dozen serviceable aircraft at a time – they went, as Gibbs had always advocated, accompanied by the even thirstier twin-engined Beaufighters in almost equal numbers.

The task of the Beaufighters (or Beaus, as they were commonly known) was to deal with any enemy fighters which might be accompanying the ships. Beauforts, though armed with front- and rear-firing guns, were no match for enemy fighters, even when flying without the impediment of a cumbersome torpedo attached. Without a torpedo they could twist and turn and perhaps score an occasional success. But with the torpedo slung underneath, and inhibited by the need to fly straight and level towards their targets when attacking, their chances against any German or Italian fighter aircraft were extremely slim. Although the Beaufighters were large and less manoeuvrable than the swift single-engined fighters such as the Spitfire or Me 109, they possessed massive firepower from their four 20-mm cannons and six machine-guns. They were also strongly built, could soak up punishment well, and were more than a match for the long-range Ju 88 fighters which the enemy normally used for convoy defence. Each Beau carried a pilot and an observer.

On 22 June 1942, a combined force of twelve each of Beauforts and Beaus set out to attack two merchant ships heavily protected by four Italian destroyers. This 2:1 ratio of escorts to supply ships is an indication of the fear which the Beauforts from Malta had already instilled in the enemy. The maritime destruction inflicted in 1941 by the Swordfish of 830 Squadron and by the U-class submarines of the Tenth Flotilla, aided by the Blenheims, had already instilled a fear of attack over the sea in the minds of the enemy planners. It was now standard practice therefore for enemy convoys, whether collected together at Naples or Taranto, to take the long route to Benghazi and the even longer one to Tripoli, in order to keep beyond Swordfish range. In part, this was because it was known that some of those FAA biplanes were still based at Hal Far, Malta. Some ships taking this route eastwards across the Adriatic direct towards the Greek islands of Corfu and Cephalonia would wait there a day or so, before commencing a dash across the Central Mediterranean towards Benghazi, making full use of the short nights of summer. Most, especially the Italian ships, then continued from off-Benghazi due west across the Gulf of Sirte to Tripoli, although the Germans always wanted everything to be unloaded closer to the front line, either at Benghazi or at the newly captured Tobruk.

Tobruk had limited unloading facilities but, like Benghazi where facilities were better, was within easy range of the Egypt-based Wellington bomber squadrons of 205 Group which, at one time, raided Benghazi so regularly at nights that it became dubbed by crews the 'Mail Run'. The Wellington aircrews of 70 Squadron were detailed to fly the Mail Run so often that they composed lyrics which they sang to the tune of 'Darling Clementine'.

> Down the flight, each ruddy morning
> Sitting waiting for a clue
> Same old notice, on the Flight board
> Maximum effort: guess where to.
>
> Seventy Squadron, Seventy Squadron,
> Though we say it with a sigh
> We must do the ruddy Mail Run
> Every night until we die.
>
> Have you lost us, navigator?
> Come up here and have a look.
> Someone's shot our starboard wing off,
> Then we're not lost: that's Tobruk.
> *Chorus*: Seventy Squadron, Seventy Squadron, etc.
>
> Oh to be in Piccadilly
> Selling matches by the score.
> Then we should not have to do the
> Ruddy Mail Run any more.
> *Chorus*: Seventy Squadron, Seventy Squadron, etc.

As a result of these activities, Axis ships were re-routed past Benghazi to Tripoli, which was now under attack only from the few Wellingtons based in Malta. During the early months of 1942, even this force was depleted as a result of Kesselring's blitz which had caused most of the Wellingtons to be withdrawn from Luqa. Tripoli at this period remained relatively untouched.

Whether the ships unloaded at Benghazi or Tripoli, the long route meant that the journey took up to twice as long: at a stroke, the attacking planes and submarines of Malta had then, in effect, greatly reduced the tonnage available to the enemy, quite apart from the number of ships which Malta-based submarines and aircraft had sent to the bottom or to the repairers' yards in the course of 1941.

The twenty-four Bristol designed aircraft, on 22 June 1942, therefore set forth to locate two merchant ships and their heavy escorts, in the open sea between the heel of Italy, Cape Santa Maria di Leuca, and the Greek islands. Despite the weight of attack and expenditure of precious petrol – and the dropping of equally precious Mark XII torpedoes – only one of the supply ships, probably the *Maria Roselli*, was damaged. For many of the crews this was their first live torpedo drop and, as with most things in wartime which depend solely upon eye and judgement, accuracy increased with experience. Beginners tended to drop too early in their excitement and when under fire for the first time. Later, it appeared that the *Maria Roselli* was beached so the big strike was not in vain. Her cargo of petrol was eventually transferred to the *Monviso*, for later despatch.

The AA fire from the four destroyers, as well as from the supply ships which often proved to be the most accurate of all, was once again withering, and Patrick Gibbs, who had led one of the three V formations, had to crash-land back at Luqa. By then, however, he had learned not to crash on the runway, but beside it.

The next sortie turned out to be even less productive. The formation failed to locate the expected enemy ships. But by the time they returned empty-handed, one of the indefatigable reconnaissance planes of Luqa's 69 Squadron had again confirmed the position of the enemy ships. As Beaufort crews only operated when a likely target was within their range, some of the weary and frustrated crews of the Beauforts now found themselves having to fly another long sortie of nearly six hours on the same day. Gibbs was one such pilot who operated twice, and by the end of that day he had flown over eleven and a half hours in an aircraft without a co-pilot, in a tense condition with the responsibility of leading a vic of three aircraft on an operation which was almost expected to lose one in three during an attack.

During this second operation the formation located the enemy ships in the open sea, near the extremity of their range, and it is thought that the *Nino Bixio* received a torpedo hit. It was seldom possible with many torpedoes running simultaneously to identify which, if any, of the several torpedoes dropped was the one which might have struck home.

The Beaufort crews in Malta were still mostly on a learning curve and better results were to come. However, with losses so heavy, every Beaufort attack included new pilots flown in as replacements.

The next strike on 21 July also scored a probable hit on a ship which may have been as big as 10,000 tons although few in the area were that large. This operation introduced a new element, and one which was to have useful repercussions. The Beaus which accompanied the five Beauforts were finding these sorties frustrating. The Beaufort sorties were being planned to catch the enemy in open waters and, as a consequence, the Beaufighter escorts found that they usually had no enemy aircraft to oppose. On this sortie, partly for their own amusement and in a more serious endeavour to terrorize the gunners aboard the enemy ships, they lobbed over the sides of their Beaus a number of empty beer bottles, having first discovered that they fell with a banshee screaming sound, akin to that of deadly bombs.

Patrick Gibbs' alert mind at once saw the significance of this. If they could carry such extras, he suggested, why should they not be equipped with real bombs? Steps were therefore taken locally to modify the Beaufighter fighters by the addition of bomb racks, and before long they were carrying two 250-pound bombs, one under each wing; and when this proved to be well within their capabilities, these bombs were upgraded to two 500-pounders. (The concept of having Beaufighters join in attacks on enemy ships not only with bombs but also by unleashing their cannons and machine-guns at the very moment when torpedo-carrying planes were running in, was also in Gibbs' fertile mind. That would come later.)

It was being realized belatedly in the UK as well as in the Middle East that the Beauforts, if used intelligently from Malta, were a prime means of stopping supplies reaching Rommel's forces in North Africa. By 24 July 1942, one of the two Flights of 86 Squadron, a unit which also operated Beauforts, was being flown from England to Malta to help make good the losses which 39 and 217 Squadrons were suffering. These were soon incorporated into the one single 'Malta Beaufort Squadron', much as the remnants of 830 Squadron Swordfish and 828 Squadron Albacores had been amalgamated into the single Royal Navy Aircraft Squadron, Malta, although the unit underwent many administrative permutations from 39 to 217 to 86, then back to 39 Squadron. London seldom caught up with the local changes which the AOC Malta was apt to decide on the spot, as required.*

With the arrival of part of 86 Squadron, Willie Davies was at last allowed to be returned to the UK. Like many others he had been told originally that he would only be in Malta a few days. This suited him fine, as he had arranged to marry his fiancée the following week. Now, many nerve-racking weeks later, he was finally able to appear at his often-postponed wedding.

With the arrival of the Beauforts of 86 Squadron, once again an officer with seniority to Patrick Gibbs appeared in Malta. Jimmy Hyde, now appointed to command the unit, was determined to lead the aircraft at the first opportunity, although he was unfamiliar with the area, the peculiarities of the job in hand and the nature of the deadly flak to be faced.

On 24 July, with Jimmy Hyde in the lead, six Beauforts took off to attack a convoy heading down the Greek coast. They flew in two vics, one led by the newly arrived CO, the other by the experienced Patrick Gibbs. Both were friends from years past and Gibbs, a prewar Regular officer, accepted the position with good grace.

Sadly, the vic of three aircraft led by Jimmy Hyde were all shot down before getting within torpedo range. He was leading his trio at a greater height than was usual and the aircraft presented a clear target silhouetted against the sky. Possibly, Hyde had kept at this height in order to extend his range of vision in his determination not to miss finding the target.

On the credit side, a possible hit was scored on the Italian *Vettor Pisani* which was believed to be carrying some of the heavy equipment of the German 164th Division. By then, having reached El Alamein, Rommel was poised to strike deeper into Egypt and had requested reinforcements. In response, the 164th Division was being moved to North Africa from Crete. The men were in the process of

---

* These discrepancies are a particular problem for writers trying to check up on events at the Public Record Office, Kew.

being flown there, partly by night, by a large group of Ju 52 transport planes. Their guns, vehicles and ammunition, which were all too heavy for air transportation, had to follow by sea. If the *Vettor Pisani* were halted, it would be a major triumph as reinforcements of men without their weapons and vehicles were a liability rather than an asset. Men had to be fed and rations, as well as petrol and ammunition, were in short supply.

Another innovation of this latest attack had been the presence of 69 Squadron – Luqa's famous photo-reconnaissance unit. Up to now, the contribution of 69 Squadron had been invaluable but passive, their pilots confirming the position of enemy ships and shadowing them both by day – using Spitfires as well as US-built Baltimores and Marylands – and by night, using ASV-equipped Wellingtons or Goofingtons.* Now, for the first time, one of its fast daylight reconnaissance planes accompanied the Beaufort/ Beaufighter strike-force in order to observe results, and also to photograph any damage done. In this case a Baltimore brought back a photograph, confirming an enemy ship on fire.

With the loss of Jimmy Hyde, Patrick Gibbs at last took official command of the Beauforts. The unit was by then a unique and comprehensive Luqa-based strike-force, composed of Beauforts from three different squadrons dropping torpedoes, Beaufighters to drop bombs, other Beaus to spray the decks of the enemy with blistering cannon fire, as well as photo-reconnaissance aircraft to record and photograph the damage being inflicted. It had almost become Gibbs' private Air Force.

To develop a better team spirit, the Beaufighters were even officially integrated into the Beaufort unit. The PR plane, which now flew alongside the attackers, was also useful in determining the exact position of any aircrew shot down into the sea. Malta possessed a highly efficient RAF Air–Sea Rescue unit which, by the war's end, had plucked more from the sea, including several dead, than any other in the RAF. Among the hundreds they had recov-

---

* 69 Squadron was unique in that it used bomber types, reconnaissance planes and Spitfire fighters to locate, shadow and photograph whatever was requested by the AOC or VAM, Malta. By September, it had also absorbed what remained of the Goofingtons of the author's previous Special Duties Flight. Officially they became 'C Flight, 69 Squadron' but were always referred to as the 'SDF Flight'.

ered were a large number of German airmen, as well as several Italians.

The apprenticeship of Malta's Beauforts was largely over. Malta was in a good position once again to menace the convoys heading for North Africa. On top of this, by late July 1942, the decision had been made for the submarines of the Tenth Flotilla, still commanded by Captain Simpson, to be based once again at Manoel Island. Just as both armies were gearing themselves for what most informed persons realized would be the decisive battle in the Desert War, Malta was back in business, much as it had been before Kesselring's rain of bombs.

The only drawback was that, by the end of July, Malta was all but starved out. The island was not just out of petrol and military supplies of every kind, from gun barrels, AA ammunition to simple fuses; more ominously, it was critically short of food and of oil to heat the food.

By advocating that Beauforts could be most effective if based in Malta, Squadron Leader Gibbs had proved himself to be an able strategist. Now, at last officially in charge of the Beauforts in Malta, he showed himself to be a wily tactician. The guiding principle behind his many changes of tactics was that a good idea was worth pursuing only twice, or possibly a third time. By then, the enemy was likely to have the measure of it and something new had to be tried. In this way he kept one step ahead.

On 28 July 1942, Squadron Leader Gibbs, now wearing the ribbons of DFC and bar, led a formation of Beauforts against the Italian *Monviso* which was carrying the fuel that had originally been on board the *Maria Roselli*. As usual, 69 Squadron confirmed by aerial reconnaissance that the ship was at sea. *Monviso* was protected by the destroyer *Freccia* and the torpedo-boat *Calliope*. Between them, these two escorts could mount nearly twenty flak or machine-guns. The *Monviso* itself was also well armed as, by then, were all merchant ships attempting to reach North Africa. The fire from these merchant ships was often as deadly as any from the escorting destroyers, as the gunners of a merchant vessel could fire straight at the attacking aircraft.

Nine Beauforts departed, accompanied this time by no Beaufighters but by a lone Baltimore which flew with them at height in order to observe and photograph the results. Gibbs had elected to intercept and attack off the south-west tip of Greece, near Sapientza, where no fighter opposition was expected. But possibly due to the absence of the Beaus, this was not a successful strike. For the loss of two Beauforts and their crews, both picked up by the destroyer, the MV *Monviso* suffered only a minor hit and was able to continue her journey.

Although laden with several thousand tons of petrol, *Monviso* was not a tanker *per se*, but by then, as few of the enemy's tankers remained afloat, virtually every ship heading for North Africa had been modified to carry fuel. The enemy was applying many of the tactics which the British were using in order to get supplies through to Malta. Just as the *Welshman*, and her sister ship *Manxman* – both fast minelayers – were being used as cargo vessels to transport urgently needed supplies to Malta, so were the Italians using cruisers to carry petrol to North Africa. Both sides made considerable use of submarines as cargo vessels and both sides had to make provision for transporting rations as well as military supplies. Neither the Desert, nor Malta, had the means of supplying the large number of persons involved with even the basic requirements of life. During the hot summer months, men on both sides were also severely rationed in regard to water, as well as food.

The sortie by the Beauforts was not entirely in vain, as the *Monviso* had to be brought into Navarino for urgent repairs. She left after a few days but never reached her destination. When almost within sight of Libya, she was detected, stalked and sunk by torpedoes fired from one of the submarines of the Tenth Flotilla then operating from a Middle East base.

It had cost the RAF several Beauforts and the combined efforts of the RAF in Malta and the Royal Navy in Alexandria to send that load of petrol to the bottom, and six weeks had passed since the Beauforts had first torpedoed the original carrier, the *Maria Roselli*. Petrol was fast becoming the single factor which would determine the outcome of the battle between the armies now lined up opposite one another at El Alamein. One vital load reaching either Malta or Rommel could swing the balance either way.

To integrate further the Beaufighters and the Beauforts, Squadron Leader Gibbs had persuaded the newly arrived AOC Malta, Keith Park, to allow him effectively to merge 235 Beaufighter Squadron into his Beaufort Wing. AOC Air Vice Marshal Park – of Battle of

Britain fame* – who replaced Hugh Pughe Lloyd[†] on 15 July 1942, was fighter-aircraft minded; he was happy to leave the attack side of Malta largely in the hands of others, such as Gibbs. Wisely he gave Patrick all the support he requested, while asking pertinent questions in order to familiarize himself thoroughly with their operations.

This integration of Beaus and Beauforts generated an enhanced fighting spirit among the personnel of the two squadrons. If the Beauforts scored a success, it became a joint success for the accompanying Beaufighters and vice versa. The two groups of pilots were briefed as one and soon came to think as one, with many useful suggestions being put forward by both.

Some of the Beaus now carried bombs, while others went ahead to blast the decks of the ships just before they came under attack. With ten guns in each Beau (four 20-mm cannons and six machine-guns), these deck-clearing aircraft became a fearful threat to the exposed ship's gunners. Also, with bomber-Beaus dropping in a dive, and torpedo-carrying aircraft operating at sea level, both attacking simultaneously, the ship's gunners were not able to concentrate all their fire upon the more deadly torpedo-carrying Beauforts. It also helped to confuse their gunners' aim that the Beaus were attacking at about twice the speed of the Beauforts. Consequently different deflection angles had to be hastily applied.

Gibbs continued to do all the planning but did not lead every strike. His physical stamina depended upon his nervous energy. Just as the food in the Desert had upset his constitution, so also did that in Malta. His constitution was not geared for such intakes and, almost uniquely in half-starved Malta, he was known to decline to eat what little was on offer.

One of his deputy leaders was 'Hank' Sharman, a robust Canadian who appeared quite fearless. He had arrived with 86 Squadron and was an able leader. Gibbs' own crew was blessed with an above-average navigator in John Creswell and Sharman also was well served in this respect. Much depended upon accurate

---

* Park had commanded 11 Group of Fighter Command.
† Lloyd was shortly promoted (and knighted), and later given command of all 'Coastal Command'-type operations in the Mediterranean, as AOC North African Coastal Air Force.

navigation by the leading aircraft as attacks were at times planned to take place near the extremity of the Beauforts' range, out in the featureless open sea where the likelihood of finding enemy planes around the convoy was more remote.

Gibbs' briefings were an inspiration to all, as Arthur Aldridge – who was critical of his former AOC's 'pep talks' – has confirmed. Every crew man knew exactly what to do, where the dangers lay and how best to avoid them. With crews steadily being lost on almost every mass attack – often several at a time – there was a steady intake of 'new boys' who had never before dropped a live torpedo in anger. Their exuberance had to be disciplined. They had much to learn. Casualties tended to be the heaviest among them, as well as among the leading aircraft which were prone to attract the maximum enemy fire.

A tanker was hit on 10 August – possibly by as many as three torpedoes. However it was proving difficult to sink tankers: their several sealed compartments gave them additional buoyancy. A formation led by Hank Sharman hit a ship trying to reach Tripoli by way of Pantelleria. The *Rosolino Pilo* – the tanker which had escaped when the *Reichenfels* was sunk – joined that German vessel at the bottom of the sea on 18 August. This was one of several joint RAF/RN triumphs. It was first hit and damaged by Gibbs' Beaufort/Beaufighter team and then finished off by a single torpedo fired by the submarine *United*.

Patrick Gibbs continued changing the tactics. After attacking in the open sea between Italy and Greece, he then tried attacks close in to the Greek shore, between the islands and the mainland. He next switched to attacking from the mainland, with the aircraft's outline almost hidden by the dark background. Another such attack was launched near the small Greek island of Paxos. At each turn he showed himself a master tactician.

Although Beaufort strikes were still being carried out during the month of August 1942, the main effort of both RAF and Navy in this month was concentrated on an attempt to relieve the siege of Malta by sending in a big convoy. This was Operation Pedestal.

Departing from Glasgow, fourteen fast merchant ships passed through the Strait of Gibraltar on the night of 10 August, hoping in the dark to avoid detection by the German-sympathizing Spaniards overlooking that famous rock. By the time the convoy was in the Mediterranean heading for Malta, Pedestal was being escorted by the largest British naval force to be assembled during the Second World War. It included two battleships, four aircraft-carriers, seven cruisers and thirty-two destroyers, as well as seven submarines, other auxiliaries and refuellers. However, most of the big ships would have to be turned round before the convoy reached the heavily mined Cape Bon area, where they would also be vulnerable to the torpedo- and dive-bombers based in Sardinia and Sicily. For the last few hundred miles, apart from the few cruisers and destroyers which would remain with the merchant ships, much would depend upon the fighter-aircraft which were to come from Malta to encircle the ships of Operation Pedestal. These, at first, would be long-range Beaufighters; later on, the ships would come within range of the Spitfires.

They would still have formidable Luftwaffe forces to contend with. When news reached Kesselring in August 1942 that a large convoy was *en route* to Malta, he concentrated everything available from both the Luftwaffe and the Regia Aeronautica in a determined effort to attack its fourteen merchant ships, in spite of their massive RN escorts. This, both sides seemed to know, was to be the battle to decide the fate of the Axis armies in North Africa.

Ranged against Pedestal, the enemy had assembled 146 German bombers, mainly Ju 88s; 72 German fighters, nearly all Me 109s; 232 Italian fighters; 16 Ju 87 dive-bombers and 139 Italian bombers, many of which were their highly effective SM 79 torpedo-bombers.

This total of 605 aircraft, based in Sardinian and Sicilian airfields, as well as a few in Pantelleria, assembled solely in order to attack a single Malta-bound convoy, is an indication of the degree of importance which Kesselring placed upon Malta, and her ability to disrupt the flow of supplies to Rommel in the Desert. Moreover, this veritable air army was assembled and brought to Sardinia and Sicily at a time when Rommel, whose rapid advance had been halted at El Alamein, was desperately trying to build up supplies so that he could launch an attack upon Alexandria and/or Cairo before the Eighth Army could receive their much-needed reinforcements.

As it was, the gunners aboard the many RN escort ships damaged and destroyed so many of their attackers that, when the Italian Navy made the decision to try to finish off the remnants of

Operation Pedestal and asked for fighter protection, the Luftwaffe and Italian Air Forces were so exhausted that no such protection could be guaranteed. The rest is history and it will never be known if Rommel would have succeeded at the Battle of Alam Halfa, which followed later that month, if he had been given the 600 aircraft which were diverted to attack Operation Pedestal instead.

Much has been written about this convoy and it is here only necessary to mention that, although 53,000 tons of the supplies desperately needed for Malta went to the bottom of the sea, 32,000 tons, including some fuel, was unloaded. This enabled Malta to fight on for another few months.

Almost nothing, however, has been written about a magnificent ploy devised by Air Vice Marshal Park, the new AOC: a stratagem which may have done as much as anything else to ensure that some ships of Operation Pedestal managed to reach Malta.

During the vital night of 12 August, after the main British battle-fleet had left the Pedestal convoy, and before the remains of the convoy could come under the protection of the daylight fighters based in Malta, a force of Italian cruisers was detected approaching from the direction of Sicily. Some of the British cruisers and destroyers which alone were then protecting the ships of Pedestal had therefore, temporarily, to leave the convoy in order to steer northwards to engage the attacking cruisers before the Italians came within gun-range of the few remaining merchant ships. As history shows, the attacking Italian cruiser force turned back even before being engaged by the defenders of Pedestal. According to the account given by Philip Vella in *Malta, Blitzed but not Beaten*:

> Fate came to the aid of the battered ships. The German and Italian Air Forces, disappointed at their failure to annihilate the entire expedition, were resolved to finish their task with an all-out effort. To achieve this, they needed all the aircraft at their disposal: none therefore could be spared to protect the Italian Naval squadron.
>
> Deprived of fighter cover, the Italian ships were consequently withdrawn just before engaging the convoy. The resulting failure of the Italian Navy to deal a death-blow to the remaining ships virtually saved Malta.

However, it was not that simple. By then, 69 Squadron was about to incorporate the few remaining Goofingtons of the original SDF into its structure. By 12 August these Fishingtons (either already in 69 Squadron as 'C' Flight or still in the SDF) were under the command of a Flight Lieutenant le Mesurier. Virtually every aircraft in Malta was then being deployed, in one way or another, to protect the ships of the approaching convoy. Photo-reconnaissance aircraft of 69 Squadron, led by Warburton who had been recalled from leave in the Middle East specifically to lead them, flew several operations daily to inspect the positions of all units of the Italian fleet. Warburton himself spent most of the day of 12 August at 20,000 feet over Taranto: firstly in Spitfire V 883 then in another Spitfire, AB 300. Patrols by Baltimores in daylight, and by the ASV-equipped Wellingtons by night, watched over and shadowed other Italian fleet movements in order to guard against surprise attack. 69 Squadron, as usual, was providing Malta with the information it needed.

On the night of 12 August, when the Italian cruisers with escorts were on the move and about to pass around the north-west point of Sicily, Keith Park sent out three Goofingtons, well stocked with flares. The instructions to one crew were to locate the enemy force, to illuminate it as if an attack was about to be made, and to send out to Malta in plain language its position, course and speed while at the same time ordering in, as if in a controller's role, an imaginary force of RAF Liberators to bomb the Italian fleet. Park knew that the Italians would pick up these signals and suspected that they had a distaste of being bombed by Liberators, as one of these had hit the *Littorio* during Operation Vigorous.

The ruse worked and the Italian cruiser force, which was timing its interception of Operation Pedestal so as to be in a position to attack at first light on 13 August – before, it was hoped, any aircraft from Malta could arrive – duly turned back.

Flying in one of these Goofingtons at the time was Wireless Operator/Air Gunner Eric Cameron, crewing with Flying Officer Fanshawe of the SDF (and/or 'C' Flight of 69 Squadron). It was a busy period for the few Goofingtons in Malta and Eric Cameron found himself operating almost all night long on 10, 11 and 12 August 1942. On the first night, his skipper scoured the area outside Taranto. 'No sightings. No bombs,' he recorded. On the 11th, the Goofington in which Eric sat again went out on patrol, this time sighting a cruiser which the crew illuminated with flares: 'No bombs dropped.' On the night of the 12th, the particular assignment given to Fanshawe and his crew was to patrol ahead of the convoy to try to detect and attack any enemy submarine, or E-boats, lurking between Pantelleria and Cape Bon. He saw the E-boats attack the ships of the Operation Pedestal convoy after the enemy had dropped flares: 'Saw HMS *Manchester* and dinghies,' he adds. (That night *Manchester* was hit, set on fire, and sunk.)

Not only did the enemy cruisers turn back, thanks to AOC Park's ploy, after rounding the north-west point of Sicily but on their way back towards Messina, they came within range of the prowling Lieutenant Alistair Mars, in the submarine *Unbroken*, who had positioned his boat west of Stromboli. It was there that he was able to hit both the cruisers *Bolzano* and *Attendolo*. As had happened on the night of 12/13 December 1941, when Commander Stokes had almost run into the enemy petrol-carrying cruisers off Cape Bon, Italian naval forces, when detected and illuminated at night by an ASV-equipped Wellington, tended to call it a day and turn back. Moreover, only aircraft based in Malta were sufficiently close at hand, at that juncture of the war, to be able to carry out this important role.

One Beaufort success this month had been to hit the Italian tanker *Pozerica*. This was carrying fuel for the Italian Army and, when it failed to arrive, the Italians had to beg and borrow fuel – scarce as it was – from their German ally. This not only depleted Rommel's slender reserves but added to the distrust which existed between the two Axis partners, as Rommel and Kesselring both knew only too well why, with their big Italian population there, the Italians preferred to route their ships to far-away Tripoli which, by August 1942, was nearly 1,000 miles by road from El Alamein where the armies stood.

Distances between ports along the African coast were colossal. Even when using Benghazi, it still took seven days to bring supplies from that port of limited unloading facilities to the front line where Rommel had been halted. To bring goods from Benghazi to El Alamein was to travel a distance equivalent to that between London and some way beyond Bulgaria. Moreover, these supplies had to be carried from a frequently bombed port along a single, constantly attacked coast road in conditions of heat and dust that reduced the life of vehicles to little more than a couple of such journeys.

Even Tobruk was more than 300 miles behind Rommel's front line and was dangerously close to attack by every kind of RAF/USAAF medium-range aircraft operating from Egypt. Moreover, the port had poor unloading facilities and, until the Germans constructed one, no oil storage tanks for any tanker which happened to reach and remain there. Much fuel was therefore being carried to North Africa in barrels. The added presence of US fast/medium-bombers, such as the Douglas Boston, had added to the RAF's strength. Some were in the hands of the SAAF (South African Air Force), a well-trained addition to the Allied strength.

In response to Rommel's demand for reinforcements for his big final push, Hitler had ordered the despatch, from Crete and else-where, of the many Axis units, including the German Ramcke Brigade, which had been assembled in preparation for the planned invasion of Malta, Operation Herkules.

Rommel was determined to attack before September 1942. He knew that massive supplies would soon be reaching the enemy and that, by mid-September, he would be outmatched in almost every respect. The US Sherman tanks were proving to be a formidable weapon which only his few recently arrived Type V Tiger tanks could match. Many Shermans were arriving in Egypt by way of the long route round South Africa and he had received intelligence that a convoy carrying 100,000 tons of supplies was due to arrive early in September.

The combination of Air Forces ranged against him now far out-numbered his African Luftwaffe, even after it had been reinforced by the aircraft which had hitherto been based in Sicily. He aimed to launch his attack on 25 August and had elected to try to break through the British line at its southern limit and then advance north to get behind the main British defences. That way all Egypt would be wide open for the taking. Hitler and Mussolini had agreed, in advance, that Rommel should become Governor-General of Egypt, and Mussolini was planning to enter Cairo astride a splendid white horse which was already being procured for this occasion.

Rommel had signalled Von Rintelen, the German Military Attaché in Rome: 'Unless I get 2,000 cubic metres of fuel, 500 tons of ammunition by the 25th [August] and a further 2,000 cubic metres of fuel by the 27th and 2,000 tons of ammunition by the 30th, I cannot proceed.' It would take no more than two or three ships to bring in these requirements. By late August Rommel also knew that he would be launching his attack against a new Allied commander. General Sir Harold Alexander, on 15 August 1942, had taken over from General Auchinleck as GOC-in-C Middle East and a Lieutenant-General Bernard Montgomery had come with him to command the Eighth Army in the field.*

August was proving to be a worrying month for the Axis. Apart from the resurgent Beauforts and their co-operating Beaufighters, another new RAF element was threatening the Axis convoys. Wellingtons modified to carry two torpedoes were beginning to make their presence felt at night. Aided by ASV, they could find targets in almost any light or weather. It was no longer a refuge, therefore, to keep a convoy in a harbour such as Argostoli in Cephalonia during daylight hours, in the hope that it could get most of the way across the Mediterranean to North Africa during the dark hours of night.

Lack of fuel was compelling Rommel to delay his planned offensive, frustratingly poised as he was only seventy miles from Alexandria, a port which had all the facilities anyone could desire. The days of 27–28 August may well have been decisive. Three Italian ships heading for the armies in the Desert were sunk. The *Dielpi* (1,527 tons), the *Manfredo Campario* and the *Istria* were all sent to the bottom by the combination of Gibbs' mixed force operating from Malta, torpedo-carrying Wellingtons operating from the Middle East and Tenth Flotilla submarines – now back, or heading back, to their former Manoel Island base in Malta.

The *Istria* was a special prize. It was carrying the vehicles and heavy equipment for the 164th German Division which was still in the process of being moved from Crete to bolster Rommel's Panzer Army.† Rommel was in a difficult position. He lacked the fuel and ammunition he needed to attack, yet every day he delayed – and he had already postponed his attack by several days because of lack of

---

* General Auchinleck's qualities were not appreciated by Churchill and others in London. The loss of Tobruk was held against him. Once he had stabilized the situation at El Alamein his days as GOC-in-C were numbered. General Bayerlein, Rommel's chief of staff, regarded him as the best British general the Germans ever faced in North Africa.

† Initially the relatively small numbers of Germans in North Africa were known as the 'Afrika Korps'. Later, when the numbers increased it was known as 'Panzer Korps Afrika'. By August 1942, it had grown in size to 'Panzer Army, Afrika'. With each change, Rommel was promoted and had advanced first to full General and then to Field Marshal.

petrol – meant that his enemy was growing in strength. In the past he had defied logic, had attacked and won the day. He now had to hang his hopes on being able, as in the past, to advance so swiftly that he could capture British supplies in order to keep up his momentum. Everything hung on that first big breakthrough which, in late August 1942, he planned to make at the south end of his Alamein line.

However, Rommel was up against a clever tactician in General Montgomery. Almost within twenty-four hours of taking command, with the assistance of Ultra information and backed by his own intuitive feel for a battleground, he had divined that a certain ridge near the southern extremity of his line (which rested in the south upon an impenetrable saltmarsh) was poorly defended. At once he moved the newly arrived 44th Division to hold that ridge. He also issued orders that when the expected attack was launched in that area, the British armour was to dig in and act more as an anti-tank force than a roving mobile one. The ridge was named Alam Halfa.

Rommel could delay no longer. He launched his attack at 2200 hours on 30 August, hoping against hope that at least the tanker *San Andrea* would be arriving as scheduled, with its cargo of 3,918 tons of petrol. It never reached its destination. A formation of Beauforts and Beaufighters from Luqa, led by Hank Sharman, sent it to the bottom. The loss was confirmed by a photograph taken by 69 Squadron's outstanding pilot and photographic ace, Squadron Leader Adrian Warburton. One Beaufighter was lost.

To give Rommel every chance of success, Kesselring, the mastermind and commander of all German forces in the Mediterranean, had transferred 1,500 tons of Luftwaffe fuel to Rommel for use by his tanks. This meant that the RAF, which had already gained a measure of air superiority over the Luftwaffe in the Desert, was poised to drum home that advantage.

The Battle of Alam Halfa was, in reality, the end of the Desert War. For the first time the Desert Fox, as some called Rommel, received a severe trouncing. His tanks gained barely a yard of ground. They attacked the Alam Halfa ridge with their usual determination, only to be repulsed almost ignominiously. After only a couple of days, to save his Panzers from complete annihilation, Rommel had to order their retreat while they still had the fuel to do so. His most formidable weapon, his tanks, had suffered heavy losses. Precious petrol had been expended, including the Luftwaffe's, for no gain. Of equal importance, British morale had been lifted and that of his Panzer Army shattered.

After the battle of Alam Halfa, both Rommel and the triumphant Montgomery knew that, barring the miracles which at times appear during a war, ultimate defeat for the Panzer Army, Afrika, was largely a matter of time. The British position and supplies could only grow stronger whereas, for as long as the combined forces of the RAF and Royal Navy, operating both from the Middle East and from Malta, continued to cut deep into Rommel's precarious supply line, that wily General would be fighting with one hand tied behind his back.

The Axis forces in Africa had been soundly defeated and the island of Malta had played a vital part in that defeat. Though all the Services in the Middle East had made their contributions to the Allied victory, the large Allied Air Forces in Egypt had mostly concentrated upon actions on the ground, leaving it to submarines and aircraft in Malta to deal with the ever-critical sea-supply problems which the enemy continued to face. In weakening the enemy's supply-lines, Malta's role was crucial.

Many in Malta had also played their part – none more so in the RAF than Wing Commander Adrian Warburton, in the long term, and in the short term, Squadron Leader Patrick Gibbs DSO, DFC and bar. It was largely due to him that the Beauforts in Malta were able to supply the offensive capacity which had been lost with the departure of the submarines of the Tenth Flotilla from their Manoel Island base.

By the time he returned to the UK, this much decorated Squadron Leader was physically and mentally played out: so much so that he had to be invalided out of the Service to which he had given his all. Always articulate, erudite and sensitive, Patrick Gibbs fought back, regained his health and became the well-known drama critic of the *Daily Telegraph*. Apart from a very slight hesitation of speech, he remains, in 1996, remarkably fit for a man in his eighties. As Arthur Aldridge recalls, 'He was an inspiration to us all.'*

---

* The second volume of Patrick Gibbs' memoirs, *Torpedo Leader* (1992), centres on his time in Malta.

10

Submarines Attack!

'We should have taken Alexandria and reached the
Suez Canal had it not been for the work of your
submarines.'

General Bayerlein,
Chief of Staff of the Africa Korps

THE EFFECTIVENESS OF the Allied submarines operating out of Malta
has already been seen. Operating under the control of Captain
Simpson (Captain (S) 10), the submarines of the Tenth Flotilla were
on almost constant patrol from Malta, except for the period
May–July 1942 when they sought temporary refuge in Alexandria
and Haifa.

Their successes were by no means easily come by, especially
as the British submarines most frequently used from Malta were
the small U-class boats, with a maximum speed of no more than
10 knots.

The Tenth Flotilla was often augmented by several larger submarines, S and T-class boats, as well as *Rorqual* and *Clyde* – the
former a minelayer, the latter modified to carry supplies: *Rorqual*
too was drafted in to serve as an emergency supply-carrier. Without
the petrol, torpedoes and other essential goods which these submarines brought in when the island was under siege, Malta's ability
to hit back would have been drastically reduced. Submarines operating in and out of the island were also occasionally employed as
miniature troop-ships, since – along with other naval vessels and
aircraft – they were often the only means available of transporting
personnel.

As a mine-laying submarine, *Rorqual* was only one of four

British submarines specifically equipped to carry out this dangerous and demanding task.* The other three were all sunk while
operating in the Mediterranean.† Named appropriately after types
of whales, these submarines were larger than many other British
types and had bulbous, less streamlined upper structures than was
normal for underwater craft. Their gross tonnage was about 1,500.
Rorqual could carry fifty mines, each weighing about a ton. While
on board they would be stowed with sinkers attached.

Sea-mines, although looking like enormous extremely heavy
cannon-balls with horns, are lighter than sea water. Unless tethered
to the sea bed by a heavy sinker, they would float on the surface of
the sea where they could be easily detected and destroyed. To be
used effectively, mines need to be laid in such a manner that they
remain only a few feet below the surface of the sea. Generally they
are laid in channels, or approaches, close to where enemy ships are
liable to be found, such as just outside major harbours. Generally
mines with sinkers had to be laid in relatively shallow waters, no
deeper than 70 fathoms.

Mines were often laid during daylight hours in order for their
exact positions to be accurately recorded. The daylight enabled
positive sights of known landmarks to be made. It was to their
disadvantage that, being bigger and less manoeuvrable than (say)
the U-class submarines, *Rorqual* and its sister submarine were
exposed to many dangers when mine-laying in daylight. During
daylight mine-laying, only a bare minimum of periscope would be
protruding above the waves.

A trick of *Rorqual*, as described by Ian Stoop, who served as First
Officer aboard *Rorqual* during her wartime service in the
Mediterranean, was to lie in wait outside an enemy harbour and
watch closely the work of the enemy minesweepers. Their job
would be to come out at first light and clear the approaches to the
port by sweeping the main channel. As soon as the minesweeper

---

* Much of the information which follows has been provided by Captain Lennox
Napier DSO, DSC, RN (Rtd) who, as Lieutenant Commander Napier, was one of
two officers who commanded this multi-purpose submarine during one of her
periods under the control of Captain (S) 10 in Malta.
† *Narwhal*, sunk December 1940; *Cachalot*, sunk July 1941; *Porpoise*, sunk (date
unknown).

had carried out its morning task, *Rorqual* would then sow its lines of deadly mines in the area just swept.

As the Allies were always hopeful of themselves being able to make use of an enemy port at a later stage of the war, each mine was equipped with a device which automatically caused it to sink to the bottom of the sea bed after forty-four days. It was essential that, as soon as a cluster of mines had been laid, a report of their exact position was sent by W/T so that friendly ships could be warned. Mines were no respecters of nationalities.

One of *Rorqual*'s most successful operations was the laying of thirty-six mines outside the channel to the port of Tunis. This took place during January 1943 during a vital stage of the land battles for Tunisia. At that time, it had become known that the German MV *Ankara* was transporting large numbers of 57-ton German Tiger tanks – one of their best weapons – to the Axis armies then fighting in Tunisia. *Ankara* was living a charmed life and had made several such journeys. She was also unusual in having derricks mounted on board which could unload those heavy tanks without the need for port assistance. *Rorqual* had orders to lay mines in the channel leading to the port of Tunis to where *Ankara* was known to be proceeding.

It was a daunting task and, given its dangers, it was decided to lay the mines at night during a period when the moon would be full. The area chosen was around the Cani Rocks which was known to be patrolled. At first, a technical hitch threatened the operation. The mine-doors would not open. This was daringly fixed by surfacing at night near the island of Zembra where the Engineer Officer and the First Lieutenant bravely went overboard in order to release the recalcitrant mine-doors. This enabled the minefield to be successfully laid. Both Engineer Officer Charles Saunders and Lieutenant Rudd-Cairs were awarded the DSC for this daring feat. The torpedo gunner's mate also received a DSM. If, during their attempts to free the doors, the submarine had been compelled to dive, they would all have been abandoned to the sea.

Almost at once, the *Ankara* obligingly ran into the minefield and was sunk along with her valuable military load. The same minefield then probably accounted for the enemy corvette *Procellaria* and possibly other vessels such as the destroyer *Saetta*.

Rorqual, once her mine-laying tasks had been completed, reverted to regular duties as a normal torpedo-carrying craft. As well as her twelve torpedoes she was equipped with an excellent 4-inch gun and her total tonnage sunk compares favourably with most submarines operating under the control of Captain (S) 10.

Rorqual was herself very nearly sunk by an Italian submarine. One explosion of what was probably a torpedo came so close that the Italians, noting the explosion, thought they had sunk the vessel; their commander was decorated by Mussolini and a plaque commemorating the success was placed in a position of honour inside the submarine. Some months later this Italian submarine was among those which surrendered at Malta after the Italians had capitulated. Ian Stoop was in Malta at the time and had the satisfaction of boarding this submarine and pointing out to her commander that neither he nor *Rorqual* had been sunk.

On another occasion, spotted on the surface at night when engaged in laying mines, *Rorqual* came under attack from a German U-boat. But *Rorqual*'s silhouette was mistaken for that of an aircraft-carrier and the torpedoes, which in German submarines could have their running depth changed even when in their tubes, were set to run deep. As a result they passed under *Rorqual*; one, which happened to be a 'circler', even did so twice.

Although it is not possible to determine with certainty how many enemy ships were sunk by mines laid by *Rorqual*, the fact that she laid more than 1,000 in the Mediterranean speaks for itself. She is thought to have accounted for over 40,000 tons of enemy shipping destroyed by mines, torpedoes or by her powerful gun.

As the supply carrier to Malta *Rorqual*, which could carry more than most other submarines, made seven journeys. Only *Clyde*, which had been specially modified to carry supplies to Malta, made more journeys. Without the aviation petrol which *Rorqual* and other makeshift supply carriers brought in, at great risk to their crews, the RAF would have been grounded. The carriage of volatile fuel imposed diving and other limitations during the journey. Also, the tins in which it was carried invariably leaked and gave away the submarines' position.

Details of one load have been made available. This consisted of 2 tons of medical stores; 62 tons of 100 octane aviation fuel; 45 tons of kerosene for use as cooking fuel by the Maltese; 24 passengers; 147 bags of mail (nothing raised morale of the isolated Servicemen more than mail from home). This load also included a complete false deck running for a good part of the boat's length, built up of packages of dehydrated cabbage. It amused the crew to wonder what might happen if water reached this cargo. On another occasion her passengers included four priests of different denominations. Priests to Malta – coals to Newcastle! Much needed spare torpedoes were carried and, unofficially but with Captain Simpson's blessing, a few cases of Navy gin.

A submarine which could take the fight to the enemy with both torpedoes and an efficient gun, which could lay mines and which became a key element in the Magic Carpet Supply Service, was valuable beyond price for Malta. It is no great surprise that her two young commanders, Lieutenant Commander Dewhurst and Lieutenant Commander Lennox Napier, between them received four DSOs and two DSCs.*

Lennox Napier, who commanded *Rorqual* during her second Malta commission, has given an account of a typical attack:

All went according to plan and at about 0400 hours I left my lurking place and proceeded without event to my chosen spot. I dived shortly before daylight and went deep. This was standard practice, since morning twilight was an awkward time for the submarine. On the surface one was increasingly vulnerable yet it would still be too dark to see much through the periscope. We would then all have breakfast and wait for full daylight while listening, of course, for screw noises. Once visibility was likely to be right, I went back to periscope depth to see what was going on. There was, in fact, not long to wait before two Italian destroyers came in sight, heading east. They were not close to us and there was no need to do anything but watch them until they disappeared over the eastern horizon. They were obvious precursors of something to come. The next thing to appear in the same direction towards which the destroyers had departed, was an aircraft, sweeping to and fro ahead of what now must surely be the approaching target.

And indeed it was. What at first seemed an armada of masts gradually resolved itself into one sizeable vessel, escorted by the two destroyers and three patrol vessels. One destroyer was disposed on each bow of the target, with one patrol vessel right ahead and one on each beam of

---

* The feats of *Rorqual* during the Second World War were portrayed in the BBC television series on submarines of the world, *Nautilus* (1995).

the target. In addition, there were two fast patrol boats, weaving at high speed between the other escorts; all in all, astonishing protection for a single ship, now seen to be a tanker. The sun is shining, the sea just rippled by a light breeze and the full extent of the problem can now be estimated.

So far nobody but myself has seen all this, though I have passed some information to those in the control room, so I invite the First Lieutenant to take a quick look. At the same time I pass a brief description of what is going on throughout the ship.

At this stage it should be noted that, in certain parts of the Mediterranean – the Adriatic Sea and waters south of the Bosphorus are two examples – there is an unusual conjunction of circumstances. Because a number of freshwater rivers pour into this sea, a layer of fresh water tends to lie on top of the more dense salt water, with which it does not readily mix. The result is that a submarine, in trim, in water of the top density needs to be made heavier in order to break through the density barrier at only slightly greater depth. This poses an additional consideration for the commander to bear in mind, when wishing to raise or lower his submarine.

As the convoy approached, I could see that I was quite well placed for a shot. I was about the right distance off the target track, on the tanker's starboard bow and easily able to turn on to a firing course without using speed. The problem were the escorts. While the tanker seemed to be holding a steady course and speed, the escorts were weaving to and fro across the general line of advance. The patrol vessel right ahead of the target did not worry me, since I felt I was outside the limit of their weave to starboard. More worrying was the patrol vessel on the tanker's starboard beam which was likely to weave out close to my desired firing position. In fact, he did just that. As the target was coming close to the bearing on which I must fire, he turned straight towards me at very short range. Of course, he might have seen the periscope though, with hindsight, he certainly had not.

At this point I had not much choice, but I judged I could go a little deeper, then come up to periscope depth astern of him and get off my salvo, perhaps with a slightly wider track angle. So I ordered 30 feet depth and told the Asdic Office to stand by to fire by hydrophone bearing if necessary. As regards the depth-change, absolutely nothing happened. We were undoubtedly sitting exactly on top of the salt-water layer. There was no point in hanging about. It was now or never for a shot. So up periscope, to find myself frighteningly close to the patrol vessel, almost under the counter of her overhanging stern, where a sailor was standing. One does not often see people during a submarine attack and his presence, so seemingly close, was almost eerie. However, he was looking away and I was falling astern of the escort so the danger was, for the moment, past.

I had intended to fire all six tubes at a target so evidently important, spread over one and a half ship's lengths, aiming the first just ahead of the target: but, as a result of the proximity of the patrol vessel, the moment for that had been lost. So I cut the salvo to four torpedoes, aiming the first at the tanker's bow, and told the operator to fire the remaining three by the (previously calculated) time interval.

As soon as the last one was gone, I turned away from the convoy track and went deep, this time using full speed and flooding Q tank – an emergency tank for quick depth-changing – in order to get through the density layer which should now prove an effective concealment from Asdic or hydrophone detection.

At this point the Asdic Office reported two hits and the depth-charging started. There were, as I recollect, some twenty charges dropped; none very close. Once we were clear of the torpedo tracks, I doubt if they ever had any idea where we were.

After about forty minutes without further enemy activity, I returned to periscope depth to see what, if anything, was going on. In the direction of the firing position, one patrol vessel lay stopped and a cloud of slowly dissipating black smoke hung over the area. There could be little doubt but that the target had been destroyed and this was confirmed on return to harbour.

The importance of this ship, the German *Wilhelmsburg* (7,020 tons), lay in the fact that, although the Germans were still exploiting the Romanian oilfields, it had become very difficult to transport the oil to places where it was needed. Little could be moved by land because of the demands on rail traffic for the Eastern Front and this ship was one of their last remaining tankers of any size which could carry it to where it was needed. Lennox Napier continues:

There is an epilogue to this story. Long after the event, Admiral Doenitz recorded in his Memoirs that he was in conference with Hitler when a signal came in reporting the loss of this ship. The Führer rounded on the Admiral, berating him for the uselessness of the German Navy and comparing them unfavourably with the Royal Navy. Doenitz replied that it was all very easy for the British, who had ample resources, to protect their convoys. Hitler went red in the face and said nothing.

Perhaps it was just as well for Doenitz that Hitler did not probe his answer further, for the escort given to this one ship was more than the Allies could have provided for a large Atlantic convoy during much of the war.*

After attacking an escorted ship or convoy, a submarine had to expect to be depth-charged in a counter-attack. One such counter-attack has been well described by Captain M.L.C. 'Tubby' Crawford, DSC and bar, RN, who during the war served in *Upholder* as First Lieutenant to the renowned Lieutenant Commander Wanklyn VC, and later, as Lieutenant Crawford, commanded *Unseen*.†

The torpedoes have been fired and the submarine is gaining depth and taking evasive action. The sonar operator has reported all torpedoes running and is now concentrating on the escorting destroyers. The Torpedo Officer has calculated the time the torpedoes should reach the target and we all await the explosion, followed a few seconds later by another. All eyes are on the Captain who smiles with satisfaction and the message soon spreads through the submarine that two torpedoes have found their mark.

Jubilation at this success is soon subordinated to the serious business of creeping away from the attacking position. Those of us in the Control Room await a report from the sonar operator.

'HE bearing Green 120 degrees, getting louder. Transmission on bearing,' reports the sonar.

While listening to further reports from the sonar operator, I hear the faint swish of a ship's propellers, which gradually increases in intensity. Everyone in the Control Room can now hear the approaching destroyer and instinctively we all grip on to some valve or fixture, in my case the back of the Hydroplane operator's chair. As the destroyer appears to be passing overhead I find myself crouching, waiting for the cascade of depth-charges that must surely come. I find I am not alone in doing this. It must be a natural reaction.

It is almost a relief when the depth-charges explode, with a series of deafening thumps which cause the whole submarine to shudder. The depth gauge needles jump wildly. A few lights go out and a shower of cork-granules drop from the deck-head.

My concentration is now on the depth gauges, hydroplanes and fore-

---

* For example, HX217, a convoy of some thirty merchant vessels, crossed the Atlantic to Britain in November–December 1942 protected by only two destroyers and four corvettes, the latter being no faster than the twenty-two Type VIIC U-boats which were poised to attack the convoy

† This account was written post-war when Captain Crawford was Command Publications Officer on the staff of Flag Officer, Submarines.

and-aft bubble, watching for the first signs of any change in trim caused by water entering the submarine. Reports come in quietly from all compartments and, fortunately, no serious damage has been caused. Attention returns to the sonar operator.

The sonar operator gives warning of another attack and soon the swish of propellers is heard again. The enemy seem to have a fairly good idea of our position, but apart from a fatalistic view that it could never happen to me, I comfort myself by the thought that the depth-charges have to be very accurate in all three planes to cause severe damage.

Attack follows attack. The only indication of their accuracy is the violence of the shuddering and damage done. Noise gives little indication, as the volume is greatly affected by the water conditions and depth of water. If the charges explode below the depth of the submarine, they will force the submarine upwards quite noticeably. Some ratings occupy themselves by keeping a tally of the number of charges dropped (these usually varied widely), while others just remain at their diving stations talking quietly, whilst remaining fully keyed up for any emergency.

Now the destroyer is clearly heard passing overhead and again we experience the deafening explosions and the shuddering of the submarine; this time more violent. Things start to happen quickly. I notice the needle on the depth gauge moving rather fast and the hydroplanes cannot hold the submarine at the ordered depth, in spite of increasing speed. The Outside ERA reports that 'Q' tank indicator shows flooded although both Kingston and outboard vent are shut. We are now down to our [theoretical maximum] safe diving-depth and still sinking. Desperate action is needed and, with the Captain's permission, I order No. 1 Main Ballast to be blown. After sinking another 100 feet, to my great relief we stop sinking and remain steady with a large bow up angle. Then, as I feared, we start to rise, slowly at first and then with increasing speed.

Drastic action is again necessary if we are not to bounce to the surface into the hands of the destroyer. I order No. 1 Main Vent to be opened and shut several times until the depth gauge steadies. This I know will send large air bubbles to the surface, and so now we wait and see how the enemy will react. We are now without our sonar, damaged in the last attack, and we creep along deaf and blind keeping our fingers crossed.

Fortunately the air bubbles must have convinced the destroyer that they had destroyed us for, mercifully, we hear no more from them and we live to fight another day.

It is obviously not possible to keep the ship's company informed of what is going on under such circumstances. Things happen too fast and all the Control Room team are kept fully occupied dealing with the situation without time for gloomy thoughts. But what goes through the

minds of the ship's company stationed throughout the submarine? They
know we have just suffered a heavy attack, they can feel the angle of the
submarine, they can see from the various depth gauges that we are well
below the safe diving-depth and then they hear (for it cannot be disguised) the Main Ballast Tank being blown.

I am very thankful that I was always in the Control Room during such
attacks as I am sure I would have found it much more of a strain to be
stationed on my own in, for example, the auxiliary machinery space.

Another of the Malta-based submarine commanders who survived the war and rose to high rank was Lieutenant Hugh, normally known as 'Rufus', Mackenzie, now Vice Admiral Sir Hugh
Mackenzie KCB, DSO and bar, DSC, who has given the author a
brief account of how he personally struck a blow at the Italian
dictator Mussolini.

Shortly after Rommel's capture of Tobruk in June 1942, Rufus
Mackenzie was on patrol in the submarine *Thrasher*, north of
Benghazi, when he received an urgent signal from Captain
Simpson. He was to get himself into position so as to intercept a
vessel of supreme importance which was expected to be reaching
Tobruk at noon on one of the next three days. He was advised that
it was a high speed tanker. Further signals followed, emphasizing
the importance of sinking this tanker.

Rufus Mackenzie's target was the *Diana*, an extremely fast 30-
knot steam yacht constructed on the hull of a destroyer. It was
Mussolini's personal yacht, his equivalent of the Royal Yacht
Britannia, which was being rushed to Tobruk with 294 port-repair
experts on board in order to get Tobruk back into working order as
rapidly as possible. It was also thought to be carrying some 200 tons
of desperately needed petrol in tins, as Tobruk had no oil storage
facilities. Rommel's advance towards the Nile was at this date –
Diana left Messina on 27 June – held up by lack of petrol.

For thirty-six hours Rufus Mackenzie in *Thrasher* awaited his
target and when it appeared, despite its vastly superior speed, he
successfully sank it on 29 June, with the loss of virtually everyone
on board: over 300 in all. After the war the German General
Hensinger attributed the failure of Rommel to reach the Nile to the
loss of the *Diana* and its precious cargo. However, post-war research
has more recently disclosed that, although the Italians had been
urged to uplift the 200 tons of petrol, even if it meant offloading the

port-repair gang, no petrol was ever put on board. Rommel's fury at the loss of the *Diana* is well described in the Rommel Papers. Might he not have been equally furious if the *Diana* had arrived without the petrol on board? In either case, the event was bound to have increased his distrust of his supposed Italian ally.

Although *Thrasher* was one of the submarines which formed part of the First Flotilla based in Alexandria, as Vice Admiral Mackenzie has advised the author: 'Occasionally we were diverted to Malta . . . In fact *Thrasher* was in Malta when I took over command in October 1941 and we maintained very close links with the Tenth Flotilla based there.'*

Also operating in Malta was Lieutenant, now Vice Admiral Sir Ian McGeoch KCB, DSO, DSC. As one of the commanders of *Ursula*, he has provided an excellent account of what it was like to be in command of a U-class submarine in the Mediterranean operating from Malta – an account which includes a useful description of some of the equipment they carried, as compared with that available to the Germans in their small, but effective Type VIIC U-boats.

The submarines used ordinary Admiralty charts on which to plot their navigational position. Some made use, also, of home-made plotting charts on which to put the range and bearing of the target at successive periscope observations. It was possible to extract therefrom an estimate of the target's speed (with a surface target its course was estimated by the observer); the other inputs to the plot, upon which its accuracy depended, were, first, one or more ranges taken with the periscope rangefinder, on which had been set the height above the water-line (in feet) of the target's mast or funnel height – neither of which could be relied upon from the information available; nor was it always possible to see the water-line of the target, so that ranging was unreliable and always subject to comparison with the Captain's experienced and considered estimate. In addition, the submarine's own movement between periscope observations had to be fed into the target speed.

The briefing in the Tenth Submarine Flotilla, which I received for the only patrol which I carried out in command, consisted of a few words from the Staff Officer (Operations). He said, roughly, 'Sail on — at — and proceed to a position — (about 30 nautical miles north of Tripoli). After twenty-four hours move towards Zuara (about 70 miles west of Tripoli) where "you may find something to your advantage".' And that was that.

---

* Letter to the author, dated 10 May 1995.

I now know that, through Ultra, Captain Simpson and his SO (O) knew precisely the route which a particular and important supply ship, heavily escorted, was to follow, bound from an Italian port to Tripoli. Not having that knowledge, I assumed that, because I had been sent to patrol off Zuara, that was the port that an enemy supply ship might be making for. Of course, I had been sent to patrol off Tripoli initially, and [then] work my way westwards, so that I would be sure of intercepting the Tripoli-bound ship.

What happened was that, just before dawn, off Zuara, I saw the lighthouse there begin to flash; so I positioned the *Ursula* about five miles off Zuara, but to the westward of the approach route from the north. Sure enough, during the morning twilight the heavily escorted ship appeared and, just as I had planned, she was silhouetted against the pre-sunrise eastern sky. Unfortunately, instead of proceeding into Zuara, she suddenly altered course about 90 degrees to port, just as I was about to fire a salvo of torpedoes. I therefore found myself almost astern of her, instead of in the optimum position to secure a hit. If only Bob Tanner (Captain Simpson's Staff Officer) had said 'we think that sometimes they may make a landfall off Zuara before turning to run along the coast of Tripoli', he would have been more helpful, without compromising Ultra.

As to minefields, I remember the relief at the base in Malta when Dick Cayley signalled that he had passed safely through the minefields south and west of Sicily, following the prescribed route. Apart from that, I do not remember worrying about mines, or knowing where they were.

The patrol areas to which we were sent were based upon the best Intelligence available from all sources. Once on patrol, we would receive reports of potential targets; and sometimes we were told to move to a certain position. Even when Ultra information lay behind such orders, this fact was concealed by sending up an RAF reconnaissance plane to make an enemy report which could account for us being in the right place at the right time.

In daytime, we often saw a Cant flying-boat or other low-flying aircraft, weaving to and fro, then there would be some smoke, probably, and eventually the tops of masts and funnels. The Officer of the Watch usually made the first sighting, and the Captain would at once go to the periscope and study the form. The order 'Diving Stations' usually followed. If the target was a warship it tended to be going fairly fast, and so you had to act very quickly to get into position to fire with a decent chance of hitting. Supply ships were usually escorted by at least two destroyers or torpedo-boats, plus aircraft. The main problem was to avoid detection by any means, or sighting from the air. In the calm Mediterranean, this could be difficult.

The periscope was operated up and down by a rating with his hand on a control lever, the power being hydraulic. The officer, whether the Captain or the Officer of the Watch, had to train it round by his own strength. As it worked in watertight glands, the effort needed to train it round was considerable. The Navigator plotted the bearings and ranges, and the Torpedo Officer set up the 'fruit machine' [i.e. the Director Angle computer] with the Captain's estimations of target course and speed. He would then, if asked, let the Captain know the Director Angle [i.e. amount of aim-off] to set on the periscope before firing, which would depend on the target's estimated speed, to be fed in at intervals. But the torpedo speed (normally a pre-set 40 knots) was needed as the third vector, with target's course and speed, to determine the correct 'DA'. When more than one torpedo was to be fired, the time interval between firing each one, so as to obtain a given spread along the target's length or a greater amount, in order to allow for error in Director Angle, could be obtained from the 'fruit machine'; and also the estimated 'distance off track' (i.e. the distance of the boat, at that moment, from the track of the target produced ahead of her, assuming that she did not alter course thereafter). An estimated range of firing and running range of the torpedo before it could hit the target, could also be obtained.

I may say that the German U-boats were able to fire their salvoes of up to four torpedoes at short and fixed intervals, each torpedo being angled by gyro in DA. This was a great advantage over our primitive 'hose-pipe' salvo firing. A system for angling one or more torpedoes through 90 degrees (but no more and no less) had been devised and fitted in some British torpedoes and submarines. But it was never used in war, I believe. The fire-control implications had not been taken fully into account.

The Germans used a tachymetric system for gauging the target's speed. The periscope bearing of the target at any instant could be automatically put into the fire-control system. A few observations then produced a 'rate of change of bearing' and this was used to predict the future bearing of the target. The correct DA at the chosen moment of firing was thus provided.

Because the Germans had envisaged mainly attacks on merchant ships, either sailing independently or in convoy, they decided to exploit the very small silhouette of a submarine on the surface, by attacking when on the surface at night. They had, therefore, developed a good night-sight mounted on the bridge. The British submarines were designed to attack, when submerged, enemy warships, usually escorted and going fast. Night attack on the surface was barely considered. The only night-sight available in 1942 was virtually useless. I had actually designed one, when I was in the Clyde, pre-war, and had it made in the depot ship. But no one else at that time was interested in it. By 1942 in *Splendid* (P228), I had a fairly good one, Admiralty pattern, and used it with success. On many nights, good visibility, moon and/or starlight, enabled one to see a fair-sized merchant ship (4,000 tons) at over a mile, and on clear moonlight nights you could see such a target 'up moon' at five miles or so. I know that, despite lack of a decent night-sight, our submarines carried out a number of successful night attacks: for example, Dudley Norman, in *Upright*, sinking the cruiser *Armando Diaz*, and Wanklyn sinking a couple of liners carrying troops.

Depth-setting was not, as a rule, a problem for us. Only in the rare event of attacking a capital ship would one wish to set the torpedoes to run at more than eight feet.

The most desirable range to attack was at about 1,200 yards when about abeam of the target, from which position the torpedoes would approach it on about a 90-degree track [i.e. at right angles to its course]. Before the days of radar, night attack was acceptable if a target presented itself; and there were times when, only by proceeding on the surface (and hence at night), could an interception of a reported target be made. An advantage of night attack was that the target could not see the track of the torpedoes approaching him. In daylight, especially when aircraft were in the escort, not only was the target alerted to approaching torpedoes and thus able to avoid them, but the submarine's position at the moment of firing could be seen from the air, and retribution usually followed.

Sir Ian McGeoch has also provided a story which well illustrates the lengths that Service storekeepers go to, to preserve their precious stores. His submarine, in Malta, was in need of a part without which it could not go on patrol. On being asked, the storekeeper advised him: 'Sorry, sir, we have run short of this item.' Not to be thwarted, the young submarine commander personally searched through the store and found what he wanted. When confronted, the storekeeper admitted that he knew of the existence of the part, but 'it was my last one and I was keeping it for an emergency.'*

---

* This confirms the author's own experience. Later in the war, at the big Coastal Command RAF station at St Eval, one of his Flight was refused a replacement article of flying clothing by a storekeeper who only issued articles of flying clothing twice a week, on certain days. When ordered to issue these articles immediately, whenever correctly indented, the veteran storekeeper, who probably had been in the RAF even before the author was born, grumbled: 'It's always the aircrew who upset the system. But for them, we could run an orderly war!'

One of the essential weapons in keeping Malta in business was the 2,000-ton submarine HMS *Clyde*, which was converted specifically for the purpose of acting as an underwater supply ship for the island. One of only three 'River'-class* boats, *Clyde* was, at 2,000 tons, a large submarine for that time, with a length of 345 feet overall. She could comfortably reach 18 knots on the surface with some still in reserve. She was not able to dive as quickly or as deep as the smaller T and U-class boats but had greater carrying capacity and operational endurance.

Clyde made nine cargo-carrying trips to Malta during the siege: more than any other submarine. With her big load-carrying capacity, these were of enormous value in enabling Malta to fight back. Jim Gilbert, who served aboard her, has provided an interesting account of one such journey when the submarine was crammed with passengers.

The actual conversion to cargo-carrying was a major operation in itself, carried out in our base in Gibraltar. *Clyde* had three battery tanks; each held 112 cells roughly 18 inches square by 5 feet high with a combined weight of 78 tons. One battery tank was emptied, the deck space timbered over, and the interior given a coat of paint. Access was by vertical ladder, and everything that went into the tank was loaded and unloaded by hand.

No. 1 battery space became a home for explosives and general stores on the way out, and a home for 40 unhappy passengers on the way back. Passengers stayed in the tank where they lived, ate, slept, and used the toilet. This last being an Elsan portable WC which had to be emptied every night by two 'volunteers', it had to be carried up two vertical ladders to the bridge (at the top of the conning tower), where it was emptied over the side. You can imagine what it was like heaving a full bucket of toilet produce up a conning tower against a howling gale of wind being sucked down to run the diesel engines! The reward for the 'volunteers' was five minutes of fresh air up on the bridge – it must have been nectar for them.

The Elsan was used because so many extra passengers trying to use the heads would have imposed a severe strain on the mechanics of discharging them when dived; this involved using a system of levers, valves and high pressure air – sometimes with disastrous results. Apart

* The other two 'River'-class boats were *Thames* and *Severn*; neither operated from Malta.

from that there would have been a continuous trail of bubble and squeak all the way from Malta to Gib!

After the conversion, the officers held a cocktail party in the vacant battery tank to celebrate the event. I was deputed to decorate it with whatever flags I could beg, borrow, or steal. The Captain's steward made use of the variety of sweets available in the shops in Gib. to produce numerous snacks. Every available WREN officer not on duty was invited or shanghaied into attendance and the total number of guests was about fifty. They came and went all evening and the lads vied with each other to help the ladies down the very steep ladders. Their visit to the No. 1 battery tank was much more pleasant than that experienced by subsequent visitors – no flags, no drinks, and not much air.

So, well topped up with stores, explosives, benzine, kerosene and extra torpedoes, off we went . . . The outward journey of approximately 1,000 miles took about six to seven days and the object was to arrive off Grand Harbour in the evening to avoid the continual air raids. Permission to enter the harbour was obtained by exchange of pre-arranged light signals. Unloading, a very slow process due mainly to all the liquid cargo having to be pumped out by hand, was done after dark. Come the dawn we submerged in the harbour and waited for night to continue unloading. Whether or not we could be seen on the bottom I do not know, but one near-miss by a bomb produced a tremendous explosion which shook the boat violently. Despite these interruptions, the stores were eventually unloaded, our first batch of passengers (some of the crew from the badly damaged HMS *Penelope*) embarked, and a few days later we left harbour to begin the return trip to Gibraltar.

The first signs that all was not well did not appear until we left harbour and made a trim dive, and then things happened rather quickly. The moment *Clyde* dived the aft hydroplanes failed in the hard-dive position; this forced the bows down at an acute angle which was made worse by the weight of water in the ballast tanks. Nearly everything that was not secured began to break loose and scatter everywhere. By blowing all the forward main ballast tanks and Q emergency tank, the Skipper tried to ease the angle of dive. All the passengers were ordered to run aft, but first they had to climb out of the battery tank, one at a time, pointed in the right direction and told to run – uphill! – through the control room, then through the engine room, separated by a circular hatch with a high step, into the motor room, another hatch, past the heads and wash room, to the aft escape chamber with a double hatch into the stokers' messdeck – which was as far as they could go. Forty-odd bodies, weighing some 10 stone each, produced an extra 2½ tons of ballast. By this time, the bows were scraping the bottom. Blowing the ballast tanks and squeezing forty bewildered passengers into the stokers' mess had the desired effect: up she went like a cork, the bows broke the surface while the stern was barely clear of the sea bed.

'Flood forward main ballast, flood Q, everyone move forward,' ordered the Skipper. Off went our mobile ballast, through the escape chamber, past the heads, through the motor room, the engine room, into the control room. 'Don't stop,' was the order, 'Keep going' – through the galley, past the Chief and POs' mess, then to the Tiffies' mess, past the Wardroom and the Officers' galley, through the forward escape chamber into the fore-ends where the seamen shared very cramped quarters, usually with six torpedoes. Before the bemused passengers had a chance to admire these luxurious lodgings, the stern came up, the bows went down, and the cry was heard 'Everybody aft.'

Off they went at a gallop, once again uphill, through the whole length of the boat, with more than one man getting a nasty knock when ducking through hatches, and finally scrambling once more into the stokers' mess. These antics went on for about thirty minutes and I recall one chap asking if he had to keep it up all the way to Gib. I know that several of *Penelope*'s lads suffered some very nasty knocks whilst negotiating the circular hatches in a hurry, and their aches and pains were doubtless magnified by their lack of understanding of what was going on.

Meanwhile, our antics having been observed by unfriendly aircraft, life was made even more miserable by the bridge being machine-gunned every time we popped up. This obviously could not go on for long as the high pressure air supply and the reduced battery (only ⅔ normal capacity) were rapidly being exhausted. So were the passengers. The Skipper finally found a level spot on the bottom where we rested until dark.

The air supply system in the (converted) battery tank was intended for ventilating the battery, which produced hydrogen gas when being charged, but it was barely adequate to serve forty smelly bodies whose every odour was only stirred around by the fans which sucked equally foul air from other parts of the boat. Everybody was ordered to remain still to conserve oxygen and we settled down to wait for night.

Surfacing was sheer bliss, but not without risk of attack by friendly forces, as we were expected to be miles away by this time. I followed the Skipper out on to the bridge, lamp in hand, and flashed the recognition signal to a blacked out coastline. Some alert soul must have been on duty that night because an answer was soon received and we groped our way back into harbour where the problem was investigated. What had happened, we finally established, was that the near-miss explosion in the harbour had damaged the after-planes which control the angle at which the submarine dives. Quite simply, a cross-connection rod had fractured which caused the planes to take up the hard-dive position as soon as they were moved.

Temporary repairs were made by lashing the planes in the amidships position which made diving more difficult and entailed constant use of auxiliary ballast tanks to control the angle, while the chap on the foreplanes worked twice as hard to control depth. However, once under way, the boat behaved reasonably well. Apart from scraping the bottom just off Sicily and losing our Asdic dome, and having to send the Second Cox'n and a Tiffy over the side when the hawser securing the afterplanes came loose, we were happy to see the familiar shape of the Rock in the early morning mist a few days later.

Several submarines were used for ferrying supplies to Malta and two were lost. *Pandora* was bombed and sunk whilst unloading alongside Hamilton Wharf with the loss of half her crew. *Olympus* with a hundred passengers and crew was mined just after leaving Malta with only nine survivors. The loss of *Olympus* was a double blow because most of the passengers were experienced submariners who had survived the loss of their own boats in Malta – *Pandora*, *P36* and *P39* – and were being sent home to commission new boats just built.

Subsequently *Clyde* made several more trips to Malta and extended them to Beirut and return. One particular load was wrapped in old sacks which were alive with fleas and cockroaches, adding to the discomfort of all on board.

There can be no doubt, as General Bayerlein and other enemy leaders have affirmed, that submarines operating under the control of Captain Simpson, and his successor Captain George Phillips, who replaced him on 23 January 1943, proved to be the most effective weapon in Malta's offensive armoury. According to an informed estimate, U-class submarines alone sank just under 650,000 tons of enemy shipping and damaged a further 400,000 tons. This achievement was augmented by a long list of submarines which visited Malta, or otherwise which came under the operational control of Captain (S) 10.

Thanks to information kindly made available by the Royal Navy Submarine Museum at Gosport, it is known that 1,790 torpedoes were supplied by HMS *Talbot*, as the Manoel Island base came officially to be called. Of these 1,289 were fired by submarines belonging to the Tenth Flotilla, of which just under 30 per cent scored direct hits. It was usual to fire about three in rapid succession in order to secure a hit, but up to four at a time could be fired by

U-class boats. These figures are borne out by there being 470 known attacks.

Most torpedoes were fired within a 1,000–3,000 yard range but one hit was scored at a mammoth 11,000 yards (at six miles, surely a stationary target?). More than half the attacks resulted in at least one hit being scored. It must also be remembered that these submarines also sank hundreds of other, usually small, ships with their main gun, even though in most cases this was an ancient, far from efficient weapon.

Not only did these submarines provide an effective check on Axis operations in North Africa, but by preventing the enemy reaching Suez they put paid to any hope that Hitler may ever have had of getting his hands on the vast oil resources of the Middle East. Without this his war machine, the once dreaded Wehrmacht, would sooner or later 'run out of gas.' The ripples created by the sinking of all those enemy ships by Malta-based submarines, spread far and wide.

11

Back to Full Strength

October 1942

'Thanks to these new supplies [via Operation Pedestal]
Malta was now capable of fighting for several weeks...
The danger of air attack on [our] supply route to North
Africa remains.'

Vice-Admiral Weichold, 'Axis Policy and
Operations in the Mediterranean'

OPERATION HARPOON – the convoy which in June 1942 had managed, at enormous cost, to force two out of its six supply ships, *Troilus* and *Orari*, through from Gibraltar to Malta – did more than enable the defenders to survive for another month or two. Quite unheralded, and almost unnoticed, three other naval ships also managed to reach Malta while the enemy concentrated upon attacking the merchant ships of Harpoon. They were three small modern minesweepers led by Commander Jerome.

Several pre-conditions had to be met before permission could be given for the return of the submarines of the Tenth Flotilla to their Malta base. One condition had been met on 10 May 1942 by the RAF which on that day had wrested air superiority away from the Luftwaffe and Reggia Aeronautica. Another was that the sea approaches to Malta had to be kept reasonably clear of the enemy mines which had accounted for the destruction, with heavy loss of life, of at least two of Malta's all too few submarines, and possibly others as well.

E-boats operating from Sicily or Pantelleria could all too easily lay mines at night almost within sight of Malta's harbours, and such approaches had to be swept almost daily. However the enemy's incessant bombing of Grand Harbour, Lazaretto Creek, and the other berths where small naval auxiliaries were kept, had sunk or damaged almost every vessel in Malta which could be used to keep clear these vital approach channels.

Enemy aircraft also dropped mines outside Malta's few harbours and, by June 1942, mines had become more sophisticated and varied. Only minesweepers fitted with modern detection equipment could successfully perform this specialized but essential task.

Vice Admiral Ford, the VAM who had done so much and for so long to sustain Allied naval forces in Malta, had been replaced in January 1942 by Vice Admiral Sir Ralph Leatham who was to carry on in much the same tradition. It was the new VAM who, on 5 July 1942, was able to send a signal to Admiral Cunningham in Alexandria announcing that, thanks to the work of Commander Jerome and his modern minesweepers, the approach channels to Malta were at last clear and that the Tenth Flotilla could again be based in Malta.

Soon steps were being taken to return the U-class submarines to their Manoel Island base and on 22 July Captain Simpson himself was flown back to Malta to prepare for their arrival.

In the absence of the Tenth Flotilla the Manoel Island base had been kept open by Captain Simpson's No. 1, Commander Hubert Marsham. Nor had he been idle. In all, the Tenth had been absent from Malta for the best part of ten weeks and during that time Commander Marsham had been hard at work using local labour. Under his directions, they had created a new series of underground bomb-proof rooms hewn out of the soft limestone. The Commander had also seen to the repairs of many of the buildings and facilities which the Luftwaffe had systematically destroyed after they had discovered where the submarines in Malta were being maintained.

As a result, when on the last day of July *P34* – the first submarine to return to Lazaretto Creek – came back to Malta, the Manoel Island base was better equipped and a safer place than it had been before. There were new underground operations rooms, bathrooms and sick quarters. Even the cinema had been repaired.

Cinemas had been the only form of recreation on the island, other than the low bars down in the area called 'The Gut' (Straight Street); but when outbreaks of polio and meningitis added to the health hazards, cinemas and public places had to be put out of bounds to Service personnel.*

Work had been slow because, in the absence of the Tenth Flotilla, the major problem facing everyone in Malta had no longer been the rain of bombs, which had dominated almost all thoughts during March and April, but food – or the lack of it. All in Malta were being starved and, in their increasingly weak and tired physical state, it was impossible to extract a full day's work from anyone, however willing. In their weakened state, diseases among the population had flourished. An outbreak of polio was difficult to control in an island lacking, not just iron lungs,[†] but almost all medical facilities.[‡] Hygiene suffered since the islanders were short even of such a basic commodity as soap. Water, too, was severely rationed in an island where summer temperatures are in the nineties, and with no fuel to heat it, hot baths were out of the question. Some Servicemen went as long as two years without a bath.[§]

John Agius, a Maltese citizen who worked tirelessly for the RAF throughout the blitz and siege, when asked which was the worst, the bombs or the food shortage, replied: 'The siege. The bombing did occasionally cease, even in April 1942, but we went hungry *all* the time.'

With regard to food, the submariners were more fortunate than almost anyone else on the island. In the first place they and the air-crews were given more food than any others. They alone, on rare occasions, could enjoy potatoes – usually tinned ones, but a luxury none the less. Uniquely, the submariners also had their own pig

---

* One cinema, the Regent, was hit by a bomb on 15 February 1942, at the cost of over 100 casualties – mainly British Servicemen. (One Serviceman, buried in the bar, was found apparently lifeless and laid with the dead. Coming round from his stupor, he asked his companion for a light, realized where he was, and let out a yell and nearly caused the death, from fright, of the local soldier guarding the corpses.)
† The Army managed to manufacture a few substitute ones.
‡ One airman reporting to Station Sick Quarters was asked, to his surprise, which colour he preferred – blue, orange or green? On selecting orange he was given a dose from a big orange-coloured bottle. 'What's in it?' he inquired. 'Water,' replied the MO. 'We have no medicines but we give you a choice of colour.'
§ Sea bathing was occasionally possible in summer. Even as an officer i/c a RAF unit, the author never saw a sheet while at Luqa and went without soap or tooth-paste for long periods. However, he was not alone in being unperturbed at the lack of button- and shoe-polish.

farm, to which rabbits and cabbages had been added, and once a week these men enjoyed a treat of roast pork. However, scraps of food from the messes with which to feed the pigs were now also in chronically short supply, and although the sows continued to have litters of piglets, most failed to survive. What discarded scraps had once been given to the pigs were now eagerly being devoured by the men.

Scabies and other skin complaints were rampant and the bugs and fleas seemed to realize that humans were about all that they had left on which to feed. Consequently they thrived and proliferated wherever the men congregated or slept. A spate of boils and carbuncles was also plaguing the airmen, all due to the poor food and the harsh, unhygienic living conditions.

Thanks to having been able to enjoy more normal living and good food for the three months they were away from Malta, the submariners returned in good heart, well fed and reasonably rested, although a few patrols had been carried out by submarines of the Tenth from bases at both Alexandria and Haifa. The submarines, too, returned in better shape, having been well maintained during their stay in well-stocked Alexandria. Many commanders had also taken the opportunity to have the bottom of their submarines scraped in Port Said, as the enormous percentage of time which the submarines had been compelled to spend under water during the terrible months of the January–April blitz had left them covered in barnacles. *Una*'s commander, for example, had spent seventy-five consecutive days submerged during daylight hours, either in port or on patrol.

Not all the young 'veteran' commanders were returning to Malta. Lieutenant Commander Tomkinson, who had been so successful in *Urge* and who had taken on the unofficial mantle of leadership after his friend Lieutenant Commander Wanklyn VC had been lost, never even reached Alexandria. After departing from Malta neither he nor *Urge* were ever seen again. In all probability he was caught by a mine, although a German U-boat was also known to be in the area where he was presumed lost. Tommo, a huge personality, 6 foot 4 inches tall, had sunk over 40,000 tons of enemy shipping including a cruiser. Although this was less than half the tonnage which had been sunk from Malta by his friend 'Wanks', it had constituted a highly creditable contribution to Malta's offensive operations. He, like 'Wanks', was a man whose loss was keenly felt by all who survived.

On the credit side of the balance sheet, Captain Simpson's Tenth Flotilla was being continually reinforced. The feats of the Malta-based submarines had been noted in London and as new U-class boats came out of British shipyards, they were sent, via Gibraltar where the Eighth Flotilla was based, to Malta. In addition, a few of the new S-class boats, both larger and faster and fitted with a more effective gun than the ancient 12-pounder* of the original U-class, were also sent on occasion to join the Tenth Flotilla in Malta.

The Tenth would soon include *P37* (*Unbending*), *P42* (*Unbroken*), *P43* (*Unison*), *P44* (*United*) and *P46* (*Unruffled*), while other old friends remained. It was significant that all the new submarine commanders were young Lieutenants; not one had a rank as senior as Lieutenant Commander. On both sides, the life of a submarine commander was apt to be tragically short and pre-war commanders were becoming increasingly scarce.

However, when the larger S-class boats began to arrive on detachment in Malta, one submarine at least was commanded by a full three-stripe Commander. Somehow Commander Ben Bryant in *P211* (*Safari*) had managed to overcome the semi-official age limit of thirty-five which seems to have been determined as the maximum allowed for British submarine commanders. *Safari*, and its elderly commander, who was now nearing forty, was to become a leading submarine and a dominant personality among the Manoel Island-based vessels.

But the first to strike back after the resuscitation of the Tenth Flotilla in Malta was one of the more youthful Lieutenants. Early in August 1942 the Royal Navy was striving, with everything that it possessed, to ensure the safe arrival at the besieged island of at least some of the fourteen supply ships of Operation Pedestal.

For once, Captain Simpson received direct orders from the Admiralty in London about what to do with his small flock. Five U-class boats were then available and three of these joined others from the Eighth Flotilla based in Gibraltar in forming a line of vessels

---

* Those who thought that this was a First World War anti-Zeppelin gun were proved wrong. One 12-pounder bore a plaque to commemorate the part it had played in the Siege of Ladysmith in 1899.

spread across an area of the Sicilian Channel. Their purpose was to intercept, and attack, any Italian cruisers which might be attempting to finish off those supply ships of Operation Pedestal which had successfully fought their way that far. By then the British aircraft-carriers and battleships, along with many of the cruisers which formed the 'heavy' part of the escorting forces of Operation Pedestal, would have turned round and be heading back towards Gibraltar. Such prize ships of the Royal Navy had orders not to proceed beyond a point where they would be within easy range of the many dive-bombing and torpedo-carrying aircraft which had congregated in Sardinian and Sicilian airfields for attacks upon the convoy. It had not helped that a U-boat had already sunk the escorting aircraft-carrier *Eagle*.

Two other submarines had special Pedestal assignments. Lieutenant Mars, in *Unbroken*, was to patrol close to, and north of, the Strait of Messina to report upon and intercept any Italian warships which might be in that area or have come from Taranto. Later he was to patrol the waters north of Sicily in the area of the volcanic island of Stromboli.

In these latter waters on 13 August 1942 *Unbroken*, having first been alerted to the presence of enemy ships by his submarine's Asdic hydrophone listening devices, sighted four cruisers approaching him – the cruiser force which had been turned back by AOC Keith Park's ploy of sending messages for the Italian listening service to intercept. They were heading almost straight for Lieutenant Mars' submarine and were accompanied by a force of destroyers, one of which passed a few feet directly over *Unbroken* as the submarine hastily dived lower. By great skill *Unbroken*'s skipper managed to fire a salvo of four torpedoes at the cruisers and, as the submarine dived and turned away from the anticipated counter-attack, two hits were heard.

The 6-inch gun cruiser *Attendolo* (7,000 tons) had been hit forwards and lost 60 feet of her bow; although she eventually scraped into Messina, she was never again able to take any part in the war. Better still, the 8-inch gun cruiser *Bolzano* (10,000 tons) was hit and set on fire. Later this burnt-out cruiser was beached and, sometime later still, finished off by another torpedo-hit from a Tenth Flotilla submarine. The retreat of this force may have saved the supply ships of Operation Pedestal from total annihilation.

Earlier in the same patrol, Lieutenant Mars had proved the 3-inch gun to be a vast improvement over the ancient 12-pounder. With his new weapon, he had cut an Italian coastal train in half with its first salvo, and later brought down the power-lines in the same section of the enemy's railways.

Una (Lt Norman) had also been given an important role to play during Operation Pedestal. Given the curious name 'Operation Why Not', her task was to land an Army commando unit near the airfield of Catania. The plan was for the soldiers to destroy the German and Italian planes which had been assembled there in readiness to attack the ships of Pedestal as soon as they came within their range. The operation was abortive, however, as the planes were found to be both illuminated and heavily guarded, and could not be reached unobserved.

In a companion operation, Wellington bombers from Egypt were flown to Luqa specifically to attack at night the aircraft assembled for the same purpose by the enemy at Cagliari airfield, Sardinia. The bomber crews on their return to Luqa reported 'large fires' among the concentration of aircraft.

No stone was being left unturned to ensure that as many supply ships as possible of Operation Pedestal reached Malta. If none had arrived, orders would have been given next day to kill all the goats and horses on the besieged island for food – although by then many animals had already ended up in various stew pots. As Christina Radcliffe, one of the island's outstanding heroines and a civilian Air Controller/Plotter who was awarded the BEM, recalled: 'When rabbit stew was offered one did not ask what had become of the cat.'

Captain Simpson's submarines, once their specific tasks associated with Operation Pedestal were over, soon began to concentrate their attacks once more upon the enemy's supply ships. In conjunction with the Beauforts of the Malta-based 86 and 39 Squadrons, which had first hit and stopped the big supply ship *Rosolino Pilo* (8,325 tons), Lieutenant Barlow in *United* finally sent her to the bottom. The *Rosolino Pilo* was obviously loaded with ammunition as well as fuel and, when hit by the torpedo from *United*, she blew up with such a massive explosion that the submarine, although over half a mile away, was quite seriously damaged by a 12-foot long iron girder which struck her close to the conning-tower. As was usual after firing a torpedo, Lieutenant Barlow had dived his submarine; now he had hastily to resurface as water began pouring in through the sections damaged by the girder. Until the holes could be plugged by wood and cotton, *United* had to remain surfaced. Fortunately no counter-attack ensued but the submarine had to return at once to Malta for more permanent repairs.

Umbra, still commanded by Lieutenant Maydon, also returned from her late August patrol flying a Jolly Roger flag which announced the sinking of another merchantman. This was the *Manfredo Campario* (5,465 tons). This supply ship was one of the three whose sinking, in late August 1942, delayed Rommel's plan to attack the Alam Halfa ridge, and caused him later to go ahead with his 'gambler's throw' of attacking, although insufficiently supplied with petrol and ammunition.

Rorqual also contributed to the enemy's plight with torpedoes and not, as was more usual with this submarine, by deadly mine-laying. On 30 August 1942, *Rorqual*, commanded by Lieutenant Lennox Napier, accounted for the 5,310-ton *Monstella* which was encountered off Cephalonia on the enemy's extended route to Benghazi.

September 1942 was clearly going to be a decisive month in the Desert War and once again, as in the past, much would depend upon whether the offensive forces operating from Malta would be able to disrupt the Axis supplies at sea. As Rommel appears to have known, massive supplies, including hundreds of American-built Sherman tanks, were due to be reaching the Eighth Army during that month, and unless he could counter this build-up, the Axis' chances of success were slight.

The rejuvenated Fleet Air Arm's contribution from Malta that September included the sinking of the *Monti* (4,301 tons); while the ubiquitous 69 Squadron, using a Wellington – probably a Fishington torpedo version – sank the tanker *Picci Fassio*. The loss of the tanker obliged Kesselring, with great reluctance, to lend the Italians some more of his precious fuel reserves. According to an Ultra intercept, the only supplies arriving in Africa for the Panzer Army between 8 and 18 September 1942 were brought in by just one ship and two submarines and amounted, in total, to 7,106 tons: 24 per cent of the Panzer Army's requirement, according to the intercepted signal.

The RAF Beauforts from Malta continued to be active and they contributed to the September total by sinking the *Menara* (7,120 tons),* although this was just one of a convoy of only two supply ships which was being escorted by eleven destroyers as well as by aircraft. A feature of this success was that Adrian Warburton, flying above the engagement as an observer, was able to confirm the result.

United contributed to the September total of enemy ships sunk by sinking a salvage vessel, the *Rostro*, and, also on 17 September, a small schooner, the *Giovanna*. Even so, enemy ships were still managing to reach North Africa and the German MV *Ankara* and the Italian ships *Ravello* and *Sestriera* all docked safely in Tobruk with vehicles, 3,500 tons of fuel and 1,100 tons of ammunition. *Rondina* and the German *Menes* likewise reached that port safely, but to counter this *Ravello*, along with *Petrusolo* and *Tripolino*, were all sunk or damaged in harbour by a night bombing raid on Benghazi.

In all, the Allies sank 33,939 tons at sea that September, which was about one-third of that landed. However, many of the supplies were brought ashore at Tripoli, far from the battle front.

Thanks to the efforts of Patrick Gibbs, Arthur Aldridge and the other Beaufort crews, coupled with the disaster of the Alam Halfa battle, Rommel was once again, by September 1942, desperately short of fuel. Even Hitler, with his hands more than fully occupied in Russia, where the greatest tank battle in history was taking place, had on at least one occasion (as was known to the Allies thanks to Ultra intercepts) taken sufficient interest in Rommel's position to order that a maximum effort be made to ensure that just one tanker – the *Aviona* – be loaded at Piraeus and be sent at once to North Africa. Forewarned, Allied aircraft, almost certainly from the Middle East, set it on fire in that Greek port. It was not too often that events in the Mediterranean could directly dent Hitler's morale; this attack must surely have done so.

The enemy was to suffer other frustrations. As Rommel required about 50,000 tons of supplies monthly as a minimum for his Panzer Army, he remained as critical as ever of the Italians' failure to deliver a total even close to this amount. As in Malta, so in North Africa the shortages of both food and water were reflected in a growing sickness rate among the Axis troops in the hot and arid Desert. This rate approached an unacceptable 10 per cent. The

---

* Tullio Marcon, from Italian records, credits the Beauforts – Middle East and Malta – with sinking, in all, ten Axis supply ships.

mauling that the German and Italian troops had received at Alam Halfa was undoubtedly a contributing factor. A triumphant army is less inclined to be handicapped by sickness among its soldiers than is a defeated one: morale comes into the equation. As in Malta, the German bread ration was cut – and cut again; there are reports that some Luftwaffe aircrew had, on occasion, to operate against the Desert Air Force on empty stomachs.

The arrival of the Fishingtons – the torpedo-carrying Wellingtons – of 38 Squadron from Egyptian airfields, where their feasibility had first been proved, gave Malta a new weapon. Now the island had aircraft which for the first time could fly all night, if needs be, in search of enemy shipping (probably under the guidance of Ultra intercepts); use radar to find enemy shipping in the dark, and themselves had the ability to destroy those ships with deadly torpedoes.

Initially, these Fishingtons also had little to fear in the way of enemy night fighters, but when they began to mount a score* in Malta they soon found themselves confronted with enemy fighter aircraft, probably Ju 88s, which also carried airborne radar against which the Wellington – with or without its torpedoes – had little defence.

The first Fishingtons arrived in Malta in mid-September 1942. Four aircraft, all captained by Royal Canadian Air Force (RCAF) pilots, were *en route* to the Middle East but, in a manner by then familiar, they were put to good use in Malta instead.† One of these was commanded by Flying Officer Paul Hartman, a US citizen who, long before Pearl Harbor was attacked and the USA joined the war, had gallantly given up his US citizenship to join the RCAF and thereby take part in the Allies' struggle against the then all-conquering Wehrmacht.

In quick time Flying Officer 'Hank' Donkersley, assisted by Flying Officers Bill Matthews and Paul Hartman, all scored successes against enemy ships. As was almost usual when a small number of

---

* Tullio Marcon credits them with five confirmed sinkings. Other hits resulted in damage.
† In the summer of 1942, the author had the privilege of training these US/Canadian pilots on Wellingtons and in the rudiments of torpedo-dropping at Limavady in Northern Ireland, and then at Abbotsinch near Glasgow. All the aircraft captains had earlier delivered twin-engined Hudson bombers across the Atlantic. They made a splendid course.

a new type aircraft arrived, or were waylaid in Malta, the Fishingtons found themselves for administrative purposes forming part of 69 Squadron, the unit now commanded by Squadron Leader Adrian Warburton who, after two years' operations, was still performing wonders in Malta.

Very quickly Donkersley and Matthews sank or damaged both the *Unione* (6,071 tons) and the *Ravenna* (1,148 tons), but as Albacores of 828 and/or 821 Squadrons also operated with torpedoes against the same ships at night, it is not clear which type scored the most deadly of the torpedo hits.

Bill Matthews, in all too short a time, was lost when he and his crew failed to return from a night sortie. The fourth pilot and his crew were also soon lost. Torpedo-dropping from aircraft was always a high risk operation whether carried out by day or night. If the chances of being hit by enemy flak by night were far less than those experienced by the Beauforts during their daylight strikes, the chances of inadvertently flying into the sea when attempting to manoeuvre at the correct Wellington dropping height of 60 feet were high, especially if star-shells or tracer gunfire were adding confusion to the situation. At that time, the Fishingtons were still fitted with Pegasus engines* which delivered at best just over 1,000 hp when new and kept in top condition. In their tired Malta state the Fishingtons could not operate on only one engine when the aircraft was fully loaded. Mathematically the chances of surviving a RAF torpedo-dropping tour of operations was about 17–18 per cent – about one in six.

Later Fishingtons were fitted not only with more powerful Bristol Hercules engines* of 1,450 hp but also with an all-important radio altimeter which gave a constant and accurate indication, on a broad-based scale, of the aircraft's height over the sea. The early models attached to 69 Squadron had no such device. Their sole indication of height over the sea came from an ordinary aircraft altimeter which had been pressure-set on departure perhaps several hours earlier: the instrument was little more than a calibrated barometer and gave the pilots false readings when the atmospheric pressure

---

* Aircraft engines are frequently up-rated. The Pegasus began life pre-war at about 850 hp or less and reached its peak at 1,030. The Hercules was soon up-rated to 1,600 hp.

changed. Moreover the face of this instrument was graduated in increments of no more than a fraction of an inch for each 100 feet.

In the often calm waters of the Mediterranean, the pilots, who were judging low-level attack parameters solely by eyesight,* were also denied the visual warning presented by the whitecaps visible on the surface of more turbulent seas. Even without banking in turns, it was all too easy for a Wellington to fly slap into the sea. When banking in turns at an indicated 60 feet, in an aircraft with an 86-foot wing-span, the likelihood of a wing-tip hitting the sea was many times greater.

United (Lt Barlow) claimed a possible hit on a ship estimated at 2,000 tons on 13 September, and definitely damaged the *Ravenna*, which had already been hit by RAF aircraft, on the night of 30 September/1 October. She was left beached.

Unruffled, commanded by Lieutenant Stevens, opened her Malta score on 21 September by sinking both the *Aquila*, a petrol-carrying schooner, by gunfire and then torpedoing the Vichy French *Liberia* (3,890 tons) the same day. Lieutenant Stevens ('Steve' to his friends) followed this up by sinking the *Leonardo Palomba* (1,110 tons) the next day. Three ships in two days was the start of a Malta career which was to lead to the sinking of a score of ships by this able submariner. Inevitably, in terms of tonnage sunk, Steve's feat, like that of other high-scoring Malta submarine commanders of 1942 and 1943, falls short of the over 100,000 tons of shipping sunk by Lieutenant Commander Wanklyn VC in the earlier days of Malta's war. As submarine commanders – and aircraft commanders too – invariably aimed to hit the biggest ships in sight, by late 1942 and thereafter most of these had already been put out of action. The enemy was now resorting to smaller ships, including schooners, for use as makeshift carriers of petrol and other war supplies.

By October, Commander Ben Bryant in *P211* (*Safari*) was well into his stride and 'Shrimp' Simpson was delighted to find himself in charge of an experienced submarine commander whom he had known pre-war and whom he came to regard as among the finest submariners then operating. Bryant arrived in Malta for the first

---

* As also were many submarine commanders. They however were moving at less than 10 knots, whilst pilots were making snap judgements when flying at about 150 m.p.h. The aircraft had no aiming sight.

time on 24 August 1942, having previously been part of the Eighth Flotilla at Gibraltar. On his way to the island on 16 August, he had sunk a small sailing-vessel – blown up by gunfire – potted a large schooner full of explosives the next day, and destroyed an empty tanker, heading northwards, on the 18th. He had also twice sighted U-boats but had failed to get into an attacking position with either.

Not until 26 September was he sent on patrol from Malta to the Adriatic. His October bag was a healthy one: three ships of various kinds sunk on 2, 5 and 10 October, for the most part while operating off Dubrovnik. On 18 October, after only four days back in Malta, *Safari* was yet again on patrol and would sink the *Titania* on the 20th before returning on the 22nd.

By this time the problems for submariners operating in the Mediterranean had, in one respect, changed for the worse. Italian destroyers and torpedo-boats had become both better equipped and more experienced in their difficult task. With both radar and Asdic devices now on board, and mastered, the enemy's anti-submarine vessels could make life very difficult for the attacking Allied submarines. When *Unbroken* had attacked and hit the Italian cruisers, Lieutenant Mars had to use all his wits to escape relatively undamaged from the hundred or more depth-charges that the destroyers lobbed downwards in his direction. These facilities enhanced an Axis fleet which was still numerous. At the start of the Mediterranean war, Italy could boast of having 59 destroyers and 134 other motor torpedo-boats, as well as 115 submarines; to which total, Germany, in the Mediterranean, added another 50–60 U-boats.

Even so, October 1942 proved to be an excellent month for the submarines belonging to, or attached to, the Manoel Island base which, now that the Spitfires had put the Luftwaffe out of action, was no longer in daily danger from enemy dive-bombers. In a tactical move designed to counter the increased efficiency of the enemy's many warships Captain Simpson would send his relatively few submarines on widely dispersed patrols so as to force the enemy to dilute their anti-submarine forces. At other times he would order a submarine commander, when sent to an unusual patrol area, to make sure that his presence was well known to the enemy, especially when his main thrust might have been elsewhere, hundreds of miles away.

Captain Simpson also devised realistic-looking dummy periscopes which his commanders would leave bobbing up and down in the water so as to attract the attention of Italian anti-submarine forces. If discovered and captured, these ingenious fakes carried a message, in Italian, indicating the region of their anatomies into which Hitler and Mussolini could insert these periscopes.

On *Safari*'s first patrol to the Adriatic Commander Bryant's instructions included the directive to stir up trouble and anti-submarine activity in that seldom patrolled sea area. This suited both the Commander and his zealous gunner, who was treating the excellent 3-inch gun fitted to *Safari* with almost reverential devotion. The crew of *Safari* and its Commander thoroughly enjoyed this patrol. In all, four relatively small ships were sunk: two by gunfire and two by torpedoes. Dummy periscopes were left in the water and generally Ben Bryant achieved the objective of diverting a number of enemy anti-submarine vessels away from their more accustomed areas. Several of the ships sunk by *Safari* on that patrol were seen to be crowded with soldiers and it is thought likely that they were troops crossing the Adriatic towards Greece and Crete as replacements for the large numbers of Germans of the 164th Division, and Italians from other units, who were being flown from those areas to the Desert.

One Ultra intercept of this period shows that, although thousands of new men were being flown to Rommel, his fighting strength remained largely unaltered as the number of those dropping out through sickness approximately equalled those being flown in. It is also indicative of the plight in which the enemy forces found themselves that petrol was being brought in by plane, although there can be no more wasteful way of transporting such fuel. Another intercepted signal revealed that a special escort was being provided for the Italian supply ship *Anna Maria*, because she was carrying food for Benghazi and Tobruk. Once again, Malta's problems were being echoed by those of the Axis armies in the Desert.

The events which befell a convoy which dared to pass to the west of Malta on 18/19 October are a good example of how the RN/RAF attack forces in Malta were operating together at that time. In the first place, the fuel situation for aircraft in Malta had only been eased because of the arrival of supplies brought in by the submarines of the Royal Navy's Magic Carpet Service. Next, flights by the PR aircraft of 69 Squadron showed enemy supply ships being loaded ready for departure from both Palermo and Naples. Accordingly, Captain Simpson positioned five of his submarines in a line where they would be likely to intercept any vessels which might be attempting to pass southwards to the west of Pantelleria.

An ASV-equipped Wellington (Goofington) duly located the convoy and, during the night of 18/19 October, passed a detailed sighting report giving the position of one tanker and three other supply ships escorted by no less than eight destroyers.

Utmost was the first of Captain Simpson's patrol line to sight the enemy next morning but was unable to score a hit. With a maximum of 10 knots, lack of speed was always the weakest feature of the Royal Navy's U-class submarines. However *Utmost*'s up-to-date position report enabled *Unbending* (Lt Stanley) to manoeuvre into a good attacking position.

Meanwhile attacking aircraft from Malta had been active at night and Hank Donkersley, in a Wellington (Fishington) HX 565, had hit and sunk the *Panuco*, a big vessel of 7,600 tons which was also thought to be carrying fuel: as indeed most enemy ships now did. An Ultra intercept records the enemy bemoaning that 'The sinking of the *Panuco* has had serious consequences.'

Unbending, during the morning of 19 October, then successfully torpedoed and sank both the *Beppe* (4,459 tons) and a big escorting destroyer, the *Da Verazzano* (2,000 tons).

The RAF, probably with another Fishington, had also hit the tanker *Petrarca* (3,329 tons), and *United* (Lt Barlow), which had been attracted to the scene by seeing the flares dropped for this attack, scored another torpedo hit against the *Petrarca*. (The flares could also have been made by an FAA Albacore of 828 Squadron who were out hunting the same quarry.) However this tanker, like the American tanker *Ohio* of Operation Pedestal fame which was hit several times on its way to Malta in August 1942, refused to sink.

Safari, another of the five submarines of Captain Simpson's line, was a large submarine with a considerably better speed. Although on the wing of the line, Commander Bryant was able to advance his submarine to intercept the convoy. Once on the scene, he found a ship stopped with two destroyers around her and duly sank the *Titania* (5,400 tons) without even being harried by any counter-attack. It is possible that *Titania* was the ship which an Albacore of 828 Squadron, or a Fishington, had hit and stopped during the night: as in many night attacks by aircraft, such hits are difficult to attribute.*

Although, like the *Ohio*, the crippled tanker *Petrarca* was towed into Tripoli in barely floating condition, the net result was that three of the four supply ships and a destroyer had been sunk and that the tanker was unlikely to be able to take part in further war service. All this had been achieved in spite of the convoy having been escorted initially by eight well-equipped destroyers.

The success was due in part to the co-operation of Royal Navy, Fleet Air Arm and RAF strike-forces acting as one. It was no surprise that within a remarkably short period of time since first arriving in Malta in September 1942, the Canadian Flying Officer 'Hank' Donkersley was awarded both the DFC and a bar to that gallantry award. The RAF in Malta tended to give immediate awards to their outstanding pilots (Gibbs was to leave Malta with DSO, DFC and bar) as, sadly, the recipients were liable to be lost in action before they could be decorated by the normal procedures. The Navy were also swift to award their outstanding submariners and, as well as Lieutenant Commander Wanklyn's VC, DSO and two bars, Tomkinson, before he was lost on his way to Alexandria, had also been awarded the DSO and bar.

Virtually every successful commander of the Malta based U-class submarines was decorated with the DSO and/or DSC for bravery, and similar awards were likewise given to other outstanding members of their crews. At war's end, by which time twenty-four U-class boats had at one time or another seen Malta service, their youthful commanders had received twenty-three DSOs and the same number of DSCs. In addition Commander Ben Bryant in *Safari* had been awarded the DSO and two bars and a DSC. *Rorqual*'s two commanders, Lieutenant Commanders Dewhurst and Lennox Napier, had between them been awarded four DSOs and a DSC, and other visiting submariners were similarly decorated.

As Winston Churchill had averred, each submarine commander was 'worth a million pounds' but to the men themselves – who, to a man, loved their skilful and responsible jobs – the decorations

---

* *Titania* (5,397 tons) had earlier been hit by a torpedo-carrying aircraft and by *Unbroken*, commanded by Lieutenant Mars. Lloyd's of London attributes her loss to both aircraft and submarine.

were sufficient recognition. Regular Navy officers also much savoured the year or two of extra seniority which a few outstanding commanders were granted, as this would obviously enhance their post-war career – always assuming they lived to witness that distant prospect. Unlike the majority of their RAF counterparts, the RN submarine commanders were at that stage of the war still all Regular pre-war trained Naval officers, whereas the 'boys in light blue' had generally had no Service experience before joining up after September 1939.*

A further success brought about by the combined strength of an FAA Albacore and the Tenth Flotilla took place on 23 October when the 8,670-ton *Amsterdam* was damaged by the former Service and sunk by the latter – by *Umbra* under Lieutenant Maydon.† *Umbra* also sank the small *Pronte* while on the same patrol.

By the end of October 1942, the final major battle of the Desert War, the second Battle of Alamein, had begun.‡ This resulted in the total defeat of the Axis armies in the Desert. Thereafter it was largely a matter of the Eighth Army, under Montgomery, chasing the retreating Panzer Army, while sensibly pausing from time to time in order to bring up supplies. This steady rout of the once invincible Rommel then continued all the way back to Tripoli, nearly 1,000 miles from Alamein, and beyond.

As had happened two months previously on the eve, and during the initial moments, of the Battle of Alam Halfa, great efforts were made by the enemy to ship in fuel and other urgent war supplies, but these efforts were matched by equally determined attempts by all Allied Services, both in Malta and in Egypt, to stop those supplies reaching Rommel and his Panzer Army. Initially Rommel, on sick-leave in Germany, was not even in Libya when General Montgomery launched the Battle of El Alamein with his now

---

* A large portion of pre-war Regular RAF operating pilots had been lost in the Battle for France in 1940 and others had come to grief during the Battle of Britain. By 1942, wartime-trained RAFVR pilots and other aircrew dominated all squadrons, and even commanded some of them.

† The *Amsterdam* was sunk almost a year to the day after the author had first hit this supply ship by night skip-bombing.

‡ Auchinleck had first stopped Rommel at this small railway halt in July 1942: this event is referred to by some as the *first* Battle of Alamein.

famous barrage fired from hundreds of massed guns, but the Desert Fox was flown back at once, although still far from fit.

Two enemy tankers, *Proserpina* carrying 3,000 tons of fuel and another with a further 1,000 tons on board, were sunk on 25 October, soon after the battle had begun, by Beauforts of 47 Squadron escorted by Bisleys* operating from Egypt. As was usual, 69 Squadron and Goofingtons from Malta had played their part in locating, shadowing and reporting the progress of the tankers as they had headed southwards. Even at the heavy cost of six of the nine attacking aircraft, the sinking of these tankers constituted a victory of prime importance at that critical moment: albeit a bloody and costly victory for the RAF in Egypt.

Three more ships followed the fate of those two tankers and, after seeing the third one sunk before his very eyes, Rommel is reported to have commented: 'Now we are really up against it.' The three ships were the *Arca*, sunk by *Taku* of the First Flotilla of submarines (Alexandria), the *Louisiana*, a tanker of 2,559 tons attributed to Hank Donkersley, and the tanker *Tergestea* (5,890 tons), brilliantly torpedoed at dusk by a Fishington of 38 Squadron. Fierce bombing attacks on Tobruk harbour also took place so that those ships which managed to reach that refuge still came under fire.

Initially, aircraft from Malta had located and shadowed the *Tergestea* but this task was then assigned to photo-reconnaissance aircraft operating from Egypt, including Goofingtons of 221 Squadron. Finally, three Fishingtons of 38 Squadron from an Egyptian airfield, led by an Australian pilot Flying Officer Lloyd Wiggins, came in for the kill. By then, the *Tergestea* had run the gauntlet of the attacking forces and was anchored just outside Tobruk harbour. With her precious fuel within sight, Rommel[†] is reported as having come to Tobruk to witness her arrival. Instead he watched her destruction, as the evening sky of 26 October descended into night. Lloyd Wiggins is still alive to tell the tale, as is another member of his crew. All aboard the Fishingtons knew that to use a torpedo-carrying Wellington in a daylight attack against a heavily defended position within gunshot range of Tobruk, was

---

* A modified Blenheim: it, too, was inadequate to its task.

† Some say that Kesselring was alongside him too.

akin to suicide. However, Wiggins skilfully manoeuvred his three Fishingtons so that they attacked out of the low setting sun. In anticipation of the hail of flak that was certain to come his way, Lloyd Wiggins was protecting his vitals with his tightly packed parachute (not much use to him as such when operating at 60 feet) perched on his lap.

All three Wellingtons were carrying two torpedoes and all six were dropped. Six may have hit home as the tanker presented an excellent stationary target and the attack took place with sufficient daylight vision still available. One Fishington was shot down, another had to crash-land in the Desert but the leader, Flying Officer Lloyd Wiggins of the RAAF, who was rightly awarded an immediate DSO for the operation, was able to bring back his aircraft, not too seriously damaged, to a safe landing. The trio of Fishingtons had left behind a blazing tanker and, it is suspected, an equally blazing Rommel who was obliged, in effect, to watch his last chance go up in smoke.

As earlier in the month *Safari* had sunk *Veglia* (ex-Yugoslavian *Kosovo*), *Unbending* the *Alga*, *Unison* the *Enchetta*, *Unruffled* both the *Una* and *Loreto* and *Utmost* the tanker *Nautilus*, it is no surprise to learn that in October 1942 the enemy lost at sea, according to official Italian figures, a total of 36,997 tons of supplies. By 26 October an Ultra intercept is referring to 'eleven ships sunk'.

As many, including the German Vice-Admiral Weichold have since affirmed, the (second) Battle of El Alamein was not only lost on land; it had been lost months earlier by the Allies' mastery of the sea and air around the Central and Eastern Mediterranean. The loss of these tankers was only rubbing salt into an old wound. The evidence is that most of the enemy's losses at sea, immediately prior to and during the vital battle period, had been brought about directly by aircraft and submarines based in Malta. Even when a successful attack had been made by an aircraft or vessel based elsewhere, Malta-based aircraft had in many cases played an indirect, but vital, role in first locating and then shadowing the enemy vessels while they were *en route* to North Africa. Had Malta not been there, the chances are that, with many possible sea routes wide open to the enemy, Allied attackers based only in Egypt would have been unable to locate and attack Rommel's supply ships without compromising the great Ultra secret.

12

The Scent of Victory

'Once again Rommel's logistic situation was extremely
serious. His troops were actually short of food and the
Panzer Army's bread ration was halved . . .
Replenishment prospects had always swung between
grim and uncertain.'

David Fraser, *Knights Cross*

As the Battle of Alamein raged into November and lasted for
much of the first week of that month, so the Malta-based attackers
continued to strike at the enemy's supply ships. Both sides seem to
sense that this was the climax of all that had gone before.

During this vital battle period, late October–early November
1942, of the eleven ships which attempted to reach and unload at
Tobruk, seven were sunk and three others heavily damaged. The
enemy then gave up all attempts to land supplies at this relatively
small but well-placed port, although it was the only one within hundreds of miles of El Alamein. There the Germans and Italians were
being mercilessly pounded, and being ground down into ultimate
defeat. For a while, the massive minefields laid by both sides
between the two armies in the Desert, held back the Eighth Army,
but after the New Zealand Division had broken through, there was
nothing for Rommel to do other than call for a general retreat while
his tanks still had sufficient fuel to do so.

At the start of November 1942, living conditions in Malta were as
difficult as they had ever been. The islanders were once again on the
brink of starvation, and starvation meant surrender. Another
convoy was needed.

Throughout the war the Royal Navy adhered as best it could to hallowed traditions and, since most responsible positions in Malta were in the hands of pre-war trained Regular officers, behaviour was generally very correct. Captain Simpson however, as befitted the unusual circumstances which pertained in the beleaguered isle, could hardly have been less formal. Taking his cue perhaps from Air Vice-Marshal Hugh Pughe Lloyd – who allowed almost anything on the ground to pass as long as men like the brilliant and undisciplined Adrian Warburton and George 'Screwball' Beurling, an ace Spitfire pilot, continued to perform wonders in the air – Captain Simpson was quick to realize that unorthodox measures were at times required if the Tenth Flotilla was to function efficiently.

Early on in his regime, some of his officers had become involved in a formal Navy court martial. It had been a long-drawn-out process and one which required several of his officers, all much in need of rest between patrols, to spend valuable hours, stiffly dressed, in court. His submariners got insufficient rest between patrols as it was and, within limits, he was happy to allow them to let off steam in whatever manner appealed to them. All he asked was that they returned for their next patrol sober and rested.

Faced with having to put another seaman on a court-martial charge for a serious offence, Captain Simpson this time sent the offender under close arrest on board a submarine bound for a refit in the UK, and gave the youthful submarine commander instructions in writing to the effect that, since close arrest inside an overcrowded submarine was not practical, the miscreant was to be placed under open arrest once the boat was well clear of Malta. He added that, if the man gave the slightest trouble or looked likely to disrupt the smooth running of the submarine, then the commander was to take him out on to the foredeck, shoot him and immediately dive, so as to prevent others from attempts to rescue him. Desperate situations call for desperate measures.

On another occasion a sailor, about to go on patrol, arrived at his submarine almost blind drunk. 'I'm not going on board any f— submarine,' he mumbled. Again a court-martial offence. This time, Captain Simpson had a rope tied to his leg and ordered the drunk to be thrown into the water. The drunken sailor, when hauled out, still swore that he was not going on board any f— submarine. Again he was thrown into the water and hauled ashore, with the same result. After his third ducking, however, he saluted as best he could and with an 'Aye, aye, sir' went on board. It is interesting to note that both these men later distinguished themselves in the submarine service either in the UK or Malta.

Like the RAF, the Royal Navy personnel based at Manoel Island from time to time lost personal equipment, including items of uniform, during bombing raids, and often from necessity tended to dress comfortably rather than formally between patrols. Sensibly, Captain Simpson did not act the martinet and, for as long as men did their work, obeyed orders unquestioningly and respected Navy discipline while on patrol, nothing was said about their irregular attire even by Admiral Cunningham during a visit he made to the Tenth in Malta.

Captain Simpson also had little regard for 'bumf' and reduced paperwork to the minimum; again in line with RAF practice in Malta, as the author can attest.* In Malta RAF aircraft and aircrew simply arrived, or were waylaid, without any accompanying administrative personnel. If extra men could be crammed on board their aircraft for the flight to Malta, inevitably the man in charge of the delivery chose to carry maintenance men. As a result virtually no administration staff were available in Malta. Of Luqa's three Intelligence Officers, two were Army officers.

Apart from the fact that neither the Tenth Flotilla nor the RAF had the office staff required to maintain full peace-time form-filling requirements, it could be argued (and was) that, with invasion expected almost any day after March 1942, it was stupid and dangerous to keep records which were likely to fall into enemy hands or which, to avoid this, would have to be burnt or otherwise destroyed, as had happened in both Greece and Crete.

Lieutenant 'Tubby' Crawford, who earlier in the campaign had been Lieutenant Commander Wanklyn's First Lieutenant in *Upholder*, was later given command of *Unseen*. He recalls receiving orders for a two-weeks patrol written on the back of a cloakroom

---

* During the author's period of command, November 1941–March 1942, the SDF had no office, no adjutant or office personnel of any kind. Consequently no records were kept. The unit consisted solely of aircraft and aircrew. From nowhere a brilliant Hatton-trained RAF Regular Flight Sergeant Dale then appeared who was familiar with Wellingtons and took over all maintenance of their ASV-equipped aircraft.

ticket. All it said was: 'Palermo and North Sicily', with dates of departure and return. Other commanders aver that their patrol orders were written on the back of a bunch of old railway tickets which Captain Simpson had come to possess. Tubby Crawford in *Unseen* also remembers being warned that he had been detected by the enemy in his patrol area by a terse signal addressed to him from Captain (S) 10, simply stating: 'Unseen has been seen.'

October 1942 was probably as bad as any month in Malta for bombing attacks combined with food shortages. Kesselring, realizing that Malta was once again threatening almost every ship destined for North Africa, had brought back to Sicily the large Fliegerkorps which, earlier in April, had rendered Malta so impotent. Having once succeeded in neutralizing the island he now hoped that, with the final battle for Egypt/Libya imminent, he could again render Malta powerless.

This time, however, things were different. Over 300 Spitfires had at various times been flown to Malta from aircraft-carriers, enabling the fighter squadrons based on the island's airfields to be maintained at full strength; even with aircraft in reserve. In the months of May–October, a number of these Spitfire pilots had also become ace killers. Foremost among these was the blunt, gruff Canadian Sergeant George Beurling – 'Screwball' to all – who had emerged as the outstanding fighter pilot on the Allied side over and around Malta.*

With the brilliant, monocle-wearing ex-First World War pilot 'Woody' Woodhall still directing the air battle from the ground, the Luftwaffe suffered a humiliating defeat and many of the October raiders found themselves bounced and shot down even before reaching the northernmost island of Gozo. Of about 700 enemy aircraft brought to Sicily in preparation for a quick strike against Malta over 350 were destroyed or damaged and, after only ten days, this assault was called off.

There were almost as many air alerts during October 1942 as there had been during April 1942 (the total in Malta now stood at over 3,000), but within two weeks Kesselring had to order what little was

---

* In a matter of a few weeks, his official score was twenty-eight enemy aircraft destroyed. Against his wishes, he was commissioned and left Malta with a DSO, DFC, DFM and bar.

left of his Fliegerkorps II back to the Desert or to Greece from whence they had come. Not only had Malta won this air battle but the losses suffered by the enemy in aircraft and other resources, almost on the eve of the Battle of Alamein, meant that when General Montgomery attacked, on 23 October 1942, the air forces available to protect the Panzer Army and their Italian brothers-in-arms were very much depleted.

The October battles for air superiority over Malta are summarized by the AOC Malta, Air Vice Marshal Keith Park, in one of the Command Reports which were submitted monthly by the AOC Malta to the Air Ministry:

> The prelude to the land engagement in North Africa was a G.A.F. [German Air Force] blitz on Malta in October 1942, which had, as its objective, the safeguarding of Rommel's supply route between his bases in Italy and his front line at El Alamein. The attack failed. The Axis had assembled an air force in Sicily of nearly 700 aircraft and of this force, the RAF defending Malta in October inflicted casualties totalling 358 aircraft destroyed or damaged. The extent to which the enemy had wasted his air effort was seen on 23 October when after only ten days, the attack was called off.

Although by November living conditions for all in Malta were perhaps even more stringent than before, a new optimism had raised morale to unprecedented heights as, on top of their own victory in the air, news of the great land victory at El Alamein filtered down. Servicemen and islanders alike knew in their hearts that the worst was over. The knowledge that German armies were being repulsed at Stalingrad added to the growing sense of euphoria and when, commencing on 8 November, it was announced that a large Anglo-American force – Operation Torch – had landed in North Africa from Gibraltar and was moving east, the scent of ultimate victory over the Axis powers hung in the air.

By 6 November, harried by the aircraft of the Middle East Air Forces, Rommel and his Army were streaming back from El Alamein in headlong retreat. But to the credit of the Allied war leaders basking in the glory of this victory, Malta's now desperate need for food was not neglected. Four merchant ships loaded with 35,000 tons of supplies set forth from Alexandria escorted by five cruisers and seventeen destroyers. This convoy, code-named Operation Stoneage, profited by having air protection virtually all the way.

Thanks to the rapid seizure of airfields in North Africa as Rommel fled west, the ships passed through the notorious Bomb Alley between Crete and North Africa relatively unscathed. Moreover when they neared Malta, long-range Beaufighters, followed later by waves of Spitfires, saw them safely into Grand Harbour. All 35,000 tons were delivered at the price of damage to the cruiser *Arethusa*.

The long-lasting siege of Malta, the longest in British history, was at last broken. When in December another four ships – larger ones – brought in another 55,000 tons, likewise without loss, the population was assured that the worst was behind them.

November 1942, however, did not turn out to be an outstanding month for the submarines and aircraft based in Malta. The latter were still heavily restricted by lack of petrol. Only a few specialist aircraft, such as the Fishingtons, could be kept at Luqa, apart from those of 69 Squadron with its mixed bag of reconnaissance aircraft ranging from Goofingtons and Baltimores down to camera-carrying unarmed Spitfires.

During the period of the Operation Torch landings in Algeria, the submarines of the Tenth Flotilla were assigned specific tasks associated with this new Mediterranean theatre of war. Built up to at least a dozen submarines by detachments sent from both Alexandria and Gibraltar, the Tenth formed lines of submarines positioned so as to intercept any attempt which the Italian Navy might make to send cruisers and battleships from Italy towards the western end of the Mediterranean, where the Allies were going ashore.

Eleven of Malta's U-class submarines, supported by *Shakespeare*, *Safari*, *Sahib*, *Saracen*, *Sibyl*, *P48*, *P222*, *Parthian* and *Turbulent*, carried out this task, at the same time having to guard against the possibility that the French fleet might emerge from its bases at Oran, Algiers and Toulon in order to protect French territory.

While *Unshaken*, *Ursula* (Oran), *Shakespeare*, *P48*, *Unrivalled* (Algiers), *Unseen*, *Sibyl*, *P222*, *Seraph* (Toulon) lay in wait outside French naval bases, *Umbra*, *Unbending*, *Unison*, *Una* and *Utmost* bottled up the Strait of Messina. In addition, a line of submarines composed of *Unruffled*, *United*, *Safari*, *Sahib*, *Saracen*, *Parthian* and *Turbulent* was positioned between Marettimo Island, Sicily, and Cape Carbonara, Sardinia, in order to intercept any threat from the Italian battleships and cruisers based in Naples or Leghorn.

It so happened that none of these sensible precautions was

required. The French Navy, after a short period of confusion regarding from whom to take orders – General de Gaulle, General Giraud or Admiral Darlan – decided that it was better to co-operate with the invading forces, especially after Germany had decided to seize hitherto neutral Vichy France as soon as the full import of the Allied landings was discovered.

The large Italian naval ships never left their bases throughout the invasion and made almost no threatening moves. But *Unruffled*, with Lieutenant 'Steve' Stevens still in charge, managed to blow the bows off the 6-inch gun cruiser *Attilio Regolo*. It was a brilliant attack as the cruiser was being protected against just such an attack by six destroyers.

Attilio Regolo did not sink and, with its heavy escort, Steve did not tarry to see what his two torpedo hits had done. After making a hasty attack report, he took *Unruffled* away as circumspectly as he could manage. This attack led to some frustration for Lieutenant Tom Barlow in charge of *United*. He also had been stalking the cruiser and its heavy escorts. His sensible tactics were to move ahead at full speed then to have a quick periscope look. It was all going to plan, except that when he rose to take his final look, with *United* now placed in an ideal firing position, all he saw was the cruiser disappearing *backwards* and well out of range. She was being towed towards a repair haven.

Commander Ben Bryant in *Safari* was also in a possible position to intercept and finish off this cruiser. He received a signal from Captain Simpson announcing its proximity just as he was holding one of his unique Sunday evening services. These consisted of crowding virtually all men not required to keep *Safari* on course at the required depth, into the tiny control room where hymns, not all found in regular prayerbooks, were sung lustily by men clad in their oily working clothes. Ben Bryant's sermons usually concentrated on what the crew had accomplished in the previous week and how things might have been done better. At least they were short and to the point. On this occasion the Commander simply read them 'Shrimp' Simpson's signal instructing them to intercept the *Attilio Regolo*, which was being towed back to Palermo accompanied (now) by eight destroyers, six E-boats and three aircraft. The service over, *Safari* put on full speed to intercept, and the men on board prayed with all the fervour they could muster. However *Safari* was too distant to intercept the cruiser. Maybe a silent prayer or two was answered?

Safari's November patrol lasted from 3–24 of that month. It had started with a bang, as Me 109s using cannons took pot shots at her almost as soon as she cleared the Lazaretto Creek boom. Having failed to reach the cruiser *Attilio Regolo* in time, she headed for the port of Sousse, on the Tunisian coast, and on the 13th sank the auxiliary brigantine with the curious name of *R. Bice*. He made a point of capturing its skipper, as he hoped to extract from him the up-to-date positions of the many enemy minefields in those waters.

Receiving a message that the now fleeing Rommel and his Panzer Army were using the tiny Tripolitanian port of Ras Ali to bring in fuel, Commander Bryant crossed the Gulf of Sirte to investigate. Here he played a cat-and-mouse game with a supply ship, the German *Hans Arp* (2,645 tons), for over twenty-four hours before sinking it with a torpedo on 16 November 1942. Fuel was apparently being off-loaded at Ras Ali by lighters and tank landing craft (TLCs). Finding a collection of these at this small port, he fired a torpedo into their midst, whereupon they all exploded in flames. Next day, 17 November 1942, he sank, with a torpedo, a 300-ton schooner anchored in nearby Mersa El Brega. This was followed up by a TLC sinking on the 18th. Before returning to Malta *Safari*, thanks to her keen gunner, sank another TLC on the 22nd, but when the ammunition on board the stricken vessel exploded, the submarine had to dive for safety.*

The Albacores from Malta scored a great triumph on the night of 17–18 November 1942, when they put two torpedoes into the 10,535-ton tanker *Giulio Giordani*, which by some margin was the largest Italian tanker still afloat. The tanker did not sink but caught fire and was burnt out. In this condition, the hulk was still afloat when it was located by *Porpoise*, now also operating from Malta. This submarine had no difficulty in sending her to the bottom with a single torpedo. At times an aircraft stopped an enemy ship and a

---

* When molesting these relatively small enemy vessels, which were trying to ferry fuel from Tripoli to places nearer to the retreating Rommel, *Turbulent*'s gunner once also attacked the trucks which were on the quayside to collect the fuel. The submarine soon stopped this when finding itself engaged in a gun battle with a German tank ashore. However, on his return to base, the Jolly Roger flag, on which successes were depicted, included a picture of a lorry.

submarine finished it off. At other times it was the other way round. Co-operation was the watchword.

Safari meanwhile had sunk the German supply ship, the 2,645-ton *Hans Arp*. When a German ship went down, it was certain that a vital military load had gone down with it. Another extremely useful sinking had earlier taken place when the T-class submarine *Turbulent* had sunk the MV *Benghazi*, the 'mother ship' for enemy submarines based at Cagliari in Sardinia. Post-war records show that forty of the latest German torpedoes, which ran without the tell-tale bubbles, were lost with her.

The SDF Flight of 69 Squadron combined with the Royal Navy and the Fishingtons in tackling an enemy convoy on the night of 21/22 November. A first-hand account is provided by Pilot Officer Hugh Fallis who was the navigator of a SDF Goofington flown by the American Flight Lieutenant 'Babe' Sutton.*

On the night of 21/22 November 1942 we were on the Marettimo–Sardinia crossover [patrol]. By ASV we picked up a return that the ASV operator thought was land twelve miles to port (south). Since I knew that there could be no land there – I'd just had an excellent pin-point a few moments previously – we turned to investigate.

We discovered a large southbound convoy. It consisted of five MVs escorted by one cruiser, four destroyers and four or more MTBs or vessels of that size. All this identification was by flare light and, except for numbers, was subject to some misidentification of the escorts, I suppose. There were certainly five MVs. They put up a lot of flak as you can imagine.

Malta instructed us to shadow, dropping flares every half hour 'for a submarine'. We complied of course. Malta sent five strike-aircraft and we 'saw' them make this run in as the flak flattened out. We saw no evidence of a hit.

We were told to continue to shadow and to drop flares every half hour until 2400 hours. Then almost exactly at 2400 hours, a searchlight came on just to the west and a force of Royal Navy surface craft crashed right

---

* Flight Lieutenant 'Babe' Sutton was another US citizen who had joined the RCAF well before America entered the war in December 1941. At Limavady, in the summer of 1942, where he came under the author for his final operational training, he stood out as the natural leader of a talented course. Later he transferred to the USAAF with the rank of Lieutenant Colonel but was soon lost on a bombing mission.

into the convoy. This force, as far as we could tell, consisted of one cruiser and four destroyers.

There followed a pyrotechnical display of giant proportions and before it was over every vessel of that convoy, except one small escort, had been sunk. The surviving escort was spotted sheltered against the south shore of Sicily the next morning by PRU [Photographic Reconnaissance Unit – the camera-carrying Spitfires of 69 Squadron].

We were out twelve hours that night but it was time well spent. We hadn't actually seen the last of it as we were getting short of petrol.

The initial sighting of the convoy was 30 miles south of Cape Carbonara.

As this cape is at the south-east tip of Sardinia, it would appear that, allowing for the time interval between first sighting and attack, the action took place about half-way between Sardinia and Bizerta.

Although the strike-aircraft from Malta did not attack success-fully that night, the subsequent successful action by the surface ships (which probably came from Algiers or Tunisia) would prob-ably never have taken place but for the Malta-based Goofingtons of the SDF Flight of 69 Squadron. It was another example of a success created by Malta's remaining in British hands.

Although the only torpedo which Babe Sutton and his crew ever dropped, on 26 November 1942, failed to register a hit, this splen-did American was awarded a DFC before leaving the RAF to join his own country's Air Force; sadly, with fatal consequences. Hugh Fallis, a Canadian, was evidently an excellent air navigator and this may be why Sutton and his crew were generally assigned on Goofington 'search-and-find' ASV missions rather than the Fishington, torpedo-dropping ones.

Another action at this period is recorded by the late Flying Officer Paul Hartman who, as one of the early Fishington pilots operating from Malta, also wore RCAF uniform:

My operational tour on night torpedo Wellingtons was largely unevent-ful. On 14 October 1942, we succeeded in hitting a 7,000-ton MV north-east of Tripoli and subsequent beaching of [this] ship [was] confirmed by RN submarine and on 3 November 42 [we] managed to sink a 6,000-ton tanker about half-way between Greece and North Africa. In the latter instance a huge oil slick, reported by recce next morning, gave us a 'probable' from the RN.

The most spectacular action occurred at approximately 23.30 hours on

1 December 1942 when an enemy force consisting of two troop-ships and four escorting Italian destroyers, which we were shadowing as it tried to slip across the Strait between Sicily and Cape Bon, was intercepted by two cruisers and four destroyers of the Royal Navy from Gibraltar [Force Q]. The two troop-ships and two of the four Italian destroyers were sunk within thirty minutes.

The surface of the sea was quite calm that night and, as we flew low at 200 feet above the surface over one of the burning troop-ships which was lying well heeled over to port and burning, the sea was thick with soldiers trying to swim.

For his 'largely uneventful' operational tour it can be no surprise to learn that Flying Officer Paul Hartman RCAF was also awarded the DFC. Unlike his compatriot Babe Sutton, Paul stayed with the RCAF throughout the war and afterwards made the RCAF his career.

Here again, as when Babe Sutton had assisted the Royal Navy ten days earlier, some credit for the successful attack by RN Force Q is due to the Malta-based Goofingtons. In a letter to the author, Paul makes the shrewd comment that 'After January 1943, it became apparent there would be little further use for night torpedo-bomber crews on Malta.' By then there were precious few ships left to sink and the RN Forces such as Q and K were at hand to do the job with better equipment. It was also becoming more dangerous to operate at night, given the Luftwaffe's response. Fishington and Goofington crews now seldom operated at night without sighting at least one German night-fighter. One crew reported as seeing as many as nine on one night. Luckily for the 69 Squadron crewmen, the Germans were using either a radar or an infra-red-ray night-detection device which glowed with a dull red, but visible, light in the aircraft's nose; otherwise they would not have been able to detect their presence. The enemy night-fighter would almost certainly be a Ju 88.* With no chance of a dog fight with a Ju 88 and well aware of how exposed, unarmoured and undefended the underneath side of the Wellington was, the tactic adopted by the 69 Squadron Wellington crewmen was to dive to the surface and there try to elude the

---

* One tail-gunner saw this red light and for minutes directed his pilot to dive, twist and turn, all to no avail. The fighter stayed on his tail, but, strangely, never attacked. Later on the ground, he confessed that the red light was not that of an enemy night-fighter but the reflection, on the perspex of the turret, of his cigarette which, against rules, he was smoking.

pursuer by violent skids and turns – an action which itself was also fraught with danger.

Sadly, half or more of the Fishington crews who operated from Malta were lost on operations, and in not one instance could the loss be positively identified with any known cause. They simply went out and were never heard from again. Night-fighters? Violent evasive action? Shot down when attacking a ship? Or was it just the vile winter weather which continued to cause aircraft to run into violent storms, to become iced up and to be tossed about like chaff? It has also to be remembered that these Wellingtons were unlikely to be able to maintain height for long on only one engine, and were being maintained on an island still lacking most regular facilities. At least one of that excellent course of Fishington crews led by Babe Sutton joined the many other Wellingtons which, on landing back at Luqa, ended up with all killed in the notorious quarry at the end of the down-hill, dimly illuminated runway.

The events of the nights of 1 and 2 December 1942 provide a good example of the difficulties which face researchers – fifty years after the events – in determining who sank what, when and how.

David Brown, head of the Navy Historical Branch at the Ministry of Defence, has produced a table which shows that fifteen enemy ships, each named, were sunk between 1 December and 3 December 1942. Of these, four are recorded as being sunk by RN Force Q – the light strike-force operating from Algiers – one by the cruiser *Aurora* which was also with Force Q, one by RN Force K, one by a mine laid by 39 Squadron (Beaufort), two (one each) by the submarines *Unrivalled* and *Umbra*, one by a mine laid by the RN's *Manxman*, one by RAF torpedo aircraft (Wellington or Beaufort) and four by FAA torpedo aircraft (Albacores). Attempts to identify these with other claims and reports have been made. Not surprisingly, with so many different attackers hunting the same quarry and all the attacks taking place at night, some difficulties occur.

For example, Lloyd's Registry of shipping losses attributes the sinking of the cargo-ship *KT1* to 'aircraft' rather than to Force Q. Another problem is that the submarine *Seraph* had also hit, on 2 December, the MV *Puccini*, which is among the ships listed as sunk by Force Q during the night engagement. This, too, took place during the night of 1/2 December 1942.

The Lloyd's list also shows the *Giorgio* (4,887 tons) as being sunk in Trapani on the night of 1/2 December 1942 – that is, on the same night that David Brown lists the *Giorgio*, a tanker, as being hit and beached by 'RN torpedo aircraft'. From another source, confirming David Brown's tabulation, Albacores sank the *Giorgio* (4,887 tons) on the night of 1 December 1942, while it was *en route* from Trapani to Tunis.

The *Puccini*, apart from being hit by *Seraph*'s torpedo and being sunk by Force Q, was also claimed by the Albacores of 821 Squadron which were out hunting the same targets on the same night. David Brown also advises that Force Q, as well as disposing of five enemy ships, also severely damaged the destroyer *Da Rocco* and the torpedo-boat *Procione*.

As the Greek submarine *Papanicolis* and the British submarine *Ursula* sank other enemy ships during the same period but in different sea areas, all that can be said with certainty is that during this short period of 1–3 December 1942, the enemy suffered crippling losses at sea at the hands of a number of different strike forces: Wellingtons of two kinds, two separate Forces of Royal Navy surface ships, submarines, mine-laying ships, RAF minelayers, torpedo-carrying Beauforts and FAA Albacores. Most, if not all, were only able to succeed because Malta was so close at hand. Much success was due to the shadowing – by day and especially by night – carried out by Malta-based aircraft.

For once, again thanks to David Brown, details of the cargoes destined for Tunisia and Tripoli – both destinations are stated – are given. The tanker *Giorgio* and four other merchant ships were carrying fuel, *KT1* was carrying ammunition, the *Aventino* and *Puccini* were carrying troops and stores, the *Asprimonte* stores and artillery and the *Sacro Cuore*, sunk by *Umbra*, was a water tanker. No doubt she, too, had been employed to carry fuel. The *Menes*, which hit the mine laid by *Manxman*, was a well-known, often-hunted carrier of German tanks. From Ultra sources, it was known that thirty-four Tiger tanks were lost when she went down.

When *Umbra* (Lt Maydon) sank the *Sacro Cuore*, she brought back to Malta a dozen Germans whom Maydon had rescued from the water. Some were Luftwaffe aircrew who had earlier been picked out of the sea. They were amazed when told that they were being brought back to Malta, as they had been led to believe that Malta had been knocked out of the war many months before.

Maydon, in *Umbra*, had scored a great success during his previous patrol. He was one of the Tenth's submarine commanders who had been involved in covering a possible Italian battlefleet intervention at the time of the Operation Torch landings in North Africa. He had sighted three battleships and fired in vain at them, although these big ships, far from rushing to attack the Anglo-American troops pouring ashore at Oran and Algeria, were apparently heading from Messina in the direction of Naples. As they were Mussolini's three finest ships, *Littorio*, *Vittorio Venuto* and *Roma*, each of about 40,000 tons, their departure away from the new front was good news. Maydon then came across the large 15,205-ton *Piemonte* which he hit and damaged: thus further reducing the enemy's ever-shrinking tonnage of merchant and troop-ships.

In spite of Malta's many tribulations during 1942, the Malta Royal Navy Air Squadron of Albacores and Swordfish, born out of the remnants of 830 and 828 FAA Squadrons during the blitz of Spring 1942, remained operational. It had been reduced to two Albacores and a couple of much damaged Swordfish, although the latter were in the process of being cannabalized into a single Air–Sea Rescue and Search aircraft.

However, on 30 November, reinforcements began to arrive in Malta from the Desert, in the form of Albacores of 821 Squadron FAA. They were an experienced unit but principally in the art of marking targets for Wellington bombers to attack at night: the squadron was, in effect, a forerunner of the Pathfinder Force which from 1943 onwards was to revolutionize the accuracy of Britain's vast Bomber Command. It was the Albacores of 821 Squadron operating from Hal Far which accounted for several enemy ships during the period 1–3 December 1942 when at least fifteen were sunk within a short range of Malta.

December 1942 was generally a successful month for Malta-based attackers who included among their number an entirely new form of offensive craft. By now, Captain Simpson was almost inundated with submarines which had come, mainly on temporary attachments, from both ends of the Mediterranean and even direct from the UK. At one time he could count on nearly thirty underwater vessels: but some of these were remarkably small.

The Admiralty, urged on by Winston Churchill, had been working on ways to emulate the amazingly successful attack by the

Italian 'human torpedoes' which had immobilized the battleships *Queen Elizabeth* and *Valiant* in Alexandria harbour. By December 1942, the time had come to try out the Navy's version. These craft, which were little more than propelled cylinders of explosive material, were known to the Navy as 'chariots' and the two men who, in diving gear, rode astride them were termed charioteers. As the chariots had a very limited speed and a range of only about 20 miles, they had first to be brought within reasonable proximity to the target earmarked for attack. Thus it was that the T-class submarines *Thunderbolt** (Lt/Cdr Crouch), *Trooper* (Lt Wraith) and *P311*, commanded by Malta's old friend Lieutenant Commander Dick Cayley, arrived in December with between them seven chariots contained in new bulbous upper structures. The chariots were still in an experimental stage of development and had barely, if at all, been used on operations.

Palermo, which was known to contain a concentration of shipping, seemed an obvious choice of a harbour to attack. Launching a chariot from a T-class submarine and then getting the charioteers fitted out in anything other than a flat calm sea, even in broad daylight, was always difficult. It took time and, for this half-hour or longer, the submarine could not dive. Moreover, of the five chariots transported to the vicinity of Palermo on the night of 2/3 January 1943, three chariots or charioteers suffered various setbacks: a battery explosion; a defective breathing bag and even severe seasickness. One chariot was recovered but two were lost; two brave men were also lost. However chariots No. XXII, with Lieutenant Greenland and Leading Seaman Ferrier, and XVI, Sub-Lieutenant Dove and Leading Seaman Freel, managed to get unshipped and safely away with their men astride their unconventional craft.

Palermo harbour was guarded by an anti-submarine net, but Greenland, in XXII, ingeniously managed to lift this by nosing

---

* *Thunderbolt* was the renamed HMS *Thetis*, which had gone down in 1938 in a accident which cost 99 lives. Lieutenant Wraith in *Upright* and Lieutenant Commander Cayley in *Utmost* were old hands at Malta, having been among the early commanders of those submarines. Both had then distinguished themselves. By the war's end Wraith could add DSO, DSC, and Cayley DSO and two bars, to their names although Cayley's days were already numbered. He did not live to see 1943.

under and blowing ballast tanks. The darkness underwater was total and the two men could barely even see one another, although only inches apart.

A prime target was a new 'Regolo'-class cruiser, the *Ulpio Traiano*, protected by its own anti-torpedo net. Again the 'human torpedo' managed to squeeze itself under this. The rest of the job was also carried out with professional efficiency. The forward part of the chariot which contained the heavy charge – 400 pounds of explosive – was clamped to the cruiser's hull and set with a two-hour clock-work fuse.

The two men still had four lighter limpet mines and they success-fully affixed one each to the destroyer *Gregale*, the torpedo-boat *Ciclone*, the *Gimma* and to another small vessel. The other surviving chariot concentrated upon attacking the 8,500-ton troop-ship, the *Viminale*, and the two 'riders' successfully planted their main charge right under her keel. The *Viminale* must have contained ammunition as her explosion awoke the entire town and for a while massive confusion reigned around the port. Soon thereafter, the *Ulpio Traiano* also went up. By then the port authorities had successfully deduced the causes of these eruptions. With some prescience, they managed to clear away the limpet mines and thus saved the other four ships.

Later in January, chariots XII and XIII were transported towards Tripoli by *Thunderbolt*. Their task was to prevent the enemy from sinking two blockships which, with the port about to fall to the Eighth Army, had been detected by aerial photographs to be strate-gically placed across the harbour entrance. The plan was to sink these ships before they could be moved to their blockship positions. It was a perilous undertaking, as the approaches to Tripoli were known to be heavily mined. However, by approaching from the west and using the route presumably used by convoys to Tripoli, Lieutenant Commander Crouch successfully launched both chari-ots when about eight miles from the harbour entrance.

Chariot XII experienced mechanical trouble but its crew managed to beach their torpedo, and both men escaped detection and managed to avoid capture until the arrival of the victorious Eighth Army, a few days later.

Chariot XIII, with Sub Lieutenant Stevens and Chief Engine Room Artificer Buxton astride, penetrated the harbour but saw that one of the blockships had already been moved to her demolition position across the entrance. Even before they could think what to do about this, that ship, the *Giovanni Batista*, exploded and sank before their eyes, almost pitchforking them off their unstable craft. However the second blockship, the *Giulio*, was still not in blocking position and the courageous pair managed to attach charges and sink her before she could be moved. However, after accomplishing their task, they had to give themselves up.

With only half the entrance blocked, when the port fell on 23 January 1943 Allied supply ships were able at once to squeeze through the unblocked 60-feet gap. This achievement – probably of greater importance to the war effort than the more spectacular blowing up of the ships in Palermo harbour – evoked high praise for all concerned. This included a congratulatory signal from Admiral Harwood, who had taken over from Admiral Cunningham as C-in-C Alexandria. The story also had a happy ending: Stevens and Buxton escaped from their POW camp near Rome and reached the Vatican City where they were well treated until repatriated, when that area fell to the Allies.

It might be thought that after the fall of Tripoli, with the enemy able now to bring supplies only to the Tunisian ports of Bizerta, Tunis with La Gaulette, Sfax and Sousse, and with Malta relatively close to all four, Captain Simpson with his enlarged Flotilla (including visitors) would have had a feast of successes. However, the difficulties counter-balanced the advantage of being so near.

Most actions of the Tenth Flotilla were now taking place in the narrow waterway between Sicily/Sardinia and Cape Bon. By 1943, this stretch of sea had been densely mined. The enemy now had few ships, although they had been able to seize several French ones. However, they still could muster a large number of destroyers, torpedo-boats and MTBs. Moreover, many of these anti-submarine craft now had Asdic and radar, and had acquired considerable experience in the difficult art of anti-submarine warfare. The relatively short route across the Sicilian Channel was also well within range of enemy fighter-aircraft based either in the vicinity of Cape Bon or at Sicilian and Sardinian airfields. The ubiquitous Ju 88s, Germany's best all-round aircraft of the war, could now patrol around their convoys for hours at a time. Each supply ship was thus protected, while *en route* to Tunisia, by at least two and sometimes several more escort vessels. To attack such ships, whether by submarine or air-craft, was to invite massive retaliation. Although the Italian battle-ships were now in distant harbours, many of their smaller warships were still capable of rushing at high speed (they were all very fast vessels) to aid one of their convoys under attack.

Other difficulties had to be faced by those in Malta, after the fall of Tripoli. The Anglo-American Army which had landed in Algeria had failed to press the attack into Tunis by Christmas 1942, as had been hoped. To invade an enemy coast in vast numbers was a new technique; there was a learning process to be absorbed. The various armies, American and British, each supported by their separate Air Forces and Navies, still needed to be organized into a coherent whole. Long before these various forces could be consolidated, exceptionally heavy winter rains, plus strong and rapidly assem-bled German defences, had brought all ground and air actions to a halt, with the invaders bogged down a hundred or more miles short of Bizerta and Tunis, their principal objectives.

The Germans had reacted to Operation Torch with swiftness and efficiency. Vichy-controlled southern France, hitherto unoccupied, was seized and, with it some further ship tonnage. Men, tanks, including even Mark VI Tiger tanks, were rushed to Tunisia, with the supply ship *Ankara* making several memorable journeys much as, a year or more earlier, *Breconshire* had done to Malta.

The French situation in North-west Africa also had to be resolved diplomatically and with delicate political acumen. French-held ter-ritory in Algeria and Tunisia had been invaded. French pride and honour had to be appeased. The many French leaders – Admiral Darlan (soon to be assassinated), General Giroud, the man on the spot, and General de Gaulle in the UK – all had their adherents and different points of view. Each was jealous of the other's authority. General de Gaulle was also furious because he had not been alerted in advance of Operation Torch.

Malta had, as usual, continued to assist the Eighth Army during its 1,000-mile trek from Alamein to Tripoli. During December 1942 and into January 1943, the Beauforts and Albacores had kept up their attacks on everything sailing southwards. Beaufighters of 227 Squadron, with their four cannons and six machine-guns, were able to sink the smaller ships by day even without bombs. Wellingtons of 40 and 104 Squadrons ceaselessly attacked both enemy ports and ships at sea. By night, ASV-equipped Wellingtons scoured the seas for further prey. 69 Squadron, as usual, kept track of enemy shipping both by day and night and 'confirmed' many Ultra-known sailings.

Submarines, either based at Malta, proceeding to Malta or temporarily visiting there, made great contributions. As submarines from the Eighth Flotilla closed in from Gibraltar and those of the First Flotilla from Alexandria, the value of Malta being so close to the enemy was never more obvious. Captain Simpson and his small staff were kept more than busy. As Vice-Admiral Sir Ian McGeoch reports of his time there: 'Although my first patrol in *P228* [*Splendid*] was from Gibraltar, to which I returned on its completion, when carrying out three subsequent patrols from Algiers, I was inevitably under the operational control of Captain (S) 10 in Malta whenever east of Longitude 8° East . . . where all the sinking was done.' In other words, submarines under Malta's control were responsible for the hundred or more sinkings by Allied submarines which denied the enemy any chance of holding out in Tunisia. It was, in effect, as if all the submarines which operated so successfully in the Central Mediterranean during the final months of the Tunisian campaign were based in Malta, although some never even touched there.

On 3 December *Ursula* sank a 1,855-ton supply vessel, the *Sainte Marguerite II*, a French ship in German hands, off the South of France. On the same day the Albacores accounted for the *Palmiola*. These FAA biplanes then went on to hit the *Foscarino* (4,500 tons) and the *Macedonia* (2,875 tons) in mid-December.* On 6 December *Tigris* sank an Italian submarine, the *Porfido*, off Bone. *Unruffled* scored a good prize when Stevens sank the *Castelverde* (6,665 tons) on 14 December. He also damaged, or sank, an unidentified tanker the next day.

The Wellington bomber raid on the night of 13/14 December on La Goulette and Tunis probably accounted for the *Sainte Bernadette* (1,596 tons) and *Saint Fernand* (4,312 tons). *Taku* sank the *Delfin* (5,320 tons) in the Aegean and *Splendid* the 5,050-ton *San Antonio* off

---

* *Macedonia* (or *Makedonia*) was damaged by the submarine *Umbra* off Sousse on 13 December 1942, was hit by the Albacore during the following night, and was finally sunk by the submarine *Unseen*, on 4 March 1943. She was by then a 'wreck with a crane alongside'.

Cape Bon. *Sahib* sank the *Honestas* (4,960 tons) and *Splendid* sent the destroyer *Aviere* to its end near Tunis.

However, the balance was not all one-sided and Captain Simpson lost several submarines with their crews. In November 1942 *Utmost*, the submarine in which the then Lieutenant Commander Dick Cayley had first made his name a year earlier, was sunk by an Italian torpedo-boat. Worse was to follow when, in December 1942, four submarines were lost: *P48* to another torpedo-boat, *P222* likewise, *Traveller* probably to a mine, and *P311*. No one could be sure how some losses occurred as accidents to submarines were not unknown and could be fatal. However *P311*, Commander Cayley's 'chariot-carrying' submarine, was probably also sunk by a mine, as no enemy warship claimed either her or *Traveller*. The loss of Dick Cayley was keenly felt by Captain Simpson and others.

Although January 1943 was free of losses, *Tigris* was sunk by depth-charges in February; *Thunderbolt*, another 'chariot-carrier', by a corvette in March and *Splendid* was lost in April 1943 – this last sunk by a rare German-manned but British-built destroyer, *Hermes*, which the Germans had seized from the Yugoslavs.

The greatest loss in the Central Mediterranean at this time, however, was *Turbulent*, which failed to return from a patrol in March 1943. Her commanding officer was Commander J.W. 'Tubby' Linton who sank over 90,000 tons of enemy shipping – second in total only to Commander Wanklyn. For this, Linton was also awarded a VC to go with his DSO and DSC. *Turbulent* had attacked a merchant vessel near Bastia, Corsica, and was lost during a determined counter-attack by escort vessels. Its commander Tubby Linton was a tough outspoken individual who had played Rugby football as a forward for the Navy at Twickenham. When lost, he was probably due a rest but, like others, was too involved to realize this. He was remembered by his No. 1 on many of *Turbulent*'s patrols, Lieutenant Tony Troup (now Admiral Sir Anthony, Rtd) as 'a wonderful man who inspired us all. If we were a trifle scared of him, it was because he was so powerful and expert at his job. He certainly taught me everything I needed to know.'

For the RAF/RCAF, 'Babe' Sutton, Hugh Fallis and their crew acted as principal conductor to another Royal Navy triumph on the night of 20/21 December 1942, as both Hugh and their Wireless

Operator/Air Gunner Alex Stittle have recounted. Hugh Fallis writes:

> We searched the entire coast of Tunisia and finally found one MV in the Gabes area. We were working with two destroyers. I think one was the Tribal Class *Jervis*. We homed the destroyer on to the target and *Jervis* (the leader) sank it by gunfire. The vessel was obviously loaded with gasoline and was on fire end-to-end in less than one minute . . . While shadowing that vessel in that brilliant moonlight night, it managed to shoot the right half of our tail plane almost right off, leaving it hanging by a thread. We stayed as long as we could (since the aircraft remained controllable), then hiked it for home as petrol was low. We were out 12 hours and 5 minutes.

Alex Stittle adds:

> It was a ship towing barges. The destroyers were on radio silence so could not ask for a report of our messages. To overcome this possible problem, it was arranged that we send our messages to Malta who signalled back 'Poor reception'. So we repeated our messages. This gave the Navy wireless operators two chances to intercept them.
>
> When the two destroyers were 12,000 yards from the target, we dropped a flare over the target . . . The target fired at us. Their AA fire gave the destroyers the exact position of the target. The AA fire put a number of holes in our aircraft. The worst damage was a shell which hit a bracket that fastened the stabilizer (tail plane) to the fuselage. Babe Sutton put the aircraft into a dive. He placed his feet on the instrument panel to extract enough leverage to recover from the dive. He put his heels through a couple of instruments. The stabilizer bent down at quite an angle but held. The destroyers destroyed the target with some 180 shells.

It is much to Vickers' credit, as the designers of the Wellington aircraft, that the tail plane did not come adrift and that, though damaged, the Wimpy remained flyable: otherwise this would have been another Wellington which simply 'never came back'.

Safari, with Commander Ben Bryant in command, was greatly enjoying her long stay with the Tenth Flotilla. With her twelve torpedoes, speed of over 12 knots, good range, and efficient 3-inch gun, Captain Simpson continued to send this boat to distant waters with terse orders (written on cloakroom tickets?) to 'stir up trouble' and, thereby, force the Italians to disperse their now more efficient anti-submarine forces more widely.

December 1942 found *Safari* concentrating upon enemy shipping in the area of the Gulf of Hammamet, off the Tunisian coast. A 49-ton schooner laden with petrol, the *Eufrasia*, was his first victim on the 17th and, five days before Christmas, Ben Bryant and his gun crew riddled the *Constantia* (345 tons) with shells before being forced by aircraft to dive below. On 24 December, he encountered another schooner which obstinately refused to sink although it was hit again and again by the shells of *Safari's* efficient 3-inch gun. It turned out to be the *Rosina* (277 tons), which had been converted into a magnetic minesweeper and was built of stout woods. It took a torpedo to end her career. Again it made sense to capture the skipper, and to extract from him up-to-date knowledge of the whereabouts of the enemy minefields in that area.

Back in Malta for only a brief stop, mainly to unload its prisoner – a stop which did not even include Christmas Day – *Safari* was once again training its gun on the small vessels laden with petrol which were trying desperately to reach some port in Tripolitania where this precious commodity could be landed. As the headlong retreat of the Axis forces brought them inexorably closer to Tripoli, their armies' only hope of being supplied *en route* lay in these smaller ports. On 27 December, the *Elenora Rosa* (54 tons, but heavy with 100 tons of petrol) went down after only a few rounds from *Safari's* gun and enabled Commander Bryant to capture a further two prisoners. This was followed by the sinking of the *Torquato Gennari* (1,012 tons), which merited a spread of three torpedoes: the engagement also dictated a hasty return to deep water, to avoid a bombing reprisal.

Safari arrived back on 30 December in time to celebrate the New Year and so make up for having had to miss the Christmas fare which, by then, was a shade less spartan than usual. It was made all the more enjoyable, now that the smell of final victory in the Desert was in the air. Thereafter, having enjoyed his successful sojourn, *Safari* departed from Malta but continued to operate in the Mediterranean from Algiers: it returned to the island again only on the eve of Operation Husky, in July 1943.

Including successes taken when operating from Gibraltar and Algiers, *Safari* was responsible for sinking more than thirty ships totalling over 40,000 tons. Not surprisingly, after the war Ben Bryant rose to Admiral's rank and became head of the Royal Navy's Submarine Service.

In addition to *Safari's* many accomplishments, 1942 closed with *Unbroken* sinking the *Djebel Diva*, an ex-Vichy French supply ship of 2,835 tons, in the Naples/Capri area. *Unrivalled* (Lt Turner), after a moonlight gun battle which cost the life of one of her gun crew, sank the schooner *Maddalena* on Christmas Day, and *Turbulent* sank *Marte* (5,290 tons) off Sardinia.

For the FAA, the Albacores of 828 and 821 Squadrons which seem to have combined, sank the *Iseo* (2,366 tons).* Malta, now relatively free from enemy bombing, was again on the offensive.

One of the RAF's main activities in December 1942 was the shooting down, both by day and night, of several of the large numbers of troop-carrying Ju 52 transport planes which were ferrying German troops to Tunisia. Here again the Beaufighters were at work. Occasionally the large 6-engined Me 323 transporters would also be encountered. Both types were slow and very vulnerable if caught without escorting fighters, as their sole defence was rifle-fire from the soldiers inside aiming through open windows.

One RAF pilot, never before having seen the enormous Me 323, was extremely cautious when first sighting one. The Beau, good and powerful as it was, was not a match for Me 109F fighters and it was some time before the pilot realized that he had not stumbled across six Me 109s flying in a tight formation but a single giant Me 323 transport plane.

Beaufighters carried out more than one kind of offensive operation from Malta during the post-Alamein period and a number of first-hand accounts from pilots of 227 Squadron provide a good indication of the work they did. 272 Squadron, another day-flying Beaufighter Squadron, was similarly involved. 227 Squadron first arrived in Malta on 25 October 1942, just after Kesselring's last desperate attempt to neutralize the island by bombing.

John Clements, a South African pilot of 227 Squadron, who flew with observer Pilot Officer Ken Pollard, describes some of the varied tasks which these day-flying Beaufighters carried out from Malta, the information coming principally from his personal pilot's Log Book.

---

* It was during this period that the Albacores scored most heavily. They accounted for most of the 33 enemy ships sunk by FAA torpedoes, according to Tullio Marcon's research of Italian records.

Oct. 25 Gib to Malta. Beau X 8074. Virtually grounded by enemy bombing and lack of fuel and ammo.

Oct. 30 Malta to Edkin (Egypt) X 8074. Only 2 Beaus flown [back] to Egypt, as rest were knocked out on ground.

By 5 November 1942, the squadron had been re-formed, given new aircraft, carried out air tests, harmonized the guns and was again ready for action in Malta.

Nov. 5 Edkin to Malta Beau X 8068. Lt. General Scobie as passenger.*

Nov. 9 Search for enemy E boats with F/Lt Schmidt. No contact. [This could have been to help clear the way for the vital convoy, Operation Stoneage – the convoy which sailed from Alexandria to relieve the Malta siege.]

Nov. 13 Fighter patrol. Destroyed 1 Ju 52, 1 Do[rnier] 24 (flying boat) shared with F/Lt Schmidt. Two other transport damaged.

Nov. 14 Fighter patrol. Destroyed 1 Ju 88 (shared with W/Cdr Masterman). On standby to attack Italian fleet. [The Italian fleet *did* leave the port of Taranto but, to the general relief of aircrews, turned NE and passed through the Strait of Messina heading for Naples.]

Nov. 20 Fighter patrol. Destroyed 1 Italian bomber (Caproni?) Polly [Pollard] dropped his dinghy attached to his Mae West to bomber crew in sea. Attacked by Me 110.

Nov. 21 Escorted Beauforts for shipping attack. No target found. Beaus successfully attacked oil supply tanker at Tunis with cannons.

Nov. 22 Shipping strike with Beauforts. Destroyer strafed. Two Beaus and 1 Beaufort shot down.

Nov. 24 Beau X 8068 still. Bombing attack on Palermo harbour. 500 lbs under each wing. Failed to return due to bad weather. Ditched off Trapani. POW. Escaped 10 Sept 1943.

In one month this pilot experienced two visits to Malta; shot down several transport planes heading for Tunisia; acted as VIP transport plane for a general; helped to protect the incoming Operation Stoneage convoy; flew as escort on some of the torpedo-carrying Beaufort strikes; tried to save an Italian airman whom he had shot down and, in return for this fine gesture, was nearly shot down by

---

* The passenger in this two-seater fighter-aircraft had no seat, so had to stand behind the pilot. While *en route* to Malta, a U-boat was sighted but it submerged before it could be strafed, much to the passenger's relief. With the aircraft being abruptly dived and flung into an attack, General Scobie had been casting anxious glances at his luggage which consisted of a suitcase and a precious case of whisky.

long-range enemy Me 110 fighters; stood by to tackle the Italian battlefleet; bombed enemy oil tanks, then the port of Palermo; strafed a destroyer; saw three colleagues shot down, only to end up a victim of Malta's vile weather. During this time, as another 227 Squadron pilot, Flying Officer Eric 'Lofty' Gittings, has advised, 'we lost at least 20–25 crews (40–50 blokes)'.*

John Clements also recalls that, when nearing Malta from Gibraltar and calling Malta for a homing bearing, he was answered from Sicily with a false one. He then arrived during an air raid and had to hold off, with fuel gauges nearing zero, orbiting around Filfla. After landing, he was directed by a soldier who had jumped on to a wing to a distant dispersal pen, passing by a number of red flags. 'Unexploded bombs,' he was later informed.

Cas de Bounevialle was another Beaufighter pilot of 227 Squadron who spent some time escorting, and later joining in the attacks with the torpedo-carrying Beauforts. 'That got expensive,' he recalls, 'as the German gunners concentrated upon the "fish"-carriers and 39 Squadron lost at least one, and sometimes more, on every torpedo strike.' Thereafter 'we did shipping strikes on our own . . . the next few months were pretty hectic, with attacks on shipping and those enormous formations of Ju 52s escorted by Me 110s and Ju 88s; also in smaller numbers Do 24 (boats), SM 82s and that big six-engined transport [Me 323]. The tally of ships sunk and aircraft destroyed was quite considerable, sometimes seven or eight or more Ju 52s in one attack.' As Cas de Bounevialle adds: 'I reckon that Malta was "value for money", in that it engaged the attention of considerable Axis forces – both sea and air – as well as causing great damage.'

Perhaps the most outstanding day-Beaufighter[†] pilot in Malta

---

* Gittings also writes: 'Skip bombing [i.e. the ducks-and-drakes bombing at low level over calm seas] led to some interesting experiences, mainly the result of bombs bouncing so high off the water that they formated on the aircraft which had dropped them. The evasive actions had to be seen to be believed!'

† The Beaufighter was primarily a well-designed, powerfully armed *night*-fighter, and in the UK and Malta was principally used as such. 89 Squadron, using Beaufighters in Malta, built up a great reputation and shot down over fifty enemy raiders at night. The populace always cheered when they heard the rattle of its four cannons and six machine-guns and saw an enemy bomber fall in flames. However, it was also an excellent long-range day-fighter and was used in Malta for PR work and low-level ship bombing.

was a Canadian, Flight Lieutenant Dallas Schmidt,* who has kindly made available his pilot's Log Book for this period. He first arrived in Malta on 26 August 1942 and flew his last – highly memorable – mission on Christmas Day 1942. Before Dallas Schmidt left Malta he had been awarded both a DFC and bar. Among his thirty-seven operations were eleven in which he accompanied the Beauforts on potential shipping strikes: on about half of these, the formation did not locate their quarry. As he was soon himself carrying bombs on these sorties, he hit a ship with these on 6 September, and scored cannon hits on another on 22 September, when the Gibbs' Beauforts attacked successfully off Paxos. Schmidt had earlier played a leading support role in two of the Beaufort attacks on tankers on the eve of the Battle of Alam Halfa. In one of these, he shot down an enemy aircraft, a Cant flying-boat.

Dallas and other Beaufighter crews went on shipping raids without the Beauforts on another eight occasions. Armed with bombs and cannons (the 250-pound bombs were soon replaced by 500-pound ones) he reckons to have sunk, or hit, a ship at only 15 yards range on 11 September, helped to damage three small coasters off Tripoli the next day, blasted his guns at two MVs on 20 November, caused a ship to be beached off Homs on 25 November, left another smoking off the coast of Tunis four days later and, on 23 December 1942, to quote directly from his Log Book: 'Beau MT 5169. Shipping strike with 500 lbs bombs, escort of 2 Beaus and 2 Spits. Scored direct hit on 1,500 ton MV with escort of 1 DR and 5 Ju 88s. That shook them. Ship blew up.'

The bomb racks were a locally made modification. The pilots had no bomb sight nor had they been trained to drop bombs. Everything depended upon the pilot's eye which is why they went so low. Throughout these operations, Schmidt's observer was Flight Sergeant Campbell and, before the pair left Malta, he was decorated with the DFM.

On other missions, Dallas Schmidt went out five times to find dinghies of brother airmen who had been shot down at sea and, prior to the epic operation on 25 December, was twice successful in locating them. He also once dropped his own one-man dinghy and

---

* Post-war he became a Cabinet Minister in the Alberta State Parliament (Canada).

Mae West life-jacket loaded with rations to an airman whom, with his quick eyesight, he happened to detect in the sea. Later he discovered that he had saved the life of a Luftwaffe pilot.

Bad weather very nearly ended his distinguished RCAF career on the Palermo night-bombing attack. Ice affected both engines and caused them to cut out, and the Beau fell from 12,000 to 2,000 feet over Sicily, when he found himself in a valley as power was restored. He regained control, went back to his task and bombed Licata instead. This was the same night, 24 November 1942, when the atrocious weather had ended John Clements' Malta career.

As with Cas, John Clements and Lofty Gittings, Flight Lieutenant Schmidt took part in several sweeps in search of the Ju 52s and other transport aircraft heading to Tunisia. In the course of these he took part in the shooting down of six Ju 52s and one Ju 88 but some were shared with John Clements and others. He also damaged several SM 82s.

The Ju 52s were generally accompanied by Ju 88s and often large numbers of Me 109s. This action by the enemy caused the Beaus, in their turn, to be accompanied by Spitfires. On three occasions Dallas Schmidt had to fly back to Malta, after an engagement, with one engine shot out, but each time he landed successfully on the remaining one. Dallas also took part in other offensive reconnaissance operations and, on one of these, he attacked with cannon-fire the railway system between Sfax and Sousse. He also escorted the cargo-carrying *Manxman* – officially a minelayer – when that Naval vessel was used to bring supplies to Malta in November 1942 in order to help break the long siege.

Although Britain's main objective was to keep Malta operational as an unsinkable aircraft-carrier and an invaluable submarine base, the plight of the Maltese population was not ignored. On this particular journey to Malta, the fast 38-knot *Manxman* was making a solo dash to Malta with supplies of dried milk for Maltese children.

If all this was not enough for Flight Lieutenant Dallas Schmidt DFC and bar, the events of Christmas Day 1942 saw the culmination, and end, of his Malta career.

Along with another Beau, Schmidt set out to find and attack a schooner and several F-boats which were protecting her. Although the pair found the enemy and Schmidt sank an F-boat, he suffered so many hits from his victim that all normal control was lost. By skill and ingenuity, although without any attitude control, he headed back for Malta using variations of engine power to raise or lower the nose as best he could. About 30 miles from Malta, with the aircraft now seemingly out of control, he ordered his observer to bale out. This change of trim which resulted from Campbell's departure made the Beau more manageable and Dallas managed to get it back over Malta where, flying at several thousand feet, he himself baled out.

The Beau, now empty, then gave an amazing five-minute long aerobatic display which astounded all who witnessed it. Several times it dived and skimmed within inches of the ground, followed by near-vertical pull-ups and further crazy dives. None of the amazed observers on the ground knew that the Beau was without a man on board and all wondered who the idiot, so clearly bent on suicide, could be. After more loops and other crazy gyrations, Beaufighter EL 232 finally dived vertically into the ground not far away from Luqa, luckily without harming anyone. This apparently senseless loss of a mad pilot and a good aircraft quite spoiled Christmas Day for some who had witnessed it.

Meanwhile Flight Sergeant Campbell, his observer, had discovered upon arriving in the sea, some 30 miles or so from Malta, that he had baled out without his one-man dinghy. With little else that he could do, he optimistically took a visual bearing from the sun and set out to swim back to Malta.

Dallas, however, had carefully remembered the estimated position where he had parted from his faithful observer and, after his own safe arrival back on *terra firma*, he was able to give such explicit information that two and a half hours after Campbell had come down in the sea, an Air–Sea Rescue Swordfish (probably all that remained of Malta's once sole strike-force, 830 Squadron) located him and dropped him a dinghy. An hour later, a launch picked him up. It was a fitting and happy ending to an amazing sortie.

In all, the Beaufighter proved itself in Malta as able an attack-aircraft as it was a robust night-defender. Once again a local improvisation – the fitting of bomb-racks – had helped Malta to strike back. Moreover this initiative was soon followed up in the UK where the Beaufighter was further modified to become, not just a low-level bomber, but also a prime torpedo-bomber.

Bomb-racks had earlier been fitted to Hurricanes and Spitfires in

Malta, having been added to Spitfires following Kesselring's unsuccessful blitz on the island in October 1942. When that attack was ignominiously and abruptly called off, the Spitfire squadrons counter-attacked by daylight bombing of the enemy's Sicilian airfields. The idea of modifying Hurricanes and Spitfire fighters to carry bombs had thereafter been taken up with good effect in the UK, and the 'fighter-bomber' became the linch-pin of British Tactical Air Forces.

The ripples emanating from Malta's successful innovations were having a beneficial effect upon the war in Europe as a whole.

By now nothing could save Tripoli, and the Eighth Army duly entered the Italian colonial capital on 23 January 1943. Thereafter it would continue its westwards march with the object of linking up, in Tunisia, with the Anglo-American force advancing from Algiers. With the fall of Tripoli and the seizure by Anglo-American land forces of the formerly Vichy-controlled territory of Algeria the emphasis of the war in the Mediterranean shifted away from the Desert to the Central Mediterranean. The French colony of Tunisia remained the only North African territory still in enemy hands.

Tunisia was the North African country in closest proximity to Malta, with most of its inhabited areas in the north-east of the country,* only about 200 miles from the British base. With the battle for Tunis raging so close at hand, Malta had become strategically well placed to play a vital part in that campaign. Once more the island's role was to sever the enemy's supply lines. The presence of Malta again became a serious threat to the enemy. While the Germans poured troops and war materials into Tunisia – ironically, in the large numbers that Rommel had so often demanded but never received – there was always the threat that Naval and Air Forces based in Malta would disrupt this supply route.

Proximity to the enemy's chosen shipping routes – Sardinia–Cape Bon or Palermo–Cape Bon – resulted in the frequent employment by Malta of Royal Navy and Allied submarines of the First and Eighth, as well as the Tenth Flotillas. Submarines of the Eighth would leave Gibraltar, perform their tasks, and replenish in

---

* South of Sfax most of Tunisia is desert. North of Sfax, it is agricultural.

Malta. Submarines of the First Flotilla operating from Alexandria would do likewise. As before, whenever operating in the Central Mediterranean, submarines from both Flotillas would come under the orders of Captain (S) 10, even if never entering Malta. As the then Lieutenant Tony Troup RN has described it: 'I cannot say honestly where precisely we started and finished each patrol. Some were from Alexandria, some from Beirut and some from Malta, but it is important to appreciate that Malta was always under our lee for use whenever required. All operations were to some extent integrated with those boats based full time in Malta.'

The importance of the Malta submarines as a key factor in the Allies' underwater successes in the Mediterraean is underlined by a report, compiled by Captain Ken Aylwin RN (Rtd), which states: 'Upwards of 500 offensive patrols by submarines took place during the period of the Siege of Malta approximately 350 of which were Malta based.'* The report also lists the large number of Allied submarines involved in these patrols: 91 in all. The fact that submarines from either end of the Mediterranean could, by 1943, be refuelled and otherwise replenished in Malta, shows the extent to which the siege of Malta had by then been lifted. It also shows how relatively safe from bombing Malta had become. The RAF had not only retained air superiority on the island but was taking the air battle to the enemy, in the many raids on Sicilian airfields by bomb-carrying Spitfires.

Hitler's determination to defend Tunisia, suicidal as it may seem in retrospect, was based on the strategic conception (right for once, as it turned out) which he expressed at a meeting of the OKW in Berlin during March 1943. 'It is necessary', he is quoted as saying, 'to confront the Italians boldly with the alternative of either making an all-out effort to get supplies through [to Tunisia] regardless of personal cost or to lose Tunisia and with that also Italy.' Moreover he matched these words with deeds. So assiduously did Hitler pour German troops into Tunisia that, despite their heavy losses *en route*, when their total surrender came in May 1943, the numbers of enemy troops who gave themselves up amounted to just under 250,000. Of

---

*'Maritime Forces supporting Malta during the Siege 1940–1943' (privately published). Information extracted from 'Naval Staff History, Second World War. Submarines', Vol. II.

these over half were German: more Germans were taken prisoner after the surrender in Tunisia than were taken by the Russians after the German surrender at Stalingrad. (Not that the Russians were over-zealous about taking prisoners!)

Towards the end of the Tunisian campaign, the transportation to Tunisia by air of hundreds, if not thousands, of men daily was an almost farcical blunder: during the final weeks of that campaign, thanks to Allied warships and aircraft, almost every ship bound for Tunisian ports was sunk. This meant that the new arrivals had little to fight with other than what they could carry in their hands. One Panzer division, for example, surrendered on foot, having walked a dozen miles to do so when completely out of fuel and almost every-thing else: including, it is thought, food.

Proximity to the Tunisian ports was not however entirely to the advantage of the Allies. Royal Navy submarines operating from, or to, Malta continued to suffer losses. It was relatively easy for the enemy to guess, with accuracy, the routes that submarines from Malta were likely to take. Many of these routes were therefore made prohibitively dangerous. Minefields were stretched much of the way across the Sicilian Channel through which submarines from Malta had to pass to order to reach the enemy's principal departure ports of Naples, Palermo, Trapani or Cagliari.

The Germans had also heavily mined the approaches to Bizerta. Other enemy minefields lay to the south of Pantelleria, in a direct line between Malta and the Tunisian port of Sousse.

It has been estimated that, during the war in the Mediterranean as a whole, the Italians and Germans laid over 100,000 mines at sea. Large minefields were laid especially in the Sardinia–Sicily–Tunisia area. These had two purposes: one was to prevent ships getting to Malta and the other was to make life difficult for surface ships and submarines operating from Malta.

It would seem likely that enemy minefields may in all have accounted for the loss of the submarines *Olympus, P33, P34, Perseus, Regent, Regulus, Talisman, Tetrarch, Thorn, Traveller, Triton, Triumph, Undaunted, Urge* and *Usk*, although other causes, such as accident or self-demolition via a 'circler', are possible. All these submarines operated, at one time or another, under Malta control. Many, such as *Olympus*, are known to have been mined off Malta when carry-ing passengers, thereby adding to the heavy loss of life.

Despite the many Allied submarine losses during the early months of 1943, the balance sheet definitely favoured the Allies. In brief, between 1 December 1942 and 13 May 1943 – the day when all Axis forces in Tunisia surrendered – well over 100 enemy ships within 350 miles of Malta were sunk by our submarines. As these sinkings all took place within the orbit of Malta rather than Alexandria or Gibraltar, it is regarded as likely that all were sunk by submarines operating under Malta control.

In addition a further half-dozen enemy ships were sunk north of 41° N – about the mid-point of Sardinia. These, also, were probably sunk by submarines operating from, or associated with, Malta. Another four were also sunk south of Sousse, and another two in the south Adriatic: again these supply ships would probably have been sunk by submarines under the control of Captain (S) 10.

Curiously, during the final seventeen days of the Tunisian campaign, only two enemy ships were sunk by Allied submarines. Yet it is known that, by then, the enemy were running out of supplies and were in desperate need of ammunition, food and petrol. Could it have been that the losses, during the period December 1942 to the end of April 1943, had been so great that the Axis powers simply gave up trying to ship goods across to their armies in Tunisia? Or had the enemy by then nearly run out of ships? What is known for certain is that very little was being landed. The supposition that there was now a grave shortage of ships is supported by the fact that a great number of small or very small vessels had been pressed into service as petrol and supply carriers and that some of these had obviously been seized from French and other sources and hastily renamed.

It is also curious to note that, even when defeat was clearly staring the Axis armies in Tunisia in the face, no serious attempt was made to evacuate the troops to Sardinia and Sicily. Less than 1,000 seem to have got back, in startling contrast to the Dunkirk evacuation of 1940. It is to the credit of those in Malta who severed the Cagliari/Palermo–Tunisia life-line that the principal enemy, Germany, was denied some 130,000 troops who, if they could have escaped drowning or capture, would have been available either to fight on the Russian Fronts or to bolster the defences, already being prepared in northern France, for the expected cross-Channel invasion from Britain.

Aircraft from Malta were busy attacking enemy shipping in the same area throughout this period. One such unit was the Wellington squadron, 221, which had been re-formed in the Desert and there converted into a Fishington squadron for employment in Malta, although it was also to be used in its former night-reconnaissance role where its ASV was so useful. After their aircraft had been modified to carry up to two torpedoes, the crews were then trained in the difficult art of dropping torpedoes by night, having first used their ASV airborne radars to locate targets. Thus equipped, 221 Squadron moved, on 21 January 1943, from Shallufa to Malta. They were able to use their radar to drop torpedoes more or less at the exact required 800 yards range as Flying Officer Les Card* had modified their ASV sets to read, on an additional scale, distances in yards rather than miles.

Although 221 Squadron had not before been based in Malta, some of its aircrews were familiar with the island, having had to land at Luqa when operating out of Egypt against enemy shipping as far west as Benghazi since the aircraft lacked the range, in certain conditions, to fly from Shallufa to Benghazi and back, especially when an extended search for the expected (often Ultra-intercepted) shipping had first been necessary. For example, Flight Sergeant Shepherd, on 3 November 1942, found a convoy off Benghazi, consisting of a tanker protected by five destroyers. Obviously, it was of vital importance to Rommel, especially as the Axis front at El Alamein was faced with collapse due, as much as anything else, to lack of petrol.

This 221 pilot, operating in a Goofington role, located the convoy by ASV, homed a number of torpedo-carrying Fishingtons of 38 Squadron towards it and, when they arrived, illuminated it for the attackers. The tanker was set on fire. As his personal Log Book records: 'Low on fuel, so diverted to Malta.' Malta's utility was once again proved, even though all the aircraft concerned with this particular attack were from two squadrons based in Egypt.

Fred Oldfield was another 221 Squadron crew member who, when operating with 38 Squadron in the Desert, had on occasion

---

* This was the same enterprising Les Card, then a Corporal in the RCAF, who had assisted Flying Officer Glazer to make the Roosters for Force K (*Aurora*) and the author's Goofington.

when low on fuel diverted to Luqa rather than try to get back to an Egyptian airfield.

Most RAF personnel arriving in Malta for the first time were struck either by the scene of almost total devastation or by the lack of food, but Lieutenant Gil Catton (SAAF),* a 221 Squadron captain, remembers most his encounter with the colourful, energetic Warburton about whom he had heard so many stories, even in Egypt: 'I was more than surprised', Gil has written, 'to see him walk in wearing civvy clothes, sports coat and flannels, and I think he wore bedroom slippers . . . We were impressed to hear that he was the only top pilot to have his own Spit and Beaufighter at his disposal.'

The Squadron arrived with a full complement of sixteen aircraft (Fishingtons) and crews. As Gil Catton recalls: 'We were given a hot reception, especially from the Ju 88 night-fighters. Within four weeks we had lost eight Wellingtons.' Gil recalls one such outing on the night of 15 February 1943 when a tanker was located midway between Sicily and Tunisia.

> There was a lot of cloud, and dark patches made it extremely difficult to see the target. Although Malta sent out all available Wellingtons and Beauforts, I was the only Wellington to launch a torpedo attack. Thanks entirely to Card's short-range scale on the ASV, we dropped the 'fish' at 800 yards, which was the ideal distance, and at the prescribed 60 feet. I had to break sharply to starboard to avoid hitting the tanker. Even so we were hit by the ship's gunfire and a fire started inside the Wimpy but the crew put it out rapidly. We had missed because, unknown to us, the tanker had stopped and we had allowed for a forward movement and had applied an appropriate deflection. Early next morning, the 39 Squadron Beauforts were sent out. They located the tanker. They couldn't believe their luck because it was stationary and had no escorts. They put several torpedoes into the tanker and she blew up.

This tanker may have been the *Capo Orso* which Lloyd's lists as

---

* The South African Air Force used Army-type ranks. Gil's rank as Lieutenant was equivalent to Flying Officer in the RAF.
† Dates and places of attacks do not always tally. Quite apart from the confusion of night-time dates, ships hit did not always sink at once. At times, they struggled on (as had the *Breconshire* into Malta) to sink a day or so later or to sink many miles away from where they had been hit, while under tow.

having been sunk by aircraft on 16 February 1943 12 miles south of Marettimo Island.† She was known to be carrying petrol and had 500 Italian soldiers on board.

While in Malta, 221 were used both to locate enemy ships by ASV at night for others to attack, and to attack the ships themselves. This is probably why, in Malta, they carried only one torpedo. Their desert training had equipped them for both roles: for night reconnaissance operations – their original Goofington role – and torpedo-dropping – the Fishington role. The Squadron's aircraft also carried flares. Later, after Tunisia had fallen to the Allies, 221 Squadron remained in Malta and operated almost entirely on reconnaissance or anti-submarine patrols, as by then there were almost no ships left to torpedo.

Jack Hoskins, a Royal Auxiliary Air Force reservist, who had risen rapidly from Sergeant Pilot to Wing Commander and to command of 221 Squadron, recalls: 'Quite frequently, when attacking targets, 38 Squadron's torpedo-carrying Wellington aircraft had insufficient fuel to return to Egypt, so opted for Malta being much nearer.' He remembers 'how strange it was, after waiting around for days on end with no reconnaissances being required, then to be told one would be required when invariably there *was* something to be found. Now, of course, it is obvious that Ultra and the "Y" Service were very much involved.' By the time that 221 Squadron got to Malta, Jack Hoskins also remarks: 'our recces were made more difficult by heavy jamming of the ASV.'

Night reconnaissance in Goofingtons had its exciting moments too, as Weston Sanders, a Wireless Operator with 221 Squadron, recalls:

We went out [from Malta] at night in the general direction and stooged around finding the target. Having found it (usually a small convoy), we then homed the Torpedo Wimps by W/T, by sending out call-signs and long dashes. They used their loop-aerials to home on to us. This was prickly-neck time. To stooge around only a few miles from enemy coast advertising your presence by standing on your morse key is not the healthiest of occupations because we were vulnerable to any Italian or German aviator anxious to make a name for himself. Why we were never shot down is, and always has been, a complete mystery to me. Dropping sticks of 4.5-inch flares to illuminate ships below, again was an occupation not recommended for those of nervous disposition. I think this was when we acquired titles:* the torpedo Wimps were Fishingtons. We were Goofingtons (ASV) but became Flashingtons when doing our illuminating. We really should have been 'Gooflashingtons' but even the AOC thought this a bit cumbersome.

Weston Sanders recalls that Wing Commander Warburton on a couple of occasions flew with them as a front-gunner 'just for the hell of it'. 'The first time he did so, I actually tore him off a strip under the impression, in the dark, that he was a substitute rear-gunner. All he did was to offer me a cigarette and ask me to put him right.'

An Australian squadron, 458 RAAF, also came to Malta with Fishingtons in the spring of 1943, as Jack Hoskins recalls. They combined with 221 Squadron and the Albacores of 821 FAA Squadron in a combined night-torpedo attack on enemy shipping during the night of 13/14 March 1943 when, according to Lloyd's, the *Caraibe* (4,048 tons) was sunk by aircraft 10 miles north-west of Marettimo Island. Ultra intercepts, however, refer to *three* supply ships being sunk at about this date. Some of the 458 Squadron aircraft dropped bombs, and hits on a destroyer were also claimed.

458 RAAF Squadron was also initially equipped with Pegasus engines, but later began to get a few Wellingtons fitted with Bristol Hercules engines which transformed their performance, as the latter engine carried more than 40 per cent additional horsepower. A Hercules-powered Wimpy, when fitted with ASV, became a Mark XIII. These engines also had the advantage of being new, whereas the old Mark VIIIs, with their Pegasus engines, were obviously tired and clapped out.

458 Squadron was in Malta from early March 1943 until the fall of Tunis some nine weeks later. One of its members, the Canadian Bryan Quinlan, who has researched its activities, records that many of his friends and colleagues, during these weeks, simply went out and 'failed to return'. In almost every case, the cause of the loss remained unknown: not a comforting thought for the survivors. The loss of crews among 458 Squadron appears to have been as high, or even higher, than the 50 per cent suffered by the similarly equipped Wellingtons of 221 Squadron which operated alongside

---

* Not so. A year earlier the author's SDF aircraft had been dubbed Goofingtons.

them – even, on occasions, using each other's aircraft. In retrospect, Bryan Quinlan writes: 'It appears to me that during our short stay in Malta the greatest dangers were the tired conditions of the aircraft and the weather. 458's most active and successful offensive period was after the conversion to Hercules-powered Wimps operating from Tunisia.'

Almost every pilot who operated out of Malta during the winters of 1941 and 1942 has commented upon the weather. David Foster DSO, DSC, an Albacore pilot of 821 Squadron who spent only a brief period there during the latter winter, has written in his autobiography *Wings Over the Sea*:

> The weather was atrocious . . . The rain clouds were almost down to sea level and when we climbed to 6,000 feet, there was still no break in the cumulus. When we finally emerged from the cloud we were met by lightning flashing all around us and a huge anvil cumulus blocking the way ahead.
>
> The return journey was sheer hell. I started to climb through the rain clouds again. When I reached the top, I was again met by lightning and the plane was bucking and yawing so much I could hardly hold it on a steady course.
>
> I have never experienced such rough weather myself and at one point I almost gave up.

The author can confirm this experience. Whenever there is mention of bad flying weather, some of those operational flights out of Malta during the winter of 1941 come immediately to mind. It seems certain that some of our aircraft losses were due to the weather: in particular to ice building up in the carburettors, on the wings and on propeller blades. Our total lack of de-icing and anti-icing equipment was an unnecessary extra hazard.* It was a long way from the

---

* The author found, during the winter of 1941/42, that ice could be cleared, with luck, off propeller blades by carrying out violent alterations of revs and throttle; also that, in extreme emergency, the only way to clear the carburettor of ice was to carry out a quick 'switch off, switch on' of the ignition leaving the throttle open. This caused a mighty backfire which could clear the ice and/or cause a cylinder head or two to blow off. He also carried a Sten gun in the vague hope of being able to shoot off an idling propeller in the event of a total engine failure. With the propeller off, the drag was much reduced and one-engine operation was then possible. A propeller feathering device would have done much to solve the single-engine difficulties.

popular view of the 'sunny Mediterranean'. In a long flying career
– before, during and after the war – only once, years later, in a trop-
ical storm over the China Sea, did the author experience such
alarming flying weather.

David Foster has a few words about the food too. 'On our first
evening we collected our weekly ration of bread (16 ozs) and other
basics such as tea and sugar which we were advised to keep in tins
because the rats were hungry too. The only meat available was
barely edible, coming from a locally bred shoat, a cross between a
sheep and a goat.'

David arrived after Operation Pedestal – the August 1942 convoy
which resulted in five out of fourteen ships reaching Malta, mostly
damaged – but remembers that the Governor-General of the time,
Field Marshal Lord Gort VC, had calculated that, if no ships of
Pedestal arrived, 7 September would have to be the target date for
the surrender of the island, as the people would, by then, have been
starved out. Fortunately, the surviving ships reached the island by
mid-August.

There is much evidence that Fishington, Flashington and
Goofington crews operating during the winter of 1942/43 with
Wellington aircraft powered by the 1,000-hp Pegasus engines, suffered heavy losses from a number of different causes. Besides the
absence of any effective device to counter ice in bad weather conditions, the tired condition of the aircraft, and the lack of normal maintenance carried out in hangars and backed up by a properly
equipped RAF spare parts/stores organization, greatly reduced the
chances of being able to operate on one engine after the other had
failed. Ju 88 night-fighters moreover were seen on almost every
operation: the aircraft had no adequate answer against them other
than to dive down and fly as close to the water as the pilot dared –
an often fatal operation. The type of operation on which they were
involved was often dangerous in itself, requiring them to deliver
their torpedoes at night down at an estimated 60 feet – the correct
dropping height – without an instrument on board which could
accurately indicate the aircraft's height over the sea. It is impossible
to tell which of these factors accounted most for the heavy losses
which Pegasus-powered Wellingtons – the Fishington units especially – suffered. Many losses may indeed have been due to a
combination of causes.

The heavy losses they suffered were not however in vain. In a period of a few months, when the enemy, on Hitler's instructions, was making a determined effort to hold firm in Tunisia, the combination of boats and aircraft operating in waters controlled by Malta sank over 200 ships: with the submarines sinking most.* The effect was to deprive the enemy almost completely of - supplies of every kind and led to the ignominious surrender of about a quarter of a million fighting men, mainly German, with no very serious engagement and relatively few casualties to the Allies.

In the minds of some, this was Malta's finest hour. To others, however, the earlier successes and heroism shown when Malta was half-starved and under murderous fire, took precedence. In the minds of others still, what was to follow was of even greater significance. Each period of the conflict seemed to those involved – whether on land, in the air, and on or under the sea – to justify the existence of Malta and its retention in Allied hands. The successive struggles – and the far-flung consequences which emanated from them – did much to ensure, not only that the Allies retained control over the Mediterranean, and consequently their control over the Middle East, but that defeat for the Axis in Europe was not only now in sight but had become almost inevitable.

Prior to the battles of El Alamein and Stalingrad, the war had been going very much in Germany's favour. After November 1942, Germany, and her Italian ally, suffered defeat after defeat. If the main ones were on land to the Russians, those in the Mediterranean were equally total, although smaller in scale. This became evident when the Allied leaders, gathered at the Casablanca Conference in January 1943, decided that nothing less than unconditional surrender should be demanded of their enemies. Six months earlier, such a pronouncement would have seemed a piece of absurd bravado but by January 1943 this edict gave notice to the world that Germany and her allies (which included Japan) had lost the war in Europe. Only a military command sure of ending victorious could make such a pronouncement.

To know that you have the measure of your opponent is one

---

* See Appendix V.

thing. To start, and to complete, the demolition process is quite another. It would take years to accomplish.

The Casablanca Conference made another important decision. The Allies were to invade enemy-held Europe. The manner and direction in which this was to be commenced again gave Malta a key role to play.

13

Operation Husky

The Invasion of Sicily

'Nearly 2,000 naval vessels and landing-craft were to
carry 115,000 British Empire and over 66,000 American
troops on the largest amphibian operation that had
ever been mounted in the history of warfare. Indeed
the number of troops and craft involved was only
exceeded in the 1944 Normandy landing, if the
follow-up formations are taken into account.'

C.A. Shepperd, *The Italian Campaign*,
1938–45 (1968)

THE CASABLANCA CONFERENCE, at which all the Allies' military
leaders as well as Winston Churchill and the American President
Franklin D. Roosevelt were present, not only made the momentous
decision to accept nothing less than unconditional surrender from
Germany, Italy and Japan. It also agreed to commence the conquest
of Axis-held Europe by an invasion of Sicily from the island base of
Malta. This far-reaching strategic decision placed Malta at the centre
of the action. The small British-held island was to be the key base
from which the largest invasion of an enemy-held territory in the
history of warfare was to be attempted.

As could be expected, a number of feints were to be made. Chief
among these were spurious plans to invade Sardinia, Greece
and/or Crete. It is much to the credit of those who planned these
phoney operations, and saw to it that the enemy got wind of those
plans, that Marshal Kesselring, sound and sensible leader as he was,
fell for them. Almost until the day when the massive forces which
had been accumulated in Malta started to land in Sicily, he remained

uncertain where the expected blow would fall. As a result, his Divisions were widely dispersed, with both Sardinia and Greece being reinforced, whilst his forces in Sicily soon proved to be inadequate to withstand the massive Anglo-American armies which began to land there, both by sea and air, in the early hours of 10 July 1943. This was Operation Husky.

What makes Marshal Kesselring's uncertainties more surprising is that, a month earlier, the Allies had paved the way for a Sicilian invasion by seizing the Italian fortress island of Pantelleria. In a foretaste of what was to come, the island was first heavily bombed: so much so that the defenders agreed to surrender even before the first troops could go ashore. A concentrated bombing attack by aircraft based in both Malta and Tunisia, supported by a naval bombardment, was enough to persuade the 11,000-strong garrison to surrender. During an aerial bombardment of several weeks, 6,000 tons were dropped on this small island, a bare seven miles by six – with 1,500 tons being dropped on a single day. Not even Malta was ever quite so heavily hit. These air raids left the defenders dazed.

Apart from removing what might have been an angry thorn in their side, the Allies had gained an additional airfield – and one with a huge bomb-proof underground hangar. By the time Allied troops went ashore, a month later, over a 100-mile front of Sicilian beaches, three squadrons of US Kittyhawk (P40) fighters, comprising 75 aircraft of the 33rd USAAF Group, were firmly established in Pantelleria.

Lampedusa, another Italian island with an airfield, but one with fewer military personnel, was also captured before Operation Husky commenced. This island, which is not far distant from the east coast of southern Tunisia, fell to a veteran Swordfish aircraft, flown by Sergeant Cohen RAF, who as a result of his conquest of the island, later became dubbed by his colleagues as 'The King of Lampedusa'.

Cohen was out in his Swordfish aircraft which, by then, had been assigned to a purely Air–Sea Rescue role. During a search for an airman downed because of compass trouble, he found himself so close to Lampedusa that a swift mental calculation showed that he was too distant from Malta to be able to return. If he headed back to Malta, he too would have to ditch his aircraft for lack of fuel.

Rather than face a ditching, Sergeant Cohen decided to land on the air strip at Lampedusa: 'Better to be a POW than to be lost at sea in the Med,' was his thought. The irony of an Air–Sea Rescue pilot being lost at sea may also have struck him.

Lampedusa was already under air attack and its fate, with Tunisia already in Allied hands, was inevitably sealed. Rather than continue the useless struggle, the garrison commander of Lampedusa – a splendidly attired Italian officer with cockade in his jaunty hat – surrenderd the island to the startled Sergeant Pilot. The surrender ceremony, however, was rudely interrupted by an American fighter-aircraft strafing the airfield – fortunately, without damaging the Swordfish. The Italians hastily refuelled Sergeant Cohen's aircraft and, with a signed surrender document in his hand, he was soon telling his story in person to Air Vice Marshal 'Mary' Coningham, at his RAF HQ near Tunis.

The plans to invade Sicily were massive. In brief, the Americans were to take beaches adjacent to Gela on the south coast of the island and the British would seize beaches further to the east.

Before an island or territory can be invaded, a prerequisite is to have full details of the beaches where troops would be going ashore, and of the enemy defences at those points. Allied submarines had landed a few brave parties, many of which were captured, but close-up photographs were also required to supplement the information thus far compiled.

As could have been predicted, it was Adrian Warburton, by now a Wing Commander and CO of 683 Squadron, who undertook to get these. 683 Squadron, which operated PR Spitfires with both high-level vertical and low-level oblique cameras, had been hived off – and increased to squadron size – from 69 Squadron where it had previously constituted 'A' Flight of that splendid, and varied, Luqa-based reconnaissance squadron which Warburton himself had commanded.

Some good examples of the photo-reconnaissance work which 683 Squadron achieved under Warburton's dynamic (if unconventional) leadership have been received from Keith Durbidge, who was a Sergeant Pilot operating PR Spitfires – mainly at high levels. According to Durbidge, the three Italian naval bases from which the Italian Navy might have emerged to threaten Operation Husky –

Naples, Messina and Taranto – were all photographed on three
occasions every day, at dawn, noon and dusk.*

Although daily breaking every rule in the book on the ground,
Warburton was a stickler for 100 per cent operational efficiency, as
Keith Durbidge can attest. Once, when on a PR sortie in his Spitfire,
Durbidge spied a southbound tanker and immediately reported it
to Malta. He had recognized it as a tanker by noticing the oil-pipes
running along the deck. A force of aircraft from Malta was scram-
bled and duly sank the ship although, far from being a tanker, it
turned out to be a ship carrying tree trunks as deck cargo. For his
faulty ship recognition, Keith Durbidge was reprimanded and had
his pilot's Log Book endorsed. Warburton expected – and generally
received – nothing short of his own high standards in the air.

Despite being CO, Warburton flew more trips than other pilots
and was prone to find excuses to take the flights which had been
assigned to others. When, thanks to his enigmatical CO's
recommendation, Keith Durbidge was commissioned, Warby was
the first to buy him a drink in the Officers' Mess. He then accused
him of drinking before going on operations and promptly took
Keith's detail himself.

Keith remembers Operation Husky well. When relatively few
Luftwaffe aircraft rose up to oppose the vast Spitfire umbrella
which protected the assault troops, the fighters went on the offensive and Keith, from above, could see them strafing the enemy airfields of Comiso, Gela and Castel Vetrano and then plastering them
with 250-pound, and even 500-pound, bombs which some of the
fighters, by then, were carrying. By 1943, some fighters were carrying bomb-loads which were equal to those carried by the 1941
Blenheim bombers.

Although the enemy never shot down Durbidge's Spitfire, the

---

* One pilot on the noon-day 'milk-run' to photograph Taranto was Sergeant Pilot
Mickey Tardif. Obliged to bale out over Italy because of engine failure, he evaded
capture for two days, but was eventually taken prisoner. Jumping from a train on
the way to a German POW camp, Tardif hid in the hills where he met, and joined,
a local partisan group specializing in waylaying enemy road convoys. Eventually
becoming leader of the group, Tardif remained with them until the Allies reached
the area. The locals were all very sorry to lose 'Captain Mickey' who was rewarded
for his efforts with the Army's Military Medal. He might even have been the only
RAF Sergeant Pilot ever to be so decorated.

Malta food got him. After having eaten tinned fish in the Sergeants' Mess, the pilot found himself so ill, at height near Tunis, that he was unable to continue. Instead, he landed at the nearest airfield, Bone, where the medics at once declared him to be too ill to fly.

Well aware that Warburton always expected every pilot to bring back vital photographs (which Durbidge had by then taken) Keith was anxious that his film magazine should somehow be flown back to Malta. As luck would have it, a UK-based PR Mosquito pilot, flying on only one engine, had problems and, soon afterwards, also landed at Bone. The pilot had departed from Benson in Oxfordshire and it was he who went on to Malta, flying Keith Durbidge's Spitfire with the precious films. Some hours earlier Keith had been reported missing.

Without skilled interpretation photographs taken from a great height are of limited value. The Malta interpreters became experts. In one corner of Palermo harbour, where local boats were usually repaired, the eagle-eyed interpreters amazed the pilots by explaining that their photographs showed that a light cruiser was being built there. They pointed to minute objects which they said were piles of seamen's kitbags waiting to go on board. They also pointed out that the slight fuzz on the photograph indicated that the ship's engines were being tested and went on to predict that, within a few days, piles of trunks and suitcases would appear on the dockside indicating that the officers were also about to board. After that, this corner of Palermo harbour was photographed two or three times a day until the interpreters announced that the new warship was ready for its sea trials and predicted when they would commence. As a result, when the cruiser did sail, it was promptly sunk.

On another occasion when on his daily run over Messina, Keith Durbidge noticed that, as usual, the three cruisers were in their accustomed places. (By then, the Spitfire PR pilots knew exactly where every major Italian warship was located.) He also saw a commotion taking place in the sea, about fifteen miles ahead. There he saw a large ship which was slowly breaking into two amidships. As he came down to investigate, he observed a destroyer and an MTB dropping depth-charges, while a Cant seaplane flew low, clearly carrying out a search.

The Sergeant Pilot took several photographs of the interesting scene below and stayed around until the stricken ship gradually sank beneath the waves. (One of these remarkable photographs is reproduced as Plate 30.) Later, he was able to present the British submarine commander with photographs and proof positive that his torpedoes had hit their mark.

When it was decided to capture Pantelleria, the Allies again needed close-up photographs of its defences. To aid the troops, mainly American, who had been assembled to storm the island, Warburton himself flew low all around Pantelleria using his oblique camera. The island has cliffs 400 feet high and Warburton actually found himself being fired *down* upon by AA guns. However, the pictures clearly revealed all the gun positions, and the Americans were sufficiently impressed to award Warburton their DFC to go with the three others which he had already been given by the RAF.

The Sicilian beaches came next. They, too, had to be photographed. Thanks to Hugh O'Neill, a Spitfire fighter leader who was given the job of accompanying Warburton as fighter escort for this extremely dangerous task, a first-hand account of Warburton's operations has become available. The task was a demanding one and Warburton could easily have assigned it to any of his pilots or, indeed, to several of them as a 100-mile wide swath of beaches had to be photographed at the lowest levels practicable, in order to reveal, in the sharpest details, the extent of the enemy's coastal defences. It was, however, never in Warburton's nature to assign dangerous missions to others. Also, as Pantelleria had shown, he knew that he was the supreme master of oblique low-level aerial photography.

Hugh O'Neill, who was then a Squadron Leader with a DSO and DFC, remembers: 'We covered the area from Gela round to Syracuse [the beaches on which the British and Canadian assault forces would be landing] on May 27, 28 and June 3 and 19. I flew about three spans out on the seaward side, while he flew along with his camera whirring. A fair amount of light flak splashed around us as we went along but this did not deter Warby, who smoked a large cigar throughout.'

In spite of his unusual way of operating with cigar in mouth (in an aircraft in which smoking was forbidden) the pictures were excellent. They were so good, in fact, that General Alexander, the GOC of the assault and the C-in-C of all land forces in the Middle

East, sent a signal to Malta asking that Warburton personally be thanked. 'The pictures', the General commented, 'are as technically perfect as if taken on a peacetime exercise. They are being distributed to the assault troops.' It is surprising that Warburton was not awarded a further decoration, but perhaps by then he had received enough. As one fellow pilot remarked, upon noticing on his medal ribbons his bar to the DSO and the two bars to the DFC – each bar being represented by a small rosette: 'It looked as if his medal ribbons had been riveted onto his tunic.'

For a washed-out pilot who had arrived in Malta nearly three years earlier as a navigator, Wing Commander Adrian Warburton had become, to all in the RAF in Malta, a living legend. As Admiral Cunningham had praised the part he had played immediately prior to the famous Swordfish attack on Taranto in November 1940 and as Air Marshal 'Mary' Coningham now added his praise to that of General Alexander for his Sicilian beaches photographs, Warburton had received a 'full house' of praise from the Middle East leaders of all three fighting Services. This was capped by Air Chief Marshal Sir Arthur Tedder's reported comment that Warburton was 'the most valuable pilot in the RAF'. Certainly, at that time no other RAF pilot – not even in Bomber or Fighter Command – had received as many as six gallantry awards.

For the invasion of the Sicilian beaches, many of the submarines based in Malta were given specific, if unusual, assignments. Their role was to ensure that the assault troops landed exactly where they were supposed to land. In all twenty-six Allied Malta-based submarines, including two Polish and one Dutch, were given individual roles to play in this great invasion.

These roles fell into two main categories. One was traditional: certain submarines would be stationed adjacent to Italian ports where the enemy's major warships were known to lie at anchor. Those submarines were to report on any attempts which the Italian Navy might make to interfere with the 2,000-strong armada of ships which would be transporting the troops, with their tanks, fuel and military material, towards their various beach-head objectives.

Since Operation Husky would involve transporting about 181,000 troops (115,000 of whom were British, including Canadian) into Sicily, this armada was formidable. If the Italian Navy could have got amongst these hundreds of small ships – tank landing-craft and the like – the carnage would have been horrifying.

As well as reporting all activities by Italian naval units, the submarines positioned outside Taranto and the other Italian naval bases of Genoa, Spezia and Livorno were also expected to attack any Italian warships within their range. Torpedoes were to be preserved mainly for naval vessels. Only large merchant vessels were otherwise to be attacked.

The other Malta-based submarines acted as essential sea- and beach-markers for the assembly points offshore where the TLCs and other assault craft would be congregating before the target date of 10 July 1943 when they would be going ashore. These 'marker' or 'beacon' submarines made sure that the invaders would be guided to their assigned beaches.* They used Asdic-transmitted sonar buoys, radio beacons and infra-red lamps to guide in craft of all kinds, commando troops having earlier been landed by folbots to set up homing devices on the beaches.

Four of the trusty U-class boats, *Unruffled*, *Unseen*, *Unison* and *Unrivalled*, who knew the coast of Sicily well from previous folbot operations, acted as marker beacons for the British and Canadian troops. As a result, these soldiers all went ashore, much as had been planned, on beaches in the south-east and east of Sicily. Although rough weather prevented some of the smaller launches from reaching their destinations, the assault troops were soon firmly established ashore. For the beaches where the US troops were to go ashore further west, the submarines *Safari* (whose crew also knew the area well), *Shakespeare* and *Seraph* likewise acted as marker beacons, enabling those troops rapidly to establish a firm base from which to break out into the mainland of Sicily.

As well as forming an iron ring around Italian naval bases, another group of Malta-based submarines were positioned just north of the Strait of Messina, in order to intercept any warships from mainland Italy which might be trying to reach the Sicilian beaches.

Lieutenant 'Tubby' Crawford in *Unseen*, one of the marker

---

* Submarines which acted as marker beacons added a lighthouse symbol to their Jolly Roger success flags which they proudly displayed on return to base.

beacons off the east coast of Sicily, has described the scene. He knew the area well as he had carried out many folbot commando operations to check upon beach gradients and the existence of beach obstructions. The particular beach where he had to lay his sonar beacons had the code-name BARK EAST. Earlier he had ensured that a beach-marker was planted there by a folbot party.

After he had landed the beach-marker, he scanned the horizon expecting to see assault boats. At first he saw nothing. It was an anxious moment. Could something have gone amiss? Then, suddenly, 'the whole horizon was one mass of dark shapes'. The Armada, 1943-style, was approaching.

One of his first recollections of this memorable event is of hearing the heavy bombing raid which preceded the sea assault. He also remembers, sadly, being aware that many of the gliders carrying the airborne troops came down into the sea. 'We saw plenty of wreckage the next day.'

Tragically, the unexpected stormy weather played havoc with both the parachutists and the towed gliders. The weather, in normal circumstances, was cause for the invasion to be postponed for a day (as indeed was D-Day nearly a year later) but, in this case, the essential back-up convoy with troops, stores, petrol and everything else that the assault troops needed to be able to maintain their initial advantage, was too deeply committed. This supply convoy had left the Clyde two weeks earlier and was already approaching Sicily.

Tubby Crawford was among several Naval officers who, at that time, were suffering physically. Captain Phillips, who had taken over from Captain Simpson as Captain (S) 10 in January 1943, was similarly stricken. Both had contracted the dreaded sandfly fever – a Maltese form of virulent malaria. It had hit many in Malta and had chosen this auspicious moment to strike the commander of *Unseen*. Sandfly fever produces a vicious, almost unbearable, headache as well as causing profound sweating.

As it would be some time before the assault craft would actually be landing on BARK EAST beach, Tubby Crawford, feeling like death, went below to lie down, after giving instructions that he was to be called if anything happened. The next thing he knew was several hours later when he awoke, went up on the bridge, found it was broad daylight and that the invasion was in full swing. With his job done, and the assault going well, *Unseen* in company with *Unruffled*, and escorted by a trawler, returned to Malta that same evening.

Another submarine commander, Lieutenant Anthony Daniel* of *Unison*, well remembers the scene – observing among a myriad of ships several well-known pre-war passenger liners which had been pressed into service as giant troop-carriers. Lieutenant Stevens in *Unruffled* was similarly impressed. He noted in his book *Never Volunteer*, 'The sky had cleared but there was dim starlight. Soon a dark shape could be discerned . . . It grew larger and larger . . . we had sighted a destroyer leading in a group of ships . . . they included many famous ocean liners being used as assault troop-ships.' He likened the scene to a pre-war good-will visit, with small craft scurrying between parent ships and shore.

The destroyers, as well as leading in convoys of vessels, also took care of the enemy's coastal guns – those guns whose positions had been so carefully noted by previous folbot raiders, and which Warburton's pictures had also disclosed.

Behind the destroyers were the cruisers, ready to take on the big ships of the Italian Navy. As a result, opposition, such as it was, soon died down, with the invaders in command of firmly held beach-heads. Those submarine commanders who were not laid low by sandfly fever had a grandstand view of a memorable occasion.

The several submarines which had been sent to report on, and deal with, possible threats from the Italian Navy in answer to this invasion of her sovereign territory, soon found that they had nothing to do. The crushing defeat of the Italian armies, first in Libya and then in Tunisia, had undermined that country's resistance. This had been apparent for some time to those submarine commanders who had taken Italian officers and men, including some submariners, prisoner after having first sunk their vessels. Almost to a man, they showed little anger at having been sunk, expressed relief that they were out of the war, and co-operated well once aboard Allied submarines. Some even assisted the work of those submarines when on the attack, and seemed quite sorry to be put ashore at the end of their captor's patrol. In some cases, their cooking had much improved the submariners' fare. Their most

---

* Now Captain A.R. Daniel DSO, DSC, RN (Rtd).

common sentiment was an utter loathing for their erstwhile German ally.

When Lieutenant John Roxburgh* sank the Italian submarine *Remo*, among his prisoners was the boat's commander, Lieutenant Vassallo. As the two submarine commanders thereafter had to spend many days cooped up together in *United*'s tiny wardroom, the intimacy of the occasion and Vassallo's good behaviour, even when Roxburgh was attacking Italian ships, created a measure of understanding between the two young naval officers. This was heightened considerably when they discovered that both their wives were about to give birth. Indeed during the patrol, before *United* could return to base, a cryptic signal informed John Roxburgh that he had a baby daughter. This event was commemorated by Roxburgh's crew who made a special 'stork flag' to be flown alongside his success-showing Jolly Roger, for his triumphal return to Malta.

Enemies at war could be friends under the right circumstances, especially if, for one, the war was over. In this case, the pair of enemy submarine commanders parted with a friendly handshake.†

Within a few days of the Operation Husky landings, many of the submarines which had been patrolling the Italian naval bases were withdrawn for other duties since the Italian Navy was clearly not prepared to contest ownership of the busy sea area between Malta and Sicily. The torpedo restrictions limiting their use to major Italian war or supply ships were also lifted. Enemy vessels of all sizes and kinds started again to be hit and sunk, both by torpedoes and gunfire.

As early as 13 July, the Dutch submarine *Dolfijn* (Lt/Cdr Van Oostram) was sinking by gunfire the schooner *Stefano Galleano*. On the same day the RN submarine *Trespasser* (Lt Favell), which was also part of the line of submarines positioned between Corsica and mainland Italy for Operation Husky, sank by gunfire a small 242-ton

---

* Now Vice-Admiral Sir John Roxburgh KCB, CBE, DSO, DSC and bar. His was the submarine which sank the ship, near Messina, which Keith Durbidge photographed from above.

† Pilots, too, could feel the same affinity in the right circumstances. On one occasion a Malta-based Air–Sea Rescue launch which had rescued a Luftwaffe pilot from the sea came upon a British pilot similarly downed. The Luftwaffe pilot helped to get his 'enemy' safely into the launch, and by the time the sea trip was over, the two exhausted pilots had fallen asleep more or less in each other's arms.

armed patrol-boat, the *Filipino. Unruly* (Lt Fyfe), which had been one of the submarines watching over the north end of the Messina Strait, went one better and fired four torpedoes at the Italian submarine *Acciaio*, which promptly sank.

The next day, *Unshaken* (Lt Whitton), which had been on watch off Taranto in the knowledge that two of Italy's battleships were known to be there, sank the MV *Cesena* off the east coast of Calabria. Lieutenant Roxburgh in *United*, which had also been part of the iron ring outside Taranto, followed this up, on 15 July, with his sinking of the *Remo*, a large Italian submarine which at 2,220 tons was nearly four times the mass of its attacker.

In all, whereas Allied submarines in the Mediterranean sank as many as twenty-one enemy submarines, including five of the highly efficient German U-boats, only one British submarine, *Triad*, appears to have been sunk by Axis submarines* – although at least one other which failed to return may have suffered this fate, as several were lost to 'unknown causes'. As Tubby Crawford has commented:

> The fact that our submarines in the Mediterranean managed to sink so many of theirs, mainly Italian, can, I believe, only be put down to the superior operation of our submarines. We always assumed that, as soon as we put to sea, we were a target for any enemy force, including U-boats [and Italian submarines] and so handled the submarine as best we could to avoid that threat. The Italians, in particular, probably felt that they were in friendly waters in the Mediterranean and spent much more time on the surface than we did: certainly around the coast of Sicily and Italy.

These comments are substantiated by the fact that sixteen of the twenty-one submarines sunk by our underwater boats were sunk in broad daylight.

Before July was out, other submarines, now released from their Operation Husky roles, but still under the operational control of Captain Phillips, Captain (S) 10, were also active, although the ships they sank tended to be on the small side. *Torbay* (Lt Clutterbuck) sank the *Pozzallo*, the *San Girolamo* and also fired at a larger vessel – these attacks taking place between Corsica and Civitavecchia, the port near Rome. *Sickle* (Lt Drummond) also sank by gunfire the

---

* However, in error, one of Italy's submarines sank a German U-boat.

small ships, or tugs, *Constante Neri*, *Rosa Madre* and *Angiolo Maria C*, while patrolling between Corsica and Livorno. *Sickle* also damaged a sizeable armed merchantman cruiser, estimated at 6,000 tons, with a torpedo hit in the same area. This was probably the *Orsini*.

Unrivalled was also active and on 24 July, after an inconclusive engagement with first a tug and then a submarine, Lieutenant Turner, her commander, sank the schooner *Impero* by gunfire. On the same day Lieutenant Clutterbuck, in *Torbay*, scored a success with the relatively large MV *Aderno* (2,609 tons) which was sunk off Civitavecchia. Malta's old friend, the ever active *Safari*, now commanded by Lieutenant Lakin, continued her successful patrols. On 18 July she sank an armed patrol-boat, the *Amalia*, and the next day sank two German barges off Porto Vecchio. On 20 July an anti-submarine yacht (by now the Germans were using almost anything that could float) was missed by one of *Safari's* torpedoes before being sunk by gunfire, again off Corsica.

Much the same happened on the 22nd when *Safari* near La Maddalena, an island off the northern tip of Sardinia, came across the small armed patrol-boat, the *Durazzo* (530 tons). She was first driven ashore by gunfire then, when stationary, sunk with a torpedo. Four days later, in the narrows between Elba and Italy, Lakin had a crack at a big tanker of nearly 10,000 tons. This was the *Champagne* – clearly a vessel of former French registration. Unfortunately, she was missed with three torpedoes.

July 1943 turned out to be one of the most memorable months of the Mediterranean war. Not only was Sicily invaded and many submarine successes scored in the Central Mediterranean but, on 25 July, the Italian Fascist dictator, Benito Mussolini, who had ruled Italy with an iron fist for over twenty years, was finally overthrown by Italian politicians and generals acting together. He was replaced by Marshal Badoglio, who assumed the powers of Prime Minister and Chief of Government, while King Vittorio Emmanuele III, who for years had been no more than an ineffectual figurehead, assumed command of the Italian armed forces. With Italian soldiers at that time surrendering in their thousands in Sicily, it did not take much guesswork to predict that Italy would soon be pulling out of the war.

Although both Badoglio and the Italian king declared over the radio that Italy would fight on, few on either side believed them.

Certainly the Germans were not fooled. By the end of July, more-over, Sicily had been largely overrun and its capital, Palermo, was firmly in Allied hands. By then the Allied Air Forces were already operating out of twenty-one Sicilian airfields or improvised air-strips.

Within days of assuming power, Marshal Badoglio, who had declared martial law in Italy in an effort to prevent civil war, had abolished the Italian Fascist Party and was sounding out, in secret, Allied peace terms, while the deposed and despised Mussolini lan-guished in jail. The invasion launched from Malta showed all the signs of toppling Italy, bringing with it the inevitable collapse of Fascism and leaving only Nazism to be overcome.

Malta's air role in Operation Husky, and the rapid conquest of Sicily, was crucial. The island, in effect, had been turned into a massive launching-pad for the purpose of providing air cover for the beaches where the assault troops would be landing in their thousands. Owing to the limited range of most Allied fighter-aircraft, Malta was the only base in the Mediterranean from which tens of thousands of troops could invade enemy-held Europe while being under the protection of a constantly maintained fighter-umbrella. Although southern Sardinia, once captured, might have offered similar opportunities, the Allies would still have been as far removed from the main body of Europe as before its capture. Sardinia, by comparison with Sicily, was a relatively unimportant part of Italy, nor did it have the many ports, good roads and airfields which the Allies themselves would soon be using.

To prepare for this historic invasion, the number of Malta and Gozo airfields had been extended from three – Hal Far, Luqa and Ta Kali – to six. Safi strip, which lies between Luqa and Hal Far and where much RAF maintenance had been carried out, was made into an airfield. Since late 1941 it had been joined to both the other air-fields by a taxi-track which wound its way through the uneven and undulating Maltese terrain.

On the west side of the island, a completely new fighter airfield had been built at Krendi or, as it is sometimes written, Qrendi (Maltese spelling is optional). It was opened in style by AOC Air Vice-Marshal Keith Park who personally flew the first Spitfire into Krendi.

As well as this, it was decided, in June 1943, that a further airfield was required and that this should be in the smaller, more northerly, companion-island of Gozo. An American battalion, part of an Aviation Engineer Regiment, arrived in June with a host of modern scrapers, bulldozers, cranes and other mechanical aids and built the new airfield, from bare fields, in an incredible nineteen days, and when it was later decided that a second runway, measuring some 4,000 × 150 feet, was needed, they added this in a further five days. Gone for ever were the days when beleaguered Malta had to construct aircraft pens by hand.

It was fitting that seventy-five of the Spitfires which soon crowded Gozo's new airfield belonged to the 31st Group of the USAAF* and were flown by American pilots, who thereby became the first to profit from the valiant work of their country's airfield engineers. In all, six of the thirty-five complete squadrons which crowded the Allied airfields in support of Operation Husky came from American Groups.

As by June 1943 the airfield at Pantelleria was also in Allied hands, the invasion forces found themselves being supported by seven airfields on which, on 10 July 1943, stood over 600 Allied aircraft. There were also half a dozen big flying-boats at anchor off Kalafrana and St Paul's Bay. Of the 608 aircraft available to the Allies on that day, over 500 were fighter types. Nearly all were Spitfires except for the 75 US-built P40 Kittyhawks, flown by American pilots based in Pantelleria. Although a few fighter squadrons were there for the defence of Malta – very necessary since the island's harbours and inlets were crammed with row upon row of tank and troop landing craft – the majority of the fighters were in Malta (and Pantelleria) in order to provide the troops going ashore with a firm air-umbrella. Apart from those in Pantelleria, all were British.

As well as warding off enemy air attacks, these fighters when over Sicily – especially after the beach-heads had been won – were used to attack almost anything that moved in the areas into which the defenders were soon being compressed. The era of the fighter-bomber, which still dominates in warfare, had arrived.

---

* A USAAF (USAF) Group is roughly equivalent to an RAF Wing.

Night defences were not neglected. Among the 173 aircraft at Luqa were 30 night-fighting Beaufighters.

Malta also became the base for the Mosquito aircraft of 23 Squadron, which had arrived in Malta in May 1943.* Initially, these aircraft were used in far-ranging daylight intruder operations, including sixty-five attacks on Italian locomotives and an attack on a 1,500-ton ship which was left in flames, near Marettimo Island.

By July, 23 Squadron was carrying four 250-pound bombs as well as cannons and machine-guns, and was attacking airfields as far north as Rome. Their aircraft also occasionally doubled as night-fighters, as required. The all-purpose Mosquito, which possessed both high speed and a good range, could be put to a wide variety of uses. Later, for the invasion of Sicily, a detachment of specially equipped night-fighting Mosquitoes of 256 Squadron, fitted with appropriate airborne radar, was also based at Luqa.

23 Squadron was exceptionally active on the offensive and, although losses on their low-level daylight strikes were heavy, replacement aircraft were regularly being flown in and by 30 August 1943 Mosquitoes had completed their thousandth operation from Malta. By then, they had hit 172 locomotives, destroyed 24 enemy aircraft and attacked 25 ships. They had also shot up airfields and enemy transports on roads. 256 Squadron also claimed 16 enemy aircraft, all shot down at night.

Virtually all the Wellingtons had been removed temporarily to Tunisian bases, to make way for the solid ranks of the best fighters that the Allies could muster; but, never out of the picture at Luqa, 69 Squadron retained half a squadron of American-built Baltimores for daylight reconnaissance and Warburton's 683 PR Squadron remained there with a full complement of fifteen high- and low-flying photographic Spitfires.

For once there were no FAA aircraft at Hal Far:† only sixty-four Spitfires plus a few ASR Walrus and communications aircraft.

---

* 23 Squadron was, at one time, commanded by Wing Commander Peter Wykeham-Barnes, a fighter-pilot who distinguished himself flying Gladiators during the early days of the Desert War. Post-war, he was to rise to Air Marshal rank.
† During the period June 1940–June 1943 when the FAA Swordfish and Albacores had been at Hal Far operating under RAF control, their crews had been awarded a remarkable 9 DSOs, 33 DSCs, 22 DSMs, 1 MBE and 47 Mentioned in Despatches, principally to aircrew of 828 and 830 Squadrons.

Sixteen FAA Albacores, however, and a few Fulmar fighters were based at Ta Kali.

The Tunisian campaign had proved that it was essential to seize, and to create, airfields alongside, or even ahead of, the advancing troops. In Sicily, at that time of the year, the melon fields were rapidly converted into fighter strips and one pilot, who had endured Malta's now adequate but still dull fare, has described the joy of waking up in the morning and stretching out a hand from under his tent in order to seize a juicy ripe pre-breakfast melon. This was in sharp contrast with the period, not many months earlier, when all in Malta had been wondering where their next meal would be coming from. Perhaps the sharpest contrast of all was the transformation which had turned an island, once defended only by a small handful of obsolescent biplanes – *Faith, Hope* and *Charity* – into the most congested area of fighter-aircraft ever assembled by the RAF and kindred Allied Air Forces.

One remarkable difference between the Malta of late 1942 and that of July 1943 was that the island, then on the verge of surrender owing to shortages of food and much else, was now, for Operation Husky, the key supply base to which the ships and planes returned again and again to be replenished.

Malta's RAF underground Ops Room at Lascaris was no longer manned (if that is the right word) by local civilian girl-plotters who had been hastily brought in to fulfil urgent requirements. Instead the Ops Room (as can be seen in the Lascaris Ops Room Exhibition of today) was honoured by the presence of all the Allied war chiefs: Generals Eisenhower and Alexander, Admiral Sir Andrew Cunningham, Air Chief Marshal (as he had become) Sir Arthur Tedder, Air Marshal 'Mary' Coningham, together with Generals Montgomery and (US) Patton and Clark, who were to lead their respective invasion armies.

Further evidence of Malta's abrupt transformation was provided in June 1943, when HM King George VI paid the island a visit – to the rapturous delight of the local populace as well as of the enormous numbers of Servicemen of all kinds who, by then, were crowded into the island's remaining serviceable buildings or who covered the area with their tents. The tents were an essential item since over 30,000 buildings had been destroyed. Six months earlier few war correspondents had dared to pay a call, nor had any been welcomed, as every unnecessary visitor meant another mouth to feed. Now they were poised *en masse* to report.

The enemy still attempted air raids but on nothing like the same scale as in early 1942 or October 1942. In any event, with hundreds of Spitfires available by day and ample Beaufighters by night, the raiders now seldom caused much harm, except to themselves.

The peak period for enemy air raids had been March–April 1942 when over 550 alerts had been sounded – an average of over nine raids per day. Despite the fact that, in June and July 1943, the island was now one big supply-dump, with both aircraft and ships massed in rows for the forthcoming Operation Husky invasion, there were only thirty air alerts in June, falling to ten in July when, during a night raid of 26 July, the last of well over 1,000 Maltese civilians to be killed by enemy bombers, lost his life.

With Sicily in Allied hands by early August 1943, the invading armies stood a bare three miles from the province of Calabria in mainland Italy, which was to be the next target and where an Allied landing could once again be protected by a massive fighter-umbrella provided by aircraft, now based in nearby Sicily as well as in Malta. Such a landing would also be supported by the several bomber squadrons which, after the conquest of Sicily, had moved up from their Tunisian bases to Malta's six airfields. To this extent, Malta now became no longer the vanguard of the Allies' invasion forces but instead, part of its back-up, along with Tunisia which was even further removed from the front line.

Another change was taking place. Up to the completion of Operation Husky, almost every one of the over 500 aircraft occupying Malta's six airfields had been British and, apart from the USAAF squadrons which operated the seventy-five Spitfires from Gozo, they had been flown by British pilots of the RAF, RAAF, RCAF and RNZAF assisted by a few brother-pilots of the SAAF.

After Husky, with the Armies subsequent move forward across the Messina Strait into Italy, and the 'left hook' landings at Salerno which soon followed, many – indeed most – of the light and medium day-bombers which came to occupy the Malta airfields were US-built Bostons, Baltimores and other types such as the B-25 Mitchells. Little by little, the American Air Forces took over the bombing role, while the British Wellingtons and other aircraft confined themselves to marine activities: continuing to attack enemy shipping, and tracking down and attacking the enemy submarines which, with thousands of targets to aim at, posed a very real threat to the Allies in the Central Mediterranean.

Even before the Allied armies which had wrested Sicily from the enemy could resume their advance and cross over to the mainland of Italy, Hitler was taking action. Fearful that the Allies would gain airfields in Italy which would enable their bombers to attack more easily the Romanian oilfields, he directed the Luftwaffe to move two operational commands from southern Russia to Italy.

The timing of the order, 26 July 1943, is significant. At that time the greatest tank battle of all times for the Kursk salient on the vital Central Russian front had just been fought, with thousands of German tanks lost. Yet, with his whole Eastern Front threatened as never before, this front was being robbed in order to face the new enemy approaching from Sicily.

On the same day, the German dictator ordered Marshal von Kluge to begin the evacuation of his troops from the Orel salient, north of and close to the Kursk salient, 'in order to prepare for the transfer of troops to Italy'.* As Ralph Bennett has written: 'Hitler's immediate reaction to the weakening of his Italian ally was to rob the Russian front and the future OVERLORD [Normandy invasion] area, to shore up his suddenly endangered southern front.' Events in the Mediterranean were again proving to be an invaluable relief to the Russian armies which were bearing the brunt of the force of the once unbeatable German Wehrmacht.

Although by May 1943 the submarines of the Tenth Flotilla had moved from Manoel Island to the island of La Maddalena on the northern tip of Sardinia, they could not have continued to maintain their operational success without having, as George Hunt‡ puts it, 'Malta under our lee'. It went further than that. As La Maddalena

---

* See Martin Gilbert, *The Second World War* (1989). As early as 23 January 1943, Hitler had told the Japanese ambassador to Germany that 'on the principle of not jeopardizing the defence of Western Europe, he had been obliged to reinforce his armies in Italy and the Balkans by thirty-five German divisions at the expense of the Eastern Front' (ibid.).

† In his *Ultra and Mediterranean Strategy 1941–1945* (1989).

‡ Now Captain RN (Rtd) with DSO and bar, DSC and bar.

had few, if any, spares or facilities, it could be regarded as a forward base of Malta, akin to an RAF advanced landing ground in the Desert.

Lieutenant George Hunt, as he then was, commanded *Ultor*, yet another new U-class submarine. Throughout 1943–4 he was the most successful submarine commander in the Central Mediterranean, as his DSO and bar, DSC and bar testify. He was responsible for sinking, or beaching, the best part of thirty enemy ships, which in numbers was more than any other submarine commander in the Mediterranean. However, as by then most of the larger enemy supply vessels were already resting at the bottom of this inland sea, his tonnage total fell far short of that sunk by either Lieutenant Commander Wanklyn or Tubby Linton. Although by the time George Hunt first appeared in Malta – April 1943 – that island was approaching wartime normality, his feats, whether operating from Malta itself or from La Maddalena, show that Malta was still striking back.

Lieutenant Hunt sank his first confirmed enemy ship in the Mediterranean when he torpedoed the supply ship *Penerf* (2,151 tons) on 14 April 1943, although he may have scored other successes two nights earlier when he had fired at, and probably hit, two unidentified merchant ships while on passage from Algiers to Malta.

On his first patrol from Malta he sank an armed anti-submarine trawler of 500 tons in Augusta harbour, on 23 May. His next patrol was more successful: on 15 June 1943 he sank the auxiliary minesweeper *Tullio* and went on to sink an Orsa-class MTB the next day. Both successes were scored off Salina Island – one in the Lipari island group north of Sicily and adjacent to the belching columns of smoke of the active volcanic island, Stromboli.

In July 1943, 'Geordie' Hunt, as some called him, sank the 6,200-ton MV, the *Valfiorita*, and in August, after first taking part in a chariot operation (cancelled at the last minute), he sank the torpedo-boat *Lince* (628 tons). It must always have been satisfying for a submarine commander in the Mediterranean to sink one of the enemy torpedo-boats which would have been at sea largely for the purpose of sinking him.

During September, off Bastia, Corsica, George Hunt had the satisfaction of hitting the 9,946-ton tanker *Champagne* and causing that vessel to be beached. This large tanker had been attacked before by our submarines, and at that stage of the war and in that particular area it must have been one of their most valuable merchant ships. On the same patrol, Lieutenant Hunt also disposed of a Siebel ferry in the same area.

Ultor, and her commander, kept up the good work in October when the *Aversa*, formerly the *Kakoulima*, a passenger ship of 3,723 tons which the Germans had taken over, was sunk off Civitavecchia. This was followed by a KT ship,* which they sank further north towards Genoa.

Part of November was spent in Algiers where *Ultor* received some much needed maintenance. In December, on her way to the La Maddalena submarine base to which the Tenth had moved, the already successful submarine skipper sank a canal barge on the 18th and on her first patrol from that uncomfortable and isolated base on the northern tip of Sardinia, *Ultor* was sent to act as a beach-marker for the Allied Anzio landings south of Rome. Here George Hunt had a grandstand view, but one which, at times, he would have been happy to forgo. In his words,

> When the time for the landings came, we duly surfaced, trimmed down very low, and anchored in our beach-marking position so that the whole assault could 'home' directly on to our beacon. As H-hour approached, we could hear them coming and then, quite suddenly, we were surrounded by vessels charging into the beach, with shells from big ships whistling over our heads.
>
> We had strict orders to remain at anchor until escorted away from the action, so, as there was nothing we could do – our part in the proceedings having been completed – we served cocoa on the bridge and enjoyed the spectacle.
>
> This was the first time we had seen the famous rocket-firing landing-craft. This vessel was very close to us, firing her rockets as she went towards the beach, which was then considered 'sanitized'. It was quite frightening to watch, let alone to be on the receiving end. Actually we knew that the beach must have been fairly free of mines because, a few days before, we had watched some Germans playing football on it.

---

* The KT (Krieg Transport) ships were merchant carriers mass-produced by, and for, the German Navy.

The La Maddalena submarine base seems to have evoked unsavoury comments from all who were based there. It had been an Italian submarine base (coincidentally, of their Tenth Flotilla) and they had left it in a filthy state. It had also suffered from Allied bombing. Being off the main island, it was remote and, when not on patrol, there was nothing to do, nor did it grow any palatable fruit or other food. Vegetables were at a premium so the crews had to live on tinned stew. It was suggested that those Italian submariners who had been at La Maddalena had only been posted there after having committed some heinous crime, such as running off with another man's wife. It even lacked decent Italian wine.

Operationally, too, the new base of the Tenth Flotilla had nothing. As George Hunt has averred: 'We could hardly have operated for very long from La Maddalena without Malta being at hand for docking, major repairs and spares.'

Lieutenant Hunt, and other submarine commanders, continued to find and sink a number of enemy warships and supply vessels, but after the Italians had surrendered on 8 September 1943 and changed sides in the war, there were relatively few anti-submarine surface craft available to oppose them. Their principal enemies, after the Italian fleet had steamed into Malta and surrendered *en masse*, were German U-boats and the aircraft of the Luftwaffe.

Another success came with the torpedoing, on 6 December 1943, of the German-operated liner, the *Vergilio*, by Lieutenant Herrick in command of *Uproar*. At 11,718 tons this liner, which had formerly belonged, first to Yugoslavia, then to Italy, was the last vessel of over 10,000 tons to be sunk by Allied submarines in the Central Mediterranean. She went down north-east of St-Tropez. According to German records, the numbers of ships sunk or beached by Allied submarines during the remainder of 1943 in Central Mediterranean waters, after the surrender of the Italians on 8 September 1943, amounted to September, 21; October, 20; November, 19 and December, 19.

Among these many sinkings were the *Humanitas* (7,980 tons), sunk in Bastia harbour by the Dutch Commander Van Oostram, in command of *Dolfijn*; the *Sinfra* (4,743 tons), sunk by the Greek submarine *Katsonis*; the *Nikolaus* (6,397 tons), sunk off Bastia by the Polish submarine *Dzik*. In addition the *Brandenburg* (3,895 tons) and

Kretas (2,600 tons) were both sunk in one brilliant attack by Tubby Crawford, still performing wonders in *Unseen*.

Uproar (Lt Herrick) can also claim to have put the final nail in the coffin of *Champagne* when she sent a further torpedo into the beached tanker, just to make sure that she could never be refloated. The Polish submarine *Sokol*, back in Malta (La Maddalena) for the second time, but this time commanded by Commander Koziolkowski, sank the *Eridania* (7,095 tons); while Lieutenant Clutterbuck in *Torbay* sent the 5,145-ton *E.H. Fisher* to the bottom, off Dubrovnik. A French submarine also aided the Allies when the *Casablanca*, commanded by Commander Bellet, caused the *Chisone* (6,168 tons), a French ship in German hands, to be beached off Toulon just after Christmas 1943. Malta's resources continued to underpin many of these successes.

Even after the Allied armies had started to work their way up the length of Italy, the tally of sinkings by Allied submarines off the coasts of Italy continued to be impressive. *Ultor* alone sank another fifteen to twenty ships, her victims in 1944 including an auxiliary minesweeper which blew up, a tug, a patrol-boat, two armed merchant cruisers the *Alice Robert* and the *UJ2201*, barges, landing-craft, many caiques and three merchant ships: the *Cap Blanc* (3,317 tons), *Pallas* (5,200 tons) and *Chietti* (3,152 tons).

A bold feat was that of Lieutenant Boyd, in *Untiring*, who fired a torpedo through the narrow entrance of Monte Carlo harbour. This blew up a minesweeper which exploded with a bang which must have broken hundreds of windows in the Principality, as well as rattling the wheel in the famous Casino.

Many other British U-class submarines continued to sink enemy ships throughout 1944, by the end of which they had sunk virtually all there was to sink. Submarines still operating here included *Usurper*, *Unrivalled*, *Unshaken* and *Unruly*. In addition *Unruffled*, still commanded by 'Steve' Stevens, had several successes, as also did *Unsparing* (Lt Piper), *Universal* (Lt Gordon), *Unseen*, with Tubby Crawford still very much in charge, *Upstart* (Lt Chapman) and *Untiring* with the enterprising Lieutenant Boyd in command.

Among the larger S and T-class boats, Lieutenant Clutterbuck in *Torbay*, and *Sportsman*, under Lieutenant Dickie Gatehouse, also scored well, as did *Sickle* (Lt Drummond). Both *Rorqual* and *Safari* also added to their already considerable scores.

As the Italian campaign approached its inescapable conclusion, with the million-strong German armies surrendering *en masse*, the new V-class submarines appeared and scored successes. By then there were very few ships left to sink: however, *Vivid*, *Vox*, *Virtue* and *Vigorous* all had their successes.

A number of enemy ships were destroyed by Allied submarines around the islands of Lemnos and Rhodes during the abortive campaign which took place in that area of the Mediterranean during 1944, but to what extent any Malta or La Maddalena-based submarines shared these successes is not clear. It would seem more likely that submarines based at Beirut or Alexandria would have been those mainly involved.

During this period many enemy ships were also sunk by Allied aircraft in their ports. By then those successes were apt to be caused by bombers – often US daylight ones – operating from North African and Italian airfields more often than from Malta. British Wellingtons and other aircraft in the Mediterranean tended to concentrate their attacks on German U-boats – a very necessary operation since by then there were thousands of Allied ships supplying the large Anglo-American forces in Italy for the U-boats to attack. Malta and its airfields continued to offer firm back-up as an intermediate port-of-call for all aircraft in difficulties and those unable to return to the more distant airfields from which they had departed. Malta was also the base for some fighter escorts.

The island's greatest days were perhaps over, but the attacks from Malta-based aircraft and submarines remained a problem for the Germans both at sea and on land, as they stubbornly retreated northwards towards the Alps. Throughout the length of Italy, the German troops had always to bear in mind that Naval forces from Malta and elsewhere were liable to be landed in their rear, as indeed happened at both Salerno and Anzio.

The landing of another Allied army in the South of France in August 1944 again brought Malta, and the Central Mediterranean Naval and Air Forces, into prominence. That event, which went almost unopposed, brought even nearer the likelihood of an overall Allied victory in Europe, and with it the prospect of Nazism following Italian Fascism into complete defeat.

14

The Consequences

'To guarantee supplies [to the Afrika Korps in Libya],
the capture of Malta was necessary and at the time
[July 1942] this was no longer possible. The
abandonment of this project was the first death blow to
the whole undertaking in North Africa . . .
Strategically, the one fatal blunder was the abandoning
of the plan to invade Malta. When this happened, the
subsequent course of events was almost inevitable.'

Field Marshal Albert Kesselring,
The War in the Mediterranean (1974)

THE CONSEQUENCES OF the various offensive operations launched
from Malta, or made possible by its being safely in British hands,
were so enormous that it could truthfully be said that without its
presence there would have been a different war in Europe; possibly,
even its outcome might have been different. Certainly, the time-
scale of the defeat ultimately inflicted on Germany would have been
greatly altered. Even assuming that the overwhelming weight of US
production would in the end have tilted the scales in the Allies'
favour, there is grave doubt whether this could have been done as
early as May 1945, when Germany admitted total defeat and her
military leaders signed the document of unconditional surrender.

There is perhaps a bigger question. As Churchill was always
acutely aware, Britain faced the terrible prospect, throughout 1941
and 1942, that the Russian leaders might sue for a separate peace
and thus leave Britain and her overseas Allies to face the full might
of the German Wehrmacht. What then? Could Britain and her
Allies have hoped to be able to mount a cross-Channel invasion
under those circumstances? Would the Americans, with their hands

full in the Pacific after December 1941, have decided not to join the battle in Europe until the Pacific battle had first been fought? How was it that Malta helped to tip the scales in favour of the USSR on the massive Eastern Fronts, which extended from Leningrad (now St Petersburg) to the Black Sea?

The key to this issue lies in the magnificent results which Malta-based submarines, splendidly supported by Force K and the strike-aircraft of the Fleet Air Arm and the RAF, achieved during the late months of 1941 when they reduced the flow of supplies to the Axis armies in North Africa so effectively that, for a while, the Axis ceased to send their ships there.

In the knowledge that Malta-based forces were responsible for these operations, Hitler, in response to pleas from General Erwin Rommel, took drastic action to try to render Malta impotent by an all-out campaign of aerial bombardment. Starting in late 1941, Hitler withdrew (Air) Field Marshal Kesselring from the Eastern Front – where he and the Air Force under his command had established an excellent working arrangement with the Army General, von Bock – and sent him to Italy, appointing him C-in-C South. To give his new C-in-C South the weapons with which to eliminate Malta from the Mediterranean war, he also withdrew Luftflotte II, one of his three Air Force headquarters facing the Russians, and transported it, and Fliegerkorps II, to Sicily. This was done at a time when advanced German troops were actually in the suburbs of Moscow.* Thereafter, the invaders of the Russian capital city got no further.

It was, of course, the great Russian 'General Winter' which was largely responsible for halting the German advance. However, the withdrawal of an entire air force, along with its bombers, fighters and reconnaissance planes, together with Germany's most able air–army co-operation expert, must have aided Britain's hard-pressed Soviet ally.

This was not the only action into which Hitler was goaded in late 1941. He took two further steps which were also intended to ensure that Malta would not be able to play any further part in the Mediterranean war.

---

* The street to which they advanced is still clearly marked.

The decision, made in November 1941, to transfer approximately half the operating U-boats from their hunting-ground in the Atlantic to the Mediterranean was taken, in part, in order to create an underwater fleet which would both harass the British Navy and also ensure that no supply ship could thereafter reach Malta. It was well known to the Germans that Malta was unable to feed its 250,000 local inhabitants – a number which had been swelled by the 20,000–30,000 British Servicemen additionally stationed there. It made sense, therefore, for the Germans to take steps to ensure that the isolated fortress should be placed under siege and cut off from replenishments of both food and war materials.

This decision greatly angered Admiral Karl Doenitz, the tactician in charge of Germany's fast-growing flotillas of deadly U-boats. By 1941, thanks to being able to operate from captured French Atlantic bases, such as Brest, Lorient, St-Nazaire, Bordeaux and La Pallice, German U-boats were already sinking Allied ships, and causing the loss of Allied seamen, at a greater rate than either men or ships could be replaced. During 1941, over a thousand Allied, mainly British, ships were sunk in the Atlantic. Moreover the numbers of new German U-boats being commissioned were increasing at the rate of between ten and twenty every month. As Vice-Admiral Otto Kretschmer, commander of *U99* and the most successful U-boat commander of the Second World War, has confirmed:* 'It is true that sending the U-boats from the Atlantic to the Mediterranean was a strategic mistake as they were much more useful in the Atlantic. Doenitz was furious. Malta should have been taken by invasion from Italy with the assistance of a German Air Force which had been moved to Sicily.'

Otto Kretschmer's reference to 'an invasion from Italy' introduces the third and final measure that Hitler took in order to neutralize Malta and so save the Afrika Korps, and the Italian armies in the Desert, from threatened annihilation. So as to make doubly sure that Malta should not threaten Axis convoys to North Africa, Hitler and Mussolini, as well as ordering the aerial bombardment of the island and its isolation by U-boats, also resuscitated and brought up to date the pre-war plans that Italy had made, as far back as 1935, for

---

* In a letter to the author, December 1994.

the seizure and occupation of the island. As Mussolini's Supremo, General Cavallero, is reported to have declared: 'If we take Malta, Libya will be safe. If not, the situation of the colony will always be precarious.'* Grand Admiral Raeder, Supreme Commander of the German Navy, was of the same mind: 'The final safeguarding of our Mediterranean supply lines . . . was possible only if we could succeed in capturing Malta.'† As early as August 1940, Vice Admiral Weichold, Head of the German Naval Liaison Staff in Rome, had reported to him: 'The elimination of Malta is the key to Axis mastery of the Central Mediterranean.'‡

Although, fortunately for all in Malta, these invasion plans – known to the Italians as Operazione C3 and to the Germans as Operation Herkules – were never put into operation, they were prepared in great detail. Men and materials were set aside for the island's invasion, effectively subtracting from the potential Russian fronts as many as 100,000 troops. These included nearly 30,000 airborne troops. The invaders of Malta would have been led by the dashing Lieutenant-General Student who, in May 1941, had successfully – although at great cost in men – dropped from the skies and seized the British-held island of Crete. Another first-class unit which was assembled for Operation Herkules – and consequently was not put to use by the Axis, in Russia or elsewhere – was the Italian Folgore airborne regiment; yet another was the renowned German Ramcke Brigade. In all, as Kurt Student remarked: 'It was an impressive force; five times as strong as we had against Crete.'§

Also, to prepare for the invasion of Malta, a crash programme to build invasion barges was instituted and, in a war which, after the initial successes by the Germans of 1940 and 1941, had partly become a war of industrial resources, any production effort expended in one direction meant less production in another. In the end, the landing-craft, the Folgore regiment, the Ramcke Brigade and much else was wasted by being hastily flung into the Desert

---

* See M. Muggeridge (ed.), *Count Ciano's Diary* (1947).
† Grand Admiral Raeder, *Struggle for the Sea*.
‡ See his 'Axis Policy and Operations in the Mediterranean'. The Admiral's strategic views always seem to have been correct.
§ Quoted from Cajus Bekker, *The Luftwaffe War Diaries* (1966).

War, often without their required heavy equipment, after Rommel's capture of Tobruk in June 1942.

As Lord James Douglas-Hamilton, nephew of Lord David Hamilton who commanded the Spitfire squadron No. 603 during the enemy's abortive October 1942 'blitz', has written in his book *The Air Battle for Malta*:

> As General Montgomery had acknowledged, the Battle of El Alamein could not have taken place if Malta had fallen earlier in 1942. If the fighter pilots, assisted by the Army, had failed to stave off invasion, or if the Navy had been unable to fend off starvation by resupplying the Island, or if the Maltese population had refused to support the Garrison, the battle of El Alamein would never have taken place. Supplies would have reached Rommel and the Afrika Korps for the most part unhindered. The Afrika Korps would rapidly have built up its strength, and would probably have seized the Nile Delta. Certainly the war for North Africa and the Middle East would have taken a different course.

This view is borne out by Squadron Leader 'Laddie' Lucas, CO of the highly successful 249 Spitfire Squadron during that same 'blitz', who cites a signal sent to General Auchinleck on 10 May 1942 by the Chief of Staff of the Defence Committee of the Allied War Cabinet.* This read: 'We are determined that Malta shall not be allowed to fall without a battle being fought by your whole army for its retention . . . Its possession would give the enemy a sure bridge to Africa . . . besides this, it would compromise any offensive against Italy and future plans.'

It was the Germans who suffered the consequences. As Rommel maintained: 'Malta should have been taken [Spring 1941] instead of Greece.'† By the time of the Battle of El Alamein, he was declaring: 'In the period from 6 September to 23 October 1942, the battle for supplies was waged with a new violence. At the end of the period, it had been finally lost by us and won by the British by a wide

---

* See P.B. Lucas, *The Thorn in Rommel's Side* (1992). Over lunch with Lucas at the RAF Club after the war, Eduard Leumann, who had commanded the Me 109-equipped JG/27 in the Desert War and been personally in touch with Rommel, confirmed to Lucas: 'Malta was the key.' He had experienced at first hand the shortages of fuel, food, ammunition and spare parts that had resulted from Malta-based operations.
† See B.H. Liddell Hart, *The Rommel Papers* (1953).

margin.' The significance of the island's operations did not escape him: 'With Malta in our hands, the British would have had little chance of exercising any further control over convoy traffic in the Mediterranean.'

The diversion of Doenitz's U-boats from the Atlantic to the Mediterranean might well have been Malta's greatest contribution to the European war. It was a process which was to continue. In all, the author has traced sixty-five U-boats which were so diverted.* Seven never managed even to get through the well-guarded Strait of Gibraltar, but were either sunk in the attempt or turned back, usually damaged. One did turn back after two abandoned attempts to get past this British-held rock without coming under attack. 'To encourage the others', Hitler thereupon had its commander, Kapitanleutnant Hirsacker of *U572*, court-martialled and shot.

Of the fifty-eight U-boats which managed to get into the Mediterranean, research indicates that only one ever escaped from it. Not that they did not have their successes. Both the British air-craft-carriers *Ark Royal* and *Eagle* were sunk in the Mediterranean by U-boats, as was also one of the all-too-few RN battleships in the Mediterranean, the *Barham*. German U-boats also played a part, but not a leading one, in attacking convoys to Malta.

As Winston Churchill wrote:[†] 'The Battle of the Atlantic was the dominating factor all through the war.' Consequently the order to Doenitz in November 1941 to transfer so many of his U-boats and their experienced commanders to the Mediterranean could well have constituted a major turning-point in the vital Atlantic battle. If Britain had become isolated from her American friends and from her stalwart Commonwealth Allies, the war against Nazi Germany could never have been won – except, possibly, by the Russians.

That is not all. With Malta holding firm, the bulk of Italian sub-marines and crews had to be retained in the Mediterranean in order to counter British Naval superiority there. If Malta had collapsed, or been abandoned, as it so nearly was in 1940 even before Italy entered the war on Germany's side, there would have been no para-mount need to concentrate the huge Italian submarine fleet – which

---

* Full details appear in Appendix VI.
† *The Second World War*, Vol. V.

was much larger than Germany's before the war – in the Mediterranean. It would have been free to carry on its depredations elsewhere. As it was, only 32 of Italy's over 100 submarines were sent to join the German U-boats in the Atlantic and, for the most part, they remained in those waters.

As was also the case with the small, effective Italian torpedo-boats, which sank about half a dozen of our Mediterranean sub-marines, including Lieutenant Commander Wanklyn's *Upholder*, this submarine force was apt to display more skill and initiative than did those manning their largely ineffective battleships and cruisers. According to the Italian naval historian Tullio Marcon, the figures show that the Italian submarines operating in the Atlantic – crewed as they were by well-trained pre-war crews – were more effective, on a ratio basis, than even the dreaded German U-boats. This may have been due, in part, to the Italian boats being bigger than their Type VII German counterparts and thus being able to range more widely to the less well-defended coasts of America and the Caribbean. Possibly, also, Italy sent only her best submarines into the Atlantic. Marcon's figures are:

Atlantic Ocean

German U-boats	Italian submarines
tons sunk per U-boats used	tons sunk per submarines used
13,000 tons	17,950 tons
tons sunk per U-boats lost	tons sunk per submarines lost
19,730 tons	35,000 tons

Tullio Marcon also draws attention to the tonnage sunk in the Atlantic by Italy's most successful submarine, the *Leonardo da Vinci*, which is credited with 120,000 tons sunk. While this falls far short of the over 265,000 tons attributed to Otto Kretschmer in his *U99*, it is a comparable figure to the tonnage sunk by Wanklyn in *Upholder*.

Had Malta been eliminated from the equation, then it can be assumed that many more Italian submarines would have been employed in the Atlantic, and with Germany also not needing to send U-boats into the Mediterranean, then the odds stacked against Britain's inadequately escorted transatlantic convoys of 1940–42 and early 1943 would have been almost overwhelming. Yet as Churchill has written, with reference to the Battle of the Atlantic,

'Everything happening elsewhere, on land, at sea or in the air, depended ultimately upon its outcome.'

After the fall of Tobruk in June 1942, when both sides were preparing for the crucial battles of Alam Halfa and El Alamein, Malta-based forces again rose to the occasion. Rommel then knew that he had to attack in August 1942 at the latest, before the massive US and British build-up of supplies would render his task of reaching Alexandria well nigh impossible. However, to attack before September, Rommel had to have supplies and reserves, especially of petrol. The story of how he was denied these needs, even after all submarines had been withdrawn from Malta, has already been told.

Again, in October 1942, in a desperate throw to neutralize Malta a second time, the misuse of the Luftwaffe, operating from Sicily, and the losses that their squadrons incurred during the ten days of that abortive air battle – an aerial equivalent of Rommel's vain effort to capture the Alam Halfa ridge – meant that when General Montgomery launched his El Alamein offensive in late October 1942, the Luftwaffe in North Africa had already been rendered largely ineffective. Thereafter the RAF in the Desert, fighting alongside the fast-growing USAAF, SAAF and other Commonwealth Air Forces, ruled the skies over that land war, all the way from El Alamein to Tripoli and beyond. Malta's Spitfires had, in October 1942, blunted the Luftwaffe just as, a month or so earlier, Montgomery's guns and armour had blunted the Panzer Army's much vaunted tank divisions at Alam Halfa. After October 1942, the triumphant fighter-aircraft based in Malta were now free to go on the offensive over Sicily, with bombs as well as cannons.

If Malta had proved valuable in 1940–42, it was to prove indispensable during the first five months of 1943 during the climax of the victorious Anglo-American Tunisian campaign. In the period December 1942–13 May 1943 – the date when the Axis surrendered all remaining forces in Africa – it is known that the Axis lost at least 180 ships to submarines and aircraft which were operating under Malta control.* Doubtless there were also more ships lost among the 646 enemy ships declared lost in the Mediterranean during the war due to 'causes unknown'.†

---

* See Appendix V.
† See Appendix VII.

As a result of these losses, just as Malta itself nearly ran out of food and other supplies during these critical months of 1942, so the Axis forces fighting in Tunisia ran short of all the materials and provisions that made it even remotely possible for them to be able to continue the fight in that former French colonial territory. German troops, especially perhaps their Panzer divisions, do not readily surrender, but in Tunisia they surrendered in such large numbers that, as we have seen, more Germans were taken prisoner there than surrendered to the Russians after the massive German defeat at Stalingrad in January 1943.

Malta, with its proximity to enemy ports in Tunisia, Sardinia and Sicily, now played a part in ensuring that these defeated armies were not able to evacuate their defeated troops to Europe, where they would once again be able to pose a danger. Fittingly, part of this Allied success was called 'Operation Retribution'. When the enemy, despairing of breaking the iron ring imposed upon their sea routes to and from Tunisia, resorted to a massive airlift of men and supplies, the Spitfires and Beaufighters from Malta were used to intercept and shoot down dozens of the transport planes which had been rushed into this emergency. Many of these planes, moreover, had been diverted from use on the Eastern Front at a time when the Germans were trying to supply their army, surrounded at Stalingrad, by air.

Referring to Operation Husky, Tullio Marcon has perhaps summed up Malta's contribution to the July 1943 invasion of Sicily as succinctly as anyone. He writes:* 'Malta's role in the invasion of Sicily was irreplaceable.' It had begun, as he explains, with 'the acquisition of data and information on [Italian] defences and beaches . . . Moreover', he adds,

> for Husky's success, it was imperative to master the sky over the landing places, with many squadrons of fighters and support planes. Considering the [short] range of the Spitfires and P-40s, this was possible only with Malta- [and Pantelleria-] based aircraft.
>
> Last but not least, Malta provided the backbone of the invasion fleet . . . These facts are sufficient to assert that if the island had fallen, then it would have been a quite different war.

---

* Letter to the author, 18 April 1995.

The German historian Professor Dr Jürgen Rohwer also writes in the following terms:*

During the Second World War from 1940 to 1942 Malta was the most important British naval and air base in the Mediterranean. It was a great mistake of the Italians in 1940 to abandon the idea of taking the then weak Malta by a forceful attack, and by the Germans in 1942 to cancel the planned operation 'Hercules' when Rommel advanced in North Africa beyond Tobruk. In 1941 Malta became the base of British attack aircraft, submarines, and even surface vessels which endangered the Italian and German supply route to North Africa, and in late 1941 almost severed it with the help of 'Ultra' decrypts. In 1942 the German air offensive could only neutralize Malta for a few weeks, before it became again the base for British air and submarine attacks against the Axis supply route to North Africa, causing with the assistance of 'Ultra' such heavy shipping losses that Rommel was almost starved, and the Eighth Army could overwhelm the German-Italian Army at El Alamein. So the great efforts of the British to supply Malta by convoys from the west and east notwithstanding heavy losses were bearing rich fruits and brought about the change of the tide in the Mediterranean.

The consequences of the successful invasion of Sicily, soon to be followed by an invasion of the mainland of Italy, were again enormous. They also had far-reaching effects upon the land battles for Europe: firstly upon Germany's massive Eastern Fronts, then upon the successful invasion of Normandy, and finally, upon the invasion of the South of France which followed.

Traditionally, German war leaders were always averse to fighting a war on two far-distant fronts. By August–September 1943, with the British and American Armies firmly entrenched in southern Italy, the Germans found themselves already faced with this problem. The almost immediate political consequence of the swift capture of Sicily by the invading British and American troops was the overthrow, by the Italian military and political leaders, of their dictator, Benito Mussolini. This was swiftly followed by Italy's decision to surrender, and to fight instead on the side of the Allies. Henceforth, the Anglo-American armies – the British advancing up the eastern side of Italy and the Americans advancing west of the Apennine mountain range – were fighting purely German forces.

---

* Letter to the author, 7 December 1995.

This had two pronounced effects upon the war in Europe, both favourable to the Allies. In the first place, as the long hard struggle by the Allies progressed up the length of Italy, more and more first-class German troops were thrown into the battle in an attempt – vain, as it turned out – to stem the gradual Anglo-American advance to the Alps. By Christmas 1944, approximately 1,100,000 German forces were engaged in Italy. This accorded with the Allies' strategic plan which was remorselessly to draw down Germany's manpower into the continuing conflict in the south. Moreover, thanks in part to ever-growing, and ever more effective, air super-iority over the battle areas and beyond, German casualties far exceeded those of the attackers. In the end, German casualties in the Italian theatre of war amounted to about 536,000, whereas those of the Allies were only about 312,000.*

Germany, which by 1943 was reeling backwards on its Russian fronts, could well have made good use of the million and more men, along with their armour, guns, transport and aircraft, on the fronts where they were opposing the advancing Russians. When the Normandy invasion commenced in June 1944, the Wehrmacht found itself fighting not on two but on three widely separated fronts. By then, approximately one-fifth of their armed forces were already committed to Italy. As Field Marshal Jodl is reported to have told Hitler: 'We are not pinning the enemy down [in Italy]. He is pinning us down.'

The invasion of southern France, Operation Dragoon, which took place in August 1944 shortly after the Allied break-out from the Normandy beach-heads, even established a fourth front for the staunch, but weary, German troops to defend – although, in this case, the new battleground scarcely merited being called a 'front' since, with so many German armies fully engaged and retreating elsewhere, this Allied invasion went ahead almost unopposed.

The Allies' second great gain, as a result of the Malta-based inva-sion of Sicily and the subsequent advances up Italy, was the lifting of morale among British and American troops. For the first time since 1940, Allied forces were fighting it out successfully against purely German forces. Hitherto, even when defeating Rommel, first

---

* Figures include wounded.

in Libya, then Tunisia, as many as half the Axis armies on the battlefields had been composed of Italians, though their strength was unevenly matched with the better equipped Germans.

Given the overwhelming defeat which the Germans had inflicted upon British as well as French troops in France during the blitzkrieg of May–June 1940, an aura of invincibility had been created around the Wehrmacht. By September 1943, this was fast disappearing, as the various German defence positions in Italy, such as their Gothic and Gustav lines, were one by one overcome by the advancing British Eighth and General Clark's Fifth US armies. By the end, the Anglo-American armies had succeeded in driving the Germans from the toe of Italy to the foot of the Alps.

The Malta-based invasion of Sicily, and the advance through Italy, served the Allies as a magnificent learning ground in preparation for the subsequent invasion of Europe, via the Normandy beaches. The Salerno and Anzio landings of troops behind the German lines, though eventually successful, were perhaps especially instructive to the Allies as, on both occasions, much went awry and casualties among the invaders, as they clung desperately to their first footholds, were heavy.

Much was also learned, during the eighteen months of fighting in Italy, about what could, and more importantly, what could not, be accomplished in the skies by the massive Anglo-American air superiority which the Allies now possessed. The word 'interdiction' (rather curiously) entered the airmen's vocabulary – indicating, in this case, the policy of attacking roads, railways and bridges behind the enemy's front-line positions in order to isolate them from their supplies. Experience in Italy showed 'interdiction' to be effective and it became a key word for those planning subsequent invasion strategies.

By both their failures and successes in Italy, the Allies learned much – especially, perhaps, that the German armies were far from invincible and that air power was an indispensable adjunct to an army's success. The Allies also learned much, from Salerno and Anzio, about the best use of sea power when invading an enemy's shore.

If these were the principal consequences of Malta's long defiance and subsequent triumphs in the Second World War, there were others, too, perhaps less obvious. It could be said that, by breaking

up the successful air–army team of Generals Kesselring and von
Bock, Malta again came to the aid of the hard-pressed Russians in
late 1941. As a team, these two leaders had done much to further the
German army's swift advance towards Moscow. Such harmony
between air and ground commanders was not always evident, on
either side.

Malta also served as a wonderful proving ground for the experts
at Bletchley Park. As all important signals between Germany and
Italy and North Africa had to be sent by W/T rather than by tele-
phone lines, which did not exist, the trans-Mediterranean use of
Enigma/C38 was enormous. Thanks to Malta's resistance, thousands of these messages were sent and the Ultra team learned, by
handling them, the best way of using such priceless information.

Much was also learned the hard way from the thirty-eight cloak-
and-dagger raiding parties which so frequently occupied (often to
Captain Simpson's annoyance) the attention of his Malta-based
submarines. For the most part, these brave men did not achieve
very much and their losses were heavy: in itself a valuable, if
painful, lesson learned. However, their advance forays into the
beach areas ahead of the main troops on the Sicilian landings
proved of great value.

It was also a significant coup for Malta that, following the early
Swordfish attacks on Augusta during which a destroyer was sunk
with a torpedo, the Italians withdrew the cruisers which would
otherwise have been based there. Had Malta not been held, and had
Italian cruisers continued to be based in Augusta as usual, the
chances of British convoys transporting goods from Gibraltar direct
to Alexandria without interference – as happened in 1940 and early
1941 – would have been greatly reduced. The same could be said
of the Italian battleships based in Taranto which, guided by
Warburton's plots and photographs, were attacked by Malta-based
Swordfish in November 1940. Soon thereafter, these ships retreated
northwards and were far removed from the west–east
Mediterranean sea lanes.

The German bombers based in Sicily during the sustained blitz
upon Malta outnumbered those based elsewhere in the
Mediterranean war zones by at least 2:1. This was to the obvious
advantage of the Eighth Army in the Desert. Likewise, the hundreds
of Ju 52s, aided by Italian transport planes, which were later used to

airlift German reinforcements into Tunisia when it became apparent that supply ships were not reaching their destinations as a result of Malta-based attacks, would undoubtedly have been of enormous value to the Germans on their Russian fronts at that time. It is also likely that the Italians were reluctant to commit their huge and fast ocean-going liners, the 50,000-ton *Rex* and the *Conte di Savoia*, for troop transportation to North Africa after Wanklyn in *Upholder*, operating from Malta, had sunk their smaller liners, *Neptunia* and *Oceania*. Both these pre-war Italian transatlantic 30-knot giants spent the entire war inactive, until sunk at their anchorages in port.

It must also have kept much of Italy's limited industrial output of iron and steel industries extremely busy having continually to repair ships damaged, but not sunk, by the aircraft and submarines operating out of Malta. Also, as has been mentioned, some of those effective daylight bombing raids of 1943/44 were, at times, only made possible because the bombers, coming from further afield, could be protected by fighters from Malta arising to meet them *en route*.

Among the units which the Luftwaffe moved to Sicily in December 1941 was 1/NJG2. This was the successful night-fighter Gruppe which had mastered the difficult art of carrying out night intruder raids upon the UK Bomber Command airfields where, prior to every big night raid on Germany, vulnerable targets were plentifully available. Over the UK in 1941, 1/NJG2 had caused Bomber Command many heavy losses. After the departure of 1/NJG2 to Sicily, as part of Fliegerkorps II, Bomber Command, for the rest of the war, remained remarkably untouched by night intruders although, as the size of their night raids increased, they were increasingly vulnerable against such attacks. Moreover, as is reported in Cajus Bekker's comprehensive *The Luftwaffe War Diaries*, 'they [the aircraft of 1/NJG2 in Sicily] flew day and night and one crew after another failed to return.' The number of first-line enemy bombers and fighter-aircraft drafted to Sicily could have been of enormous use elsewhere.

Finally, with the invasion of Italy successfully launched, Malta's unique role as an isolated and independent outpost of attack began to recede into history. By then, however, many on the island who had lived through the bombing and siege of 1941–43, as well as those who had supplied and defended the island, had surely done enough. Many Servicemen who had manned the airfields, army bases and harbours had been there for years and seen it through, often without leave or respite. Once in Malta, it had been almost impossible to get away.

Argument will continue to rage over whether the late-1941 period, the pre-Alamein period of 1942, the Tunisian period or the Operation Husky period of 1943 constituted the island's greatest contribution to the Allied war effort. All four periods have valid claims.

To have cut deep into Rommel's supply lines during September–December 1941, as Allied submarines had done, and thereby to force the enemy into taking the extended sea-route to North Africa was a magnificent achievement. It was crowned, perhaps, by Force K's sinking of the *Duisberg* convoy: although the greatest damage undoubtedly was caused by our submarines, backed up by the magnificent Swordfish of 830 Squadron, and not forgetting the Albacores and brave, but badly mauled, Blenheims. The Beauforts and Beaufighters who entered the fray in summer 1942 served a vital purpose, helping to deny Rommel the fuel and ammunition he needed at both Alam Halfa and El Alamein. By the winter of 1942/43, all eyes in Malta were turned towards Tunisia where again the submarines scored heavily, supported this time by Albacores and Fishingtons as well as by the then well-established Beaufort/Beaufighter team. During this period the fighter-aircraft also operated on the offensive.

During Operation Husky the eyes of the world were on the tiny island whose presence alone made that vast undertaking a reality and helped to turn the invasion of Sicily into another great Allied victory. Again, the submarines had a key role to play and the sub-mariners were magnificent. It is no coincidence that many of those young submarine commanders who survived – and tragically many other did not – rose to become Admirals: Ben Bryant, Tony Troup, Rufus Mackenzie, John Roxburgh, Arthur Hezlet, Ian McGeoch, among them; never forgetting their first great leader 'Shrimp' Simpson.

Throughout all these periods, two RAF elements shone. Firstly, it is doubtful whether any PR unit throughout the war ever played a more vital and important role than did 69 Squadron in Malta. From as early as September 1940 onwards, its many types of aircraft and inspiring leaders kept the Allied war-leaders, in Malta and the Middle East, constantly informed about enemy merchant and navy shipping. As Air Vice Marshal Hugh Pughe Lloyd has written: 'Every time the enemy moved a row boat, we knew about it.' If not strictly true, this is in spirit correct. The combination of 69 Squadron and Ultra was a never-failing asset throughout Malta's war. As the German General Werner von Fritsch wrote with foresight in 1939: 'The military organization with the best aerial photo-reconnaissance will win the next war.'

Secondly, there were the Wellingtons in their various guises: bombers, night reconnaissance (Goofingtons), flare droppers (Flashingtons), torpedo carriers (Fishingtons) and, finally, anti-submarine hunters. Luqa, from late 1940 onwards, up to the time when Operation Husky dominated all thoughts, was never without a Wimpy or two on that battered airfield. Many innovations were first attempted from there with these pre-war designed aircraft which, from 1941 onwards, were becoming an obsolescent bomber type in the UK.

FAA and RAF aircraft, and up to about 100 Allied submarines, along with occasional surface ships, all played a part. Nor should the Army's role be neglected. At times, there seemed to be as many Army personnel on Malta's airfields as there were airmen. They helped to build and extend the runways, the winding taxi-tracks to distant dispersal points and the hundreds of vital aircraft pens. They almost took over refuelling and, in some instances, lent a hand at rearming and even aircraft maintenance. Their officers became RAF Intelligence Officers. In the dockyards, under fire, they assisted with the unloading, and all the while defended the island with an AA barrage that Luftwaffe pilots came to admit was the heaviest they had experienced.

If the boat was sometimes almost sinking, everyone was in it together and it didn't matter who pulled at the oars. There was no need for committees or edicts about co-operation. The three fighting Services, aided by many loyal Maltese, fought as one and did so with whatever they could get hold of. Moreover, the little that was available had been brought in, at enormous cost, by a gallant Merchant Service. Malta operated a do-it-yourself war. The harsh conditions broke the fibre of some but made many heroes out of minions. Malta, under her magnificent leaders – men such as Vice

Admiral Ford, Major General Beak VC (GOC, Malta), Air Vice Marshal Lloyd, their successors and those who served under them – made her own rules: rules which worked.

It was a fitting and magnificent gesture when, in 1992, the Malta Government issued a Commemorative Medal to those who had served there. Her Majesty the Queen added her tribute by decreeing that this foreign-given award could be worn alongside other British awards. Her father King George VI had, uniquely, awarded the George Cross to the peoples and island of Malta. The Queen's tribute may also be unique, as were so many of Malta's contributions to victory. To those who were privileged to play a part, it was a period in their lives that few can ever, or ever wish, to forget.

Perhaps President Roosevelt, in an address delivered during a visit to the island on the second anniversary of Pearl Harbor, found the most appropriate words – words still proudly on display in Malta:

> In the name of the people of the United States of America, I salute the Island of Malta, its people and defenders who, in the cause of freedom and justice and decency throughout the world, have rendered valorous service far and beyond the call of duty.
>
> Under repeated fire from the skies, Malta stood alone and unafraid in the centre of the sea, one bright flame in the darkness – a beacon of hope for the clearer days which have come.
>
> Malta's bright story of human fortitude and courage will be read by posterity with wonder and gratitude through all the ages.
>
> What was done in this island maintains the highest traditions of gallant men and women who, from the beginning of time, have lived and died to preserve civilization for all mankind.

APPENDIX I

Ultra intercepts

28 November 1941

These copies of a series of Italian signals, sent via Enigma, or C38, machines in the late hours of 28 November 1941, were despatched by the Admiralty in Rome to various enemy naval bases and to Italian ships at sea. Those in Italian have been translated into English.

They give very precise information about the routes to be followed by the merchant vessels *Adriatico*, *Venerio*, *Iseo* and *Capo Faro* along with their destinations, speeds and ETAs (Estimated Times of Arrival). The signals also describe the types and numbers of escorting vessels which would be accompanying these merchant vessels. They further indicate the area where the Italian battleship *Duilio** is expected to be and where the cruiser force *Aosta*, also at sea, will be at certain specific times.

This series of Top Secret signals was sent at a time when, almost in despair of getting any supplies to Rommel in North Africa, the enemy resorted to sending a number of single ships and small convoys across the sea by different routes in order to ensure that some, at least, might reach their destinations (which were divided between Tripoli and Benghazi), although others might be intercepted and sunk. By then, the reputation of Force K operating from Malta filled the Italian Navy and merchant navy with trepidation. To meet her challenge, the Italians for once ventured to put a battleship to sea as well as a cruiser force.

This mass of supposedly undecipherable information was intercepted by British monitoring stations and passed to the team at Bletchley Park. Within minutes, it was unscrambled, translated into English and transmitted to the very few who were in on the Ultra secret. In this case, they appear to have been sent only to the Navy C-in-C Mediterranean, the Vice

---

* Although a second battleship, *Littorio*, is included in Rome's distribution list, she appears not to have been involved in any way.

Admiral Malta and the Intelligence Chief at Alexandria. Clearly the Admiralty in London was also advised.

As well as putting the Italian signals into comprehensible plain English, the experts at Bletchley Park also added their own helpful comments.

It is little wonder, therefore, that the *Adriatico* was in due course despatched by Force K with its usual lethal efficiency, guided to it in the darkness by their friendly Wellington of the SDF, Luqa.* The *Capo Faro*, which was probably first located by 69 Squadron, was also hit and sunk by marauding Blenheims of 18 Squadron operating from Malta. The same squadron also damaged the *Iseo*. Of the four merchant ships mentioned in this batch of signals, only the *Venerio* escaped unscathed. Worse was to come. The big tanker, *Iridio Mantovani* (not included in this batch of signals), was first hit and stopped by Blenheims and then, when under tow by the destroyer *Alvise da Mosta*, sunk by Force K, on the morning after Captain Agnew and his cruiser force had dealt so clinically with the *Adriatico*. *Iridio Mantovani* was carrying 1,870 tons of petrol, 1,727 tons of benzine and 5,032 tons of gas-oil and naphtha.

Referring to these attacks in his diary Count Ciano, the Italian Foreign Minister and Mussolini's son-in-law, records:

> December 1   Out of the whole convoy two arrived [presumably the *Iseo* and *Venerio*], one was forced to beach at Suda Bay and two were sunk, the result is not brilliant but it could have been worse.

The next day he laments:

> Another of our ships has been sunk, almost at the entrance of the port of Tripoli. It was the *Mantovani* loaded with 7,000 tons of petrol. It cannot be denied that this is a hard blow.

What became of the battleship *Duilio* and the cruiser force? Apparently one of the cruisers, the *Garibaldi*, developed engine trouble and its speed was reduced to 14 knots. This was deemed sufficient reason for all the Italian capital ships, and their destroyer screens, to return to Taranto.†

Of the signals included here those marked A1, A2, etc., originated the series at 17.28 hours, 28 November 1941. They are English translations of the original signals sent by the Admiralty, Rome. They provide full details of the sailing, routes, destinations, times and escorts of a number of mer-

---

* Flown by the author.

† This last is one example where Ultra unwittingly misled those who received its information. When events did not turn out as planned by the enemy, because those who received the Enigma signals did not do what they were supposed to do, then the Enigma signals, and the subsequent Ultra intercepts regarding those events, were apt to be misleading to the Allies.

chant and naval vessels heading for North Africa. This was clearly information of the greatest value to the Allies. The 'Dept. Notes', in brackets, appear to be points of clarification which have been added by the Bletchley team.

Those marked B1, B2, etc., were issued by the Ultra team at Bletchley. It can be seen that, within three hours, they have intercepted the enemy signals, unscrambled them via the bombe (their early form of computer), translated them into English and transmitted them. They have also added their own elucidating comments. It is presumed that these would have been transmitted to Alexandria and Malta and to other interested Commands. Clearly, they also went to the Admiralty in London.

Those marked C1, C2, etc., were issued by the Admiralty, London. They went only to C-in-C Mediterranean, Vice-Admiral Malta and to what is thought to be an Intelligence Office in Alexandria. They concentrate upon the movements of the Italian Navy's big ships with only a passing reference to the merchant ships at sea. Even these were issued within three hours of the first signals originated by the Admiralty in Rome.

*Original Italian signals**

A1

ADM ZIP/ZTPI/2617
To ID 8
From NS
9065 KC/S   TOO 1305. 1430. 1450.   TOI 1239/1315/1320/
28/11/41.

Rome to Patras
From   Admiralty Rome
To   Naval Command Peloponnese, Patras, repeated to the *Littorio* for the Squadron, Naval Headquarters Taranto, *Duilio* for the Division, *Aosta* for the Division and Naval Headquarters Benghazi.
22895   Decypher in person.

Make arrangements for the motor vessel *Adriatico* to sail at 2300/29. Speed 12 knots, routeing: point 40 miles, 241 degrees Point Feminile at 0700/30. Point 33 miles, 250 degrees Point Colla at 1900/30. Point Ora, then steer so as to make the lighthouse on a course of 161 degrees.

Naval Headquarters Benghazi is to make arrangements for pilotage and protection in the area where she is to arrive.

The M/V *Adriatico* might sight the *Duilio* towards the west in the hours

* Extracted from DEFE3/834 at PRO, Kew.

before noon on 30/11, and, on the afternoon of the same day, the Seventh Division, both of which will be cruising on protective operations.

(Dept. Note: The last mention of the *Adriatico* is in ZTPI/2421. Point Feminile is approx 37 degs. 15 min N, 20 degs. 40 min E. Point Colla is approx 34 degs. 40 min N, 20 degs. E. Point Ora is approx 32 degs. 27 min N, 20 degs. 3 min E.)

1725/28/11/41/CEL/LLB.

A2

ADM   ZIP/ZTPI/2623
To ID 8
From NS
9370 KC/S   TOO 1300, 1600, 1630.   TOI 1512, 1617, 1602/
                                                                28/11/41.

Rome to Tripoli   *Most Immediate*
From   Admiralty Rome
To   Naval Headquarters Taranto, Naval Command Libya, repeated
    Littorio for Squadron, *Duilio* for Division, *Aosta* for Division.
34336   Decypher in person.

Naval Headquarters Taranto is to arrange for the sailing of motor vessel *Venerio* escorted by destroyer *Da Verazzano* at 1200/29. Speed 14 knots.

Routeing: Point Carbone. Point 37 miles 93 degrees, Point Ministero at 1200/30.

Set course for Point Fumo.

At nightfall alter course for Point Giovedi passing at 0700/01. Point 10 miles south of Point Isola.

Expected arrival at Point 23 miles 140 degrees from Point Azia at 1700/01.

During the day of the 30/11, convoy *Venerio* may perhaps be able to join convoy *Iseo* and *Capo Faro* escorted by torpedo boat which is following the same route to Point Forza.

Naval Command Libya to arrange for protective pilotage on the day of arrival.

Naval Headquarters Taranto is to communicate to convoy *Venerio* all information concerning protection by *Duilio* and Seventh Division.

2010/28/11/41   CEL/AC.

ADM   ZIP/ZTPI/2623A.
To   ID 8
From   NS

(Dept. Note: It is thought that Point Carbone is in approx position 38 degrees 32 minutes N and 18 degrees 20 minutes E. Fumo approx position 32 degrees 55 minutes N and 19 degrees E. Giovedi approx 32 degrees 40 minutes N 16 degrees E.)

A3

ADM   ZIP/ZTPI/2669.
To   ID 8
From   NS
153.8 KC/S   TOO 1035, 1110.   TOI 1457/1534/29/11/41.

Rome to   ?   *Important*
From   Admiralty Rome
To   *Duilio* for Division, *Aosta* for Division, Naval Headquarters Taranto, repeated to *Littorio* for Squadron and Naval Headquarters Messina.
85215   Decypher in person   Reference cypher message no. 76131/28/11.

Cruising area for *Duilio* group from 0900/30 to 1900/30 is between parallels 36 degrees 40 minutes and 35 degrees 40 minutes and meridians 19 degrees 0 minutes and 19 degrees 40 minutes.

(Dept. Note: No. 76131 not received.)
2035/29/11/41.   CEL/AC.

A4

ADM   ZIP/ZTPI/2696.
To   ID 8
From   NS
153.8 KC/S   TOO 1155/30   TOI 1045/30/11/41.

Rome to ? Messina   *Most Immediate*
From   Admiralty Rome
To   *Duilio* for Division, repeated *Aosta* for Division.

65216   *Duilio* force is to proceed to a position 20 miles from *Aosta* group and remain at that distance.

(Dept. Note: See ZTPI/2669 for protection of *Duilio* group.)

1328/30/11/41.   LWF/VSN.

A5

ADM   ZIP/ZTPI/2710.
To   ID 8
From   NS
5455KC/S   TOO 1230/30   TOI 1110/30/11/41.

Rome to ?   *Most Immediate*
From   Admiralty Rome

42677   *Duilio* force, instead of keeping 20 miles distance, is to proceed within sight of the *Aosta* force. The *Aosta* force will change course in order to proceed to within sight of *Duilio*. From thence it will resume its original course. *Venerio* with *Da Verazzano* is to steer east until sunset thence to Point Violenza. *Aosta* to inform *Da Verazzano*.

(Dept. Note: Point Violenza thought to be Benghazi – see ZTPI/2696 – of which this is an amendment.)

1337/30/11/41.   LWF/LLB.
RD TKS

Ultra signals issued from Bletchley*

B1   MK307, AL297, MA200, AIC.

Emergency

Para 1. *Adriatico* had orders today 28th to leave ARCOSTOLI see MK168 at 21 hours Saturday 29th for Benghazi. Speed 12 knots, (MK307, AL297, MA200, AIC in two parts, part 1) passing through 36 Degrees 44 Minutes by 19 degrees 58 minutes at 05 hours Sunday 30th then through 34 degrees 26 minutes by 19 degrees 28 minutes at 1700 hours 30th, then through 32 degrees 27 minutes by 20 degrees 03 minutes. Arrive Benghazi 05 hours Monday December 1st.

Comment: Points approximate.

Para 2. *Littorio* for Squadron as well as *Duilio* and *Aosta* for their respective divisions were also notified of above. *Adriatico* may sight *Duilio* to west-wards towards 10 hours 30th or a few hours before then and 7th Cruiser division after 10 hours same day. Both will be cruising on protective operations.

Comment: At 10 hours on Sunday 30th *Adriatico* should be about 35 degrees 46 minutes by 19 degrees 44 minutes.

---

* Extracted from DEFE3/745 at PRO, Kew.

Para 3. From further reports the following will be at sea in the area between latitudes 37 and 34 and longitude 20 and 18 with mean course south on Sunday 30th: firstly *Adriatico* unescorted: secondly convoy *Capo Faro* and *Iseo* escorted by one torpedo boat: thirdly *Venerio* escorted by destroyer *Da Verazzano*; fourthly the 7th Cruiser division with 3 destroyers, *Duilio* with 4 destroyers will remain in support on the same longitude, north of 36 Degrees.

(part 2 and final of MK307)

The naval forces will be on their return passage on the next day, that is Monday. FliegerKorps 10 to provide reconnaissance on both days. Above was also to be communicated by PATRAS to MAESTRALE for Squadron comment. Although as mentioned under Para 2 above, *Littorio* was also advised of these movements, there is no mention of her in the report under Para 3. Western Desert has not been sent a copy of this signal. Details of convoy routes will follow.

Time 2020/28/11/41. GMT.

B2 MK346, AL334, MA227, AIC.

Emergency

Cruising area for *Duilio* group (see MK307) from 0700 to 1700 Sunday 30th is between (MK346, AL334, MA227, AIC) 36 Degrees 40 minutes and meridians 19 Degrees and 19 Degrees 40 minutes.

Time 2040/29/11/41. GMT.

B3 MK346, AL363, MA252, AIC.

Emergency

At 1030 hours today 30th *Duilio* group and 7th Cruiser Division had orders to proceed within sight of each other, this necessitating a change of course for cruiser group. (MK376, AL363, MA252, AIC). Cruisers were immediately afterwards to resume original course. At the same time *Venerio* and *Da Verazzano* were to proceed eastwards until sunset and then in the direction of BENGHAZI.

Time 1330/30/11/41. GMT.

*Ultra signals issued by Admiralty, London**

C1

Most Secret

Serial No.F944
2010A/28 November. OUT.

To: C in C Mediterranean   470 B1
      COIS Alexandria
      VA Malta   270

Date: 28.11.41.

Naval Cypher Special One Time Table

From: Admiralty
Immediate   AIDAC

Italian Battleship *Duilio* will be in the vicinity of 36 degs. North 20 degs. East AM on 30th November.

Three 6" cruisers will be in vicinity of 35 degs. 00' North 15 degs. 30' East PM on 30th November.

Both the above units are acting as cover to ships proceeding to North Africa.

Comment: MK follows.   2010A/28. DDIC Green 3.

C2

Most Secret

Serial No.F ?
1628A/30 November

To: C in C Mediterranean   525 B1
      VA Malta   290
      COIS Alexandria

Date: 30.11.41.

Naval Cypher Special One Time Table

From: Admiralty
Immediate   AIDAC

Estimated position, course and speed of *Duilio* at 1345B/30 was approximately 36 degrees 47' N 19 degs. 23' E South, fifteen knots.

1628A/30. DDIC.

---

* Extracted from ADM223/103 at PRO, Kew.

C3
Most Secret   Serial No.F956.
                                              1908A/30 November. OUT.
To: CS 7   Date: 30.11.41.
      Repeated: C in C Mediterranean   530
      VA Malta   291
      COIS Alexandria

                     Flag Officer Cypher

From: Admiralty
Immediate   AIDAC

For your personal information not to be retransmitted.

Italian Battleship and cruiser divisions are proceeding South in company until 2000Z/30 to cover merchant vessels proceeding to Benghazi from British forces coming from the West.

                                      1908A/30. DDIC.

APPENDIX II

Merchant ships sunk by Allied aircraft in enemy harbours

> Rommel's difficulties were due rather to the dramatic fall in the shipping tonnage plying the African route: of the 1,748,841 tons of Italian shipping of January 1940, 1,259,001 tons had been sunk by the end of 1942.*

In the excellent library of London's famous Guildhall can be found a tome entitled *Lloyd's War Losses: the Second World War*, Volume II. It lists enemy shipping losses (presumably of insured ships) sunk in the Mediterranean in this period. Many details of each ship are listed as well as the manner in which each vessel was sunk – whether by a surface ship, submarine, aircraft, mine or 'other causes'. The location of where each ship was sunk is also given. From these details it is easy to determine which ships were sunk in enemy harbours by Allied aircraft on bombing raids. Ships were being sunk, in harbours as at sea, at a greater rate than they were being replaced.

In the knowledge that bomber-aircraft were based in Malta for almost the whole of the war in the Mediterranean, with the Wellington type predominating, it can confidently be deduced that, of the over 250 ships listed as having been sunk in enemy ports by Allied aircraft, at least 100 are likely to have been sunk by aircraft based in Malta. This gives ample proof that what Sir Archibald Sinclair describes in his congratulatory signal to AOC Malta as 'the steady and deadly slogging of Wellingtons at enemy ports' was far from being an unproductive tactic.

After subtracting from the total number of ships those more likely to have been sunk by aircraft based in either the Middle East or west of Tunisia, the Lloyd's list contains the names of 194 commercial vessels sunk in ports which were well within range of the Wellingtons based in Malta,

---

* Vice-Admiral Weichold.

and which were closer to Malta than to other Allied airfields where bombers were also based.

This total of 194 enemy ships sunk compares favourably with the numbers which were sunk by Allied surface ships and submarines while based in Malta.

However, the sinkings which were accomplished in open sea were by far the more damaging to the enemy. A ship sunk at sea goes down with its valuable cargo and generally results in the losses of hard-to-replace seamen. A ship sunk in port can at times be refloated and used again: indeed, the list shows several enemy ships which had the distinction of being sunk by aircraft in enemy ports on *two* separate occasions.

Moreover, many of the vessels sunk by aircraft in ports were of the small kind that rarely venture far from port: tugs, dredgers, service vessels, ferries, barges, lighters and other auxiliary harbour vessels. About 30 per cent of the ships sunk in their harbours were of less than 500 tons. However, without these small but essential vessels, a port is not able to function efficiently, especially after the various port installations have been damaged, as unquestionably also occurred. Malta herself experienced this when, after 1941, there was a great scarcity of small ships available to help unload the few ships which did arrive or to sweep up the mines which lay outside her harbours.

Since RAF records in Malta are not thought to be reliable, it is not possible to determine which ships in enemy ports were sunk by aircraft based in Malta and which were sunk by aircraft based further afield. It can, however, be stated with some assurance that virtually all the twenty-one enemy ships which are listed as having been sunk in Tripoli by aircraft were victims of aircraft based in Malta. Even the one which is shown as having been sunk by a mine most probably struck a mine which had been laid by a Swordfish or a Wellington.

The list of enemy ships sunk in Tripoli is probably typical of the 'mixed bag' of victims sunk by aircraft in their harbours. These sinkings began on 25 February 1941, when the auxiliary vessel *Guidonia* (86 tons) was hit and ended when, on 15 January 1943, the tanker *Argostino Bertani* (8,329 tons) was sunk, only a few days before the Eighth Army marched in.

The other ships sunk in Tripoli were: *Annunziatino* (small), *Capo Doglio*, *Eritrea*, *Flammetta*, *Fluvior* (sunk by mine), *Giulia*, *Giuseppina*, *Luciana* (small), *Marocchino*, *Neptunis*, *Nereo*, *Quarto* (dredger), *Riv*, *Romagna*, *Rosa* (commercial auxiliary), *Sirio*, *Terere* (hospital ship in harbour for repairs), *Tomaseo* (tug), and the small *Usodi Mare* (24 tons).

Likewise, it is a fair assumption that those enemy ships which were sunk during bombing raids while in harbours in, or adjacent to, Sicily were also sunk by Malta-based bombers. One or two may have been sunk by

Swordfish, Blenheims or even Beaufighters but most were due to Wellingtons. In all, forty-four ships are listed as having been sunk by aircraft in Sicilian ports: seventeen in Palermo, fifteen in Messina, six in Trapani, four in Reggio di Calabria and one each in Catania and Syracuse. The raid carried out on 3 March 1942 sank three ships, including the *Cuma* (6,652 tons) and the *Securitas* (5,316 tons). The raid by Wellingtons on Palermo on 22 March 1943 accounted for the *Jacques Schlafigno* (1,797 tons), the *Labor* (510 tons), the *Moderna* (3,050 tons), the *Trentino* (671 tons) and the *Volta* (1,191 tons). Generally, there were larger ships to sink in 1942 than in 1943.

Another twenty ships were sunk in Genoa, including the *Augustus* (30,418 tons), but as this port is at the limit of Wellington range from Malta, and as it was raided later in the war by both the 'heavies' of the USAAF from African and, later, probably Italian bases, and as bombers of the RAF's Bomber Command also raided this port from UK bases, it is not considered that Malta-based aircraft made many, if any, contributions.

Another twenty-five ships were sunk in Benghazi harbour, making it almost impossible to berth and unload ships there. To what extent these were sunk by aircraft based in the Middle East, on the 'Mail Run' attacks mentioned in 70 Squadron's verses, or by Wellingtons from Luqa, is not known. There are, however, a few instances where crew members of Wimpys based in Malta definitely mention that they had hit ships in that harbour during the several periods when Benghazi was nearer to Malta than to any airfield available to our Middle East Air Forces.

Uncertainty also attaches to the fourteen ships sunk in the port of Civitavecchia. No fewer than nine were sunk in one raid on 14 May 1943 – the day after all Axis forces in Tunisia had surrendered. Did the aircraft come from Malta or from some newly captured, but more distant, Tunisian airfield? Possibly it was a combined raid from a number of different bases by squadrons which, after the surrender of Tunis, found themselves in want of other fields to conquer? Nine of the six ships sunk were supply ships and this one raid did much to deplete further the already diminished supply of enemy ships to which Vice-Admiral Weichold referred in the quotation at the start of this Appendix.

However, it can be assumed that most of the enemy ships sunk in Naples were sent to the bottom of that harbour by Wellingtons based in Malta. Apart from Tripoli, Naples was probably the port most often attacked by these bomber-aircraft. Commencing 13 December 1940, when the small auxiliary *Immacolate II* was sunk, eight other vessels, totalling 53,175 tons, were sunk, with the 20,006-ton *Lombardia*, sunk on 3 April 1943, being the enemy's biggest loss. The same raid also sank the *Sicilla* (9,646 tons). The attack on Naples of 4 August 1943 accounted for the *Catania* (ex-*St Marin*)

(6,176 tons) and the *Santagata* (4,299 tons). The warehouses, nearby Royal Arsenal and dock area were frequently the causes of large fires seen for miles by the tail-gunners of the departing raiders. The proximity of the ever-smoking Mount Vesuvius made it almost impossible for aircraft crews not to locate this large target.

Malta-based aircraft were of enormous assistance in attacking enemy ports during the months of the Tunisian campaign, first, when the enemy was pouring troops and supplies into that former French possession, and later when the reverse was happening and the enemy was endeavouring to get what remained of the defeated armies back to Sardinia and Sicily.

The enemy's principal ports of Bizerta, Tunis and adjacent La Goulette, Sousse, and Sfax all came under heavy attacks.

In Bizerta, four ships were sunk by Malta-based bombers, including the *Noto* (3,188 tons) sunk on 30 January 1943, and the *Spoleto* (7,960 tons) sunk on the following night.

Six ships were sunk by aircraft in Sousse during December 1942. Three more were later sunk in Tunis and La Goulette. The four which were sunk in Sfax, including the one which Warburton blew up, were sunk long before Tripoli fell, at a time when the enemy were trying to use this neutral port as a refuge on their way to Tripoli. Finding the RAF in pursuit, they soon abandoned this ploy. Later still, many enemy ships were sunk in the Sardinian harbours of Cagliari and Porto Torres.

Smaller numbers of enemy ships were sunk in the Italian ports of Porto Maurizio, Porto Vecchio, Spezia, Ancona, Livorno, San Antonio, Chioggia, Valona, and in such places as Corfu, Argostoli (Cephalonia), off Kuriat Island, Navarino, Pantelleria, Dubrovnik and Zuara. In short, there was no safe port within Wellington-range of Malta where enemy vessels could hide.

Lloyd's, wisely, do not insure Navy vessels. There is therefore no corresponding list issued by Lloyd's of enemy warships sunk by aircraft in the Mediterranean during the Second World War. If Malta is any guide, many warships would also have been sunk in enemy ports, especially when it is remembered that the Italians started the war with several hundred of these.

In Malta itself, whereas only three merchant ships were sunk in port – namely the *Pampas*, *Talabot* and the *Breconshire* (which was a Navy supply ship and was first crippled when about ten miles from Malta), many times that number of warships in Malta were sent to the bottom by enemy aircraft. These included three submarines, four destroyers and several minesweepers, drifters, anti-submarine trawlers and the tug *Helispond*.

While the above list is not intended to imply that hundreds of enemy warships were sunk by Malta-based bombers, there can be no doubt that a number of Italian warships and naval auxiliaries were victims of the many bombing raids upon their poorly defended ports, and that many of the bombers came from Malta.

Whatever were the total losses which the enemy suffered in ports as a result of Malta-based raids, the policy of basing Wellingtons, Blenheims and other bomb-carrying aircraft in Malta – never forgetting the gallant contributions of the Fleet Air Arm – paid handsome dividends, even though hundreds of these bombers were destroyed on Malta's airfields by enemy aircraft.

To have sunk, by the end of 1942, over one and a quarter million tons of enemy shipping (as Weichold avers) even before the enormous sinkings around Tunisia took place during the first five months of 1943, was a great triumph for all concerned: surface ships, submarines and aircraft.

Malta was strategically well placed to inflict such damage and played a leading part in this crippling of the enemy's ability to carry out military campaigns in North Africa. The long list of their losses at sea explains why so many of the Ultra intercepts deciphered by the team at Bletchley Park consist of increasingly desperate pleas for supplies, made by an increasingly frustrated and anxious Rommel.

APPENDIX III

Attacks on MV Victoria

1. MVs *Monviso*, *Ravello*, *Monginervo* and *Pisani*, with eight destroyers or torpedo-boats, pass through the Strait of Messina and head north-east. The intention is to give the impression to any reconnaissance aircraft from Malta that the convoy is proceeding to Taranto and not to North Africa.

2. The 'Pearl of the Italian merchant fleet', *Victoria*, leaves Taranto protected by battleship *Duilio* and her destroyers. They head southwards but keep sufficiently east so as to remain outside the 190 nautical mile range of the Malta-based Swordfish of 830 Squadron.

3. Cruisers *Duca d'Aosta*, *Attendolo* and *Montecuccoli* – the *Aosta* division – with four more destroyers leave Taranto and head south to rendezvous with the *Vivaldi–Monviso* group. After doing so, they proceed independently southwards, while also keeping outside Swordfish range. They eventually join the *Duilio–Victoria* group at a point about half-way between Malta and Benghazi, at 1500 hrs 23 January 1942 (point 4).

5. SDF Goofington (F/O Spooner) departs Luqa and, using ASV, locates what is reported as 'One battleship, one liner,* three destroyers and two or more unknown ships.' With the ASV iced up and behaving irrationally, it was reported as just one convoy but it is now thought that both the *Duilio–Victoria* group and the *Aosta* division were located. At the time, when homing towards an ASV blip on the tiny cathode-ray screen, the distances increased. It now seems possible that this was because there were two adjacent groups and not one and the iced-up ASV aerials were occasionally picking up ships behind, instead of in front of, the aircraft. (See Chart.) It did not help that the many aerials all 'sang' with a continuous loud and eerie note due to the ice on them. In general, the weather was as bad as it could be for flying: ice, hail, rain, lightning with very strong winds and low clouds.

---

* In Malta, *Victoria* was thought to be a liner. She looked like one.

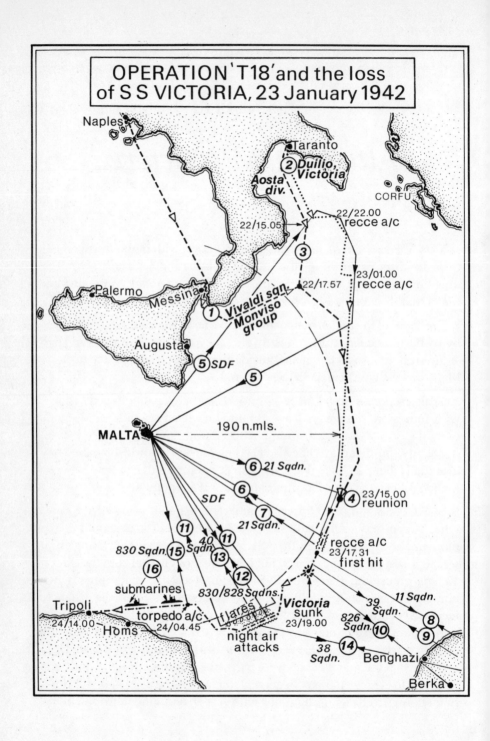

OPERATION 'T18' and the loss
of S S VICTORIA, 23 January 1942

6. A Blenheim of 21 Squadron is sent on a daylight reconnaissance. It finds the ships at the point where the two groups are about to join one other (at 1500 hrs on 23 January). The enlarged convoy now becomes 'T18'.

7. Two other Blenheims of 21 Squadron are sent to attack but are unable to do so. Ironically, between the two stormy nights, the weather is clear, without the required cloud-cover.

8. Meanwhile, six Blenheims of 11 Squadron based in Egypt make an attack but the convoy is not slowed or damaged. By then, up to a dozen Ju 88 long-range fighters have been sent to increase the protection around T18 (which was transporting a Panzer division and its supplies). One Blenheim is shot down.

9. At about the time when the Blenheims of 11 Squadron are attacking, three torpedo-carrying Beauforts of 39 Squadron, also based in Egypt, make an attack. They score a hit on the stern of the *Victoria* which, with several destroyers remaining behind to protect her, drops behind the rest of convoy T18. Some of the Ju 88s also orbit around. The simultaneous Blenheim attack may have diverted attention away from the Beauforts.*

10. FAA Albacores of 826 Squadron from Berka, near Benghazi (still in British hands), led by Lieutenant Commander Corbett attack with torpedoes. Lieutenant 'Ferret' Ellis scores a hit. A possible hit is also scored by Lieutenant Commander Corbett but Corbett is shot down. (He was picked up later by one of the ships picking up survivors from the stricken *Victoria*.) Half an hour after being hit, *Victoria* sinks but Ellis and his colleagues are well away by then and this information is not known to the Allies. (Many hits which are claimed, unfortunately, turn out to be near-misses.)

11. An SDF Wellington (the same Z8725 which had departed twenty-four hours previously), this time flown by Flying Officer David Beaty,† departs from Luqa, dodging the ninety-seven bomb craters made on the runway that day. The ASV fails (owing to ice, damp or Malta's general lack of service facilities) but Beaty locates T18 visually and reports: 'One battleship, four cruisers, fifteen destroyers, one liner, three MVs.' Knowing that the 'liner' *Victoria* had become a part of convoy T18, and unaware that she had been sunk, Beaty naturally assumed that the largest MV was the *Victoria*. Beaty shadows for most of the night and, in response to a signal

---

* A high-flying Liberator was also sighted by those on board and this may also have diverted *Victoria*'s gunners away from the Beauforts.
† Now the successful author of over a dozen books. His *Cone of Silence* was made into a film.

from Malta, begins to drop a flare about every five minutes for the next three or more hours. This is to guide attacking aircraft to T18.

12. Meanwhile, Frank Hopkins, the Observer CO of Swordfish 830 Squadron, has departed from Hal Far (which only had thirty-seven bomb craters that day) in an ASV Swordfish with four other Swordfish and two torpedo Albacores of 828 Squadron. Owing to the atrocious flying weather, only one of his small flock are able to stay in formation with him. He locates T18 and, like others in Malta (and probably in the Middle East, too), he is unaware that the *Victoria* has already been sunk. With only one torpedo-carrying aircraft still with him, he decides to return to Malta and to do it all over again with four Swordfish and one Albacore alongside him.

13. Eight Wellingtons of 40 Squadron depart from Luqa and, guided by Beaty's flares, drop bombs on T18 without any visible result. (The men on board the ships of T18 refer to their ships being 'continually illuminated virtually all night').

14. Wellingtons of 38 Squadron, based in Egypt, are also guided to T18 by Beaty's flares. They also drop bombs, but again claims of probable hits cannot be confirmed. One crew fly low and gunners fire at one of the escorts.

15. Frank Hopkins, this time in an aircraft piloted by Lieutenant Cedric Coxon, again departs from Hal Far, locates the convoy, although his ASV is now playing up. Two Swordfish who have managed to stay with him drop torpedoes. Claims of probable hits are made but the convoy neither slows nor stops. The attackers are still unaware that *Victoria* is no longer with the convoy. This last misconception has led to both the Wellingtons and the Swordfish believing that they have sunk the 'Pearl of the Italian merchant fleet'.

16. Malta-based submarine *P36* (Lt Edmunds) attacks 'three cruisers' but misses. Later he attacks an MV, also with no noticeable result.

Apart from the fact that no one seems to have been aware, for about twenty-four hours, that *Victoria* had been sunk by Lieutenant Ellis, the co-operation between the three Services – Royal Navy, RAF and Fleet Air Arm – was splendid; as also was the co-operation between Malta and the Middle East.

The overall result was probably a slight advantage to the enemy as four loaded supply ships reached Tripoli at a time when Rommel was just starting another surprise, and successful, counter-attack. He needed every drop of fuel which they brought, every new tank and every round of ammunition. However, the expenditure by the enemy of petrol, and especially of naphtha oil, was costly and the Italians were left to mourn the loss of their biggest and finest supply ship. As only 1,064 of the 1,455 men on board the *Victoria* were picked up, the enemy lost many soldiers. Most were probably highly trained Panzer experts.

These details show that the enemy were frightened of the torpedo, and other aircraft, based in Malta. The semi-circular route from Taranto to Tripoli which they felt obliged to take added a further 150 nautical miles to the convoy's journey. If Malta had not been there, then an even shorter route direct from Messina or Palermo could have been chosen. Taranto was only involved because the battleship *Duilio*, which was based there, was thought to be required.

Although the sinking of the *Victoria* was a Middle East, rather than a Malta, success, Malta-based aircraft played an important supporting role. Without its presence, it is doubtful whether the progress of the enemy ships, almost from the moment when they first left Taranto, would have been so accurately known to the FAA and RAF in the Middle East.

APPENDIX IV

Personnel and supplies shipped to Libya

June 1940–January 1943

As can be seen in the table opposite, the enemy lost *en route* to North Africa by sea 17,240 personnel. This is only a few thousand less than the estimated 22,000 fatalities that the enemy lost during the battles on land.

In supplies, the enemy lost at sea 315,090 tons. This was more than was landed in Malta during the entire period.

It is significant that during the months of February–April 1941, the bulk of the original Afrika Korps was transported to North Africa with only minor losses. This was before the Malta strike-forces, submarines and aircraft, had fully learned their trade. How much, it is wondered, would have arrived safely if Malta-based strike-forces had never existed, or, as Captain Simpson has put it, 'acquired the knack'?

The all-too-brief period when Force K was at full strength in Malta – for about two months from mid-October 1941 onwards – is indicated by the enemy's great losses of supplies during November 1941. The considerable losses of supplies during the months immediately prior to the Battles of Alam Halfa (which commenced on 30 August 1942) and El Alamein (which commenced on 23 October 1942) is also noteworthy.

It also notable that, after losing about 50 per cent of the personnel transported by sea during September 1941, the enemy thereafter sent relatively few men by ship. Instead, thousands of troops were later airlifted to North Africa, at a considerable expenditure of precious petrol.

It can also be seen that the determined bombing of Malta, which began in January 1942, had an immediate beneficial result upon the enemy's losses at sea. During both January and February 1942, the enemy landed over 99 per cent of the supplies which they shipped.

Year & Month 1940	Personnel		Supplies	
	Shipped No.	Reached No.	Shipped Tons	Reached Tons
June	1,358	1,308	3,618	3,608
July	6,407	6,407	40,875	40,875
August	1,221	1,221	50,669	50,669
September	4,602	4,602	53,635	53,635
October	2,823	2,823	29,306	29,306
November	3,157	3,157	60,778	60,778
December	9,731	9,731	65,556	58,574
1941				
January	12,491	12,214	50,505	49,084
February	19,557	19,557	80,357	79,173
March	20,975	20,184	101,800	92,753
April	20,968	19,926	88,597	81,472
May	12,552	9,958	73,367	69,331
June	12,886	12,886	133,331	125,076
July	16,141	15,767	77,012	62,276
August	18,288	16,753	96,021	83,956
September	12,717	6,630	94,115	67,513
October	4,046	3,451	92,449	73,614
November	4,872	4,628	79,208	29,843
December	1,748	1,074	47,680	39,092
1942				
January	2,480	1,355	66,214	66,170
February	531	531	59,468	58,965
March	391	284	57,541	47,588
April	1,349	1,349	151,578	150,389
May	4,396	4,241	93,188	86,439
June	1,474	1,249	41,519	32,327
July	4,566	4,435	97,794	91,491
August	1,281	790	77,134	51,655
September	1,367	959	96,903	77,526
October	1,011	631	83,695	46,698
November	1,031	1,031	85,970	63,736
December	5	5	12,981	6,151
TOTALS	206,402	189,162	2,244,893	1,929,803

Luftwaffe in Sicily

10th Submarine Flotilla

Force K

Luftwaffe in Sicily

10th Flotilla

Beauforts

Luftwaffe

These figures appear to apply only to personnel and supplies shipped from Italy to North Africa. They do not apply to personnel and supplies shipped from Greece/Crete and it is known that, after Rommel had advanced as far as El Alamein in June 1942, taking Tobruk on the way, the transportation of men and supplies via Greece/Crete was used more frequently, although the route was under threat from Greek and other guerrilla forces which disrupted the single railway line on which much depended.

These figures were supplied by Tullio Marcon.

APPENDIX V

Tunisian campaign: enemy ships sunk

1 December 1942–13 May 1943

The chart overleaf maps the sinkings of enemy ships in the Central Mediterranean during the Tunisian campaign, the accompanying tables recording relevant details. The names of warships in the following table are indicated by asterisks. The 'UJ' type were probably small merchant ships converted into patrol-boats; the 'APM' type probably armed minesweepers. When two attackers are indicated, this is because of overlapping claims. Unless otherwise stated, all sinkings by Royal Navy ships were accomplished by submarines. The *Dolfijn* was a Dutch submarine.

Most of the ships were sunk in waters around Tunisia. Others are thought to have been heading for Tunisia. However, a few sunk during December 1942 may have been heading for Tripolitania, where Rommel was still in full retreat. The number of small ships sunk by submarines indicates the parlous state of affairs into which the enemy had fallen. By March 1943 onwards, they were making use of almost anything that could float in order to bring in supplies.

SHIPS SUNK BY THE ROYAL NAVY

NAME	TONS	DATE	CHART NUMBER	ATTACKER
Adelina	85	13.5.43		*Shakespeare*
Amabile Carolina	38	23.1.43	37	*Unruffled*
Angela	56	8.2.43	52	*Unison*
Aniello	77	3.1.43	43	*Safari*
Ankara	4768	18.1.43	23	Mine, laid by *Rorqual*
Anna Maria Gualdi	U/K	1.12.42		Mine, laid by Beaufort

The chart shows 180 sinkings, concentrated in NW Sicily; around the Tunisian coast, and with lesser groups around the departure ports of Cagliari and Naples and in the area of the Messina Strait. To reduce clutter, ships sunk by air in ports are shown near the ports.

I = SUBMARINE SINKINGS

Ⅰ = AIRCRAFT SINKINGS

NAME	TONS	DATE	CHART NUMBER	ATTACKER
*APM 31	150	20.1.43		*Unrivalled*
*APM 36	150	20.1.43		*Unrivalled*
Ardito	120	21.1.43	36	*Unrivalled*
Aspromonte	U/K	2.12.42		Force Q/Fishington
Aventino	U/K	2.12.42		Force Q/Fishington
*Aviere (Dr)	1620	17.12.42	10	*Splendid*
Baalbeck	2115	21.2.43	61	*Unruffled*
Bella Italia	124	9.4.43	86	*Safari*
Bivona	164	19.4.43	93	*Unrivalled*
Bois Rose	1374	29.3.43		*Unrivalled*
*Bombardiere (Dr)	1654	17.1.43	22	*United*
Carlo Margottini	855	10.2.43		*Unbending*
Carlo P	64	8.2.43	51	*Unison*
Castelverde	6685	14.12.42		*Unruffled*
Citta di Bergamo	2163	14.3.43	70	*Unbending*
Citta di Trapani	2465	2.12.42		*Unrivalled*
Cleopatra	44	19.1.43	33	*Splendid*
* Climene (TB)	652	28.4.43		*Unshaken*
Colomba lo Faro	900	5.3.43		*Triumph*
Commercio	4765	19.1.43	34	*Splendid*
Constantia	345	20.12.42	12	*Safari*
Cosala	4260	10.2.43	55	*Una*
Cosenza	1471	14.3.43	71	*Unbending*
Devoli	3175	17.3.43	73	*Splendid*
Dora	U/K	U/K		Force Q
Edda	6107	19.1.43		*Unbroken*/Albacores
Egle	1145	29.3.43	79	*Dolfijn*
Elenora Rosa	54	27.12.42	15	*Safari*
Emilio Morandi	1522	9.1.43	17	*Umbra*
Emma	7930	16.1.43	20	*Splendid*
Entella	2690	11.4.43	89	*Safari*
Eritrea	2517	8.2.43	53	*Unbending*
Esterel	3100	12.2.43	68	*Thunderbolt*
Eufrasia	49	18.12.42	11	*Safari*
Fabriano	2940	18.12.42	90	*Safari*
Favor	1323	18.1.43	31	*United*
Foggia	1245	8.4.43		*Unshaken*
*Folgore (Dr)	1500	2.12.42		Force K
Forli	1525	17.3.43	72	*Trooper*
Francesco Crispi	7600	19.4.43		*Saracen*
Galiola	1428	20.4.43	98	*Sahib*
Gemma	67	3.1.43	44	*Splendid*

NAME	TONS	DATE	CHART NUMBER	ATTACKER
Genova	90	17.1.43	21	Unrivalled
Gerd St Raymond	1700	24.2.43	62	Splendid/aircraft (U/K)
Ghrib	82	13.3.43		Taurus
Giacomo C	4638	26.4.43	99	Umbra/aircraft (U/K)
Giorgio	4887	21.3.43	74/1	Splendid
Gran	4140	28.12.42	16	Ursula
Graz	1870	8.12.42	4	Mine, laid by Rorqual
Grete	1503	11.2.43		Torbay
*Grondin (Dr)	1500	17.1.43		Unrivalled
Honestas	4960	14.12.42	8	Sahib
Ischia	5100	20.2.43		Torbay
Isongo	3335	10.4.43	88	Safari
KT 1	795	2.12.42		Force Q/Fishington
KT 7	795	19.4.43	92	Unrivalled
KT 13	795	1.4.43	83	Mine
KT ?	795	21.4.43	95	Unison
La Foce	2495	18.2.43		Universal
L'Angelo Raffaelo	75	12.2.43	60	Unruffled
Le Tre Marie	1085	4.2.43	48	Unseen
Lillois	3680	28.3.43	78	Torbay
*Lince (TB)	679	28.3.43		Ultor
Lisboa	1799	31.3.43	45	Unruffled
Liv	3069	U/K		U/K
Loredan	1355	10.4.43	87	Safari
Luigi	433	15.4.43		Taurus
Luigi Verni	50	8.2.43	50	Unison
Luni	337	23.1.43	38	Unbending
*Lupo (TB)	679	1.12.42		Force K
Maddalena	345	31.12.42		Unrivalled
Makedonia	2875	4.3.43	64/10	Unseen
*Malachite (Sub)	615	8.2.43	54	Dolfijn
Marco Foscarini	6400	26.4.43	94	Unison
Margherita	69	26.12.42	14	Unrivalled
Maria Angeletta	214	20.1.43	35	Saracen
Marseilles V	124	12.2.43		Saracen
Marte	U/K	29.12.42		Turbulent
Menes	5603	3.12.42		Mine, laid by Manxman
Michello	39	23.1.43	40	Unrivalled
Milano	379	12.4.43	97	Unbroken
*Narvalo (Sub)	810	14.12.42	20A	Drs: Hurley, Pakenham & Beauforts
Nasello	314	3.4.43	84	Safari

NAME	TONS	DATE	CHART NUMBER	ATTACKER
Onda	98	8.5.43		*Safari*
Oued Tiflet	U/K	14.1.43		*Sahib*
Parma	2548	31.1.43	25	*Mine*
Pasubia	2216	16.2.43	58	*Unrivalled*
Pegli	1595	14.3.43	69	*Sibyl*
Petrarca	3330	15.2.43	56	*Una*
Pia	385	5.5.43		*Tactician*
Pippino Palomba	2035	8.5.43		*Safari*
*Porfido (Sub)	697	6.12.42	3	*Tigris*
Pozzuoli	5345	21.1.43	46	*Turbulent*
President H. Schmidt	9103	22.3.43		*Tribune*
*Prestinari (TB)	635	31.1.43	26	*Mine*
*Procellaria (TB)	565	31.1.43	27	*Mine*
Provencale II	1254	12.3.43		*Saracen*
Puccini	2422	2.12.42	2	*Force Q/Albacore/ Fishington*
Redentore	46	25.1.43	42	*Unruffled*
Regina	9545	4.4.43	85	*Unbroken*
Rosalina S	297	22.12.42	13	*Safari*
Rosario	5470	10.3.43	66	*Trooper*
Ruhr	5354	22.1.43	24	*Rorqual*
Sacro Cuore	1097	2.12.42	1	*Umbra*
*Saetta (Dr)	1206	3.2.43	28	*Mine*
San Antonio	6013	11.1.43		*Sahib*
Sant' Anna M	156	13.5.43		*Shakespeare*
Sant' Antioco	5050	14.12.42	9	*Splendid*
Santa Irene	520	12.4.43		*Trident*
Santa Maria Salina	765	9.5.43	101	*Unrivalled*
San Vicenzo	865	1.3.43	63	*Turbulent*
Sempre Avanti	135	5.5.43	100	*Tactician/aircraft (U/K)*
Sidamo	2385	27.3.43	77	*Sahib*
Siena	4000	17.2.43		*Splendid*
Sogiola	307	2.5.43		*Safari*
Sparviero	498	16.2.43	57	*Unrivalled*
Sportivo	1598	18.1.43		*Unseen*
Stefano M	69	9.3.43	65	*Thunderbolt*
Ste Rosaline	1323	19.1.43	32	*Splendid*
St Lucian	1255	12.4.43		*Unruly*
St Teresa	20	18.2.43		*Sahib*
Sullberg	1669	9.12.43	5	*Umbra*
Tabarca	606	1.12.42		*U/K*
Tagliamento	5450	22.4.43	96	*Saracen*

NAME	TONS	DATE	CHART NUMBER	ATTACKER
Teodolinda	361	25.1.43	41	*Unruffled*
Thorsheimer	9555	10.1.43	18	*Umbra*/Beauforts
Togo	105	1.12.42		*Ursula*
Torquato Gennari	1010	29.12.42		*Safari*
Tosca	474	24.3.43	76	*Sahib*
Triglav	231	1.4.43	82	*Unrivalled*
*U301	769	2.1.43		*Sahib*
*U340	769	1.1.43		Destroyer/Wellington
*U562	769	10.2.43		Drs: *Isis* & *Hurley*/ Wellington
*UJ2201 (PV)	1375	29.3.43	80	*Unrivalled*
*UJ2204 (PV)	1188	29.3.43	81	*Unrivalled*
*UJ2205 (PV)	1168	19.4.43	91	*Unseen*
*Ulpio Traiano (Cr)	3362	3.1.43		*Charioteers*
Uragano	1204	3.2.43	29	Mine, laid possibly by *Abdiel*
Utilitas	5342	5.2.43	49	*Turbulent*
Valsavoia	5733	2.2.43	47	*Safari*
Viminale	8657	3.1.43		*Charioteers*
Viminale	8657	23.1.43	39	*Unbending* (on tow)
Vittorio Beraldo	547	11.1.43	19	*Turbulent*
Westmark	2835	26.12.42		*Unbroken*
XXI Aprile	4787	7.2.43	59	*Splendid*
Zeila	1835	23.3.43	75	*Unison*
Zenobia Martini	1454	17.1.43		*Unseen*

SHIPS SUNK BY RAF (INCLUDING RAAF, RCAF, USAAF)

Those listed as 'Lloyd's' appear in Lloyd's list of ships sunk by aircraft but whose sinking has not been traced to any particular aircraft. Where a harbour is named, the ship was sunk in that port during a bombing raid.

NAME	TONS	DATE	CHART NUMBER	ATTACKER
Albisola	4087	21.3.43	51	Cagliari
Alcambo	6887	24.2.43	34	Beauforts
Alfieri	4573	29.1.43		Beauforts
Anna Maria	1205	28.12.42	17	Sousse
Anna Maria Giuldi	3259	28.12.42		Beauforts
Aquila	3386	9.8.43		Lloyd's

NAME	TONS	DATE	CHART NUMBER	ATTACKER
Aquino	5079	14.4.43	69	Beauforts
Arlessiana	5702	7.5.43	72	Tunis
Armando	1541	28.12.42	18	Sousse
Audace	1459	2.12.42	3	Beauforts/Fishington
Balzac	1947	7.3.43		Lloyd's
Bellino	4279	9.5.43		Lloyd's
Capo Figaro	2811	31.3.43	52	Cagliari
Capo Mele	3860	31.3.43	53	Cagliari
Capo Orso	3149	15.2.43	30	Wellingtons
Capri	154	1.5.43		Beaufighters
Capua	424	17.4.43	61	Albacores
Caraibe	4048	13.4.43	45	Albacores/Wellingtons
Caucaso	2065	14.12.42	12	La Goulette
Cerere	1198	24.12.42	16	Liberators
Chiete	5487	17.4.43	63	Palermo
Chisone	6118	22.1.43		Lloyd's
Col de Lama	3804	18.2.43	31	Wellingtons/Liberators
Esmeralda	146	15.1.43	22	Tunis
Etruria	2633	21.12.42		Albacores
Fabriano	2845	11.4.43	58	Fishington
Foscolo	4500	13.12.42	8	Albacores
*FR III (Sub *Phoque*)	974	28.2.43	35A	RAF/FAA
Gerd St Raymond	1700	22.2.43		Lloyd's/*Splendid*
Giacomo C	4638	16.4.43		Palermo
Giorgio (tug)	169	21.3.43	49	Beauforts
Giorgio	4887	1.12.42	1/74	Albacores
Giuseppe Lara	1430	29.12.42	19	Sousse
Giuseppina Chiesa	213	13.12.42	9	Sousse
Henri Ester	1904	7.3.43		Lloyd's
*Hermes (Dr)	1414	7.5.43	71A	La Goulette
Inas Corrado	6200	7.3.43		Lloyd's
Jacques Schlafigno	1757	22.3.43	40	Palermo
Jutland	1160	6.4.43	56	Trapani
KT 1	795	2.12.42	5	Lloyd's/Force Q
KT 9	795	9.5.43		Lloyd's
KT 12	795	1.4.43		Lloyd's
KT 21	795	9.5.43		Lloyd's
Labor	510	22.3.43	41	Palermo
La Ditta	38	14.12.42	21	Tunis, Wellingtons
*Lavanzo (Gunboat)	226	6.5.43	79	RAF/USAAF
Lecce	1956	15.2.43	28	Naples
Lentini	1068	17.4.43	64	Tunis

NAME	TONS	DATE	CHART NUMBER	ATTACKER
Lilibeo	191	28.2.43	35	Livorno
Liv	3069	18.4.43	67	Porto Torres
Lombardia	20006	4.4.43	54	Naples
Luigi Razza	4334	18.4.43	65	Porto Torres
Maggio	331	7.3.43		Lloyd's
Makedonia	2875	13.3.43	10/64	Albacores/*Unseen*
Manzoni	4550	22.3.43	46	Fishington
Maria Grazia	295	29.4.43	71	Wellingtons/ Liberators
MF 'p'	120	–	16A	Beaufighters
Minerva	1905	3.12.42	7	Albacores
Minerva	1905	3.4.43		Albacores
Moderna	3050	22.3.43	42	Palermo
Modica	3161	15.2.43	29	Naples
Mondori	461	11.4.43		Lloyd's
Monginervo	5324	17.4.43	62	Albacores/Wellingtons
Monti	4301	22.3.43	47	Lloyd's
Mostagnem	1942	19.4.43	68	Fishingtons
Motol	268	15.12.42	15	Sousse
Narenta	1362	6.4.43	59	Trapani
**Narvalo* (Sub)	810	13.1.43	20A	Beauforts & Navy
Noto	3168	30.1.43	26	Bizerta
Ombrina	6400	22.3.43		Lloyd's
Orione	291	9.5.43	77	Palermo
Palmiola	1880	2.12.42	6	Albacores
Pantelleria	1408	11.4.43	60	Trapani, Wellingtons
Paolina	196	28.2.43	36	Cagliari
Paolo	3925	28.2.43	37	Cagliari
Partnico	4425	11.5.43	76	Catania
Pistoia	2448	31.1.43	25	Fishingtons
Potestas	5237	23.12.42		Lloyd's
Pozzuoli	5345	1.2.43	27	Wellington/*Turbulent*
Pro Patria	541	29.12.42	20	Sfax
Rabelais	4999	5.4.43	55	Palermo
**RD 44* (Naval auxiliary)	155	5.5.43	78	RAF/USAAF
Regina	9645	4.4.43		Lloyd's/*Unbroken*
Rhea	1388	28.2.43	50	Naples
Roverto	8564	6.4.43		Lloyd's
Ruhr	5054	22.1.43		Albacores/Beauforts
San Antonio	6013	5.5.43		Lloyd's (after refloating?)

NAME	TONS	DATE	CHART NUMBER	ATTACKER
San Diego	6013	6.4.43		Lloyd's
Santa Maria	399	15.1.43	23	Beaufighters
Santa Rita	5191	13.5.43		Cagliari
Saturno	5022	20.1.43		Lloyd's
Scilla	2807	9.5.43	75	Messina
Scotfos	1465	6.4.43		Trapani
Sempre Avanti	134	5.5.43		Lloyd's/*Tactician*
Seneglaise	120	18.12.42	14	Albacores
Seneglaise	120	17.3.43		Bizerta (refloated?)
Sicilla	9649	4.4.43	57	Naples
Spoleto	7960	31.1.43	32	Bizerte, Wellingtons
Sterope	10495	12.3.43	39	Beauforts/Albacores
St Bernadette	1586	13.12.43	11	Tunis, Wellingtons
St Fernand	4312	14.12.42	13	La Goulette
St Sauveur	1394	6.5.43	73	Reggio di Calabria
Teil	1349	28.2.43	38	Cagliari
Tenace	250	23.3.43	48	Trapani
Teramo	1599	29.4.43	70	Fighter aircraft
Thorsheimer	9555	21.2.43	33/18	Beauforts/damaged by *Umbra*
Tiziano	1333	18.4.43	66	Trapani
Trentino	671	22.3.43	43	Palermo
Valverdi	138	23.1.43		Livorno
Veloce	5464	2.12.43	4	Albacores
Vercelli	3091	29.1.43		Lloyd's
Verona	4459	23.1.43	24	Fishingtons/Beauforts
Villa	932	6.5.43	74	Reggio di Calabria
Volta	1191	22.3.43	44	Palermo

These names add up to 247 ships sunk but, allowing for overlapping claims, the total is nearer 230. However, 230 ships sunk (and two ships were sunk twice, presumably having been refloated) in only 164 days represents a rate of sinking which was never before approached or reached again after the fall of Tunis on 13 May 1943. Of the 247 ships listed, those sunk by the Royal Navy amounted to 144, with 103 being attributed to air-craft. There must also have been several more which have not been recorded, as it is known that, in the Mediterranean as a whole, 646 enemy ships were sunk by 'causes unknown' in the course of the Second World War. However, they are believed to have been mostly small ships.

In retrospect, it seems to have been bordering on the irrational for the Germans to attempt to supply and defend Tunisia at a time when

Tripolitania was all but lost and Malta so close at hand. With air superiority being maintained over Malta, the island fortress could harbour, or service, more submarines, strike-planes and even a few destroyers with relative impunity. Yet Hitler, guided by false intuition, continued to attempt to pour troops and supplies into Tunisia in the kind of numbers that, a month earlier, Rommel would have given his hind teeth to have received.

Again, the folly of flying in thousands of men without their heavy equipment, much of which ended up at the bottom of the Mediterranean, was pursued. As a result, when the final surrender came, without even a particularly fierce battle, of the nearly quarter of a million troops who surrendered ignominiously, more than half were found to be Germans. To try to reinforce Tunisia at a time when submarines and strike-aircraft were in Malta was optimistic in the extreme, and bordered on the suicidal. Possibly Hitler believed that Malta had been rendered innocuous.

Only two ships were sunk in the last seventeen days of the campaign. Were Italian sailors refusing to depart, or had the enemy simply run out of ships?

APPENDIX VI

U-boat losses in the Mediterranean war

It has been contended that Malta's greatest accomplishment was to goad Hitler into the decision to divert many of his U-boats from their hunting-grounds in the Atlantic into the Mediterranean. Virtually all the U-boats which made the perilous journey past the Strait of Gibraltar – where several met their end or were driven back – were subsequently sunk. Aircraft and submarines operating from Malta contributed to the demise of several of these U-boats.

Hitler's decision was taken shortly after Force K had sunk the entire *Duisberg* convoy, even though that spectacular action was only a relatively small part of the many sinkings of enemy supply ships which were at that time (November 1941) being accomplished by the submarines of the Tenth Flotilla backed up by the aircraft of the FAA and RAF based in Malta.

U-boat no.	Sunk / Damaged	Date	Area	Details
71	N/A	5.12.41	N/A	Returned to base. Engine trouble
73	S	16.12.43	not known	Surface ships
74	S	2.5.43	Western Med.	Drs *Wishart* & *Wrestler* plus F-boat of 202 Sqdn
75	S	28.12.41	Eastern Med.	Dr *Kipling*
77	S	28.3.43	Eastern Med.	Hudson L/233 Sqdn & Hudson L/48 Sqdn
79	S	23.12.41	Eastern Med.	Drs *Hasty* & *Hotspur*
81	S	9.1.44	not known	USAAF. She sank *Ark Royal*
83	S	4.3.43	Western Med.	Hudson 500 Sqdn
95	S	28.11.41	East of Gib.	Dutch sub *021*

U-boat no.	Sunk / Damaged	Date	Area	Details
96	D	1.12.41	Gib. Strait	Swordfish 812 Sqdn (*Das Boot* of book & TV series)
97	S	16.6.43	Western Med.	Wellington J & P/179 Sqdn and/or 459 Sqdn, RAAF
98	S	19.11.42	West of Gib.	Hudson 608 Sqdn
127	S	15.12.41	West of Gib.	Dr *Nestor*
133	S	14.3.42	Aegean	Mine
138	S	18.6.41	Gib. Strait	5 F-class Drs
202	D	21.12.41	Gib. Strait	Swordfish 812 Sqdn. Returned France
204	S	19.11.41	West of Gib.	Drs *Marlow* & *Rochester*
205	S	17.2.43	NW of Derna	Bisley 15 SAAF Sqdn & Dr *Paladin*
206	S	unknown	to Gib.	Mine, possibly air-laid
208	S	?7.12.41	off Gib.	Dr *Bluebell*
224	S	13.1.43	Western Med.	RCN *Ville de Quebec*
259	S	15.11.41	off Algiers	Hudson 500 Sqdn (S/Ldr Ensor)
301	S	2.1.43	W. Corsica	Sub *Sahib*
303	S	21.5.43	off Toulon	Sub *Sickle*
331	S	17.11.42	unknown	Hudson 500 Sqdn & Albacore*
340	S	1.11.43	West of Gib.	Wellington R/179 Sqdn & Dr?
371	S	4.5.44	unknown	Surface ships
372	S	4.8.42	unknown	Wellington M/221 Sqdn & Drs *Sikh* & *Zulu*
374	S	12.1.42	Eastern Med.	Sub *Unbeaten*
375	S	30.7.43	Eastern Med.	Surface craft
392	S	16.3.43	Gib. Strait	Catalinas 12 Sqdn (US) & 63 Sqdn (USN)
411	S	15.11.42	off Algiers	Hudson D/500 Sqdn & Drs *Quiberon* or *Quentin* or *Wrestler*?
414	S	25.5.43	Western Med.	Dr *Vetch* or sub *Vetch*?
431	S	21.10.43	Western Med.	Wellington Z/179 Sqdn[†]

---

* *U331* surrendered to the Hudson and was on the surface awaiting crew pick-up when sunk by an Albacore from the aircraft-carrier *Formidable*.

† Paul Tenholt, crew member, advises that *U431* was also attacked by aircraft on 21.5.42, 10.6.42, 3.11.42, 14.11.42, 23.3.43 and 11.5.43 before being sunk by the Wellington on 21.10.43: in most cases the U-boat was able to dive to safety with only minor damage, if any. Life for U-boats in the Mediterranean was precarious.

U-boat no.	Sunk / Damaged	Date	Area	Details
432	D	17.12.41	Gib. Strait	Swordfish 812 Sqdn. Returned France
433	S	16.11.41	East of Gib.	Dr *Marigold*
442	S	12.2.43	West of Gib.	Hudson 48 Sqdn
443	S	23.2.43	off Algiers	Drs *Bicester, Laverton* & *Wheatland*
447	S	7.5.43	Western Gib.	Hudsons X/233 & I/48
451	S	21.12.41	off Gib.	Swordfish 812 Sqdn
453	S	21.5.44	unknown	Surface ships
557	S	16.12.41	unknown	Italian MTB (own goal!)
558	D	3.12.41	Gib. Strait	Swordfish 812. Returned France
559	S	30.10.42	Eastern Med.	Wellington 47 Sqdn & 5 Drs
561	S	12.7.43	unknown	MTB
562	S	19.2.42	NE Benghazi	Drs *Isis* & *Hurley* & Wellington 38 Sqdn
563	S	1.12.41	unknown	502 Sqdn
565	S	24.9.44	unknown	USAAF bombing raid
568	S	28.5.42	Eastern Med.	Drs *Eridge, Hero* & *Hurworth*
569	D	16.12.42	Gib. Strait	Swordfish 812 Sqdn. Returned France
572	D?	15.1.42	Gib. area	Abandoned attempt to enter*
573	D	1.5.42	Western Med.	Hudson M/233 Sqdn. Interned Cartagena
577	S	9.1.42	Eastern Med.	Sunderland X/230 Sqdn & ?815 Sqdn
591	S	Appears to have survived		
594	S	4.6.43	West of Gib.	Hudson F/48 Sqdn
595	S	14.11.43	Western Med.	5 Hudsons of 500 Sqdn
602	S	23.4.43	off Algiers	Drs *Lotus* & *Starwort*
616	S	16.5.44	Western Med.	Wellingtons A, H & X/36 Sqdn & US Dr
617	S	12.9.43	Western Med.	Wellingtons J & P/179 Sqdn

* As recorded in the text, one U-boat commander was court-martialled and shot for cowardice. Yet it was always extremely difficult to get past the Strait of Gibraltar, as the losses above show. Having once arrived in the Mediterranean, it was even more difficult to get out. For one thing, the strong underwater current flowing from the Atlantic into the Mediterranean made it much harder to travel out against the current than it was to drift in at a very deep level, as skilled U-boat commanders succeeded in doing.

U-boat no.	Sunk / Damaged	Date	Area	Details
652	S	2.6.42	unknown	815 Sqdn & Sunderland 203 Sqdn. Finished off by *U81*. Crew rescued
660	S	12.11.42	Western Med.	Drs *Lotus* & *Starwort*
731	S	15.5.44	Western Med.	Wellingtons A, H & X & US Dr
755	D/S?	28.5.43	Western Med.	Hudson M/608 Sqdn, using rocket projectiles
761	S	24.2.44	West of Gib.	127 & 202 Sqdns, Catalinas 63 USN Sqdns & US Dr
960	S	19.5.44	Western Med.	36 & 500 Sqdns & Drs

APPENDIX VII

Total enemy shipping losses in the Mediterranean

In the Mediterranean as a whole, the total number of ships, including warships, which the enemy lost – sunk, captured, scuttled, surrendered or lost by accidental action – was enormous. According to the report in the Public Record Office, Air 20/9598, the enemy lost 4,472 ships, totalling 5,192,245 tons, plus a few more unknown vessels of low tonnage. In numbers of ships lost, but not in tonnage, this is comparable to the numbers sunk during the Battle of the Atlantic.

Ignoring the 524 small ships of unknown tonnage, these losses are attributed to:

	Ships sunk	Tonnages
Navy	773	1,342,789
Mines	179	214,109
Navy/Air shared	25	106,085
Navy/Mine shared	1	1,778
Air	1,326	1,466,208
TOTAL	2,304	3,130,969

The other two million tons which the Germans and Italian forces lost were due almost entirely to two factors. Over one million tons was surrendered when the Italians decided to change sides in September 1943. A further large tonnage was lost due to 'causes unknown'. A few ships were also lost as a result of self-inflicted actions, being fired on, in error, by their own forces.*

It seems likely that some of the losses due to 'causes unknown' resulted from the over 100,000 mines laid by both sides in the waters around Sicily, Pantelleria, Yugoslavia, the Greek islands, Malta, Tunisia and Libya.

---

* The Germans even lost a U-boat, *U557*, to an Italian MTB.

The lists in Air 20/9598 do not attempt to divide losses between the West, Central or Eastern Mediterranean, but since most of the enemy shipping was employed in the Central Mediterranean, it is evident that some 60–70 per cent, possibly more, may have been lost within easy range of the submarines and aircraft based in Malta.

The lists are, however, divided into merchant and war ships. They show that the Allies sank 863 warships and that another 527 gave themselves up when Italy capitulated in September 1943, or were scuttled at that time. Others were lost due to 'causes unknown'.

From the number of Italian warships which surrendered – five battleships, nine cruisers, ten destroyers, nineteen torpedo-boats and twenty corvettes, as well as many hundreds of smaller vessels – it can be seen that Allied Naval forces and submarines operating from Malta were up against a formidable opposition. The feats of the relatively few submarines of the Tenth Flotilla were, in these circumstances, all the more meritorious. The Allies' heavy losses of submarines are also made more understandable.

It was not all one way in the submarine warfare. Losses were extremely heavy on both sides. In all, the enemy lost 76 Italian submarines at sea and another 31 either surrendered, as most of this number did, or took refuge and were interned in Spanish harbours. Five of the much feared midget submarines also surrendered. In addition, at least 54 German U-boats were lost in the Mediterranean.*

Air 20/9598 also lists the enemy losses on a month-by-month basis. From these statistics it can be seen that only for the first month of the Mediterranean war – June 1940 – were mines the principal cause of sinkings, with 11 of the total of 12 enemy ships so sunk during that month.

From July 1940 onwards, losses due to Allied naval actions, mostly due to submarines, dominate although losses due to aircraft begin to mount. Many of these latter losses were due at first to the FAA Swordfish of 830 Squadron and might, if compiled by a different authority, be attributed to a Navy, rather than an aircraft, source.

During 1941, 125 merchant ships were deemed to have been sunk by the Navy. Most of these sinkings were attributable to submarines, although it was during this period that Force K and Captain Mack's destroyers of the 14th Destroyer Flotilla inflicted total losses on enemy convoys. During the same period, aircraft accounted for another 70 ships sunk, some of these caused by bombing raids on enemy harbours.

During 1942, 108 merchant vessels were sent to the bottom by the Navy and 88 by the Air Force, the significant feature being the sharp rise in sink-

---

* See Appendix VI.

ings during November–December 1942 when the Anglo-American land-ings in French North-west Africa increased the scale of the Mediterranean war and thus the size of the forces engaged.

For the four-month period following December 1942, the enemy lost on average over 100,000 tons of merchant shipping per month. This was a figure not before attained and never again to be reached.

After May 1943, by when all enemy forces in North Africa had surren-dered, enemy losses at sea greatly diminished. However, their losses in ports continued to be heavy, owing to a greatly increased number of raids upon their ports. Henceforth, especially once large formations of USAAF four-engined bombers began to raid these ports during daylight hours, most of the enemy's shipping losses were accounted for in this manner.

In this year, large numbers of enemy ships either surrendered or were scuttled rather than surrender. During 1943, 186 enemy ships were sunk by the Navy before the Italian surrender, but only 30 thereafter. Those sunk by aircraft numbered 316 before the surrender, and 24 thereafter: a total of 340 – almost one per day.

By 1944, when there were relatively few ships to sink at sea, the Navy accounted for 64 whereas the Air Force count amounted to 225, virtually all due to bombing of enemy ports. Such action was still important as the almost complete air superiority which the Allied Air Forces had by then gained over all Italian battle areas, and the deliberate policy of destroying road and rail transport behind the enemy lines – the so-called policy of interdiction – had left the enemy unduly dependent upon coastal shipping.

Towards the end of the Mediterranean war, the once plentiful transport fleets available to the enemy – several million tons in 1940 – and which had been fortified by seizures of ships from Yugoslavia, Greece, France and other overrun territories, had been reduced to almost zero.

Surface ships, submarines and aircraft based in Malta did much to account for this state of affairs, as is confirmed by the tables of losses in Air 20/9598, when allied to the knowledge of what was based in Malta. Together they show that the Central Mediterranean proved to be a grave-yard for the Italian and German merchant service and a constant drain on the resources of the enemy, which was reduced to attempts by the Germans to mass-produce merchant vessels: their KT series. Throughout, the position of Malta was crucial to the outcome and showed that, in the battles for supplies which were to dominate the campaigns in the Mediterranean theatres of war, Britain had been right to hold, and to maintain, that small and isolated fortress.

Bibliography

Bailey, E.A.S. (ed.), *Malta Defiant and Triumphant*, privately printed, 1992.

Baker, R., *The Ship Busters*, Chatto & Windus, 1957.

Bekker, Cajus, *The Luftwaffe War Diaries*, Macdonald, 1966.

Bennett, Ralph, *Ultra and Mediterranean Strategy*, Hamish Hamilton, 1989.

Bryant, Ben, *One Man Band*, William Kimber, 1958.

Churchill, W.S., *The History of the Second World War*, Cassell, 1954.

Ciano, Count, *see* Muggeridge, M.

Doenitz, Grand Admiral Karl, *Memoirs: Ten Years and Twenty Days*, Greenhill Books, 1990.

Douglas-Hamilton, James, *The Air Battle for Malta*, Mainstream Publications, 1991.

Foss, Pat, *Climbing Turns*, Linden Hall, 1986.

Foster, David R., *Wings Over the Sea*, Harrap Press, 1990.

Fraser, David, *Knights Cross*.

Gabriele, Mariano, *Operazione C-3*, Rome, 1965.

Gibbs, Patrick, *Torpedo Leader*, Grubb Street, 1992.

Gilbert, Martin, *The Second World War*, Weidenfeld & Nicolson, 1989.

Gillman, R.E., *The Ship-Hunters*, John Murray, 1976.

Ginn, Robert, *Strike Hard*, 104 Squadron RAF Association, 1990.

Gunby, David, *Sweeping the Skies: A History of No. 40 Squadron, RFC and RAF, 1916–56*, Bishop Auckland: Pentland Press, 1984.

Kesselring, Albert, *The Memoirs of Field-Marshal Kesselring*, William Kimber, 1953.

Lamb, Charles, *War in a Stringbag*, Cassell, 1977.

Liddell Hart, B.H., *The Rommel Papers*, Collins, 1953.

Lloyd, H.P., *Briefed to Attack*, Hodder & Stoughton, 1959.

Lucas, P.B., *The Thorn in Rommel's Side*, Stanley Paul, 1992.

Marcon, Tullio, 'Operazione Malta Due', *Rivista Marittima*, 1976.

McGeoch, Ian, *An Affair of Chance*, Imperial War Museum, 1991.

Muggeridge, Malcolm, *Ciano's Diary, 1939–1943*, Heinemann, 1947.

Nesbit, Roy C., *Torpedo Airmen*, William Kimber, 1983.

Poolman, Kenneth, *Night Strike from Malta*, Janes, 1980.

Preston, Antony, *Decisive Battles of Hitler's War*, New Burlington Books, n.d.

'The Second World War 1939–1945. Royal Air Force Narrative. The Middle East Campaign', Vol. XI: 'Malta, June 1940–May 1945'. MSS held in the Air Historical Branch, MOD, Whitehall.

Shepperd, C.A., *The Italian Campaign, 1938–45*, Arthur Barker, 1968.

Shores, Christopher, Cull, Brian and Milizia, Nicola, *Malta: The Hurricane Years*, Grubb Street, 1987.

Simpson, G.W.G., *Periscope View*, Macmillan, 1972.

Smith, Peter C. and Walker, Edwin, *The Battles of the Malta Striking Forces*, Ian Allan, 1974.

Spooner, Tony, *In Full Flight*, Macdonald, 1965.

——, *Warburton's War*, William Kimber, 1987.

——, *Faith, Hope and Malta GC*, Newton Press, 1992.

——, *Clean Sweep*, Crecy Books, 1994.

Tedder, Lord, *With Prejudice*, Cassell, 1966.

Terraine, John, *The Right of the Line*, Hodder & Stoughton, 1985.

Vella, Philip, *Malta, Blitzed but not Beaten*, Valletta: Progress Press, 1985.

Weichold, Vice-Admiral E., 'Axis Policy and Operations in the Mediterranean'. MSS held in the Naval Historical Branch, Ministry of Defence.

Wingate, John, *The Fighting Tenth*, Leo Cooper, 1971.

Index